THE
20
GREATEST MOMENTS IN
NEW YORK
SPORTS
HISTORY

THE 20

GREATEST MOMENTS IN

NEW YORK SPORTS HISTORY

OUR GENERATION OF MEMORIES, FROM 1960 TO TODAY

TODD EHRLICH & GARY MYERS
FOREWORD BY DAVID TYREE

SPORTS
PUBLISHING

Sports Publishing books may be purchased in bulk at special discounts for
sales promotion, corporate gifts, fund-raising, or educational purposes. Special
editions can also be created to specifications. For details, contact the Special Sales
Department, Sports Publishing, 307 West 36th Street, 11th Floor, New York,
NY 10018 or sportspubbooks@skyhorsepublishing.com.

Sports Publishing® is a registered trademark of Skyhorse Publishing, Inc.®,
a Delaware corporation.

Visit our website at www.sportspubbooks.com.

10 9 8 7 6 5 4 3 2

Library of Congress Cataloging-in-Publication Data is available on file.

Cover design by David Ter-Avanesyan
Cover and interior photographs: Getty Images

Print ISBN: 978-1-68358-457-5
Ebook ISBN: 978-1-68358-458-2

Printed in the United States of America

For my mom, Dr. Carole Owens:
my editor and lifetime supporter

For my wife, Debbie Ehrlich:
my lifetime companion and supporter

For my son, Jagger Ehrlich:
my inspiration and whom I support

For my dad, Jay Ehrlich:
who inspired my passion for sports
and the teams we support

—Todd Ehrlich

CONTENTS

FOREWORD

BY DAVID TYREE

I grew up in Essex Country, New Jersey, and moved to Montclair in 1990 where athletics really came alive for me. The town has such a rich tradition in sports. Long before my success, there were a number of other people from Montclair that became professional athletes. Sports gave my life a sense of purpose, direction and discipline. It allowed me to dream, set goals and achieve them.

When I think about New York sports, the word that comes to mind is *passion*. There is a strong sense of pride evoking high standards and expectations. I was a solid sports fan growing up, I was captivated with the '86 Mets with Doc Gooden and Darryl Strawberry. But in my heart of hearts, it was all about the Knicks. For me to be from Jersey, then getting drafted by the Giants in 2003, was a dream come true. I was just anxious to find a role and prove I belonged with the Giants, who are such an iconic franchise. I wanted to be a part of that legacy. It really brought everything together for me. It was a script that couldn't have been written better for me.

Now to be told that I am a part of the number one moment in the history of New York sports is humbling. There's no city in the world like New York City. There are very few things that New York isn't at the pinnacle of including sports, media, finance. And with my honest opinion, yeah, I'm in full agreement with the Helmet Catch being the best moment in New York sports history.

When you think about Joe Namath, Willis Reed, Reggie, and Phil Simms, it sounds surreal. There have been so many incredible sports moments in our city, so even to be considered in the conversation with these heroes is an honor. It is a little overwhelming, honestly, because there's so many great athletes who have played in the city. The meaning and gratitude . . . it is difficult to find words. NYC, we did it!!

When I made the Helmet Catch, I had no clue how good it was. In the postgame press conference, I gave Eli all the credit and I meant it. He did an amazing job breaking free from the Patriots' pass rush and getting that pass off to me. I knew that it was a good catch, but I didn't know that the ball was actually pinned to my helmet. So, the entire time, I'm giving postgame interviews, I knew I had the game of my life. I knew we won the Super Bowl, upset the undefeated Patriots and prevented them from making NFL history, and that I actually played a big role in it, but I didn't see the catch until I got back to the hotel and saw the replay and the ball stuck on the side of my head. For the first time in my life, I was actually impressed with my own work. After seeing it, I was definitely a little surprised that I held onto the ball. That being said, I am a man of faith and I believe in miracles. I also knew that catch was an appointment with destiny. No four-leaf clovers here.

I don't call it luck because it meant far more to myself and so many others in a way that that transcends happenstance. I've had people tell me that they've had family members who were terminally sick and their lives extended eight months longer after watching our Super Bowl together as a family. So, to me with the Helmet Catch, it was a moment of significance, a moment where all my years of effort finally paid off. I was one of the best special teams players in the NFL always looking to prove myself as a wide receiver. The Super Bowl provided that moment of validation for me. It showed others I could play the position at a high level, and deliver when it counted the most. It was definitely a miracle. It happened when it was supposed to happen, for the team that it was supposed to happen to, and for the city that deserved it most.

It was great to turn the Patriots into an 18–1 team rather than finish their season at 19–0. It may be a little petty—but no one is perfect. They are still one of the best teams to ever play in the NFL. It just goes to show how difficult it is to win a Super Bowl. What a gritty outfit the Giants were in 2007. It was a traditional David vs. Goliath story. It was a test of our resolve against a little bit of overconfidence from our competitors from New England. We were a special team and a special group of guys that had a special bond. Those are usually the teams that win championships.

I'm excited to rejoice in the other nineteen moments. As I get older, my respect for the game, the history of each sport, and heroes that build eternal memories increase exponentially. I'm actually really, really excited and intrigued by this project, because I've always been more interested in other people than myself. I can't wait to learn a little bit more about the moments that have been chosen. I'm excited to celebrate those achievements, and to lift up the crowd, in honor of them as well.

We couldn't have asked for two more credible people to write this book than Todd Ehrlich and Gary Myers. Let's start with Gary. In my experience as a player, you start to understand the role of the newspaper writers and columnists and you appreciate the demands on them. They have to share the storylines and feed the hysteria. There's only a handful of people that actually have command of these moments and understand their importance and significance. There couldn't be a better voice to write about New York sports history and shape what they meant to the city than Gary's, who grew up in Fresh Meadows, Queens, less than ten miles from Shea Stadium.

Todd Ehrlich's credibility is unquestioned. He is an incredibly passionate TV producer and executive. He's been committed to formulating and delivering the storylines and significant moments throughout New York sports since the mid-eighties. I've had a chance to work with him on multiple occasions, and it's been nothing but fruitful. I am excited about his contributions to the New York sports community and really excited about this book. This is an important project.

I'm humbled that I was asked to write the foreword. I want to express my gratitude to Todd and Gary for this honor. That's the biggest thing I can say. I also want to say thank you, New York, New Jersey, and all the local sports fans that cherish these moments as much as we cherish the opportunity to deliver them. The shared connection that we have with our unique city, and its sports fans, is what makes this opportunity special for me. When I reflect on the significance of studying history, it shows us not only where we've been, but where we're going. New York is the greatest sports city in the country, and in the world for that matter. There are very few places that have sports moments that can measure up to New York's. There is a lot to celebrate on the pages of this book. We get a chance to tip our hats to the past and perhaps get a glimpse of the future.

INTRODUCTION

The 20 Greatest Moments in New York Sports History was written for sports fans of every generation. It will bring back memories for those who lived through these historic moments and shine a light for those who didn't. Where were you when the "Miracle Mets" won the World Series? When Bucky Dent earned a new middle name? When Mark Messier made his historic guarantee? For fans who were not alive for some or any of these moments, this book was written with the hope that it will spark conversations with their parents and grandparents. Hopefully, this book will bring families closer together and create dinner table conversations that can last a lifetime.

We not only want to revisit some of the happiest moments of your fandom, but also take you down the road that led into history, supplemented by never told until now anecdotes. How was the team constructed, what were the key plays, games, or decisions along the road? Some of the paths were a straight line, some were a winding road, but all will surprise, thrill, and enlighten you.

The best way to take a trip down memory lane is by talking to those who were there. As such, this book includes more than one hundred original interviews with players, broadcasters, writers, and even a director/comedian (you need to read the book to uncover his name). As you flip through these pages you will be treated to stories from your sports heroes detailing how they got there, what the moment meant to them, and how it changed their lives. You will be treated to stories that will make you think, "I didn't know that." The one phrase that made me the happiest when conducting these interviews was "I have never told this story publicly before." I hope that you will come away both entertained and educated about sports history in New York.

One day, my dad dropped me off at the train station. I was running late—really late. I ran into a bookstore, with seconds to spare, to grab a book to read during my train ride. I went directly to the sports section and selected a book by the colors of my favorite football team. Once I sat down and caught my breath, it dawned on me that sports fans were both hyperlocal and passionate primarily about their home teams. That's when I decided to write a book about the greatest moments in New York sports history. As a New York television sports producer—whose jobs included interviewing athletes and producing shows with live sports guests—it dawned on me that I had relationships and the contact information for many of the most prominent athletes in the history of sports here in the Big Apple. So, that was a leg up in getting the project off the ground. I also have worked in the New York market covering sports since 1984. I grew up watching or covering most of the moments in the book.

Steve Serby of the *New York Post* was the first person to believe in the project and partner with me on pitching the book. Then Elliott Kalb came on board when I offered to dust off the book proposal and search for a publisher for a second time. Finally, Gary Myers, a *New York Times* best-selling author and former long-time columnist for the *Daily News*, helped get the book across the finish line. There are no overnight sensations in sports or literary pursuits, as this book took over two decades from concept to your hands.

There isn't a person that I shared the book's concept with that didn't immediately list their top memories. Most people came up with a lot of the same moments, but the ranking depended on the teams that they support. We are open to any and all debate about the ranking, but I dare say that each of the moments will bring back happy memories to all who start turning these pages.

Thank you for buying the book, and I hope that you enjoy reading it as much as I did in researching and writing it.

Todd Ehrlich

#1

SUPER BOWL XLII: NEW YORK GIANTS vs. NEW ENGLAND PATRIOTS

FEBRUARY 3, 2008

THE HELMET CATCH

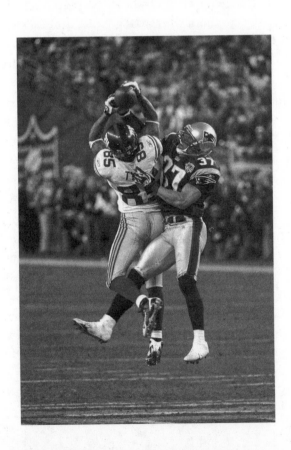

TIME CAPSULE

- Mayor of New York: Mike Bloomberg
- Oscar, Best Picture: *The Departed*
- Oscar, Best Actor: Forest Whitaker, *The Last King of Scotland*
- Oscar, Best Actress: Helen Mirren, *The Queen*
- Grammy, Album of the Year: Herbie Hancock, *River: The Joni Letters*
- Grammy, Record of the Year: Amy Winehouse, "Rehab," *Back to Black*
- President of the US: George W. Bush
- Price of Gas: $2.84/Gallon
- Heisman Trophy: Tim Tebow, quarterback, Florida

PREGAME

Question: Can an inanimate object catch a ball?

Answer: In the history of man, the answer was only 'yes' on February 3, 2008.

Apparently, a football helmet can catch a ball. However, we have a long road to travel before we can tell that story. When you hear the term *road trip*, what comes to mind? *Thelma and Louise*, *Easy Rider*, *Midnight Run*, or even a trip you took with some college friends?

Arguably the greatest road trip in sports history was taken by the 2007 New York Giants. As all good road trips, it began right at home with a glorious—if seemingly unattainable—destination in mind, and carried right over into the new year. This one started at Giants Stadium, on the evening of December 29, 2007, with a hard-fought 38–35 loss to Bill Belichick's New England Patriots, which enabled the Pats to finish off the first 16–0 regular season in NFL history. The Giants already had their playoff seeding locked up, but instead of resting his starters for the wild-card game the following week in Tampa Bay as many coaches would have done—Giants coach Tom Coughlin decided to go all out rather than just laying down and allowing New England to finish off its undefeated season. Coughlin also felt that, if his team played well against the

New England powerhouse machine, it could establish momentum going into the playoffs. Being old school, he firmly believed it was crucial for the integrity of the league for the Giants not to mail it in.

It turned out to be a brilliant decision. The Giants held a fourth quarter lead, scared the heck out of the Patriots, and even though they would end up losing, gained a psychological advantage in the longshot event that the teams would meet in the Super Bowl.

"I'll never forget. I was also working for Sirius XM NFL radio, and Dan Koppen of the Patriots had a weekly spot on my show," recalled Bob Papa, the radio voice of the Giants. "In the old Giants Stadium, I take the elevator down, I had to go to the locker room to do the Giants postgame interviews—which means we have to walk past the visiting team's locker room. And I see Dan Koppen and I stopped and said, 'Hey Dan, congratulations on the undefeated season.' He says, 'Hey thanks, bud,' but he said, 'I hope we don't see those guys again. That was one tough game.' So, the Giants had left their mark on the Patriots that day."

Coughlin walked into his office at 5 a.m. the morning after the three-point loss to a message on his answering machine from the legendary John Madden:

> Just called to congratulate you and your team for a great effort last night. Not good, but great. I think it is one of the best things to happen to the NFL in the last ten years, and I don't know if they all know it, but they should be very grateful to you and your team for what you did. I believe so firmly in this: That there is only one way to play the game, and it is a regular-season game, and you go out to win the darn game. I was just so proud being a part of the NFL and what your guys did and the way you did it. You proved that it's a game and there's only one way to play the game and you did it. The NFL needed it. We've gotten too much of, "Well, they're going to rest their players and don't need to win, therefore they won't win." Well, that's not sports and that's not competition. I'm a little emotional about it. I'm just so proud.

The character of the 2007 Giants was on full display for the world to see in that Week 17 game. They honored the sports credo: play every minute of every game to the best of your ability and with the singular goal of winning. Nothing less is acceptable.

"Obviously, we had so much respect for John Madden, and it just kind of confirmed that it was the right thing to do and that we trusted Coach Coughlin and whatever he said we did," said Eli Manning. "He was our leader. And he said we're playing and, hey, we went out there and competed our tails off, and we did the right thing. And football's about playing the game and you play the game hard all the time. We definitely used that game as motivation and my mentality was let's go out there and see how we compete against the best team in the NFL right now, these guys are undefeated. And to go out there and hang with them into the fourth quarter gave us confidence going into the playoffs. We felt like we can beat them. It just prepared us and gave us a little momentum going into that Tampa game and then later into Dallas and Green Bay."

The road trip went through Florida (a 24–14 win over the Bucs), Big D (a 21–17 nail-biter over the Cowboys) and the frozen tundra (a 23–20 overtime victory over the Packers), and the last stop was in Glendale, Arizona, on February 3, 2008, at Super Bowl XLII. It's where the Giants created one of the most enduring memories in not only the history of New York sports, but in the history of sports, period.

The David Tyree "Helmet Catch."

That catch led to one of the most stunning upset victories in Super Bowl history, over a Patriots team that added playoff victories over the Jaguars (31–20) and Chargers (21–12) to come into the game at 18–0, needing one more victory to match the '72 Dolphins (who were 17–0, including three postseason victories) with the only perfect seasons in league history.

The helmet catch was only the end of the play. First, there was an equally improbable escape by Eli Manning to avoid a sack and get the pass off when he somehow worked himself free from his jersey being grabbed, stepped back in the pocket, and let it fly down the middle of the field to the most unexpected receiver on the team—one who had a dreadful practice that Friday, dropping everything thrown his way.

Whew. That's a lot of stuff happening.

Tyree was one of the top special team players in the league. As a receiver? Not as much.

Tyree's catch—with All-Pro safety Rodney Harrison draped all over him—is an all-time great. It never would have happened if Manning hadn't first pulled off his Houdini act—with future Hall of Famer Richard Seymour having a chunk of his jersey in his left hand and referee Mike Carey coming so close to ruling the play dead—with Manning in the grasp.

"I think it is the biggest play ever in a Super Bowl game," said Giants defensive end Justin Tuck, who easily could have been named Super Bowl MVP after sacking Tom Brady twice and providing constant pressure. "The most remarkable play ever in a Super Bowl game. Considering as unathletic as Eli is, for him to break the tackles, and stay out of the grasp of that sack, and then throw a pass to one of the most unlikely of recipients for a pass in David Tyree going against one of the most feared defensive players of his time in Rodney Harrison—there are so many storylines in that one play."

There were important stops along the way in Florida, Texas, and Wisconsin, but before we get to that, we need to start with what happened between the Giants' last championship in Super Bowl XXV and how they even got to this point.

* * *

It all started with Bill Belichick, the head coach of the Patriots, on that December night that left such an impression on John Madden. Belichick came into the public eye years before as the Giants' defensive coordinator under Bill Parcells. They led the New York Giants to two Super Bowl wins: Super Bowl XXI, breaking a 30-year championship drought for Big Blue, and Super Bowl and XXV.

In 1996, the two Bills reunited in New England. Belichick served as the Patriots' assistant head coach and defensive backfield coach under Parcells. The two led the Patriots to Super Bowl XXXI, where they lost to the Packers. They then packed up and headed back to the Big Apple, joining the New York Jets in 1997, which caused acrimony, to say the least, with the Patriots and their owner, Robert Kraft. It cost the Jets picks in the first four rounds of the draft, spread over three years.

Following the 1999 season, Parcells resigned as the Jets' coach, contractually elevating Belichick as his successor. The next day, Belichick put in his resignation letter on a piece of note paper, inking that he resigned as "HC of the NYJ," preempting the press conference that was to introduce him as the Jets' new head coach. Belichick was the Jets coach for a day.

Kraft and the Patriots hired Belichick as their head coach and, for releasing Belichick from his contract, the Jets received the Patriots' first-round pick in the 2000 draft, along with exchanging other picks in the 2001 and 2002 drafts. It may have been the most lopsided trade in the history of the NFL, and the Jets were not on the winning side.

What happened? Well, the Patriots drafted Tom Brady and won three Super Bowls in four years. In 2006, the Patriots made it all the way to the AFC Championship Game, where they lost a 21–3 lead to Peyton Manning and the Indianapolis Colts. The following year, looking to avenge that bitter disappointment, the Patriots were on a mission.

The Jets were first up to start the 2007 regular season. On September 9, 2007, Matt Estrella, a Patriots video assistant, was caught illegally taping the signals of Jets defensive coaches during the season opener at Giants Stadium. When an NFL security official confiscated his video camera and videotape, the jig was up. The incident was dubbed "Spygate."

From 2000 to 2005, Jets head coach Eric Mangini was a Belichick assistant and possessed an insider's knowledge. The commissioner ruled that the Patriots had indeed violated league rules, fining Belichick $500,000, taking away a first-round pick and fining the team $250,000 . . . but Belichick was not suspended. The league confiscated and destroyed all the evidence of the scandal.

On the field, the 2007 Patriots could not be stopped. The NFL played forty-four seasons (1978–2021) with a 16-game schedule. This 2007 team was the only one to finish a perfect regular season, at 16–0. But it's not that they just won . . . they dominated. Belichick not only wanted to beat other teams to prove the videotaping, and the entire Spygate scandal, was meaningless and it was wrong to label him a cheater, he wanted to utterly destroy them.

New England scored a record 589 points (134 more than the next-closest team, the Dallas Cowboys), averaging more than 36 points per game. Only four times did the Patriots fail to score at least 30 points. They outscored their opponents by 315 points, an average margin of 19.7 per game. (The only other team to have a win margin over 10 was the Colts, with 11.8.) Brady threw a record 50 touchdowns, and Randy Moss caught a record 23 TDs. Brady and Moss set the record in the fourth quarter of the final game of the regular season against the Giants.

* * *

The New York Giants were a good, but not great, team. They were led by Manning who, in his fourth season, tossed 23 touchdown passes—not even half of Brady's total. Four of the twenty-three came in the season finale against the Patriots. One thing the Giants had going for them: Manning, at twenty-six, was unflappable. Brady, meanwhile, was a perfectionist. The Giants knew he hated pressure up the middle and if they could show that early, they felt they could rattle him. They did have tremendous respect for him. After all, the Giants led the regular season meeting by 12 points in the third quarter—the Patriots' largest deficit of the season—though could not make it stick.

The Super Bowl road trip started with a win in Tampa Bay, 24–14. Next stop: Dallas. Swept by the No. 1 seed Cowboys during the regular season, the Giants staged an upset in the first-ever postseason meeting between the long-time rivals, winning 21–17. The 13–3 'Boys had won three more games than the 10–6 Giants during the season.

The Giants next traveled to the frozen tundra of Lambeau Field to take on the Packers and the ghost of Vince Lombardi in the NFC Champion-ship Game. It wasn't just the tundra that was frozen that day. Everything was frozen, including Coughlin's rosy-red face. The game-time temperature was minus 1, with a minus 23-degree windchill. It ranked as the fifth coldest game day in NFL history. But the Giants left the field feeling warm all over with an overtime win and an all-expenses paid trip to thaw out in sunny Phoenix, with a shot at the Lombardi Trophy.

"We knew we were good on the road, we just kind of had that road warrior mentality. It was our motto going into the playoffs," Manning said. "We knew we were going to have to win three on the road and then one in the Super Bowl to be champions. That was the mindset, we're a good road team. We lost the first game of the season on the road to the Cowboys, but we put up a ton of points and played Dallas tough. We figured out that we can hang with any-body. And we found the way we needed to play and just kind of rode with it."

Manning played one of the most clutch games of his career, overcoming subhuman conditions in Green Bay, but if the Giants were going to win the Super Bowl, the defense was going to have to bring it home. There was no resemblance to the defense that gave up a combined 80 points in the first two games of the season against Dallas and Green Bay, but just held those teams to a total of 37 points in back-to-back playoff games. The defensive ends, Osi Umenyiora and Michael Strahan, combined for 22 sacks in the regular season, with Justin Tuck contributing 10 more. The Giants led the NFL with 53 sacks. Defensive coordinator Steve Spagnuolo knew he was going to have to devise a game plan to put plenty of pressure on Brady.

When asked for a prediction in the week leading up to the Super Bowl, Giants wide receiver Plaxico Burress picked his team to emerge with a 23–17 victory. This amused and insulted Brady, and he replied with a laugh, "We are only going to score 17 points, OK. Is Plax going to play defense? I wish he said 45 to 42 or something like that. At least he gave us a little more credit for scoring a few points."

As it would turn out, Burress was not giving his defensive teammates enough credit. Strong leadership and focus would be one of the keys heading into the game, if the Giants wanted to stop the Patriots from being the first ever 19-win undefeated Super Bowl champion.

"We didn't think about that, to be honest with you," Tuck said. "We thought about it from perspective of this is just another game. I think Coach Coughlin and the leadership on our team did a really good job of keeping people focused and not to get into the hoopla of being 19–0 and that story-line. Because none of that mattered, we were a team there to win a football game. They were a team there to win a football game. It's the Super Bowl, you can throw all the records out, you can throw all the previous matchups out, all that doesn't matter. So, I think the reason why we were so successful is because we held that Super Bowl as what it was, it was another game, and it was just one game. And we didn't think about what they had previously did, you know, obviously studied them. But that had no bearing on how we were gonna play that night. So, I think it obviously means a lot we add in the fact that that's a Boston-New York rivalry. It's a great defense versus a great offense. There's a lot of storylines you can take from it. But at the end of the day, the storyline for us was just the opportunity that we had to win a Super Bowl."

There was serious preparation that went into the game plan. Every minute would count when it came to setting the tone, as it had all season long under Coughlin.

"After our first practice session in Phoenix, they had In-N-Out Burger for all of us," says Tuck. "And we're all on the bus, getting ready to leave. And we're like, why isn't the bus leaving and we're looking out the windows and Coach Coughlin is sitting on the curb eating In-N-Out Burger. He had ketchup all over his face and it was like the best thing he had ever had, and he finally gotten In-N-Out Burger and he was enjoying it. I'm not saying we were late leaving, but let's just say we didn't leave as promptly as we normally would have left because of Coach Coughlin. Which was funny because of his rule of being five minutes early and now he's the one who is holding us up."

Maybe a little balanced leadership and In-N-Out Burgers helped as well. There were a lot of questions leading into the Super Bowl. Could the New York Giants beat New England and their record-setting offense? Could the Giants give an ounce of pleasure to the fan base of their co-tenants, the New York Jets, who had watched the Patriots steal their head coach, spy on their signals, and trounce them repeatedly for a generation?

The answer was in Tyree's helmet. He had never caught more than 19 passes in a season, and heading into the Super Bowl had caught just four balls for 35 yards and no touchdowns. In New York's first three playoff games, he had one catch for all of four yards. Tyree overcame it all, used his head (and helmet) to help the Giants win Super Bowl XLII and end the road trip happily in the desert of Big Blue dreams.

TYREE, ELI ARE MIRACLE WORKERS

BY PETER BOTTE

You can pardon David Tyree for borrowing the classic broadcasting call from likely the most memorable and significant sporting result in history.

Tyree's pinned catch against his helmet on the Giants' winning drive in Super Bowl XLII in Glendale, Arizona, in 2008 may not quite have been akin to the group of unheralded American amateur hockey players upsetting the heavily favored Russians on their unlikely path to gold medal at the 1980 Winter Olympics in Lake Placid.

In a word, however, it certainly was miraculous.

"Do you believe in miracles?" David Tyree responded with a laugh when asked how he held onto the ball. "Because as much as any man can say he's prepared for that moment, that moment can never be recreated. So, there's nothing that I could have done to practice or prepare to defy both physics and logic and come up with that catch—an instance that was that iconic. So that's why I always approached it with a lot of humility."

Of course, everything about the circumstances surrounding this moment fit under the miraculous and legendary headings. Former Giants assistant coach Bill Belichick, now regarded as the greatest coach in NFL history, future Hall of Fame quarterback Tom Brady, and the New England Patriots were gunning for a perfect 19–0 season.

The Tom Coughlin–coached Giants, a wild card entry who had posted three consecutive road wins in the NFC playoffs, had just given up a touchdown pass from Brady to Randy Moss and trailed 14–10 when they got the ball back with 2:39 remaining.

On third-and-five from the Giants' 44-yard line—one play after Manning nearly was (and should have been) picked off on the right sideline by Patriots cornerback Asante Samuel—Peyton's kid brother somehow escaped the temporary grasp of defensive linemen Richard Seymour and Jarvis Green and scrambled to his right.

Manning then heaved the ball down the middle of the field towards the Super Bowl logo, where Tyree—with safety Rodney Harrison draped all over him—leapt and snared the ball against his helmet for an unreal 32-yard reception and a first down at the New England 24-yard line.

Four plays later, Manning—the Super Bowl MVP for the first of two times in five years—found Plaxico Burress in the corner of the end zone for a 14-yard score with 35 seconds on the clock.

The Giants would upend the Pats again behind another late Manning scoring drive in Super Bowl XLVI and only made the playoffs one more time in the decade.

Tyree's miraculous "Catch 42" remains the greatest play in Super Bowl history.

"I remember being in the locker room and saying I want to watch *SportsCenter*, I want to see the catch. Everybody keeps talking about this catch and I didn't really see it," Manning said three years after his retirement from football. "It wasn't until later that night that I really got to see what an impressive catch it was."

POSTGAME

Greatest Road Trip in the History of the NFL

SHAUN O'HARA (GIANTS CENTER): There are two things that travel well, having a running game, and a great defense. We had those two that year. We had Brandon Jacobs, Ahmad Bradshaw, those were our one-two punch. In 2007 our defense was phenomenal. We have etched on our Super Bowl rings, "11 straight on the road," that had never been done before.

AMANI TOOMER (GIANTS WIDE RECEIVER): We were a veteran team. When you're on the road, you realize how you really need each other. There was a lot of guys that played a lot of years together on that team. I just know, I really enjoyed playing on the road. I enjoyed silencing crowds. That was one of my favorite things to do.

SHAUN O'HARA: Ironically, that year, we played in the very first London game. Traveling on long flights and staying in a motel for three or four days. Talking to some of the guys, those were times we bonded as a team. We talked about what it would be like to play in the Super Bowl. You're in a neutral site, both teams are traveling. We're here for business. We're here to work. We're here to win a football game. So that was kind of a little foreshadowing for us as to what was to come. But I think all of those things were all factors.

We just kind of took that mindset anytime we went on the road. That's when Strahan started his "us against the world." We fit that underdog narrative to a T, the whole year. I felt we thrived when we were on the road. Our focus was that it was a business trip.

Friday's Practice

AMANI TOOMER: David had a horrible practice on Friday. I mean, he dropped so many balls.

DAVID TYREE (GIANTS WIDE RECEIVER): That Friday practice, which is supposed to be a dress rehearsal, which means it's supposed to be buttoned up and clean, Plaxico Burress was injured. They were a little uncertain about his status going into Sunday. I was taking a lot of reps, and I was dropping everything. It was probably the worst practice I've ever had in my entire history of being an athlete. It wasn't a fun experience at the moment, but it didn't carry over into the game.

Eli kind of encouraged me afterward saying, "You're a gamer, I know you'll be ready."

ELI MANNING (GIANTS QUARTERBACK): David had a terrible practice on that Friday, he dropped everything. He caught a touchdown early in the Super Bowl. We had a special play for him that we put in on a kind of fake block and run and a little pop pass that he got the touchdown. I always believe and trust my guys. If you don't trust your gut, you'll be hesitant on everything.

A Giant Standard to Maintain

SHAUN O'HARA: I remember Harry Carson coming in to talk to the team. I remember, George Martin was always around along with Howard Cross and Carl Banks.

You would see these guys and as players you always kind of felt that you wanted to get to a level to make them proud. It's a proud organization. It's one of the flagship franchises in the NFL. I think that we all felt that as players when you have those championships like they had in '87 and '91. You feel like that's our standard, we've got to get to that.

What's Under an Underdog

SHAUN O'HARA: Nobody gave us a chance to win that game.

JIM NANTZ (CBS SPORTS ANNOUNCER): The amazing thing to me is I had the perspective on what was about to be the completion of the perfect season. At CBS we're the network of the AFC. I called half of the Patriots' games during the regular season and I had all the playoff games through the AFC Championship Game. So, I felt like we were handing off the eventual undefeated Super Bowl champion, New England Patriots, to FOX Sports for the Super Bowl. They seemed destined to be the first team since the '72 Dolphins to run the table. You knew it was going to take a great game plan, a hell of a lot of determination, and maybe a freakish bounce of the ball or an odd play for the Giants to be able to pull it off. And that's exactly what happened with the Helmet Catch.

BOB PAPA (RADIO VOICE OF THE GIANTS): At that time, I was also working for NFL Network. The Patriots were the first media session on media day, the Giants went second. They asked if I would come on the NFL Network set for the last two segments with Solomon Wilcots to talk about the game. So, I said sure.

So, I'm on the set with Solomon Wilcots, and I'm giving all the reasons why I think the Giants could win the football game. They're hot, they went down to Dallas and beat the Cowboys; they went to Lambeau Field and beat

Brett Favre; their pass rush was playing well, and they can get there with just four guys.

In the regular season finale, the Giants had given the Patriots all they can handle. It was a one-score game. The Giants had a bad call go against them and then Randy Moss scores a long touchdown and the Patriots wind up winning that game to go undefeated in the regular season.

The producer tells Solly, "Ask Bob to make a prediction."

Solly says, "Bob, you gave us all these reasons why you think the Giants can win the game, who do you think is going to win?"

I'm hemming and hawing.

He finally says, "Well, who do you think is going to win?"

I said, "I don't know. Brady and Belichick are 3–0 in Super Bowls, and they're undefeated this season. I mean, this is the Giants' first Super Bowl with this group. How could you pick against the Patriots?"

So long story short, the show ends. Little did I know that in the locker room that the Giants were in, they had the NFL Network on all the TVs. Now the Giants come out and it's right in front of where I am. I've never forgotten Amani Toomer's face.

Toomer looks at me and says, "Our own play-by-play guy picked against us."

I'm like, "I didn't really pick against you."

So, he busted my chops. And then in the hotel after the Giants won the Super Bowl, he was giving it to me.

I said, "Tooms, I gave like 15 reasons in three minutes on the air of why I thought you guys could win."

He said, "Yeah, but at the end of the day you picked against us."

I was like, "All right."

That's a funny story that I'll never forget about that Super Bowl, and Amani Toomer reminds me all the time that I had picked the Patriots.

AMANI TOOMER: It was one of these situations where I felt like our whole team was getting so disrespected the whole time. Then for our own "Voice of the Giants" to be adding on to it was just infuriating. We felt so disrespected because we had played them the last game of the year, and we had them beat and just ended up making a couple of mistakes, giving them an opportunity to get back in the game. We weren't intimidated by them at all. We were thinking that everybody was on crazy pills. Because we matched up really well with that team. And we had just almost beat them.

SHAUN O'HARA: It was going to be a historic win no matter what, right? I mean, if they won, it would have been unprecedented that they went 19–0. That had never ever been done before. So, it was going to be a monumental Super Bowl, no matter which way it went. There's been all kinds of terms for the game including David slaying Goliath.

76 Max Union Y Sail

ELI MANNING: It was a base play—we ran up a ton of different versions off it. It was a popular two-minute play. We'd run to the right side of the field where you have kind of a sail concept, a corner and a post, and it's good versus lots of coverages, Cover 3, man, quarters coverage and that's the coverage we got. It was quarters coverage. The middle safety either runs with the corner route, which would have been Steve Smith, or he gets deep and covers the post.

SHAUN O'HARA: I think that play, right out of the gate, was not how you draw it up. The play call was "76 Max Union Y Sail." We didn't block it exceptionally well. I still remember just kind of feeling like Eli was about to be sacked and I was trying to squeeze and push and do whatever I could to get the defensive guys off him. I remember seeing them have a hold on his jersey and then, somehow, he broke free.

ELI MANNING: I'm trying to read the coverage off [the safety]. He covered Steve Smith, so I was going to throw it to Tyree. That was my first read if I could have thrown it on time, but because of the pass rush, I was trying to step up hard but was getting grabbed by the jersey so I couldn't throw it in at that point. I was thinking how do I avoid a sack on third-and-five, which you never want to take? We would have to go for it there and I just don't want it to be a fourth-and-twelve. So, I'm just trying to kind of throw it away and get out of the situation, but they never tackled me. They had hold of me, but the offensive line is still blocking these guys. They had a good push, grabbed me, but the offensive line blocked the guys off of me. I was able to somehow get out of the pocket to the right. David Tyree is in the middle of the field, normally it's not a great idea to throw a ball up into the middle of the field with a couple of defenders around because if it gets tipped up, it's probably going to get intercepted because they got more defenders around. But I saw a little room and just knew we were running out of time, and we needed to make a play.

AMANI TOOMER: I just remember looking back and seeing Eli scrambling and I thought, *Oh my gosh, it's going to be fourth-and-long.* Then I saw him drop his shoulders and throw the ball deep. As a receiver, you read body language when you're looking at the quarterback. Then I thought, *No, he's throwing it to David?*

ZAK DeOSSIE (GIANTS LONG SNAPPER): I was on the Patriots' 40-yard line, so that side of the 50, holding hands with [defensive back] Craig Dahl. I was looking to my left and saw Eli getting chased, his jersey being ripped and pulled, and then all of a sudden, he spurted and stumbled out and my heart was sinking. I saw him throw it. It was this big old Hail Mary duck.

I was thinking, *Oh, my Gooosh.*

SHAUN O'HARA: I'll be honest, when he launched the ball, my first reaction was, *Oh no.* That's one thing you don't do. You don't throw a Hail Mary, up the middle of the field, at that point in the game. I thought it was destined to be a pick.

ZAK DeOSSIE: It was one of the longest throws and plays that I can ever remember watching. It felt like an hour from start to finish.

The "Helmet Catch"

JIM NANTZ: Well, on the improbable meter it's up there in the top five of most unlikely plays.

BOB PAPA: The broadcast booth [for the Super Bowl] in [the Cardinals' stadium] was down by the goal line. It was a very interesting perspective because we're watching Eli do all these things to get away from the sacks. The thing I remember most about the play was when the ball was snapped, Eli had David Tyree streaking down the middle of the field wide open.

BOB PAPA: I see Tyree is a wide open. My field of vision had the drop back and Eli is suddenly under pressure, but I see Tyree flashing. Eli avoids all these sacks and then heaves it down the middle of the field. So, my call, as Eli is throwing the ball was, "wide-open Tyree." Well, at this point, he's no longer wide open. Then after Eli avoided like 18 sacks, let's face it: Tyree was covered. So, I get a little grief for that.

HOWARD CROSS (FORMER GIANTS TIGHT END/WFAN SIDELINE REPORTER): I'm looking up, and somebody has Eli in his grasp. He's spinning and turning, and the ball gets released. I'm listening to the call because I'm part of the broadcast team. Bob Papa says David Tyree is open down the middle, the ball is thrown, and I'm thinking, *He's not open.*

BOB PAPA: I'm calling it in real time staying in the moment, "It's David Tyree and he makes the catch."

HOWARD CROSS: Then he jumps up, catches it, and pulls it down. You're like, "Holy smokes." You knew right then, seeing the play live, *That's got to be the greatest catch in Super Bowl history.*

BOB PAPA: You don't really see the helmet part of it right away. And because now the Giants are in the last two minutes of the game, I have to continue with the flow of the play-by-play. So I was caught in the moment, and it wasn't until we went to a break and saw the replays and you're like, *He caught the ball with his helmet.*

ELI MANNING: I trusted David there. And he came through! It was one of those deals, I probably didn't give it the proper reaction and credit it deserved because you're so in the moment at that time, and I really just kind of disregarded the helmet part of it. And I was just kind of looking to see in the replay whether it hit the ground or not. I saw it didn't hit the ground. I was like "All right, we've got to go and score a touchdown."

SHAUN O'HARA: I feel like there were really two miracles on that play. Number one was Eli breaking that tackle. I don't know if he had ever done that before in his career. Then, of course, miracle number two was Tyree not just catching the football but pinning it against his helmet with one hand while Rodney Harrison is yanking him down with both hands.

MATHIAS KIWANUKA (GIANTS DEFENSIVE END): I was on the bench with [tight end] Jeremy Shockey and [running back] Derrick Ward—we were all injured. For the Helmet Catch, I just remember the energy, the enthusiasm on the sidelines, and the sense that there was no quit in this team. My reaction to the catch was, "Oh, let's go (laughing)." Tyree and I were on special teams together. We'd spend a lot of time together outside of the team. So I was just floored and amazed because he was such a good person and the good things in football don't always happen to the good people. That was an instance where the good person got the good thing to happen to them, and at the perfect time.

DAVID TYREE: I was satisfied with my career as an All-Pro special teams player, but always striving to make a mark as a receiver. To have one moment where I'm still able to be a part of the conversation of the NFL, it's something that most people will never have. And maybe they deserve it, but it's something that I just wear with extreme humility and honor.

BOB PAPA: The Tyree catch is one of the greatest catches in Super Bowl history . . . but it's the most iconic in Super Bowl history because it's not just a throw and catch. It's a near sack about four different times. Then the second part of it is Tyree going up, pulling the ball against his helmet, and being pulled down on Rodney Harrison.

DAVID TYREE: I've never talked about the catch with Rodney Harrison outside of TV interviews. He did everything he could do on the play, but it was something that was meant to happen. That's the easiest way that I can summarize it. It was beyond someone's talent or ability level—myself included—and despite Rodney's desire to break up the play for his team. I'm a special teams guy who made the most of my opportunity. He has had many moments on the mountaintop.

DAVID TYREE: I think it has changed my life immensely. For a guy who had minimal expectations for an NFL career, but always tried to have a meaningful impact for my team, to have a place in NFL history is something I never could have imagined.

What Just Happened???

SHAUN O'HARA: I was saying to Eli, "Let's go, let's run a play so that they can't review it or challenge it in case he didn't catch it."

AMANI TOOMER: I remember running up to the line, and we had a specific signal. We would say "FedEx" if he wanted to snap the ball right away so that they couldn't review the play. I remember I was lining up in the slot and I was like, "Eli, Eli, Eli, FedEx, FedEx, FedEx."

He looks over at me so calmly, just kind of puts his hand up, as to say, like, *Calm down, he caught it. Just like one you caught.* And then I remember thinking, *Oh my goodness, we're so close.* I just knew we were gonna score.

ELI MANNING: I wasn't quite sure if he caught it or not. We called timeout, I would have loved to get up there and spike it but we just didn't have the time to do that. We couldn't let that much time run off and so called the timeout immediately to save time. I went up to David Tyree and asked him, "David, did you catch it?" And he's like, "Yeah, I caught it." I said don't lie to me. You know receivers have lied to me so many times before when I asked, "Were you open on this last play?"

I'm like, you gotta tell me the truth now, otherwise there's a big difference in thinking about your first-and-ten play call from the 24-yard line or a fourth-and-five play call back on your own 43.

He ensured me that he caught it and the ball didn't hit the ground and then you saw the replay and it didn't hit the ground. It's just an unbelievable effort by David!

SHAUN O'HARA: Man, there was just so many things that had to go right for us to win. The Helmet Catch was one of them. Ironically, we still had to score a touchdown. So as big as that catch was, we realized, hey, we got to go run a play.

ZAK DeOSSIE: When it was officially ruled upon as a catch, I said, "All right, the football gods are bouncing the ball our way today."

JUSTIN TUCK: So at the moment I think, we as defensive players, we're thinking *Okay, we gotta go back and stop Tom Brady if we score here.*

Helmet Catch Payoff—Plax Touchdown

ELI MANNING: New England had a tendency when you got to the red zone that they were going to play coverage, coverage, coverage, and eventually they're going to come out on an all-out blitz. So we kind of kept calling a similar play to the right with Steve Smith and Amani Toomer. I knew on that play they played off coverage on Plaxico and we had a fade route, which is not always the perfect play—I thought about changing it to a slant, but I had six on five DBs. I mean basically I'm gonna throw this up and kind of just play jump ball and let him go get this thing.

Because of the all-out blitz, I had to throw it a little bit early so I wouldn't take a hit. When I threw it he had not broken open. He gave a little stick, like he was gonna run a slant and the DB jumped it and now the ball's in the air and he's wide open, and I'm just hoping, I'm just thinking, *Please come down inbounds*, and it seemed to hang up there forever. You know, sure enough, he catches it and gets the touchdown.

ELI MANNING: I remember someone trying to give me a Super Bowl champion hat after that drive, and I'm like get that thing away from me! I'm not even going to look at that thing or touch it until there's zeroes on the clock.

Still Gotta Stop the GOAT

ZAK DeOSSIE: Right after Plaxico puts us in the lead, the Patriots get the ball. Behind my back, I hear, "'Psssst Zak, Psssst Zak." I'm like who the hell could that be, it's third down and long, I look behind me and it's my dad (former Giant Steve DeOssie). Somehow, he is standing behind our bench. He finagled his way onto the field with his press credentials. I turned around and looked at him.

He said, "Psssssst Zack, I think you guys are gonna win." (Laughing)

I turned to my dad and said, "Shut up, Dad, you are going to jinx us." I turn back to the game and started praying again.

BOB PAPA: What everybody forgets about that game was that New England still got the ball back. Brady got sacked by Jay Alford on the first snap. Then Brady threw a laser to Randy Moss that Corey Webster got a fingertip on the ball right in front of the Giants' bench down the left side. Or else history might have been rewritten in another way.

ELI MANNING: We got a sack early on, but you know, Brady throws a ball down the left sideline with Randy Moss streaking that Corey Webster just got a hand on. It was a little closer of a play than I would have liked to see. We got the ball back on fourth down, and that's when you kind of knew we did it: we just pulled off an unbelievable, unbelievable, upset. But, more importantly, we're Super Bowl champions.

BOB PAPA: If it wasn't for a Giant defensive play, after Brady had been battered, the Patriots still might have gone undefeated.

Underdogs No More—Simply Call Them "Champions"

SHAUN O'HARA: They were clearly the best team in the NFL, and the best offense in the NFL. It was why sports are great: you still have to play the game, and you just never know how things are going to turn out.

I think Super Bowl XLII is the perfect example of that. I think it's great, it gives hope to every underdog and every team, regardless of sport, it can happen to you, too.

ZAK DeOSSIE: At that point you've reached the pinnacle. You were watching those long Brady passes to Randy Moss in the waning seconds and are losing years off your life. Then finally it ticks to zero and all hell breaks loose!

JUSTIN TUCK: I think we're disappointed that they scored 14, to be honest with you. I think whenever you play a team as dominant as that Patriots team had been, you're going in and you feel like you have nothing to lose, because no one is really even thinking you have a chance. So, for us, it loosened us up and just allowed us to really play freely. I'll take that defense, and that D-line—especially against any O-line and any offense—any day.

ZAK DeOSSIE: I was thinking, *We did it. We did the impossible. We beat the undefeated Patriots.* Combine that with reaching the top, it's just like a double whammy of elation, satisfaction, and appreciation for everyone on that sideline. It was just absolute bananas.

BOB PAPA: The Miami Dolphins from 1972 still toast champagne every year as the only undefeated season in Super Bowl history. They are still the only one because of what the Giants did. I mean, the Patriots were that close to pulling off 19–0.

Say What, Stray?

JUSTIN TUCK: I'd been with my family for a little bit and I went up to I think it was Osi's room. And when I got there, and we are just sitting there talking and reminiscing about the journey, and Strahan told us that he was going to retire. And I got mad at him. I was like, "Man, why didn't you tell me this earlier, I would have held out for more money (laughs)." But no, I think that moment was pretty surreal. It was just Strahan, Osi and myself and it was Stray's way to signal to us that he was passing the torch. Which was significant, and I mean, you can't write it any better because the career he had and getting the opportunity to go out with one of the biggest upsets in NFL history. And obviously Michael means a lot to this franchise and means a lot to this city and to me, and getting the opportunity to kind of embrace him and tell him how special it was to play with him.

A Championship Tradition Continues

JUSTIN TUCK: Man, listen, you're talking to a guy who grew up in the hometown of Kellyton, Alabama, where 212 people have lived in the last century. So, you put me on a float with, I don't know, with 2 to 4 million people. I mean, I was like a kid in a candy store. My eyes were probably as big as a saucer. Because it was just unreal, the amount of people and the amount of confetti. And plus, and just knowing the history of the people who have come through that Canyon of Heroes. Obviously, sports teams but also war heroes. So, to have your name somewhat linked with so many great people that have been celebrated in the Canyon of Heroes was just tremendous.

SHAUN O'HARA: It was great to give the Giants fans a recent championship memory. As opposed to "I remember watching that Super Bowl with my dad. I was five years old, like, I don't really remember it." It definitely gives you an appreciation for all the guys that came before you.

JUSTIN TUCK: When it first happened, I didn't know what it meant to be honest with you (laughs). I knew the fan base was going to absolutely love it when we came back to New York. But like, honestly, that game is still talked about just about every day that I talk about sports to anybody, that is the game that is brought up. The outpouring of support and pride that this city and our fan base had for us during that time. I don't know how to put it into words, it still to this day gives me goosebumps just thinking about being a part of it.

Seeing is Believing

ELI MANNING: Later that night we had the Super Bowl party, and you have friends and family all talking about the catch. I knew that the next morning I was gonna have to go to a press conference early in the morning, at eight. It's three o'clock in the morning and my wife said, "Let's go to bed."

I remember being in the room and saying I want to watch *SportsCenter*, I want to see the catch. Everybody keeps talking about this catch and I didn't really see it, I want to see how it happened, who was around him. I didn't know which player was trying to tackle him and how it all played out. I remember sitting there waiting to see the play so I could just analyze it. And I think that was the first time I was like, Oh my goodness, this guy, Rodney Harrison was draped all over all him and he catches it one-handed to the helmet and holding on to it, getting bent over backwards.

The Impact of the "Helmet Catch"

DAVID TYREE: People come up to me all the time and share their reaction to the moment I made the Helmet Catch. One Giants fan came up to me and shared that his grandfather was on his deathbed and they all watched the game together. They were expecting him to die within the month, but he ended up living six months longer. They told me it was because they shared so much joy watching my catch and the team's Super Bowl victory.

The moment really transcended football for so many people. The fact that my moment was shared with Giants fans all over the world, and someone's time on earth was extended beyond expectation is humbling. It's really overwhelming.

Keeping It Lighthearted from Training Camp to the
Super Bowl and Beyond

SHAUN O'HARA: Eli's always had a great knack for playing pranks. We were in the last day of training camp up in Albany. After practice, everybody already packed up the car and it's like the Indy 500 coming down the New York State Thruway with everybody trying to get home. I stole Eli's E-Z Pass. As he was flying home to get to Hoboken and passing all these tolls, he was in the E-Z Pass lane, and it kept saying, "Toll unpaid."

He's looking at it like what's going on? He got a ticket for every E-Z Pass violation all the way home. It was the gift that kept on giving all year long. He didn't know who did it, and then my wife told his wife.

My wife said, "I feel so bad that Shaun did that to Eli's car."

She asked me, "Didn't you tell Eli about it?"

I was like, "Noooooooooooooooooo!" That was payback, we had roomed together in training camp so there were all kinds of shenanigans going on.

SHAUN O'HARA: There was another good prank that happened the week before we went out to Arizona for the Super Bowl. We practiced at home that week. Our strength coach, Jerry Palmieri, is one of the nicest dudes you'll ever meet. We used to tease him a lot. But strength coaches have a good relationship with the players because that's kind of our sanctuary. Jerry was always getting on everybody about their workouts. Strahan used to bust his chops whenever we would do stretches, because he would kind of marble mouth sometimes. One of the practices, we're jogging and warming up, going back and forth down the field. And there's this huge climbing rope, you know, it's probably like six feet long and it's in the middle of the field. Everybody stops and gets into their spots for the stretching and takes their helmet off and they're about to start stretching and Jerry walks over to the big piece of rope.

He grabs it and he screams, "Hey, Stray, what is this?"

Strahan is looking at him and says "what?"

(Editor's Note: Strahan has a large gap between two of his upper front teeth.)

Jerry says "Hey, Stray, I thought I told you to quit leaving your dental floss out here on the field." Everybody busts out laughing, even Tom's laughing. A week before the Super Bowl, Jerry finally got his revenge. It was well thought out. It was great strategy.

Even Strahan was chuckling and said, "Jerry, that was a good one. You got me on that one."

So, there was some good humor in that one.

SHAUN O'HARA: There were a lot of good moments and a lot of good laughs that Super Bowl season. There was a great prank that Eli pulled. Here we are getting ready to play the biggest game of our lives and Eli was still able to add some levity to the team flight.

ELI MANNING (ON THE PRANK HE PLAYED BEFORE THE SUPER BOWL): On the way to Arizona for our first Super Bowl, we had a short practice that morning on a Monday. And when we were at practice, I knew we had to wear a coat and tie and dress shoes on the plane to fly out there.

So, while we were at our practice, I had our managers get all the linemen's shoes and purchased similar sizes and similar shoes and they spray painted them this bright purple. You know, there's always that shot, as you land in the Super Bowl site, of the team walking off the plane when they arrived. You know, the Giants have arrived at the Super Bowl in Arizona and then there are my linemen wearing purple shoes. They were all kind of freaking out, didn't know where their shoes were. I went out and delivered their real shoes to them on the plane. So I just had them freaking out for a little bit.

SHAUN O'HARA: Anytime that I've done an event with Eli after we won the Super Bowl and we're talking about the Helmet Catch or the Super Bowl, he always starts off with "Yeah, first, I have to thank my offensive linemen for not doing their job." Eli does not miss any opportunity to bust balls. He loves busting chops. I feel like, Eli has a lot of brothers, the guys that he played with and the guys that he loves and his friends, nobody is safe from Eli busting chops.

A Giant Legacy

The Only Father and Son to Win a Super Bowl with the Same Franchise

STEVE DeOSSIE (FORMER GIANTS LINEBACKER AND FATHER OF ZAK DeOSSIE): The Giants were a huge part of my life. It was not simply because we won a championship, the Giants helped me turn my life around. When my son got drafted by the Giants, I was so happy that he was going to a place that I loved and that I knew was an organization that cared about its players.

ZAK DeOSSIE: I didn't know at the time being a rookie just how truly special it was to be a part of a championship winning team in New York. Every year I get away from the 2007 season, it feels even more special because this is New York City and it's the best sports city in the whole universe.

STEVE DeOSSIE: To watch them win a Super Bowl brought back the feeling that I had when we won. Then to know that your own child is experiencing something that was monumental in my life. I was one of the few people in that building that knew what he was feeling. I knew that very few people get to feel that. Knowing as the years went along, that my son felt the same way I did about the Giants organization was another factor. It was just a joy to watch my son play.

ZAK DeOSSIE: I was very, very proud. For me personally, my dad is my hero. To reach the Super Bowl championship level with the same exact team he did made it even more special.

2

SUPER BOWL III: NEW YORK JETS vs. BALTIMORE COLTS

JANUARY 12, 1969

NAMATH'S PREDICTION

TIME CAPSULE

- Mayor of New York: John Lindsay
- Oscar, Best Picture: *In the Heat of the Night*
- Oscar, Best Actor: Ron Steiger, *In the Heat of the Night*
- Oscar, Best Actress: Katharine Hepburn, *Guess Who's Coming to Dinner*
- Grammy, Album of the Year: Glen Campbell, *By the Time I Get to Phoenix*
- Grammy, Record of the Year: Simon & Garfunkel, "Mrs. Robinson," *The Graduate: The Motion Picture Soundtrack*
- President of the US: Lyndon B. Johnson
- Price of Gas: $0.34/Gallon
- Heisman Trophy: O. J. Simpson, running back, USC

PREGAME

guar·an·tee
noun

> • **a formal promise or assurance**

a sports guarantee (guar·an·tee)
noun

> • **See Joe Namath before Super Bowl III**
> **for the definition**

It's debatable which is the more memorable moment: Joe Namath guaranteeing the disrespected Jets of the laughed-at American Football League would beat the big, bad Baltimore Colts of the established National Football League in Super Bowl III; or Joe Willie and the boys actually going out and doing it.

Namath set a new standard for trash talking, and then led the Jets to the greatest upset in sports history as 18-point underdogs. It set the tone for the most amazing 18 months in New York sports, as the precocious

Mets—in the eighth year of their infancy—followed up the Jets victory with an incredibly easy five-game win over the powerhouse Baltimore Orioles in the World Series, *then* followed by the Knicks beating the Lakers in seven thrilling games for the NBA title.

In each case, it was the first championship for each franchise. The Mets and Knicks have each won only one more title since, while the Jets have been stuck on one for more than a half century. That is why January 12, 1969, remains such an iconic moment.

And it all started with Namath's guarantee.

The Colts could not make Namath eat his words, and Namath immediately became an icon both on and off the field for his fashion statements by wearing fur coats, endorsing panty hose, and co-starring with Ann Margret in the 1970 classic *C.C. and Company* (kind of kidding about it being a classic). Joe set the stage for Madison Avenue embracing high-profile athletes as pitchmen.

But his impact on football runs much deeper.

The original eight teams of the AFL started in 1960, including the New York Titans, who would become the Jets in 1963. The NFL didn't consider the AFL much of a threat at first, although when the Houston Oilers offered Tom Landry its first coaching job in 1960, Giants owner Wellington Mara suggested to Tex Schramm—the president and general manager of the expansion Dallas Cowboys—that he hire the Giants' defensive coordinator. That worked out well for the Cowboys. Essentially, the NFL considered the AFL nothing more than a nuisance.

But with the AFL having some owners with deep pockets added to the financial support and visibility provided by NBC, the league refused to go away. And in 1965, the Jets made quarterback Joe Namath from Alabama— by way of Beaver Falls, Pennsylvania—the first pick of the AFL draft. The St. Louis Cardinals selected Namath with the 12th pick of the NFL draft. The Cardinals offered a three-year $200,000 deal. The Jets topped that with a three-year $427,000 deal.

That's how Namath made it to New York and became "Broadway Joe."

The bidding war for Namath was the most high profile of the competition for college talent that had developed between the NFL and AFL. They were driving up the prices on each other, which was bad for business. On June 8, 1966, after Schramm and Kansas City Chiefs owner Lamar Hunt had done the legwork, the NFL and AFL came to an agreement on a merger. Although the two leagues would not officially become one and play regular season games against each other until 1970, there was the matter of crowning a world champion for the next four seasons.

It was decided that the champion of the NFL would play the champion of the AFL. The first two games were known simply as the AFL-NFL World Championship Game. Hunt came up with the idea to call it the Super Bowl, and it became so for Super Bowl III. In the first two championship games, the AFL was embarrassed by the Green Bay Packers. First, Vince Lombardi and the Packers beat the Chiefs 35–10, followed by a 33–14 victory over the Oakland Raiders.

The two games made it clear that the AFL had some catching up to do, and it would be up to Namath to close the gap in Super Bowl III. The Jets finished the 1968 season with an 11–3 record, with Namath passing for a pedestrian 15 touchdowns and 17 interceptions. It wasn't until the following season that he threw more touchdowns than interceptions for what turned out to be the only time in his career. In the Super Bowl season, he completed just 49.2 percent of his passes. If a quarterback put up those numbers today, he would likely be benched or cut after the season. But the game was so different five decades ago. There was more of a reliance on the running game—truth be told, Matt Snell, not Namath, should have been the MVP of the Super Bowl after rushing for 121 yards and the game's only touchdown, with an additional 40 receiving yards. The rule changes that opened up the passing game were decades away. As a result, wide receivers not only had a tough time breaking free at the line of scrimmage, but once they made their way into the secondary, cornerbacks and safeties did things that today would routinely draw flags, if not arrest warrants.

The Jets beat the Raiders in the AFL Championship Game at Shea Stadium. The two teams had a bitter rivalry, and this game was actually more competitive than the Super Bowl, as New York escaped with a hard-fought 27–23 victory. The Colts, meanwhile, were a powerhouse. They were 13–1 on the season and beat the Vikings 24–14 and the Browns 34–0 in the playoffs. In the regular season, the Colts scored 402 points and gave up 144, barely 10 points per game.

Naturally, all the pre–Super Bowl talk was about how the Colts would embarrass the Jets, just as the Packers had done to the Chiefs and Raiders.

That provided even further motivation for the Jets . . . not that they needed it.

On January 9, the Thursday night before the game, Namath was honored by the Miami Touchdown Club at the Miami Springs Villas as professional football's player of the year. It was the first time the award went to a player in the AFL. Namath went to the podium, unaware he was expected to make a speech. In the back of the room came the words that inspired one of the most famous quotes in sports history. After a heckling Colts fan shouted, "Namath, we're going to kick your butt," Joe Willie Namath responded, "The Jets will win Sunday, I guarantee it."

Jets coach Weeb Ewbank had warned his players all week about providing any bulletin board material for the Colts. Ewbank had spent the first nine years of his head coaching career at the helm of the Colts (winning championships in 1958 and 1959), and beating his old team meant an awful lot to him. Let them think the Jets were pushovers. But at that moment, Namath let his pride—and mouth—take over. One reporter was at the banquet and his story didn't even make the top of the *Miami Herald* sports section the next day despite the headline, "Namath Guarantees Jets Victory." If that happened today, the room would have been full of reporters and Namath's words would have been blasted around the world on social media before he even took his seat.

The next morning, Namath was having breakfast with some teammates. Ewbank had just became aware of Namath's brash guarantee and scolded him for waking up the Colts. "I asked Joe what possessed him to do such a thing," Ewbank said. "I said, 'Don't you know [Don] Shula will use this to fire up his team?' Joe said, 'Coach, if they need press clippings to get ready, they're in trouble.'"

Trash talking is one thing in a sport like boxing. Muhammad Ali made a living out of opening his mouth and, more often than not, he was able to back it up. Individual sports are different. The only pressure is on the person doing the bragging. But Namath was not going to have to block Bubba Smith or cover John Mackey. Realistically, how many players go into a game believing they are going to lose? Namath was simply vocalizing what just about every athlete believes: they are going to be victorious. Namath was just twenty-five years old. He owned New York. He loved the ladies and the ladies loved him. If the Jets won the game, they would love him even more.

Nobody expected the Jets to win except the Jets, and Joe just made sure everyone knew it.

"Look, I had some great coaches in my time," Namath said. "And I have three older brothers and I never ran my mouth. You know what I mean? You don't pat yourself on the shoulder. But this was the Thursday night before the game and I got up to the podium to speak and a wise guy in the back of the room said, 'Hey, Namath, we're gonna kick your [bleep], ya know.' And I said, 'Hey man, wait a minute. You folks have been talking for two weeks now. You know you're big favorites. Well, I got news for you. We're going to win the game. I guarantee it.'"

Namath was fired up that night, and it carried right over into Sunday. "It was a little anger coming out of there," he said. "But we believed it. You're never going out there thinking you're going to lose. Our college coach told us in our first meeting as a freshman at Alabama, Paul 'Bear' Bryant, he said if you think you can't, you won't, and that applies to everything in life. Argue for your limitations and you can have them."

Jets running back Emerson Boozer was not disappointed that Namath publicly guaranteed victory. "I think he was pretty much echoing the sentiments of the whole group of guys, that we felt that we were as good or better than the club that we're about to face," Boozer said. "I was pretty confident because I had seen the Colts play a lot."

The lack of respect for the AFL was felt not only by the Jets, but the rest of the league. AFL players dropped by the Jets' hotel in Fort Lauderdale in the week leading up to the game, imploring Joe and the Jets to win it for all of them. The Jets knew they were carrying the AFL banner into this game.

Who knew the Jets could win with Namath completing just 17 of 28 passes for only 206 yards, or with Don Maynard not even catching a pass? Or Namath not even attempting a pass in the fourth quarter? But Snell was a star, George Sauer caught eight passes for 133 yards, and Namath kept the Colts' defense off balance by calling the plays at the line of scrimmage and going in the opposite direction of where he thought the Colts were anticipating the play to be run. Namath made headlines with his mouth, made his money with his arm, but won this game with his head.

Namath ran off the field wagging his right index finger in the air signifying the Jets were number one, and champions of the football world. It gave the AFL credibility one year away from when it would begin playing regular season games against NFL teams. The Steelers, Browns, and Colts (of all teams) agreed to switch from what was to be the National Football Conference to the new American Football Conference in 1970, giving each conference thirteen teams. In the last Super Bowl between the NFL and the AFL, the Chiefs easily beat the Minnesota Vikings to get the AFL even at 2–2 before the merger took effect.

More than fifty years later, the Jets are still in search of their second Super Bowl. Since January 12, 1969, only one other team that have been around for every one of those seasons has not made it to the Super Bowl—the Detroit Lions. Not exactly the type of company the Jets want to keep.

But as Jets Nation prays for the day Gang Green can make it back to the Super Bowl, those old enough to remember will always have Super Bowl III and just as important the most outrageous and famous guarantee of them all.

BROADWAY JOE BACKS UP GUARANTEE

BY PETER BOTTE

Perhaps the incomparable Muhammad Ali was brash enough to pull it off in the 1960s and '70s, but professional athletes in team sports—football, especially—never would dare to guarantee a victory.

Especially not a relatively young and unproven player from an upstart league about to face a heavily favored juggernaut in the more established NFL, right?

Then again, anyone saying that somehow must not have known much about the swashbuckling New York legend known as Broadway Joe Namath.

The Pennsylvania native and former Alabama quarterback immediately etched his name in Big Apple sports lore when he guaranteed and backed up his midweek words that the Jets—18-point underdogs to the Colts—would become the first AFL team to defeat an NFL team in Super Bowl III in January 1969. It was the first of three New York sporting championships in a 16-month span, with the Mets and the Knicks to follow.

"My reaction was 'Oh, my God, he didn't say that, did he?' offensive lineman and longtime teammate Randy Rasmussen said. "You know, the one thing that [Jets coach] Weeb [Ewbank] had been preaching to us leading up to the game is just don't say anything and don't give them anything that they can put up on their bulletin board.

"And here comes Joe on the Thursday before the game and he says, 'We're gonna win and I guarantee it.' So, it kind of shocked me a little bit, but yet it didn't because that was Joe. I think it kind of actually helped us psychologically."

Namath didn't exactly dominate on the field that day in Miami—throwing for 206 yards and no touchdowns in the 16–7 Jets victory. Their lone TD—to go along with three Jim Turner field goals—was scored in the second quarter on a four-yard plunge by running back Matt Snell.

Namath went on to throw more interceptions than touchdowns in his career. And the Jets, of course, didn't reach the Super Bowl in more than five laugh-track decades since the ever-brash Namath fittingly exited the field that night in Miami while wagging his right index finger in the air.

"Boy, you know, it was just like that, yeah, we did it!" Namath said. "There were a bunch of Jets fans right there. I was running by them and they were so happy. And it was just yeah, we did it. That's what [the No. 1 finger] was about. Those people that were up there did that first."

"I never did that before in my life. I never did it at Alabama. We didn't do that, you know, that kind of thing, but we were Number 1. And I mean that humbly."

A word rarely associated with Broadway Joe, and for good reason.

POSTGAME

The Guarantee

MIKE D'AMATO (JETS DEFENSIVE BACK): I was with Joe the night that he said that. We were out at dinner and, earlier in the day, Weeb told us not to throw any wood on the fire with the press so that we wouldn't give any incentive to Baltimore.

When Joe said that there were a couple of us sitting at the table, and he said, "I guarantee it." We all kind of cringed, because we said, "Oh, God, we've just went over that, you know." He said back to us, "Well, don't you think we're gonna win?"

JOHN SCHMITT (JETS CENTER): We all laughed when we heard it and said, "We can't let Joe down, we better win."

RANDY RASMUSSEN (JETS GUARD): Watching the films, we matched up so well with the style of game that the Colts were playing. I said we should win; we should win but nobody could say it. Well, Joe said it for us. I think it was okay, but it did shock me when it first came out.

GREG BUTTLE (JETS LINEBACKER, 1976-84/PRE AND POSTGAME RADIO HOST): The media promoted Joe's guarantee. The whole football team thought that they were going to win the game, Namath just verbalized it. Every single player on that team felt that way. Weeb Ewbank's biggest job during practice was making sure they weren't overconfident. He did that. I know that as a fact from all the players I've talked to.

Us Against the World

GREG BUTTLE: Vegas made the Colts an 18-point favorite against the Jets. Nobody in pro football believed that the Jets were going to go in there and beat those mighty Baltimore Colts. The only exceptions were the 40 some players on the Jets roster. They all looked at the film and said, "Let's just not beat ourselves." And they didn't.

JOHN SCHMITT: Coach Ewbank stopped letting us watch film on Thursday because he thought we were getting overconfident. He really did.

MIKE D'AMATO: We had a pretty tight team that year. And we felt we could win. I mean, we weren't out there thinking that we're going to lose.

JOE NAMATH (JETS QUARTERBACK): I remember standing on the sideline before the game, talking to a player who was a little too happy, and I said, "You're a little too happy. The gun hasn't gone off yet." If the gun hadn't gone off yet and, you know, they have [Johnny] Unitas over there. Trust me it wasn't over till that gun went off. That's the way I felt.

GREG BUTTLE: The Jets felt disrespected that they were such a big underdog. Namath and I've talked about it many times, after watching film of the Colts defense and in practice they were just overconfident about beating the Colts.

JOHN SCHMITT: I contracted pneumonia after the championship game against the Oakland Raiders. I was the only center. Coach Ewbank didn't like to spend any extra money on having a backup. So, I didn't have a backup. Coach came up to me and they thought I was allergic to penicillin. So, they didn't give me anything for the pneumonia. By Thursday of the week of the Super Bowl,

I was coughing up this blood and green and yellow stuff. I was dying. I could barely walk.

Coach came up to me and said, "Schmitty, you got to go out there. We're going to have a press day. You can't let anybody know that you're sick because they'll pick up on it. We won't let anybody hit you, but you got to practice."

So that's the way we went during the week and Thursday, just before the Super Bowl, I went to the coach and said, "Look, Coach, if you don't give me penicillin, I'm not playing in the game because I can't walk, I can't even hardly get out of bed."

So, they gave me the penicillin and it worked. But it was too late, basically.

Game Time

JOHN SCHMITT: It was big getting the game's first score, because almost no one had scored a touchdown on the ground against the Colts all season. Also, when we scored on the ground, they were like in shock. They couldn't believe it. That's when things turned because the first quarter, they were really kicking our rear end. They really came out after us because of that article, where Joe guaranteed the win. They really came out after us real hard, but then when we scored that touchdown on the ground with Matt [Snell], that really took the air out of their balloon. It really started to get things going in our direction.

GREG BUTTLE: Namath called all the plays in the Super Bowl. They studied the Colts, and they couldn't believe how well they matched up with them and knew they were going to beat them.

JOHN SCHMITT: I played in the game and you saw me coming out of the huddle in the first quarter, and I'm running out of the huddle to the line of scrimmage, and then in the second quarter, you see me jogging out of the huddle. And in the third quarter, you see me walking out of the huddle. And in the fourth quarter, you see me with Dave Herman and Randy Rasmussen, helping me to the line of scrimmage.

When the Clock Hit Zero

JOE NAMATH: There was just so much emotion as I was running off the field.

EMERSON BOOZER (JETS RUNNING BACK): It meant everything because we were in a supposedly weaker league than the Colts. The Jets, we were the new league, the weaker league. So, it meant a lot to me that Joe guaranteed it and it was a good feeling to me that we backed it up.

GREG BUTTLE: The game plan was a masterpiece. It was perfectly executed.

EMERSON BOOZER: When we won the game, it was basically what I thought in the first place: that we had enough talent to defeat the Colts, and that thought was: *we had accomplished it, finally.*

RANDY RASMUSSEN: Well, I couldn't believe it. I will tell you; I grew up being a Baltimore Colts' fan. In high school, and even in college, I remember watching the Colts and they were my team. All of a sudden, I'm out on the field playing against this team. The first thing I thought was, *Wait a minute, you're out here and you're out playing, and these guys are not invincible.* That was kind of my feeling about the game. When the game was over, I said there's one thing I have to do—shake Johnny Unitas's hand. After everything, I went over. I caught him just under the goalposts and gave him a handshake. He's got pride, too. He lost and wasn't in the best of moods, but that was okay. I got to meet him. He was my guy. So, when the clock struck zero, it was a celebration first, then find Unitas, and shake his hand.

JOHN SCHMITT: I was so weak after the game was over—this is terrible, but I'll tell you the story anyway. We were kneeling down saying a prayer after the game and Joe Namath was right next to me as usual. I started losing it and I started wetting myself.

Joe hit me and said, "Schmitty, it's really nothing against you, but I'm out of here."

I said, "I don't blame you, Joe, get out of here because I can't control this (laughs)." That's how weak I was, that's really how weak I was.

Pop the Champagne!

EMERSON BOOZER: In the locker room we certainly all were totally elated that we had done what a lot of folks thought we couldn't do. That was to beat the NFL. We were the AFL.

MIKE D'AMATO: Winning the Super Bowl meant everything in the world. To make the Jets team and then go on to win the Super Bowl. I mean, that's the dream of a lifetime for anybody.

JOHN SCHMITT: We were a second-rate team in New York next to the Giants. I mean, we were just Joe-bag-of-doughnuts, okay? That's the way we got treated. If I went out to make a speech, I got $100 for the speech. A Giant got $500. It was crazy what the difference was, but that game changed everything.

MIKE D'AMATO: It kind of legitimized everything. It made the merger seem legitimate. I think it was very important that we that we won that Super Bowl.

RANDY RASMUSSEN: It was a great feeling. During the whole ceremony downtown at City Hall, you are kind of floating. It was still sinking in that we won this game. Even though, going into it, we knew we were going to win. So, I don't know. Your mind can play tricks on you, I guess.

How the Jets' Win Changed the NFL

EMERSON BOOZER: It was a great feeling for me and I'm sure for all the other guys as well. We, as the supposedly weaker league, showed we could defeat the big boys from the other side of town. It was just something we thought we could do, and we did it.

GREG BUTTLE: That's how big this game was because it was an AFL team that needed to prove that the AFL was not only worthy of being a joint member of the National Football League, but that they could beat them. Which they hadn't done in the championship game until that game, and they did it with the weight of the world on the Jets.

EMERSON BOOZER: It's still a great feeling, those that remember that we were an AFL club, not originally part of the NFL. So, you got the AFL defeating the NFL, so to speak. We were from that AFL side of the ball. I am sure most folks didn't think about how that one win helped to create the NFL as it is aligned today. It all came from these upstarts from the new league, the AFL and our answer to the question, could you defeat the NFL?

GREG BUTTLE: The Jets' Super Bowl III win had a major impact on all New Yorkers and the entire AFL. Because the AFL had lost the first two Super Bowls in such a fashion that it was an embarrassment.

If the Jets Ever Won a Second Lombardi Trophy. . .

GREG BUTTLE: Jets fans are always dreaming of another Super Bowl. Giants fans win one every five or six years, or so it seems. Jets fans hang on every single play and have since the last time they won the Super Bowl. New York never sleeps, but man, Jets fans are all dreaming of another championship.

What Do a Chicken and a Jet Have in Common?

RANDY RASMUSSEN: We played hard, and we partied hard also. Yet when we came in on any Sunday morning for the game, it was time to work; it was all business. We had some real characters on that team. [Punter Curley] Johnson was our storyteller and, oh my gosh, I could sit and laugh for an hour with him with all the stories he had to tell. His famous saying, "A chicken ain't nothing but a bird, and that ain't nothing but another football game." I remember reading that in the papers back then, Curley would just say it all the time.

3

1977 WORLD SERIES: NEW YORK YANKEES vs. LOS ANGELES DODGERS, GAME 6

OCTOBER 18, 1977

REGGIE! REGGIE! REGGIE!

TIME CAPSULE

- Mayor of New York: Abraham Beame
- Oscar, Best Picture: *Rocky*
- Oscar, Best Actor: Peter Finch, *Network*
- Oscar, Best Actress: Faye Dunaway, *Network*
- Grammy, Album of the Year: Stevie Wonder, *Songs in the Key of Life*
- Grammy, Record of the Year: George Benson, "This Masquerade," *Breezin'*
- President of the US: Jimmy Carter
- Price of Gas: $0.59/Gallon
- Heisman Tropy: Earl Campbell, running back, Texas

PREGAME

Three's a Charm for Reggie
Reggie!
Reggie!
Reggie!

Reggie Jackson famously was quoted as saying he was "the straw that stirs the drink" with the New York Yankees.

Well, the drink special being served on the 18th of October 1977 had three shots in it. The drink was the *Mr. October,* and it tasted as sweet as a Reggie! bar to Yankees fans and helped secure the Bronx Bombers a long-overdue World Series championship.

The building blocks to that championship were set by the Yankees of the previous season. But "The House that Ruth Built'" wouldn't get a championship without the final brick in the wall. On November 29, 1976, George Steinbrenner signed Jackson to a five-year, $3.5-million free-agent contract. Reggie wanted to be a Yankee and gave the Boss credit for outworking all the other teams to secure his services. The signing made Jackson the highest paid player in baseball. And Jackson would soon make the Boss a champion. There were other suitors in the free-agent sweepstakes, but Jackson wasn't going to miss his chance to play on the biggest stage a few miles from the bright lights of Broadway. In a move that may have foreshadowed Reggie's October heroics, he selected the number 44 in honor of the home run king, Hank Aaron.

The Yankees were a team on the rise. The previous season, they finished in first place for the first time in twelve years, winning the pennant on a thrilling walk-off in the winner-take-all Game 5 on a Chris Chambliss home run to beat the Kansas City Royals. Unfortunately for that season's club, they couldn't finish the job in the World Series, losing in four games to the Cincinnati Reds' "Big Red Machine."

However, just getting to the World Series was not good enough for the winningest franchise in baseball history . . . and it was *definitely* not good enough for the Boss. Steinbrenner was not going to sit back and hope his 97-win team would improve organically. There was a frenzy of activity surrounding the Yankees after getting swept in the World Series. As such, Steinbrenner opened up his checkbook—which was not good for the rest of baseball. Gabe Paul, the team's president and architect, acquired shortstop Bucky Dent, a couple of days before the season started, in a trade with the White Sox (sending Oscar Gamble, LaMarr Hoyt, Bob Polinsky, and $200,000 to Chicago). The Yankees weren't done, just weeks later completing a trade with Oakland to acquire starting pitcher Mike Torrez (and shipping out Dock Ellis, Larry Murray, and Marty Perez). They further bolstered their starting pitching by inking free agent pitcher Don Gullett to a six-year, $2 million contract. After Gullett started and beat the Yankees 5–1 in Game 1 of the 1976 World Series, the team leaned on the old adage of "if you can't beat them, sign them."

Then came the coup de grâce: bringing in Reggie Jackson—a three-time World Series champ and MVP of the '73 series as a member of the Swingin' A's.

To no one's surprise, the Boss reveled in the media fury that surrounded the negotiations with Jackson. Similar to the Wiz, nobody was going to beat out the Boss. But that didn't stop San Diego, the New York Mets, and even a last-minute attempt by the Montreal Expos (with former A's manager Dick Williams at the helm) from making a run at the slugger. But the Yankees were a first-place team, while Montreal was a last-place squad, and so Reggie's ego demanded Yankee pinstripes. Steinbrenner now had his man.

"They would name a candy bar after me if I played in New York," Reggie said in 1976 while still playing in Baltimore.

And he was right. The Reggie! bar hit candy stores in 1978. By the way, Reggie! bars—a luscious combination of chocolate, caramel, and peanuts—were handed out to fans for the home opener in '78. When Jackson hit a three-run bomb in his first at-bat of the game, a flurry of Reggie! bars greeted him when he returned to right field in the top of the next inning.

The Boss and Gabe Paul had put together an incredible collection of talent. But how would they mix in the clubhouse? They sure were a group of very different personalities, and the main question was if Jackson would either fit right in or destroy the locker room camaraderie. Would he be accepted by his teammates and Billy Martin, the team's fiery manager? How would he gel with the team's captain, Thurman Munson?

Well, three months into the season, an interview from spring training with Robert Ward was turned into a piece in *Sport* magazine (released in June), those concerns that probably should have been addressed behind closed doors were now in print for everyone to see.

"This team, it all flows from me. I'm the straw that stirs the drink," Jackson was quoted. "Maybe I should say me and Munson, but he can only stir it bad."

Aside from the fact that Reggie said (in print, mind you) he was the team leader and Munson could *never* be a team leader (because the Yankees had been swept the previous October by the Reds), Thurman had a gentleman's agreement with owner Steinbrenner that he would be the highest paid Yankee player (aside from pitcher Catfish Hunter).

Let's just say the Yankees were supremely talented, but team chemistry would be a question mark all season long.

THE GEORGE & BILLY SHOW

Martin was hired by Steinbrenner midway through the 1975 season, after being fired thirteen days earlier by the Texas Rangers. Martin was a player on the Yankees' dynasty teams in the 1950s and played under Hall of Fame skipper Casey Stengel. By the 1977 season, the honeymoon was long over. Billy was fighting with everyone. He was fighting verbally with Reggie. He took the fight with Reggie to another level. He was also fighting with the Boss. A battle he was sure to lose.

What a group of diverse personalities. On May 23, after hitting a homer, Jackson ignored his teammates and manager who had gathered at the dugout entrance for handshakes. "I had a bad hand," Reggie explained afterward. "He's a frigging liar," responded Munson.

Hmmm, that doesn't sound like the chemistry of a championship team—but just wait, as there were more fireworks before they would even get to July 4. On June 18, it all came to a head between Martin and Jackson. The manager replaced Reggie in right field in the middle of an inning at Fenway after Martin felt Jackson was "dogging it" in chasing down a base hit, which resulted in a double. In the dugout, Reggie confronted Martin, escalating into an altercation clearly visible to everyone—including a large television audience. Reggie, clearly irritated, ran directly to the dugout and sought out Billy. They went nose to nose screaming at each other. Seeing what was transpiring, Yankees legend and coach Elston Howard got between them, less than 10 seconds into the altercation. As the jawing continued, Howard stayed with Billy to keep them apart. Yogi Berra then helped Howard keep Billy away from Reggie. The scene wasn't over as Billy escaped from Howard only to be wrestled down by Yogi and coach Dick Howser. All of this was in full view of the WPIX broadcast cameras and the fans in Fenway Park. The game was also the national *Game of the Week* on NBC and over a minute of it was in full view of baseball fans from coast-to-coast as well before a Yankee put a towel over their cameras. But the damage was done at that point. The result was that Steinbrenner ordered his manager to bat Reggie in the cleanup spot or to look for other employment.

The Yankees were so talented that they eventually began rolling, going 50–20 following the All-Star break with the game that year being played in Yankee Stadium.

1977 ALCS

The Yankees and Royals finished in first place in their divisions and would meet for a second straight season in the ALCS. The Yankees had improved from 97 wins to 100, though the Royals improved even more, with Whitey Herzog's team winning 102 games (compared to 90 the previous season).

In 1976, the Royals entered the ALCS on the heels of a huge late-season slump. In 1977, they had won 16 straight at one point in September, part of a torrid 24–1 stretch.

With all that said, the Yanks laid an egg in Game 1, losing 7–2 at Yankee Stadium. Their ace, Gullett, left after two innings with a bad shoulder.

That forced Martin to bring in high-leverage reliever Dick Tidrow for 6 2/3 innings and facing 27 batters. Oh, Catfish Hunter (9–9, 4.71 ERA) had not pitched in a month, and Ed Figueroa (16–11, 3.57 ERA) hadn't pitched in two weeks with nerve damage in his right index finger. Plus Mike Torrez (14–12, 3.82 ERA) had just come back from a stiff shoulder.

So, for Game 2, New York turned to rookie Ron Guidry for the start. "Louisiana Lightning" went the distance, giving up just two runs while scattering three hits to even up the series. The play everyone remembers from this game is when Kansas City's Hal McRae leveled second baseman Willie Randolph with a football block to break up a potential inning-ending double play in the sixth, which enabled Freddie Patek to score from second and tie the game at 2–2. As unsportsmanlike as the play was, it was legal at the time. (Following the season, the league would actually implement a new rule to avoid such a play, often referred to as the "Hal McRae Rule.")

But that play may have been just what the Yankees needed, as they would score three runs in the bottom of the inning on their way to a 6–2 victory, tying the series.

Dennis Leonard (20–12, 3.04 ERA) was saved for Game 3 by Herzog, who wanted his left-handed pitchers to start at Yankee Stadium. Leonard, a right-hander, was the right man for the Game 3 start, as he went the distance, giving up only two runs on four hits. The Royals won easily, 6–2, bringing the club one win away from their first World Series appearance in franchise history.

It's hard to believe, but rumors were swirling that Steinbrenner would fire Martin if the Yankees lost this playoff series. Martin was managing to save his job. The Yankees' three left-handed sluggers (Jackson, Chris Chambliss, and Graig Nettles) were a paltry 3-for-31 in the first three games.

In Game 4, the Yankees evened the series to extend the ALCS to a fifth and deciding game. New York won, 6–4, after fighting off Kansas City, who were nipping at their heels the entire game.

Though forcing a fifth and final game, Martin was forced to use his Cy Young–winning reliever, Sparky Lyle, who pitched 5 1/3 innings when he was the winning pitcher in Game 4, after using him for 2 1/3 innings the day before. But could the Yankees really turn to Sparky in Game 5 after nearly eight innings of work the previous two games? "The most I can go is five or six innings. After that, we'll play it by ear," Lyle joked.

But while the team hoped their pitching would hold up for the deciding game, there were further issues that the Yankees needed to address. Mickey Rivers, who had four hits in the Game 4 victory, said after the game that he wanted to be traded. Why he wanted to be traded was anyone's guess. One thing for certain was that his timing was awful.

Unlike most teams, however, these Yankees thrived on controversy.

Well, Martin pulled quite a move even before Game 5 started. After going 1-for-14 in the series, he refused to start Jackson in the deciding game against Royals left-handed starter Paul Splittorff. Martin also gave the ball to Guidry, who would be working on two days' rest . . . for the first time in his career . . . after he had just thrown a complete game.

The gamble didn't work out, as Guidry was rocked and departed in the third inning. Down 3–1, Martin turned to Game 3 starter Mike Torrez—who had given up five runs over eight hits in just 5 2/3 innings—he came in and delivered 5 1/3 brilliant innings to hold down the Royals until Lyle could enter in the eighth.

But the biggest, most controversial move, of course, was sitting Reggie. Martin had his reasons. Aside from his 1-for-14 in the series, Reggie was just 2-for-15 against Splittorff that season. And Martin wasn't in love with Reggie's defense. But not one to go out without a fight—and on the verge of being fired—he took one last shot with Jackson. Now, in retrospect, all of Martin's reasons to bench Reggie could be justified, especially on Royals Stadium's artificial turf. But make no mistake: benching Reggie was a slap in the face to Jackson *and* Steinbrenner.

In the top of the eighth, down 3–1, Martin sent up Jackson as a pinch-hitter with two on and one out. After all his struggles, Reggie came through when the team needed him, singling in Randolph to cut the deficit to 3–2. In the ninth, the Yankees would rally for three runs to take the lead, with Sparky throwing multiple innings for a third straight game and shut the Royals down. The thirty-three-year-old was the winning pitcher in Games 4 and 5. He would also be the winning pitcher in Game 1 of the World Series, notching a victory in three consecutive postseason games.

The Yankees—dramatically, of course—advanced to the World Series for a second straight year for the first time since they made it to five in a row from 1960 to 1964. New Yorkers were swept up in the excitement of another World Series, this time with the volatile and tenuous Jackson-Martin relationship providing a great sideshow.

Clinching Game 5 against the Royals after 10 p.m. on Sunday night, the team plane landed at Newark Airport at 4 a.m. on Monday. There was a large group of fans (estimated by police between three and four thousand) gathered to greet the team, breaking police barricades. That same night/early morning, police—and plenty of them—were needed at Yankee Stadium, where fans had lined up to buy World Series tickets. They did this at 3 a.m., and the ticket windows wouldn't even open up until 9 a.m. Thousands of fans were lined up, eight abreast, hoping for a chance to buy a few of the five thousand bleacher seats for each of the first two World Series games at $4 a ticket, which was a pretty good deal.

Reportedly, some of the Yankee wives were worried about the fans' presence at the airport. Upon landing, Steinbrenner was overheard to say, "Can you believe this?" A fan, who had heard, replied, "We believe it. But keep Billy." And that led to the fans chanting "We want Billy! We want Billy!"

1977 WORLD SERIES

Make no mistake: the Yankees owned New York. The Mets were irrelevant in 1977, trading away Tom Seaver ("The Franchise") at the deadline in June, and hiring player-manager Joe Torre, who would later go on to win four World Series as the Yankees manager.

After disposing of the Phillies in four games, the 1977 World Series would be a clash of familiar foes: the Dodgers vs. the Yankees. It would be the ninth time the two teams would face off in the Fall Classic, and the first since 1963.

In classic fashion (for both the Yankees and the rivalry), there was back-and-forth drama in Game 1. With the score tied 2–2, Munson drove in the go-ahead run in the bottom of the eighth. Martin left in his starter Don Gullett to open the ninth, but took out Reggie and replaced him with Paul Blair for defense.

Dusty Baker led off with a single. After a flyout by Manny Mota, Gullett walked Steve Yeager, with Lee Lacy on deck. Martin then turned to Lyle, but he gave up a single to Lacy that tied the game.

Unfazed, Lyle proceeded to get the next eleven Dodgers out to win his third straight game. The Yankees won on a walk-off in the bottom of the 12th, when Blair drove in the game-winner. Reggie may not have liked the move, but it paid off and put the Yankees ahead to start the Series.

Game 2 in the Bronx was something else. Martin had used Ron Guidry and Mike Torrez to survive Game 5 against the Royals, and had to turn to the sore-armed Catfish Hunter. Unfortunately, Hunter didn't make it out of the third inning, giving up home runs in in the first, second, and third. The game was delayed in the ninth after somebody tossed a smoke bomb into center field near Mickey Rivers. Jackson drove in the only Yankees run of the night in the fourth inning, but the game was already out of hand with the Dodgers leading 5–1, on the way to an easy 6–1 victory.

The second game may be remembered more for what the ABC cameras caught off the field. During the coverage, ABC cut to a helicopter shot of the surrounding neighborhood where a large fire was shown raging out of control. That was the genesis of a documentary on the Yankees, based on a book titled *The Bronx is Burning*.

In bizarre fashion, the teams split the first two games, and were now headed out west for the next three. The first game at Dodger Stadium started with a moment of silence for crooner and Hollywood movie star Bing Crosby. After that, an emotional ceremonial first pitch by paraplegic Roy Campanella, who had competed in so many Yankees-Dodgers World Series in the 1950s, added to the energy already pulsing throughout the stadium. The national anthem was sung in center field by superstar rocker Linda Ronstadt, wearing a Dodgers warmup jacket.

But once the game started, it was the Yankees who were singing, as they put three runs on the board off starter Tommy John before the Dodgers had even come up to bat. Maybe skipper Tommy Lasorda should have thought about asking Ronstadt to take off the warm-up jacket and come in for John during that first inning. After a double by Rivers to start the game and a groundout by Randolph to move Rivers to third, the heart of the order came through with back-to-back-to-back RBI hits by Munson (double), Jackson (single), and Lou Piniella (single)

Not to be counted out, the Dodgers put up their own three-spot in the third, after a three-run shot by Baker. Unfortunately for them, that would be all the offense they'd be able to muster. A rested Torrez got the win with a complete game that featured nine strikeouts, and the Yankees took back the series lead, 2–1, with a 5–3 victory.

In Game 4, Jackson began to heat up. He doubled. He homered. And Guidry scattered four hits in a complete-game victory, giving the Yankees a commanding 3–1 Series lead.

The Yankees would try to end the Series in Los Angeles, but the Dodgers extended their season. This time, it was former Brooklyn Dodger great Pee Wee Reese who threw out the first pitch. Gullett's day started out rough, needing 25 pitches to get the Dodgers out in the first inning and not making it through the fifth. Munson and Jackson hit back-to-back homers in the eighth, but the game was already out of reach by then. Don Sutton pitched a complete game, and the Dodgers beat the Yankees 10–4 to move the Series back to New York. Now in front of their home fans, the Bombers hoped to wrap up the title in Game 6.

On the travel day, the soap opera Yankees were still the talk of baseball. And the questions were endless for a team on the brink of a title.

Jackson will be with the New York Yankees next season, Steinbrenner declared. He then answered the question surrounding the skipper, sorta, by saying he would leave the decision to keep or dismiss Martin up to club president Gabe Paul. Meanwhile, just a few hours before the first pitch of Game 6, Ed Figueroa threatened to leave the team and return to Puerto Rico, demanding to be traded.

During the clubhouse quarrel, Martin told the *New York Times* that Figueroa was "not 100 percent," suffering from nerve damage in his right index finger. The pitcher replied, "I'm ready to work." Figgy had gone 16–11 with a 3.57 ERA for the season, but in his only playoff appearance (Game 4 of the ALCS) had given up four earned runs in just 3 1/3 innings. So, that was now two Yankees who wanted out *during* the playoffs. Adding insult to injury (at least in Figueroa's mind), Martin had told the pitcher that if the Series headed back to New York, he would start Game 6. Martin had obviously changed his mind, and told Figueroa on the cross-country flight he wouldn't be pitching.

It was also no secret that Munson also wanted to be traded; specifically to Cleveland, to be closer to his family.

When the microphones were turned off, and it was time to play ball, Torrez (a free-agent-to-be) started for New York. If a Game 7 was necessary, Guidry would get the ball.

Martin was called in by his bosses early, around 1:30 p.m., on the day of Game 6. Turns out, they would be giving him a bonus and told him he would be back for the 1978 season.

And with that, the stage was set.

GAME 6

A championship in sight.

The drink was poured.

The straw was a baseball bat.

And it would take Reggie three swings to cement himself as an immortal Yankee.

Reggie Jackson was indeed the straw that stirs the drink.

Forever Mr. October.

THEY NAMED A CANDY BAR AFTER HIM

BY PETER BOTTE

The Yankees have a record twenty-three players and managers who've had their uniform numbers retired in Monument Park at Yankee Stadium and Reggie Jackson spent the fewest seasons in the fabled pinstripes.

More than any of the other honorees, Reggie's impact over his five seasons in the Bronx can be traced to a singular signature moment.

Jackson's three home runs on three straight pitches from three different Dodgers pitchers in Game 6 of the 1977 Fall Classic not only sealed the Yankees' first World Series title since 1962, but it forever earned him the fitting moniker "Mr. October."

It also perfectly capped an imperfect and tumultuous first year in New York for the former Oakland A's slugger, who feuded with star teammate Thurman Munson and manager Billy Martin during the regular season. He also had been benched by Martin earlier in the American League playoffs against the Kansas City Royals.

"It certainly was clutch. But I got to tell you, if anybody was going to do that, it would be Reggie. Reggie lived for those moments," former Yankees closer Sparky Lyle said. "In the time that he was there with us, I never saw Reggie miss his home run pitch. Not once.

"You know, a lot of guys foul the ball off or pop it up. You can tell when the ball is on the way to the plate. 'Uh-Oh' and there it goes and that's exactly what he did that day. Each one of those pitches was in a different spot and he got all of them."

Years before signing a five-year contract worth $3.5 million with George Steinbrenner as a free agent ahead of the 1977 season, Jackson had vowed he'd have a candy bar named after him if he ever played in New York. Of course early the following season, a few months after his World Series heroics, fans at the Stadium flooded the field with Reggie! bars that were handed out before one game. Of course, the press conference to introduce the new candy was held at the swanky 21 Club in midtown Manhattan.

The Yanks would go on to repeat as World Series champions in 1978—after Martin was fired and replaced by Bob Lemon at midseason—but the franchise did not win it all again until the four titles in five years under manager Joe Torre beginning in 1996. In the interim, Steinbrenner even insultingly dubbed another high-priced import, Dave Winfield, "Mr. May," in comparison to Reggie's postseason exploits.

Indeed, Jackson's individual feat easily stands among the greatest championship-winning performances in New York sports lore.

"It's hard to think of a comparable in any sport—the stakes, the stage, the perfection and the efficiency," former longtime *New York Post* baseball columnist Ken Davidoff said. "It would be like Tom Brady completing every Super Bowl pass he threw for touchdowns, or Steph Curry hitting every single three-point shot attempt in the clinching NBA championship game."

POSTGAME

Setting the Table

JOHN HARPER (*NY DAILY NEWS* BASEBALL COLUMNIST/SNY CONTRIBUTOR): Jackson claimed to have a flair for the dramatic, going back to his days with the Oakland A's, and he proved it in that Game 6.

Ray Negron, who would go on to become an executive for the Yankees, worked that 1977 season as a twenty-one-year-old batboy and clubhouse attendant, and developed a strong relationship with Jackson, even working for him part-time answering his fan mail and doing personal errands.

He once gave me a behind-the-scenes reminiscence of that famous day and night.

"Reggie had worked through his issues with Billy and Thurman by that point. He had gone to lunch with Thurman about a month earlier to talk about a lot of the stuff that had been building in the clubhouse, all going back to the *Sport* magazine article, and Reggie told me they cleared the air that day because they both wanted to focus on winning a championship. So, Reggie's head was in the right place during that postseason."

The Storm Before the Calm

MARTY APPEL (YANKEES HISTORIAN AND BESTSELLING AUTHOR): To think of Reggie's three-home run night in the World Series, you have to take the full season in context. It was the culmination of what at times seemed like a nightmare. Billy Martin wouldn't hit him cleanup, a way of one-upping Reggie by the manager who never wanted him in the first place. Reggie had foolishly gone to war with team captain Thurman Munson, saying "I'm the straw that stirs the drink, Munson can only stir it bad." But look at the smile on Munson's face in the dugout as Reggie entered following [home run] number 3. The smile says it all; all the pain of the season, the "Bronx Zoo" season, was over.

BUCKY DENT (YANKEES SHORTSTOP): Well, I mean, it was just electrifying. There was so much that went into that moment. Reggie went through a lot in 1977. We both did with Billy.

[...] hat World Series, you're thinking we're finally there, the Yan[kees...] a World Series in I don't know how many years.

[...] put together by George Steinbrenner. They had lost in the [...] 1976. It meant so much to be a part of it and to see history [...] nt of your eyes.

[...]ON (*NY DAILY NEWS* BASEBALL COLUMNIST/SNY CONTRIBUTOR): It's a moment that will never be forgotten, especially since the man who had come to New York with such fanfare had delivered on the biggest stage for a team that hadn't won in a while. It was a rough era for the city of New York and that added to everything that Jackson delivered. I think of the quotes about Jackson, the idea that there wasn't enough mustard in the world to cover that hot dog. But what can you say when he authors a sequence like that? He said he'd soar in New York. He sure did.

MICKEY RIVERS (YANKEES OUTFIELDER): Well, we were glad to get Reggie on our team. Mr. October like he was called. He did his job in October and we appreciate that. He was a good player out there, he just never got along with the manager. Other than that, everything was nice.

JOHN HARPER: Ray Negron shared his memories of Game 6, "I went to Reggie's apartment in the city that day and drove with him to the ballpark. He drove his Rolls-Royce and I remember that he was more quiet than usual, not making the usual chitchat. He was really focused, wanting to get the job done and close out the Dodgers in Game 6 that night. At the ballpark he put on a show in batting practice, hitting like fifteen balls to the back of the bleachers in right-center, and he didn't stop to admire any of them. Then after BP I remember he was looking for a little more information than the scouting report the Yankees had given him on Burt Hooton, the starting pitcher.

3 HRs on 3 Swings vs. 3 Different Pitchers

REGGIE JACKSON (TO BILL WHITE ON ABC SPORTS, SEPTEMBER 18, 1977): I think the word *superstar* is overused a lot. And you [White] played in an era where the word really originated with guys like DiMaggio, [Willie] Mays, [Hank] Aaron, and [Roberto] Clemente. I can now say that I have had one day that was like those guys.

JOHN HARPER: For sheer drama nothing topped Reggie's three home runs as he made good on all of his talk in his first season as a Yankee, going all the way back to spring training when he offended some his new teammates by telling a writer from *Sport* magazine that he, not captain Thurman Munson, was "the straw that stirs the drink."

MARTY APPEL: Forget the chemistry. Just throw Reggie Jackson three meatballs in the deciding game. Case closed.

SPARKY LYLE (YANKEES PITCHER): I can remember turning to the guys in the bullpen and saying in the sixth or seventh inning, "You know, we've already won the World Series."

We all started laughing. They said, "You know what, you're right, holy hell."

When Reggie got his pitch and he hit the ball, as soon as you heard the sound it was already halfway to the seats. I mean, the ball just literally jumped off his bat. When he hit the third one it was like, "Oh my god here we go."

CHRIS CHAMBLISS (YANKEES FIRST BASEMAN): I was on deck for Reggie's three home runs in Game 6. I hit behind Reggie, so I met him at home plate on all three of those home runs. That was another thrill of a lifetime. My favorite thrill in that game, believe it or not, was before Reggie hit a home run, I hit the first home run in that game, in the second inning. I hit a two-run homer, which was my only World Series home run. So that day, I love to talk about it because I know it was Reggie's day. But it was my only World Series home run also.

BUCKY DENT: The crowd was just electric the whole game. We got down in the game then Roy [White] hit a home run and Reggie hit a home run, and Reggie hit another home run. And he came up in the eighth inning and you go, "Is he going to do it again?"

The first pitch he hits it in the black section in center field and the crowd just went crazy. Your adrenaline is just pumping and you're just excited. It's hard to explain because that's the moment you dream of and it's starting to happen. You just need three more outs.

JOHN STERLING (RADIO VOICE OF THE YANKEES): That was phenomenal. Each home run was more exciting than the other. The last one was on the first pitch from the knuckleballer Charlie Hough and he hit it in the center field bleachers which was "in the black" as they call it, which was a long home run. You don't expect to see someone hit three consecutive home runs. That was in the last game of the World Series that the Yankees won, and it was more than helped by those home runs.

JOHN HARPER: Ray Negron shared these memories with me, "Reggie told me that Stick told him, 'look for the fastball in. He's going to try to keep you from getting your arms extended.' So Reggie looked in and, sure enough, he got a pitch to pull and didn't miss it. So he comes into the dugout after the first home run, and the crowd is still going wild and I told him he should take a curtain call. He wouldn't do it, and then after he hit the second home run off [Elias] Sosa, the crowd was even louder and again I told him to take the curtain call. He said no, he wasn't going to do it because the fans had booed at him times during that season and he wasn't going to give them the satisfaction. I said, 'Okay, but when you hit the third one, you've got to take the curtain call.'" He just laughed and said ok. Then he hit the one off Charlie Hough and you can see it on the video from that night, me in his ear, telling him, "You said you'd do it," and him saying, "Okay, okay" as he goes up the steps and gives the fans what they wanted.

Mr. October

RAY NEGRON (AS TOLD TO JOHN HARPER): That was the night he became Mr. October. The funny thing was, the nickname came from Thurman, of all people. Late in the game, I heard Munson say to Reggie, "You sure put on a show tonight, 'Mr. October,'" and he was kind of messing with him the way he said it, but you could see it hit home with Reggie right away. He said, "Hey, I like that," and Thurman laughed and said, "Don't say I never gave you anything." From then on, he was Mr. October.

SPARKY LYLE: There isn't anything like finishing that stuff off and knowing that you're world champions and I mean, that's what you play for from opening day to the end of the season.

BUCKY DENT: Like I said, standing at shortstop the year before, I remember with the White Sox, I was watching the game when Chambliss hit the home run and the people started running on the field, and I'm standing [at] shortstop and I'm going, "Oh my God, am I gonna run for the mound and jump on Torrez, or am I gonna run for my life?"

Just that quick, [Lacy] popped the ball up and Torrez caught it. I'm telling you, before you can get to the mound, there had to be a thousand people running on the field. So, I just kind of ran by and patted him on the back and then just took off running for my life for the dugout.

It's not like today where everybody can celebrate on the field, and they keep the people off the field. Back then you just took off for your life, but it was electric. I mean, it was the greatest feeling ever.

RON GUIDRY (YANKEES PITCHER): It was special, not only was it special for Reggie, but the team won the World Series. They hadn't had a World Series title here since 1962. So, to bring back a title to New York City, that was great. So it was a great moment for Reggie. But it was a great moment for New York.

ANTHONY McCARRON: It was the righting of the ship, a return to the baseball world that had been the norm through most of the history of the game. The Yanks had been just loping along as the dynasty of the sixties faded, had some solid teams in the seventies, but this one made memories. The shipbuilder from Ohio who had said he was going to stay out of things had delivered a title.

4

NBA FINALS: NEW YORK KNICKS vs. LOS ANGELES LAKERS, GAME 7

MAY 8, 1970

REED HOBBLES INTO HISTORY

<table>
<tr><td colspan="2"><h2 style="text-align:center">TIME CAPSULE</h2></td></tr>
</table>

TIME CAPSULE

- Mayor of New York: John Lindsay
- Oscar, Best Picture: *Midnight Cowboy*
- Oscar, Best Actor: John Wayne, *True Grit*
- Oscar, Best Actress: Maggie Smith, *The Prime of Miss Jean Brodie*
- Grammy, Album of the Year: Blood, Sweat & Tears, *Blood, Sweat & Tears*
- Grammy, Record of the Year: 5th Dimension, "Aquarius/Let The Sunshine In," *The Age of Aquarius*
- President of the US: Richard Nixon
- Price of Gas: $0.35/Gallon
- Heisman Trophy: Jim Plunkett, quarterback, Stanford

PREGAME

Willis Walks, Clyde Glides, and the Knicks Become Champs

The road to the Knicks first championship was "marvelous." So why not call on "the voice of the Knicks" and an all-time New York legend, "Marvelous" Marv Alert, to be our tour guide down that championship road?

The New York Knickerbockers started playing basketball in 1946 in the BAA (who would merge with the NBL to create the NBA). They shortened their name to the Knicks but the fans expectations were never short of a championship. This is New York, you know? The Big Apple has the best of everything . . . so why not the best basketball team? New York, after all, is a basketball town. The center of many of the city neighborhoods is the basketball court. That demand for a championship started on those courts and emanated out to the five boroughs and tri-state area.

Marv Albert: Basketball has always been a game that is appreciated in New York. You see it even today with the Knicks, having problems, the fans still have such hope when they go to the Garden. And if things do work out on that particular night, you can hear the crowd and hope that they're going to turn things around. It's a basketball city.

The Knicks and the city were a perfect match: they were smart, hardworking, and played as a team. They had some early success under coach Joe Lapchick, who led them to three consecutive Finals appearances, from 1951 to '53, but never broke through with a championship. Their success on the court didn't elevate their status as tenants at the World's Most Famous Arena.

Marv Albert: In the '50s and '60s, Knicks games were like second- and third-class citizens. If the circus or the dog show was scheduled, the Knicks games would be shifted to the 69th Regiment Armory down on Lexington Avenue, between 25th and 26th Street. I remember the bathrooms for the team were used by the public as well—it was a part of the team's locker room. I remember one time Harry Gallatin was at a urinal, in full uniform, and there were fans right next to him.

The sixties started off about as well for the Knicks as playing in the 69th Regiment Armory indicated. In fact, on March 2, 1962—at a neutral site in Hersey, Pennsylvania—Wilt Chamberlain scored an NBA record 100 points, which stands to this day. We all have seen the picture of Wilt holding a homemade sign with the number 100 written on it (in Hershey chocolate, I presume).

The Knicks' fortunes got sweeter starting in 1964, when they drafted Willis Reed tenth overall with the first pick of the second round. He would go on to average 19.5 points and 14.7 rebounds per game, winning the league's Rookie of the Year award. The following season, they added center Walt Bellamy, who had won the same award in 1962. Walt was a great player, a four-time All-Star (1962–65) and future Hall of Famer, but he was also clogging Willis's path to his preferred position.

Marv Albert: Willis Reed may have been one the most competitive players in the NBA. And I recall how, as a rookie, he was really inspired by the fact that he was drafted behind a guy named Jim "Bad News" Barnes, who was a first-round pick—along with several other centers—while Willis was a second-round pick. (Barnes was drafted by the Knicks with the first overall pick in that draft.) That really spurred Willis on. He felt he was passed by because he was from a small school. (Reed had gone to Grambling State, and had been only the seventh player drafted from that school.) The Knicks first looked at Willis as a forward, and really didn't become a center until they traded Walt Bellamy to the Detroit Pistons (along with Howard Komives) in the deal for Dave DeBusschere.

The trade not only moved Reed to center but also added DeBusschere, a coach on the floor and future Hall of Famer.

Marv Albert: At age twenty-four, DeBusschere was a player-coach for the Detroit Pistons. In that era, teams would have player-coaches to basically save money. Here's a good story about DeBusschere that I have never before seen written, but it's true. When Dave was with the Pistons, they were always struggling—a really poor team. As a player-coach, he tried to work out a trade that would have sent him to the Boston Celtics, who were perennial champions. Dave would always laugh when he told the story, so people thought he was kidding, but he told the story all the time.

Well, it is 100 percent true that, on December 19, 1968, DeBusschere was in fact traded to the Knicks—not the Celtics, and as Marv said, that opened up moving Willis to the center position. The building blocks were being put into place to create a championship team. The Knicks had their center in Willis Reed.

One short mile may have been the difference in the Knicks winning a championship with 1965 being the last year of the NBA territorial draft. "Dollar Bill" Bradley played basketball at Princeton. Both the university and the town are one mile closer to New York City then to the City of Brotherly Love, Philadelphia. It's certain that 76ers fans may not have felt the love from their New York brothers who used the slim advantage, in location, to grab a key piece to their championship puzzle. He was a Knicks territorial draft pick in 1965 (taken second overall). And with that, another key to the championship puzzle was added. There was no detail that Bradley left to chance, as Marv will now share.

Marv Albert: He told one of the referees before a game that one of the baskets was infinitesimally lower, maybe a quarter of an inch too low. And when they measured it, he was, of course, right. He saw that just with his naked eye. And then he was very conscious of the basketball being just right. And if he didn't like it—whether it had too much air or not enough—he carried a pin with him in the [waistband] of his uniform shorts and he had the players surround him. So if he thought there should be air taken out of it, he utilized the pin and would make the ball more to their liking. I mean, that's incredible.

Bradley was an Ivy League graduate, yet didn't take the court for the Knicks until the 1967–68 season. Instead of playing those first two years in New York, he instead went to Oxford as a Rhodes Scholar following graduation. Trust me: he was worth the wait.

Marv Albert: I can recall doing an interview with him and he was talking about the fact that after Princeton he went to Oxford. He said he would always play on a court at the university just to stay in shape, because he knew he was eventually gonna come to the Knicks. And he said he would do play-by-play as he would shoot around. He said he didn't want to do it for me and warned me it would break my heart to hear it (laughing).

Considering Bradley was a Rhodes Scholar and became a three-term US senator, his play-by-play was certainly first class. But in the class of Marv Albert, not quite as sure.

The Knicks got their head coach in late December 1967, when the 15–23 team fired Dick McGuire, who would go 75–103 during his tenure with the team. The Knicks had yet to have a winning season in the 1960s, and at the point of McGuire's dismissal they were a paltry 205–393. They hired Red Holzman, who hadn't coached since his firing from the St. Louis Hawks a decade before. Though his career coaching record (over four seasons with the St. Louis/Milwaukee Hawks) had only been 83–120, Holzman went 28–16 the rest of the way, leading the team into the playoffs, though they would fall to the 76ers in six games of the Eastern Division semifinals. It was clear that Red had the right temperament for this team.

<u>Marv Albert</u>: Red really didn't like to say much to the media. He was very close to a number of writers, but he always held back. He would be very careful with the way he would be quoted. He didn't care to be interviewed. But when I was doing TV a little after the championship year, he would reluctantly do interviews. I would kind of rate him—I would say that's a strong six, you know, for his performance. But he didn't want to say anything that might be taken wrong. So that's just the way he was and it worked. He was very good at handling the players. Very well liked and he had a good sense of humor.

. . . and with the fifth pick in the first round of the 1967 draft, the Knicks took Walt Frazier out of Southern Illinois.

<u>Marv Albert</u>: Clyde actually was very quiet as I got to know him. We were together as broadcasters as well. He was the nicest person with fans, he was always very personable as he is today. You know the same way. He loved the flamboyance aspects. He loved having a picture spread in *Look* magazine or in the newspapers. He lived it up like that. He liked the attention, but at the same time I thought he was really a shy person.

Based on Albert's comments on Frazier's shyness, I asked the man himself if he would consider himself as such.

<u>Walt "Clyde" Frazier</u>: You just brought up something that Marv said about me, and he's right: I was a very shy person. Clyde was my alter ego. Clyde was a guy that operated between midnight and 4 a.m. (laughing). I never drank in high school. In college, I started drinking beer. So when I came to New York, I was trying to be hip, I would drink Tanqueray and orange juice or rum and coke and, man, I'd wake up with terrible headaches.

One day I said, "Man, that's it, I'm through drinking." Then I found I could drink white wine and, the next day at practice, I wouldn't feel hungover. Then when I went out, I would have a couple of glasses of wine and that is where Clyde would come out (laughs). Clyde likes the limelight. I've got the mink coat on. I got the Rolls-Royce. I've got the suits. The rest of the time I'm just Walt—a quiet, shy guy. I never had an entourage. I'm usually at home by myself. We were winning. I'm out of town and we're losing. I don't even answer my phone, I've become reclusive. I don't even talk to people. So, basketball was my whole life. Everything revolved around that: playing well and winning.

Shy when out of the public eye? If you say so, Walt. But boy was his off-court personality flamboyant—so much so that backup center Nate Bowman came up with his nickname, "Clyde" (or Knickname, if you will).

Marv Albert: Nate Bowman felt that Walt was as smooth and silky as Warren Beatty, who played Clyde in the movie *Bonnie and Clyde*. Clyde, at the time, was constantly photographed in magazine spreads. He was basically such a personality around New York, even though he was shy at his core. He had a chauffeur-driven Rolls-Royce and was always a terrific quote for newspapers and radio and TV, as he still is to this day.

Walt "Clyde" Frazier: When I was a rookie, I wasn't playing well. So to pacify myself, I went shopping. That made me happy.

I would go back to my room and dress up and would think, *I'm not playing good, but I still look good* (laughing).

I was in Baltimore and went to a hat store. I see this Borsalino hat. It was brown velour, but it had a wide brim. In those days they were wearing narrow brims. So, the first time I wore the hat my teammates all laughed at me and were making fun of the hat.

I said, "Hey, man. I look good. I'm going to keep it on."

Two weeks later, the movie *Bonnie and Clyde* comes out and Clyde wears a hat like mine. I was "stealing" the ball on the court. That's how it all evolved with the nickname "Clyde," and I'm very proud of that name. Most of my endorsements and commercials were related to Clyde. I can tell where you know me from; if you call me Walt, you know me from college or my early upbringing in Atlanta, Georgia. If you call me Clyde, you know me from my exploits as a Knick.

. . . and with the 17th pick in the second round of the 1967 draft, the Knicks drafted lanky forward Phil Jackson out of North Dakota. He was a gritty, hardworking defensive player for the Knicks, even though he would miss the first championship season with a back injury. He was a key member on the court for the Knicks 1973 championship team. Jackson brought an inquisitive mind to the Knicks locker room.

> Marv Albert: Phil Jackson was always very curious. He was hurt for the 1970 Finals, and was more a part of the 1973 team. He always asked a lot of questions about broadcasting. He watched a lot of hockey, which he still does, because I was doing the Rangers games at the time. He compared the way the game was played. He was interested in the passing in hockey and compared it to what he saw in basketball.

It was quite an eclectic bunch, but when they played together they were in perfect harmony.

> Marv Albert: They loved being together on the court. On the court, the '69–'70 Knicks was a great group, the way they played together. You know they had the great teamwork with guys looking for each other in terms of passing the ball. But that was on the court. Off the court, they were a little different. I mean, they liked each other, but I don't think they were that close.

Now that you have met the team, how did they start the season? Well, like a house on fire is the answer. The Knicks were clearly a team on the rise. They had made the Eastern Division Finals and won 54 games in 1968–69. That team chemistry was on full display to start the 1969–70 season, as the club began the season with an astounding 23–1 record.

But by the time the Knicks were good enough to potentially bring a championship to the Big Apple, New York's other teams had taken over the mantle as the best in their sport.

On January 12, 1969, the New York Jets shocked the Baltimore Colts—and the world—with their Super Bowl III upset win over the heavily favored Colts.

On October 16, 1969, the "Miracle Mets" shocked the Baltimore Orioles—and the world—with their World Series upset win over the heavily favored Orioles.

The Knicks, on their own path to greatness, would *also* need to go through Baltimore—in the form of the Bullets—on their way to a championship.

The Knicks sent notice to Jets and Mets fans right from the start of the season that something special was happening at the Garden as well.

Marv Albert: That was a magical team. I believe they started out winning their first five games then lost one game. Then they won 18 in a row. So, they started the season 23–1. That team was really so intriguing because of the personalities from Willis to Frazier to Bradley to DeBusschere to [Dick] Barnett.

The Knicks rode that hot start to the best regular season record in the NBA. They finished with 60 wins and only 22 losses. Reed led the team in scoring (21.7) and rebounding (13.9). Clyde led them in assists (8.2). And the city went Knicks crazy. It was the hottest ticket in town.

Marv Albert: They got a lot of publicity. They were getting a lot of attention from fans and the media. There were a lot of celebrities coming to the games. The games were sellouts and you couldn't get a ticket. And there was this hope that, finally, there was going to be a Knick championship. I think most fans were pessimists—similar to what Mets and Jets fans had gone through before winning in 1969. So, I don't think there was a lot of overall confidence in the Knicks. But the hope was there when they started out 23–1. That was pretty good.

The Knicks had a real window of opportunity to win their first championship entering the 1969–70 season. What may have also helped was the retirement of Celtics great Bill Russell. After defeating the Knicks in the Eastern Division Finals, on their way to their tenth championship in eleven years—the club dropped to a 34–48 record, paving a path for a new team to step into the limelight and be crowned as NBA champions.

But their old rivals from Baltimore also felt that it was their time to shine. The Bullets had finished with the best record in basketball the year before (57–25), but were swept by the Knicks in the semifinals. And even with the best record in the league, the Knicks had owned the league and were looking to keep their dominance into the playoffs, but nothing was guaranteed versus the always tough Bullets. The Knicks-Bullets games featured five incredible matchups: Reed vs. Wes Unseld, DeBusschere vs. Gus Johnson, Bradley vs. Jack Marin, Barnett vs. Kevin Loughery, and Frazier vs. Earl "The Pearl" Monroe. (Spoiler Alert: The Knicks would later trade for the Pearl, who would help them win the title in 1973. But back to the chase for their first championship and the first round of the playoffs.)

It took the Knicks two overtimes to win Game 1, behind 30 points by Reed and a ridiculous 24 rebounds by DeBusschere. The Knicks took a 2–0 lead in the series the next night—this time at the Baltimore Civic Center. But the Bullets would not go quietly, winning the next two games by 14 and 10 points, respectively. It was a classic series that went the distance, with the Knicks winning the series in the seventh and deciding game. How close was the series? Well, the Knicks outscored the Bullets by a razor-thin margin of 11 points total.

On June 3, 1971, Lew Alcindor, out of New York's Power Memorial High School, changed his name to Kareem Abdul-Jabbar. But before his name change, he tried to change the fortunes of the Knicks in the 1970 Eastern Division Finals. It took the Knicks just five games to dispatch of the Bucks, yet Alcindor scored 35, 38, 33, 38, and 27 points (along with 89 total rebounds). In just his rookie season, his sky hook was unstoppable . . . but his Bucks were stopped in the series, four games to one. And with that, New York had advanced to the NBA Finals for the first time since 1953. There would be no stopping the Bucks the following season, as they would win an NBA title of their own with the help of the Big O, Oscar Robertson, and Bobby Dandridge. So it was an impressive series win by the Knicks, to say the least.

> Marv Albert: In the playoffs they knocked off Baltimore in a tough seven-game series. Then they beat Milwaukee with Lew Alcindor—which was Kareem's name at the time—and they outplayed them. And then it was on to the Finals.

The team that would be facing the Knicks in the Finals would be the Los Angeles Lakers—another team happy to *not* see Russell and the Celtics in the playoffs. After losing to Boston in each of their last seven Finals appearances—including the previous two seasons—they also felt that it was now their time to be crowned as the best in the league.

Furthermore, the Knicks were also looking for retribution, as they'd lost two of their three previous Finals appearances to the Lakers—then in Minnesota—in 1952 and 1953.

As expected, the Finals were highly competitive, with the teams splitting the first two games in New York.

That led to a classic in Game 3, in which the Lakers jumped out to a 14-point lead at the half. Looking to take a 2–1 series lead, the Knicks knew that they had to come back onto the court ready for battle.

After tying the game—and with just three seconds to go in regulation—DeBusschere hit a jump shot from the top of the key to give the Knicks a two-point lead, 102–100. That's when Jerry West, "The Logo"—who was known as "Mr. Clutch"—did what he did best, which was nailing a desperation shot—from the other side of half court—to send the game into overtime. It's lucky for the Knicks that West hit the shot in the NBA and not the American Basketball Association (ABA), where it would have counted for three points and won the game for the Lakers. The NBA did not adopt the three-point shot until the 1979–80 season. The resilient Knicks stayed together as a team and didn't let the buzzer beater rattle them, and outscored the Lakers 9–6 in overtime to take Game 3 and the series lead.

Marv Albert: I didn't do the game because at the time we didn't do the games in LA on radio. That obviously has changed. But I remember hearing the story that Bradley and DeBusschere said in the huddle very adamantly that the game is not over when they were going into overtime. This is not over just because he hit a long shot. I remember when West hit the shot, Wilt Chamberlain had walked off the floor thinking the game was over. I think the Knicks handled it in a very mature fashion saying we can still win this game.

This seesaw series saw Los Angeles bounce back from their devastating overtime loss to get one of their own in Game 4. Behind West—who scored 37 points, along with 18 assists—and Chamberlain (who added 18 points and 25 rebounds)—the Lakers tied the series at 2–2 with a 121–115 overtime victory.

Back in New York for Game 5, the unthinkable happened. Willis Reed, who had been the rock for the Knicks in the first four games of the series, got hurt on a drive to the basket just eight minutes into the game. Though they would win the battle, 107–100, it seemed as though they would not be able to win the game. After all, how could they beat Chamberlain, West, and the Lakers without their leader on the floor?

Marv Albert: Knicks fans were always accustomed to see their team fall short. The powerhouse teams at the time were either the Boston Celtics or the old Minneapolis Lakers. So, they expected to be disappointed in the Finals. Clyde said, "that will do it, no championship this season" when Willis got hurt in Game 5. The general feeling was that there was no shot without Willis. As it turned out, they won two games with the four different players playing center against Chamberlain in that game. Though Willis went down in Game 5, it was a sensational Knicks victory. People forget about Game 5, that when Willis went down with a hip injury late in the first quarter the Knicks were trailing by 15. That's when they came together, with Bradley and DeBusschere conferring with Red Holzman and coming up with a slightly different controlling style. And then they went to LA and lost Game 6, which tied the series. The feeling was that when they came back to the Garden, if Willis didn't play, they had no shot. As it turned out, he didn't play that much, but it was just enough.

Walt "Clyde" Frazier: When Willis went down in Game 5, we didn't think anything because we were still playing in the game. We had to go on. That's what Red Holzman would always say. Willis wasn't here, we still have to play the game. So, we didn't know how severely he was injured. We were able to prevail in Game 5. At that point we thought he definitely would be back for Game 7. We wanted him back for Game 6, but if he couldn't play the Game 6, we knew we had the homecourt advantage in Game 7.

Though up 3–2 in the series, any fears in the locker room also became apparent on the court, when Chamberlain scored 45 points and added 27 rebounds to lead the Lakers, helping them tie the series with a commanding 135–113 victory.

It all came down to a Game 7, winner-take-all bout. The question was: would Willis play?

Marv Albert: In the forty hours leading up to Game 7, Willis had so many different procedures done. On the injured hip, he had hot packs, massages, ultrasound treatments, and whirlpool baths. It was really a crash-type project, followed by the cortisone shot. They tried everything.

But was the treatment enough? The New York fans had not had luck on their side in the past, and were not optimistic that this would be the night that lady luck would shine on them . . . even though this was the night they needed it most.

<u>Marv Albert</u>: I don't think there was a great deal of positivity regarding Willis playing that night. There was a buzz in the Garden with the anticipation of the possibility that "Hey, maybe Willis will play." But I don't think any of the fans really thought that he would play.

Marv was sure going to try and find out during his pregame radio show and share with Knicks fans if there was any shot that Reed could play.

<u>Marv Albert</u>: I did the pregame show with Willis, who was a question mark as to whether he was going to play. And usually when I'd asked the question, "Are you going to play?" with somebody being injured, they would say, "Of course." You didn't necessarily believe them. But with Willis, first I saw him take a shot. He was given an injection by the trainer, and he was kind of limping around the room when I did the interview. But he said there's no question he was going to play. So I didn't know what to expect. I went up to the radio booth and the teams came out. First the Lakers, and then the Knicks . . . but there was no Willis. And then as we got closer to the start of the game, the fans began chanting for Willis. And right down below me—this is like a moment or two before they were going to do the anthem and the lineups—he walks out; kind of limping out. The Lakers stopped and stared. They couldn't believe it. I remember Chamberlain and West looking in the direction where the Knicks were warming up on my left, and the Lakers were on my right. They looked like they were aghast that Willis was going to play. Then he took a couple of warm-up shots and the crowd went crazy. In fact, that crowd throughout the game was the loudest I'd ever heard at Madison Square Garden. But I hadn't heard anything as loud and as enthusiastic as when Willis walked on the floor and took his warm up shots. When they announced him, he kind of hobbled out and I don't think anybody expected much from him, but it was so inspirational.

<u>Walt "Clyde" Frazier</u>: When Willis walked out of the tunnel, everybody thought it was premeditated. There were no cell phones at the time, so we couldn't find out any information until we got to the game. I didn't find out until later that Willis had been there since like eight o'clock in the morning getting treatment. We were all in the training room asking Willis if he was going to play.

Holzman said, "Hey, get out of here. Whether he plays tonight or not, you have to play. Go get mentally ready to play."

So, when we left the locker room, we had no idea what he would do. Willis wasn't in the team meeting. He was still in a training room. First it was Cazzie Russell who came out, and people thought it was Willis. The next time it was Willis. I was mesmerized like everybody else, but no one was more mesmerized than Jerry West, Elgin Baylor, and Wilt Chamberlain. They stopped doing what they were doing and just stared at Willis, holding their basketballs.

When I saw that I got so much confidence, I thought, *Man, we got these guys.*

I don't know, just seeing how they were looking at Willis and the apprehension on their faces. Then the way the crowd was erupting, now add that Willis came in and made not one but his first two shots.

Laughing, I said to myself, *There's nothing wrong with this guy.* He didn't make another basket—he didn't need to. The die was cast.

The Knicks road to a championship was about to end, at the World's Most Famous Arena, in marvelous fashion.

WILLIS REED'S GONNA PLAY?

BY PETER BOTTE

People often reference the film *The Karate Kid* whenever an athlete returns to the playing arena after departing with what appeared to be a serious injury.

As in, "Daniel LaRusso's gonna fight?"

New York has its own famous instance of such hobbled heroics, when Knicks captain Willis Reed limped out of the tunnel at Madison Square Garden on a gimpy right upper leg to play in their Game 7 victory over the Lakers to seal the 1970 NBA Finals—their first of two championships in a four-season span and still the most-recent titles in franchise history.

The Hall of Fame big man had sat out Game 6 but helped thwart Lakers center Wilt Chamberlain in the clincher, while also raising the roof at the Garden by nailing his first two jumpers for his only four points in 27 inspiring minutes.

"It almost sounded like the Garden exploded when he hit the [first] jumper," longtime Knicks radio announcer Marv Albert said. "To think that he would actually hit his first two was amazing. I remember my voice raising up when he hit them. Like a lot of NBA games in those days it was on tape delay, even the finals on ABC. We were live and it was one of the largest radio audiences which is why so many people have told me that they heard the broadcast.

"I'm sure it's the same thing with so many people saying that they were at the game. But when he hit those first two shots, the sound of the crowd was like an explosion."

Point guard Walt "Clyde" Frazier, who has been enshrined in the Basketball Hall of Fame as both a player and a broadcaster, led the Knicks that night in an amazing performance with 36 points, 19 assists, and seven rebounds in 44 minutes.

Decades later, the tunnel Reed emerged from was removed and replaced with seats when the Garden was renovated. Still, he rightly was named MVP of the 1970 Finals with averages of 23.0 points and 10.5 rebounds in his six appearances.

"I never anticipated that I would come up with those numbers, but, if Willis Reed didn't do what he did, I would not have had that game," Frazier said. "When I saw him come onto the court, and I saw Chamberlain and [Lakers stars Elgin] Baylor and [Jerry] West and how they were, like, mesmerized, then the crowd went berserk, it gave me so much confidence.

"Then Willis made his first two shots, and we were riding on Cloud Nine, man. That was it."

POSTGAME

Knicks First Championship

WALT "CLYDE" FRAZIER (KNICKS GUARD/TELEVISION ANALYST): To me we were a team of destiny.

Never Get a Second Chance to Make a First Impression

WALT "CLYDE" FRAZIER: The Captain was supposed to pick me up my first time coming to New York. And he was late man, over an hour. When I left home, my parents and grandparents were there because they were so concerned with me going to New York. New York is provocative. People would do anything there, because they were all crazy compared to the south. My parents were telling me, don't leave your bag, don't talk to anybody. I was petrified now this guy is late. I gotta go to the bathroom but was too afraid. Finally, Willis drives up in a convertible and screams, "Hey, Frazier came on." So, I hop in the car and he's speeding down the highway going like 75 or 80 and a cop stops him and pulls us over. Willis starts berating the cop telling him he wasn't speeding. I'm coming from the South, from Atlanta Georgia, I can't believe it, I'm gonna see this guy gets shot, right (laughing). He talked the cop out of the ticket. He took me to the hotel and that night he got me a date. We went to Wilt Chamberlain's place Smalls Paradise. We walk in the back and they have the go-go girls in the in the dancing cages and all of that. It was something out of a movie for me, man. I never saw anything like it. They introduced Willis and they gave him a standing ovation. And then they introduced me as the Knicks' number one draft pick and I got a few applauses. But I was like at a tennis match. My head was going back and forth looking at women in the cages, I can recall that like yesterday. I will never forget that. He drove me downtown to Times Square in the convertible and we could see all the lights. I was just mesmerized hypnotizing, thinking man, and I wish I could be a star in this town.

Yes!

MARV ALBERT (HALL OF FAME BROADCASTER, FORMER VOICE OF THE KNICKS): In New York, so many of us would live in the schoolyards. And actually, that's the way I came up with the "Yes" phrase, there's was always someone who's doing play by play of our 3-on-3 games in Manhattan Beach. A friend of mine would mimic a referee by the name Sid Borgia who was very colorful. He would make gyrations and if a player would score and was fouled, he would say, "Yes, and it counts." And my friend did that. And I just happened to do it also. Early in my career, I remember was a playoff game against the Sixers. Dick Barnett hit one of his fallback baby jumpers, and I just said "Yes," when he hit it. People started to throw it back at me, fans and even players started mentioning it to me, so that's why I incorporated it in important shots. I would say it but it came from a friend who used to do play-by-play as we were playing 3-on-3 in the schoolyard.

Pushing the "Red" Button

WALT "CLYDE" FRAZIER: When I was a rookie, I wasn't playing that much.

I would get dejected a lot when I lost games, and Red would say, "Come on, Clyde, the sun is gonna come up tomorrow, I gotta go get my Scotch now." He was always like that.

When I became Clyde, he would say, "Hey, Clyde, you saving any money? You can't spend all your money; you got to save for a rainy day."

He was always giving me good advice, man. He was hard but fair. I mean, he was just like my parents—hard and strict—but if you do what you were supposed to do, he was very fair.

The ultimate honor that I gave Red Holzman was when I was inducted into the basketball Hall of Fame, I had him do my induction speech, to present me, because he was so instrumental in my being there.

WALT "CLYDE" FRAZIER: He was my surrogate father. I'll never forget one time we played in Philadelphia. I wasn't playing very well. Red said, Clyde, "I want you to sit by me on the bus." We used to take the bus to Philly, he said, "Sit next to me on the bus on the way back to New York."

I thought, *Oh shoot, I got to ride with him for two hours.*

He asked, "What's wrong with you?"

I replied, "What do you mean?"

He said, "I saw you play in college. I know you can do much better than what I have seen you do on the court."

I told him, "I don't know. I'm kind of nervous."

He thought about it and said, "You can't be nervous. because I believe in you. I'm going to give you more playing time, and I want you to play with confidence. Get out there and do what you can do. I know you can do it."

It sounds mundane, but from that one little talk, my game changed. I started to play better.

WALT "CLYDE" FRAZIER: Red Holzman was the catalyst for that. If you didn't play as a team player, you weren't going to play. if you didn't play defense you weren't going to play.

MARV ALBERT: The Knicks were very well coached. Red Holzman was a guy who also believed in letting his players participate in the coaching like Bradley in Game 5 when Willis went down late in the first quarter, the Knicks were down by 15, and I remember Walt Frazier saying we are done we won't win the championship. Bradley and DeBusschere suggested changes in the huddle and they did that often with Red. In those days they didn't have assistant coaches, so Red would listen to Bill and Dave. In that game, they used four or five different players at center against Wilt. Wilt was also hurt, but not as serious, people forget that he wasn't himself either in that Game 7, I don't want to ruin the story (laughs). But you know, it was toward the end of his career too. The Knicks in Game 5, and they did some of this in Game 7, had shorter guys like, compared to Wilt who was 7 feet, 1 inch—DeBusschere, Nate Bowman, Dave Stallworth, Bill Hosket, who was a guy off the bench. They were the guys who went up against Chamberlain in both games. And they just swarmed all over him.

The Mecca of Basketball

WALT "CLYDE" FRAZIER: In 1969–70, the Vietnam War was going on and there was a lot of racism. You alluded to the fact that it was tumultuous times. That's why we captivated New York. Because for three hours, you could come to the Garden and forget about the woes of the world. You could watch five guys that are playing like one.

WALT "CLYDE" FRAZIER: When the Knicks were good, they talked about us. When the Knicks were bad, they talk about us. We cast this giant shadow over any Knick team because of the personalities, Frazier, Bradley, DeBusschere,

Willis Reed, and Barnett, you know, the way we carried ourselves, and the way we captivated New York with our unselfish play, being colorblind on the court, no one saw color, hit the open man and teamwork and defense.

Captain Courageous

MARV ALBERT: I hate to use the word *courageous* for playing basketball, but that was the type of player Willis was. He was going to push himself. As other guys have played hurt in certain situations. I can recall games I did with Michael Jordan in the playoffs, the "flu game" or other games when he was hurt and they would carry him back to the bench and he'd come right back out and have a big game. But with Willis it was so unexpected to see him on the court.

WALT "CLYDE" FRAZIER: Whenever I would leave the locker room Holzman would always pull me over and give me instructions on what to do in that game.

Like if we're playing the Bullets, he would say, "Clyde, forget about offense, just focus on defense—on Earl Monroe."

This game [Game 7], he pulled me over, he said, "Clyde, hit the open man, make sure everybody gets involved."

So, when I went on the court that was that was my philosophy. I was going to get the ball, move the ball around, and hit the open man. As the game progressed, I was the open man (laugh) I came off of a pick and roll and I'm open. I came up with a steal and was open for the layup. So, I had no idea that I will be shooting that much and having that type of game because my focus when I went onto the court was to get everybody involved like I always did. You know, more dishing than swishing. I never anticipated that I would come up with those numbers, but, if Willis Reed didn't do what he did, I would not have had that game.

Game 7: The Best Two Words in Sports

MARV ALBERT: The radio audience, because the TV broadcast was on tape delay, was said to be the largest sports radio rating ever in New York City's history.

WALT "CLYDE" FRAZIER: We felt invincible at home.

MARV ALBERT: Reed comes out and he hits his first two shots, they were jumpers. And again, the crowd goes just wild. And he basically from an offensive point of view. That's all he did. He had the right hip injury, which he hurt in Game 5, but the team rallied around him and they just went on a tear.

MARV ALBERT: People often forget that Walt Frazier actually had one of the great games in playoff history. Clyde had 36 points 19 assists and 7 rebounds. It was just a constant flow from the Knicks from DeBusschere or Bradley or Frazier or Barnett. They just they just destroyed the Lakers.

WALT "CLYDE" FRAZIER: The Lakers never really threatened us in that game. They were trailing most of the time by double digits. And you know, I still get goosebumps. I'm getting goosebumps now just thinking about it. I'll never forget it.

WALT "CLYDE" FRAZIER: We felt that, the fans, they were our sixth men. Without the crowd, we would not have beaten the Lakers in Game 7. They catapulted us to that win. They gave us the confidence that we needed. So, it was an extraordinary time. That's why it was my sanctuary when I got there, I felt like I was the king.

MARV ALBERT: I will tell you one other thing that I remember that people may not know, when time was running out, they were swinging the ball as they often did in the final minute. But when the Knicks actually won the game and when the buzzer sounded, they had only four players on the court because Clyde had run into the safe haven of the locker room with about four or five seconds left. He anticipated that the crowd would swarm the court at the final buzzer and was fearful of being mobbed. So, I remember looking down, you see just four Knicks on the court.

Nothing Like Your First Championship

WALT "CLYDE" FRAZIER: Obviously, I went out on the town after the game, and I drank so much champagne that I don't even like it anymore. Everywhere I went people were buying me drinks for months and months and years and even now today.

Sometimes, I can get a taxi and the guy goes, "Clyde, you know I'm not charging you. Thanks for the championship."

WALT "CLYDE" FRAZIER: The Knick fans were denied for so many years. Boston dominated us for so long. Philadelphia did the same. Finally, the Knicks fans could walk in pride that they finally won a championship. Man, they showed us the city. I still can't spend money in New York. We're talking 50 years; we're talking about 50 years ago we won the championship. You're calling me about something that happened almost 50 years ago. People still talk about that team like we're currently playing.

It's just incredible man that this thing is still going on. I know the Mets don't have that. The Jets don't have that. The Lakers don't have that. None of those guys are revered like our 1970 Knicks team.

WALT "CLYDE" FRAZIER: We still do Zoom calls around the holidays. Bradley is the catalyst getting us all together, checking on each other. It's that championship bond and it's still very strong.

#5

1969 WORLD SERIES: NEW YORK METS vs. BALTIMORE ORIOLES, GAME 5

OCTOBER 16, 1969

THE MIRACLE METS

TIME CAPSULE

- Mayor of New York: John Lindsay
- Oscar, Best Picture: *Oliver!*
- Oscar, Best Actor: Cliff Robertson, *Charly*
- Oscar, Best Actress: Katharine Hepburn, *The Lion in Winter*; Barbra Streisand, *Funny Girl*
- Grammy, Album of the Year: Glen Campbell, *By the Time I Get to Phoenix*
- Grammy, Record of the Year: Simon & Garfunkel, "Mrs. Robinson," *Bookends*
- President of the US: Richard Nixon
- Price of Gas: $0.34/Gallon
- Heisman Trophy: Steve Owens, running back, Oklahoma

PREGAME

**Once upon a time, Bobby Weir sang,
"I Need a Miracle Everyday."**

**In the Summer of 1969, the Mets provided
just that, day after day.**

In 1969, it seemed as if the Mets provided a miracle every day.

The Mets had never finished above ninth place in the National League. Seven years after their expansion season of 1962—where they won just 40 games and lost 120—not much was expected of the lovable losers from Queens. Then, in 1968, they jumped to 73–89—good for another next-to-last place finish. For these Mets to win the World Series would be nothing short of a miracle.

So how did we get to October 1969 and still have baseball being played at Shea Stadium? Well, let's take a look.

Everything about the 1969 season was guaranteed to look different from any other season in the sport's 100-year history. America's Pastime was going to add four new expansion teams—including one from Canada, the Montreal

Expos. Along with the Expos, the San Diego Padres also joined the National League. In the American League, there were expansion teams in Kansas City (Royals) and Seattle (Pilots). The expansion would also trigger a realignment of the traditional leagues; there would now be two divisions in both the AL and NL, with the division winners playing a five-game playoff series for the right to advance to the World Series. Baseball would have extended playoffs for the first time ever; the regular season winner of each league would no longer advance directly to the World Series. They would have to earn the right in the newly formed playoff format.

One thing was virtually certain, however: the World Series (and for the first time ever, the League Championship Series) would almost certainly bypass New York. The Yankees started a season without Mickey Mantle for the first time since 1950, as he announced his retirement on March 1, 1969. The Yankees were coming off a fifth-place finish in 1968, which was actually an improvement from their ninth- and tenth-place finishes the previous two seasons. In very un-Yankee-like fashion, the mighty boys from the Bronx had not won a World Series since 1962, and had not played in one since 1964.

Did that leave the door open for the Mets to take over the Big Apple? That was certainly not the common wisdom going into the Summer of '69. The Yankees were still a better team than the Mets, who had yet to produce anything close to a winning season. In fact, the Mets had never finished any higher than ninth place in the 10-team NL standings.

So as the song goes:

Meet the Mets, meet the Mets, step right up and greet the Mets. Bring your kiddies, bring your wife, guaranteed to have the time of your life.

Well, in the early days of this song—written by Ruth Roberts and Bill Katz—they may have oversold the "time of your life" part. They were a few miracles short of that in the early days. Here is a miracle that came in 1966 to start to turn things around. Get a load of this and tell me if anything short of miraculous could describe how Tom Seaver became a Met.

The Atlanta Braves—who would win 85 games and featured a lineup that included Hank Aaron, Eddie Mathews, Felipe Alou, and Rick Carty—drafted Tom Seaver in the first round (20th overall) of the January Draft-Secondary Phase. Commissioner William Eckert, however, voided Seaver's contract with the Braves because the University of Southern California had played in two exhibition games. Did Seaver play in either of those games? The answer was no. Was Seaver's contract with the Braves valid? The answer was also no—according to the commissioner. Even though Seaver did not play in those games, his team did. Was Seaver allowed to go back and play college ball with USC? The NCAA said the answer was no because he signed a pro contract. Seaver was a man without a professional or collegiate team. He threatened to sue MLB, which prompted Eckert to set up a lottery to equal Atlanta's offer. The Mets won the lottery, beating out the Phillies and Indians for the right to match the Braves contract offer and sign Tom Terrific.

The date of the lottery, April 3, 1966, was the beginning of something special at Shea. Seaver was the lone bright spot during a dismal 1967 season, which produced only 61 wins. Seaver was, well, terrific. He instantly made the franchise worth watching, as he pitched to a 16–13 record and a 2.76 ERA and Rookie of the Year honors. In addition, if you take into account Seaver's 16 wins, along with the four games the Mets won in which he started (and did not have a decision), he personally had a hand in a third of the team's victories . . . and that was as a rookie!

While Seaver was the superstar-in-waiting in that '67 season, his catcher—the twenty-two-year-old Jerry Grote—was already there. Signed by the Houston Colt .45s (Astros) as an amateur free agent in 1962, he was traded to the Mets for a player to be named later and cash after the 1965 season. Grote is charged with handling the young pitching staff, to go along with his outstanding defense. He may have been a light-hitting catcher, but was credited with helping the Mets crawl out of the cellar for the first time. The Mets won 66 games in 1966 with Grote behind the plate, and finished in ninth place for the first time ever. Progress was being made at Shea.

With all this young talent, the Mets needed a manager to help mold them. And on November 27, 1967, they traded for one. Former Brooklyn Dodgers first baseman Gil Hodges—then managing the Washington Senators—was acquired by the Mets in exchange for $100,000 and pitcher Bill Denehy. Hodges brought traditional National League magic to the Mets. He was already a local legend from his playing days with the Dodgers; a Gold Glove first baseman who could hit for power. And get this: he was the Mets original first baseman in 1962. Destiny and a shrewd trade brought Hodges home to lead the Mets.

Less than three weeks later, they acquired their center fielder and lead-off hitter Tommie Agee from the Chicago White Sox. It was a big move, as they traded Tommy Davis—who was their best hitter—as well as frontline starter Jack Fisher, Buddy Booker, and Billy Wynne—in exchange for Agee and backup infielder Al Weis.

In 1968, the Mets finished 73–89—their best season in the franchise's short history. Still, it was only good for ninth place.

To help usher in this new era in Mets baseball, allow me to present another miracle. Jerry Koosman was "scouted," "discovered," and "found" by, of all people, a son of a Shea Stadium usher. That is correct. John Lucchese caught Jerry when he pitched for Army in Fort Bliss. That Texas pairing turned into an ace for the Mets. The Mets waited for Koosman to be discharged from the Army and then offered him a contract. Things were starting to come together in Queens.

What would you call it for a team to draft a kid out of high school in the 12th round and to have him turn out to be one of the best pitchers in the history of the game? A first ballot Hall of Famer, with 98.7 percent of the votes; an eight-time All-Star, and author of seven career no-hitters. Umm, I am going with another miracle. His name was Nolan Ryan.

Every major league team had trouble hitting in 1968 ("The Year of the Pitcher"), but the Mets were particularly feeble. However, similar to other teams, their pitching was top-notch, Including Jerry Koosman finishing second to Reds catcher and future Hall of Famer Johnny Bench for the 1968 Rookie of the Year. Koosman went 19–12 on the season—including seven shutouts—with a slim 2.08 ERA. The rookie Ryan would also emerge in 1968, throwing 134 innings with a 3.09 ERA.

* * *

Finishing 16 games under .500, no one expected the Mets to contend in 1969—even a quarter of the way through the season, when they were 18–23 following a loss on May 27. They were again in ninth place in the NL, and nine games behind the first place Chicago Cubs.

But then something happened. The Mets didn't just get good, they got great. They went on to win 11 straight games and went 19–9 for the month of June.

Then, after starting July with an 8–2 record, Seaver pitched a gem and was two outs from a perfect game at Shea against the Cubs in one of the most intense game in the history of the franchise. Behind dominant pitching and clutch hitting, they went an incredible 82–39 after May 27 to finish with the first winning season in franchise history, at 100–62.

The only trouble was, the Cubs were peaking as well. Manager Leo Durocher had a team of future Hall of Famers (Ferguson Jenkins, Ernie Banks, Billy Williams, Ron Santo), who were running on all cylinders. As late as August 16—even with the Mets being 13 games over .500—they were still nine games back of the Cubs and tied for third with the defending NL champion Cardinals.

With the twilight of the regular season approaching, an early September match-up between the Mets and Cubs would be one to remember.

Let me set the scene: it was September 9, 1969, and the first place Cubs were in town. They were still leading the newly formed NL East division, and both teams had their aces on the mound. It was Ferguson Jenkins vs. Tom Seaver. This was a statement game for sure. And who made the statement? A black cat. The cat appeared in front of the Cubs' third-base dugout in the top of the fourth inning. In Chicago, they could now add the curse of the black cat to the curse of the billy goat. The Mets went on to win the game, 7–1. The black cat helped to make the statement that Mets would not quit, and were on their way to becoming division champions. Call it an omen, a jinx, or whatever you want, but the Mets finished on a torrid 38–11 mark down the stretch while the Cubs limped in, finishing the season 16–25. That was enough to give the Mets their first ever NL East division title.

As a reward for winning the division, the Mets didn't go to the World Series but instead had to defeat the Atlanta Braves—the team that originally drafted Seaver—to punch their World Series ticket. Even though the club finished with 100 wins, and Atlanta 93, the Mets weren't even favored to win the series.

Atlanta was hot going into the playoffs, winners of 27 of their final 38 games to win the NL West. Isn't Atlanta in the eastern part of the United States, you may be asking yourself? Well, yes it is, but the Braves had been put in the West to preserve the Cubs-Cards rivalry, with both St. Louis and Chicago staying in the NL East. Well, after losing Seaver to the Mets, this was feeling like a rivalry in the making.

Although the Mets finished with a better record, the NLCS opened with the first two games in Atlanta. Game 1 would start at 4 p.m. Eastern for television (the ALCS would start at 1 p.m.). This meant shadows, which would presumably mean a big advantage for power pitchers like Seaver—the day's starter.

But Seaver faltered, giving up an uncharacteristic five runs and eight hits over seven innings, including a home run and RBI double to his hero, Hank Aaron. The Mets offense picked up Seaver, however, and scored five runs in the eighth to come through with a 9–5 victory.

In Game 2, the Mets jumped out to an early 8–0 lead, but surprisingly, Koosman couldn't hold it and was knocked out in the fifth, giving up six runs over seven hits. Ron Taylor restored order, and Tug McGraw got the save as the Mets won 11–6, sending it back to Shea for a potential series sweep.

Down 2–0 and 4–3, the Mets kept battling on their way to a 7–4 win, completing a sweep of the Braves in front of 54,195 delirious fans. Ryan replaced starter Gary Gentry in the third inning, and pitched seven strong innings to get the win, while Agee and Wayne Garrett each had two RBIs. Ken Boswell added to the party as well, going 3-for-4 with three RBIs of his own as the Mets advanced to their first World Series. Just 78 days after the miracle of man first walking on the moon, the Mets were going to the World Series.

Two miracles in one summer.

If Mets fans thought the Braves were a rough opponent in the NLCS, their World Series opponents were the 109-win Baltimore Orioles. The Orioles featured 20-game winners in Dave McNally (20–7, 3.22 ERA) and Mike Cuellar (23–11, 2.38 ERA). They also had the best third baseman in baseball: the Human Vacuum Cleaner, Brooks Robinson. Add to that slugger Frank Robinson, who had led the Orioles to the 1966 World Series title as the league MVP—and you could say that the Birds were stacked, to say the least. They were not only the most dominant team in baseball, but had civic pride, and revenge on their minds. This was just nine months after the heavily favored Baltimore Colts lost to the New York Jets in Super Bowl III.

When Game 1 of the World Series began, it looked like the Mets may just come back down to earth. Don Buford took Tom Seaver's second pitch and knocked it over right fielder Ron Swoboda's head for a home run, and from there it was smooth sailing, as the Orioles cruised to an easy 4–1 win. Brooks Robinson said after the game, "We are here to prove there is no Santa Claus."

Gil Hodges may not have been Santa Claus, but he was there to lend a steady hand. He gathered his team together in the clubhouse after the game and told them to try not to do too much, just be yourselves, and you'll be fine. They listened. In Game 2, Jerry Koosman was unhittable. In Game 3, Agee saved five runs on a pair of spectacular catches. In Game 4, Ron Swoboda made the catch of his life and the team pulled out an extra-inning victory. In Game 5, the Mets were going for four wins in a row and the most unlikely championship in the history of baseball.

Beating the Baltimore Orioles in the World Series would indeed be a miracle.

AMAZIN' METS: OUT OF THIS WORLD

BY PETER BOTTE

A few months after Apollo 11 landed on the moon, the 1969 "Miracle Mets" pulled off an otherworldly feat that some probably thought was even more improbable.

Lovable losers since their 1962 expansion season as the National League replacement in New York for the departed Dodgers and Giants, the Mets of manager Gil Hodges and alpha ace Tom Seaver advanced from ninth place in the National League in 1968 to World Series champions in an Amazin' one-year turnaround.

Their defeat of the Baltimore Orioles in five games in the Fall Classic—with lefty Jerry Koosman going the distance in a 5–3 clinching victory—marked the Mets' first of only two championships in their 60-plus-year existence. The final out was made by Orioles second baseman Davey Johnson, who managed the Mets to their second championship in 1986.

"All these years later, when you describe the 1969 Mets, I think one of the things that was more important than anything else is that Gil Hodges was able to get the most out of everybody on that team," former Mets outfielder Art Shamsky said. "When you talk about the Mets, you just don't talk about Tom Seaver, Koosman, [Cleon] Jones, [Donn] Clendenon, and [Tommie] Agee.

"You talk about Rod Gaspar, Ed Charles, Wayne Garrett, Buddy Harrelson, Ken Boswell, Al Weis, Ed Kranepool, Jerry Grote, too. That's important because when you talk to people nowadays, [more than fifty] years later, they know everybody who played on that team. And I think that's a real tribute to the legacy."

Another was Hodges's overdue enshrinement in the Baseball Hall of Fame in July 2022. The longtime Brooklyn Dodgers first baseman died in 1972 at forty-seven years old, and his family waited fifty years for the call from Cooperstown.

The honor was the latest example of how tales of the '69 Mets always will endure in New York.

"There's always been 'Man on the Moon' comparisons with the unlikelihood of the Mets winning, and those seem apt, considering the Mets had never previously finished higher than ninth," said Anthony McCarron, a longtime New York baseball writer who most recently has served as an analyst for SNY, the Mets' home station. "The players' celebrity soared; there were parades, commercials, even TV appearances (on the *Ed Sullivan Show*) where they, gulp, sang.

"The '69 Mets are sort of frozen in that moment in some ways since then. No matter what any of them did or didn't do in their careers following that, they were part of something that few outside the club thought possible only months earlier."

POSTGAME

The "Miracle Mets"

ART SHAMSKY (METS OUTFIELDER): Well, you're talking about a team that finished in ninth place in 1968, a half-game out of last place when it was all over. I don't think anybody in their right mind would have thought that we would have turned it around as much as we did.

KEN DAVIDOFF (FORMER *NY POST* BASEBALL COLUMNIST/PIX11 BASEBALL HISTORIAN): In their seven previous seasons of existence, the Mets had never gotten within sniffing distance of so much as a .500 record and hadn't finished higher than ninth place in the National League. They had lost more than 100 games in five of those years and only once, in 1968, had they avoided the 90-loss mark—and just barely, as they went 73–89. While the '68 season saw championship seeds planted with the rise of youngsters like Tom Seaver, Jerry Koosman, and Cleon Jones—and the '69 season marked the splitting of the leagues into two divisions—there was still little reason to think these Mets were capable of such a leap. Hence their success became known as a "miracle," still cherished to this day.

OMAR MINAYA (FORMER METS GM): There was something about that youthfulness of that Mets team. There was a war going on. There were a lot of social conversations about the civil rights movement as well. Everything was changing for us as kids growing up at that time. The Mets were something that everybody got behind. The 1969 Mets was the team that played in my neighborhood where I grew up in Corona, Queens. Here was this National League team of young guys that really connected with the baseball fans. They also connected socially to the fans. Then it was just a buildup where they made a late run when they were not expected to win. The Mets were a movement that everyone got behind.

The 1969 Season

ART SHAMSKY: During spring training in 1969, [Gil Hodges] said, you guys lost a lot of one-run games, just find ways to win some of those close games and you won't be the lovable losers anymore. That was the beginning and we just started to find ways to win.

ANTHONY McCARRON: Tom Seaver had arrived two years earlier and not only was he a mega-talent, he was a culture-changer. Being lovable losers wasn't acceptable anymore. Jerry Koosman had shown in '68 that the Mets had more dangerous pitching at the top of the rotation. A key trade for Donn Clendenon boosted the lineup and, with his veteran, needling influence, the clubhouse, too. Gil Hodges's platoon system, while not loved by the players who were sacrificing at-bats, worked wonders. And the players would do anything for Hodges.

ART SHAMSKY: At the beginning of the season, we didn't play well, although we did play better than in 1968. I just think that for some point in the season, we started to find ways to win those games that we normally lose. The early Mets knew how to lose games. And even in '68, we were not a team that was able to close out games. Then we just started to believe that we could find a way to win.

We were still nine games behind the Cubs the first couple of weeks in August. Then I think it just kind of clicked. Here's the thing that people tend to forget, Gil Hodges was a master. He got the most out of everybody on that team. People platooned in five positions and everybody who came off the bench contributed to the success of that team. The thing about it is we had great pitching and really good defense. And so, if we stayed close in the games, we were always going to find a way to win.

RON SWOBODA (METS OUTFIELDER): We felt like we were surfing on this wondrous sense of discovery the whole year long. We kind of cruised around in Nowhere Land until July. Then we started playing a little better and then we started playing even better and were playing about as good as we could play going into August and still couldn't catch the Cubs. They went through a swoon for about 10 or 11 days. In that process, we kept winning three out of four and blew by them and never looked back. And that was amazing.

The Black Cat (September 9, 1969)

RON SWOBODA: This black cat came out and ran up and down in front of the Cubs dugout like we had worked with him. They saw him and we saw him. This cat was terrifying. This cat was in there, and it was out of its mind. But in that craziness, it's just running back and forth in front of the Cubs dugout, and we're like, "This is an omen, this is classic."

Down the Stretch They Come

ANTHONY McCARRON: The '69 Mets are sort of frozen in that moment in some ways since then—no matter what any of them did or didn't do in their careers following that, they were part of something that few outside the club thought possible only months earlier.

ART SHAMSKY: Miracles come from nowhere, but all of a sudden, you start believing. The reality was we started to play great baseball and then were unbeatable from about the third week in August on. We won 100 games during the regular season everybody forgets that. We'd beat a team that was really a terrific team in Baltimore, they won 109 games. So, the "miracle" nickname kind of fits for that team.

World Series

RON SWOBODA: Well, there was a little sense that the Orioles could have been looking down their nose at this team. We were a heavy underdog to them and that's okay. I think the best advantage in sports has been a quality underdog. I really do.

ART SHAMSKY: We had a team that was resilient. We had really good pitching and we were able to handle Baltimore who was a terrific team.

Game 1 Loss

RON SWOBODA: After we lost Game 1 in Baltimore, Gil said, "You guys don't have to be anything but what got you here, you don't have to be bigger than life." I'm paraphrasing him now. But the sense was, what got you here is good enough. So don't try to be anything more than that. Just play the game the way you know how.

Four in a Row

ART SHAMSKY: We played a great game the next day [in Game 2], and we came back to New York, tied at one game apiece after losing the first game in Baltimore. We won the next three. We had some breaks, there's no doubt about it. So, for me, to be able to be in that situation and be on a championship team was unbelievable.

RON SWOBODA: The most nervous I was in the whole process was when we got the lead in Game 5, and if we hold it, we win . . . now it was ours to lose, and that was scary as hell.

Final Out

ART SHAMSKY: When Cleon caught that ball? it was just a feeling of, I don't know, as if you just accomplished so much in a short period of time. I remember

I made the last out of the first game—that was the only game we lost. A lot of people thought we were going to lose four in a row.

RON SWOBODA: You know that last catch in Game 5 of the '69 World Series, Davey Johnson swore he thought he hit it hard enough to hit it out. But when Cleon went back and I saw him and it looked like it was staying in the yard, you know it's caught and that was just electric and an iconic moment you're always going to remember.

Celebrate Good Times, Come On (the Field)

ART SHAMSKY: That was a third celebration at Shea. Remember we won the division and they all ran on the field then because the Mets had never won anything. Then we won the pennant against the Braves and they all ran on the field and then we won the World Series. They all ran on the field. So, Shea Stadium took a pretty good beating. But all three of those celebrations were vivid in my mind.

ART SHAMSKY: People who weren't even born talk about their parents who did it or the grandparents who did it (ran on the field). I'll tell you really funny thing, I probably have had a hundred thousand people telling me over the years they were at Shea Stadium October 16, 1969. I said, that's great. And I think about the ballpark. And I think it held about fifty-three thousand. So I said, "Forty-seven thousand people are not telling the truth (laughing)."

RON SWOBODA: Well, I know one thing when they were swarming on, we were trying to swarm off, because their eyes were big as saucers, and they did look a little crazy. You just didn't want your hat ripped off your head or your glove taken away from you. It wasn't comfortable. It wasn't comfortable at all (laughing).

Canyon of Heroes

RON SWOBODA: Living in New York, everyone knows about the ticker-tape parades. if you talk to anyone who has ever lived here or spent time in New York, they know what it means to take part in that. To think that we were in a position to take part, put a smile on everybody's face. That is what it felt like and what a privilege and an honor it was.

6

1994 NHL STANLEY CUP: NEW YORK RANGERS vs. VANCOUVER CANUCKS, GAME 7

JUNE 15, 1994

1940 NO MORE!

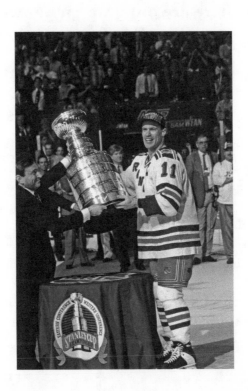

TIME CAPSULE

- Mayor of New York: Rudy Giuliani
- Oscar, Best Picture: *Schindler's List*
- Oscar, Best Actor: Tom Hanks, *Philadelphia*
- Oscar Best Actress: Holly Hunter, *The Piano*
- Grammy, Album of the Year: Whitney Houston, *The Bodyguard: The Motion Picture Soundtrack*
- Grammy, Record of the Year: Whitney Houston, "I Will Always Love You," *The Bodyguard: The Motion Picture Soundtrack*
- President of the US: Bill Clinton
- Price of Gas: $1.11/Gallon
- Heisman Trophy: Rashaan Salaam, running back, Colorado

PREGAME

They say there are only two guarantees in life: Death & Taxes.

There are also only two guarantees in New York sports: Namath & Messier.

In 1969, Joe Namath predicted the biggest upset in Super Bowl history. Even though they were an 18-point underdog, his New York Jets defeated the Baltimore Colts in Super Bowl III.

A quarter of a century later, in 1994, Mark Messier made his guarantee before Game 6 of the 1994 NHL Eastern Conference finals. He, too, was facing long odds when he made his prediction. The Rangers had lost two games in a row against their Hudson River rivals, the New Jersey Devils. They were facing elimination.

When asked about Game 6 against the Devils, the Rangers' captain's confidence sparked the famous backpage headline, "We Will Win Tonight."

<u>Mark Messier</u>: I think it all starts with believing that we could win. At that point in my career, I had enough experience to know what our team was made of and how we were able to win all year long.

We found ourselves in a tough series against a great team with a goalie that was playing really well. We lost momentum. One of the biggest things that you need to win a game, is belief. So, the impetus behind making the guarantee was to make sure that our players believed that we could win that game. I was really trying to reinstill the confidence that we had shown all year. We needed to find a way to play better. We weren't playing poorly by any stretch of imagination, but we needed to find a way to play better. So that was the thinking behind it.

The guarantee not only made for a splashy back page headline, but also inspired his team. "I think, personally, for me, it was a shot of confidence." Adam Graves said of the guarantee. "It was at the most intense time in the season, it was one of the biggest games of our life. And the person that you admire most in the locker room is putting it all on the line. It was inspiring. His leadership was easy to follow."

"Mark Messier is one of a very few athletes on the planet that could have pulled off making that guarantee." Stéphane Matteau said. "A lot of people talk but not a lot of them back it up. I would never have had the guts to make that prediction because the pressure I would have put on my shoulder would have been too big."

Just like Joe Namath, Messier backed it up. Going into the third period in Game 6, the Rangers were facing a one-goal deficit and the frightening possibility of elimination. That is when Messier stepped up and delivered a natural hat trick—and the win—for the Rangers.

"The Devils basically dominated us for the better part of two periods. If it wasn't for Richter, we would have never been in that position to begin with, but [Alexei] Kovalev scored at the end of the second period and for all the great play that the Devils had shown, they were only up 2–1 going into the third period. As you know, when you're up one goal going into a third period, you have a tendency to sit back and try to protect that lead. That gave us an opportunity to get our offense going and sure enough, that's what happened," Messier said. "I was on the receiving end of some good scoring chances and scored a couple goals and then got the empty net goal. You know what I mean.

I don't really know how to explain it, because I didn't really look at it as me scoring a hat trick. I looked at it more as we found a way to win—the hat trick was a byproduct of that."

"Certainly, his performance in scoring three goals and, you know, the magic of that guarantees is legendary, and one that only Mark, could accomplish," Graves said. "And for all of us it was just a privilege to be a part a small part of it and to follow our captain's lead. It was it was terrific." Backing up his guarantee, Messier firmly etched his name into the pantheon of New York sports figures. The Game 6, 4–2 victory set up a dramatic Game 7 on home ice at MSG.

"For him to have been able to score a hat trick alone in the third period was extremely courageous," Matteau said. "That shows the leadership that we had. It also showed that he believed in us, believed in our team, and he believed in his own ability. He didn't guarantee that he was going to score a hat trick, he guarantee that the team was good enough for us to win the game. And that's exactly what it did."

"Game Six against the Devils everybody, of course, remembers Messier's hat trick and his guarantee. That's part of the lore of 1994," said Don La Greca, currently a Rangers broadcaster. "I remember talking to Messier and confirmed for me that none of that ever happens if Kovalev doesn't score at the end of the second period and nobody ever gives him credit for that. He said that they were down 2–0, and it didn't look like it was going to happen for them. They were going to lose in six games. Kovalev scored late in the second period to make it 2–1 and the building erupted. The Ranger fans roared. And they went into that room and felt like they could do it."

In Game 7, the Devils were looking to punch their ticket to their first-ever Stanley Cup Finals while the Rangers were looking to end a fifty-four-year championship drought. New York looked like they were going to back up their captain's prognostication with a one-goal lead until Valeri Zelepukin tied the game with just 7.7 seconds on the clock. The MSG crowd was stunned. The Rangers were stunned.

"It was a huge disappointment," Matteau said. "It was a huge kick in the butt, or should I say kick in the head. When Zelepukin scored we felt like exactly like the crowd did. We felt shocked. We only had seven seconds to finish the game. When the [third period] ended, we went in the locker room in shock. And we realize how close we were to go to the Stanley Cup Finals.

He took that away from us. But it didn't take long for Messier to speak up after we were in the locker room. It took maybe three or four minutes. The guys got undressed, fixed their sticks and skates, and that is when our great leaders started talking, one after the other, to the team. I wished we had a camera in the locker to witness what I witnessed from the leadership. The old Edmonton Oilers all stood up [Craig] MacTavish, [Glenn] Anderson, Kevin Lowe, Messier, and Graves. They all stood up and they were cheering, and they kept the room very positive. And I think that's why we were able to come back and come back from a huge disappointment and win the series."

Anderson, who was one of the former Oilers who had won championships, remembers the locker room after Zelepukin's tying goal. "For Stéphane Matteau to say something like that was kind of awesome that he would think of us and say we helped build the confidence up at that point. The funniest thing about that is that we haven't hadn't won anything yet. We're still in the conference finals, we weren't even in the Stanley Cup Finals yet. In our minds, we're taking one shift at a time, one shot at a time. We're not thinking too far ahead because we have to get through this first task at hand. It could have been that some of the guys weren't high on the hog. But as soon as that goal went in, and the buzzer went into overtime, I know for a fact that I was thinking this is a great opportunity for someone to come up large. I was thinking all right, that happened, that's sad that we got scored on with 7.7 seconds to play. But as far as our attitude, it was very positive. I was thinking, *Oh my God, this is a great chance for someone to come up large,* and this is what makes it more exciting. And you wouldn't want to be in any other position, because I don't care who you are, all you ever wanted growing up as a little kid is to be playing a Game 7 situation. Since you were like five, six, or seven years old playing ball hockey in the backyard with a tennis ball, all you would say on a regular basis is "this is Game 7 of the Stanley Cup," that's all you talk about. It was more of an opportunity than sadness or disappointment. That would have dissipated immediately before we even got into the dressing room. We changed that attitude of the dressing room around quickly."

And they did win the series in double overtime, when Matteau stunned the Devils by scoring one of the biggest goals in the Rangers franchise history. Here is how it sounded when Howie Rose made his equally famous call, "Fetisov for the Devils plays it across ice into the corner, Matteau swoops in to intercept, Matteau behind the net, sweeps it in front, he scores! Matteau!

Matteau! Matteau! Stéphane Matteau and the Rangers have one more hill to climb baby, but it's Mount Vancouver, the Rangers are headed to the Finals!"

"The emotion was surreal," Matteau said. "A lot of happiness and a lot of relief, because we were going to the Stanley Cup Finals. A lot of stress was lifted because we were down by one game, 3–2 in the series, and had to win both Game 6 and Game 7. There was a lot of relief, but a lot of happiness, that's for sure."

The win in Game 6 kept the Rangers' chances alive. But what made Messier's guarantee even more memorable was it gave them the chance to permanently put to rest the dreaded "1940, 1940, 1940" chant.

Back in 1940 no one imagined it would be over a half-century between New York championships. They had captured three Cups in just twelve years. Then came the endless quest for Lord Stanley's Cup and the equally endless chants, from fans in Long Island.

The tide turned on July 17, 1989, when Neil Smith was hired as the general manager of the Rangers. He was tasked with breaking the drought. A couple years later, Smith signed Adam Graves as a free agent on September 3, 1991. Graves was a leader on an off the ice. He was almost an annual winner of the Rangers' Steven McDonald Extra Effort Award. He was recognized after the 1991–92, 1992–93, 1993–94, 1998–99 and 1999–2000 seasons.

That award demonstrated Graves's immediate and lasting impact on his teammates. The McDonald Award is given the player that "goes above and beyond the call of duty." It is named after the New York police officer who was shot in the summer of 1996 by a fifteen-year-old in Central Park. McDonald was paralyzed from the neck down but forgave his shooter and publicly hoped for his redemption. As a Rangers fan, he was a constant presence at the Garden.

"I will say this as clearly as possible; Steven McDonald is a person that defines what a hero is." Graves said. "The power of forgiveness and the power of belief. He represented everything that was great in humanity and someone that I admired greatly. And for me, when you're lucky enough to be associated with him and even to be a small part of his life, you consider yourself very, very fortunate., It's much bigger than the game, it's much bigger than then pretty much anything. What he represented was just very, very special."

In 1994, the NHL recognized Graves with the King Clancy Memorial Trophy. The award is given leaguewide to the NHL player who exhibits leadership and makes a significant humanitarian contribution to the community. So, it's clear that he was a man of high character and had a tremendous impact on his teammates and community.

Graves also had a championship pedigree, winning a cup with the Edmonton Oilers in 1990. On the ice, Graves topped the 50-goal mark in 1993–94 and was selected to represent the Rangers in the All-Star Game. His first three years with the Rangers he scored 26, 36, and 52 goals and dished out 33, 29, and 27 assists. He was a complete player and a complete teammate.

Smith wasn't done. On October 4, 1991, in what turned out to be the most important trade of his career, Smith acquired team captain Mark Messier from Edmonton. You know what, it may have been one of the most important trades in NHL history, not just in Smith's career. Messier delivered dividends in his very first season. He led the Rangers to the best record in the NHL and the Presidents' Trophy. Messier was always a team-first player and was awarded the Hart Trophy, given to the player that was the "most valuable to his team." If the voters thought he was valuable in 1991–92 they just had to hold on to their ballots, they hadn't seen anything yet.

Former Edmonton Stanley Cup champions, Messier and Graves, were joined by former Oilers teammate Craig MacTavish in 1994. That made seven former Oilers on the Rangers, including Kevin Lowe, Glenn Anderson, Esa Tikkanen, and Jeff Beukeboom.

"We talk about Mark's leadership; he is one of the greatest leaders in the history of the sport," said Graves. "But I do believe that he leaned on his teammates, and certainly when you think of Kevin Lowe, and Craig McTavish and their experience, Kevin winning five Stanley Cups with Mark in Edmonton, and then Craig McTavish, winning multiple Stanley Cups and Jeff Beukeboom, and being able to draw on that experience meant a lot. Esa Tikkanen was as big, big-game player who always saved his best hockey for the playoffs. And when you can look to those players in the locker room and on the ice and we know that experience is the greatest teacher, so we all were able to draw on their experience. It was pretty special. I would tell you that Mark would probably say the same thing that he drew a lot of confidence having them on his side and certainly some of the other players that came from Edmonton that he had won multiple Stanley Cups with him brought a quiet confidence with them."

Smith added the final piece of the puzzle by hiring hardnosed head coach Mike Keenan to lead the 1993–94 Blueshirts. On March 21, 1994, Smith traded the popular Tony Amonte, at the 1994 trade deadline, to the Chicago Blackhawks for Brian Noonan and Matteau. Keenan who coached Matteau in Chicago, had his fingerprints on the trade. Boy, would it pay dividends.

What a season 1994 was for the Rangers, the All-Star Game was held at "The World's Most Famous Arena" and featured four Rangers—Adam Graves, Brian Leetch, Mark Messier, and Mike Richter. The Eastern Conference stars, stocked with Rangers, defeated the Western Conference, 9–8. Goaltender Mike Richter was named the MVP of the game, saving an incredible 19 of 21 shots. Messier scored a goal and had two assists. Graves had two assists, including one on the Messier's goal. Not a bad afternoon for the Blueshirts, who then went home and slept in their own beds.

They rolled to the Atlantic Division crown and the Presidents' Trophy, leading the NHL with 112 points. Mount Vancouver was all that stood in the way of the Rangers and their coveted championship.

Game 1 of the finals was rolling along for the Rangers until they gave up a late goal. This one with one minute to go in the game was netted by Martin Gelinas to tie the game at two. Counting Game 7 against the Devils, that was the third time in the playoffs that they gave up a last-minute goal to tie the game. Brian Leetch clanked a possible game winner off the crossbar in overtime. Instead of triggering a euphoric MSG reaction with a goal, the rebound gave Vancouver an odd man rush the other way that ended with a Greg Adams goal and devastating 3–2 overtime loss to the Canucks.

Game 2 was also at the Garden, and the Rangers won the game 3–1 highlighted by a shorthanded goal by Glenn Anderson with an assist by Mark Messier. They all headed to the Pacific Northwest and Game 3, with the series tied at one win apiece.

It took Vancouver took just over a minute into the game to grab the lead. But the Rangers scored five straight goals, turning the game into a laugher as New York won 5–1 and took a 2–1 lead in the series.

Game 4 was also held in Vancouver. The Canucks were looking to tie up the series with a win. They came out on fire with two first-period goals. Leetch stepped to the forefront of the game in the second period, first with a blistering slap shot that cut the lead in half, 2–1. Then Leetch was handling the puck in his own zone when he misplayed it and Pavel Bure was there to take control. Bure streaked past Leech at center ice and by the time he was at the blue line there was nothing but clear ice between him and the goal. Leetch used his stick to hook him and take him down to the ice from behind. Bure was awarded a penalty shot on the play. The game, the series, and history all seemed to be squarely on goalie Richter's shoulders. But it would turn out to be his right leg, not his shoulders, that saved the Rangers.

Here is what it sounded like on CBC, Canadian Broadcasting Corporation's call, "It's 2 to 1 Vancouver leading the New York Rangers and the exciting Pavel Bure with the exciting penalty shot play, he is in, stopped by Richter! Look how far out he is, he backs up, his timing is perfect, he goes to the right, great angle, that could be a great psychological move for his Rangers."

The Rangers survived the penalty shot and added a power-play goal late in the second period to tie the game at two apiece. Alexei Kovalev and Steve Larmer added two more goals in the third period and the Rangers won the game handily 4–2 and took what appeared to be a commanding 3–1 lead in the series.

Game 5, at The World's Most Famous Arena, was set to host the hockey world's most famous victory party. The Rangers had a commanding three-games-to-one lead. They were 60 minutes away for extinguishing the curse. The fans were ready to celebrate. They city had already set the date for the victory parade. They forgot to issue parade tickets to the Canucks, who had other plans. Bure scored at 2:48 of the third period and Vancouver took what seemed to be an insurmountable 3–0 lead. In just under six minutes the Rangers stormed back on goals by Doug Lidster, Steve Larmer and, you guessed it, the captain, Messier, and the game was tied at three. The Stanley Cup was in the house and the Rangers could almost taste the champagne. The lead lasted only 29 seconds, Bure found Dave Babych, who found the back of the net and gave Vancouver the lead again. The Canucks scored three straight goals of their own, delaying the celebration and the parade. Truth be told the Rangers were just outplayed in the game. Yes, Rangers fans point to a disallowed goal by Esa Tikkanen but they lost by three goals and had a five-hour flight back to Vancouver to think about what could have been in MSG.

Graves shared his post–Game 5 thoughts, "It was disappointing, and I will tell you that nothing is ever easy. We came back it seemed like it was too easy. And then Vancouver went right back down the ice and scored, I think you have to give credit where credit is due and they were an excellent hockey club. They weren't going to be an easy team to defeat. When we went back to

Vancouver, we had a lot to think about. Obviously losing the first game but had bounced back and won three in a row. Then coming back to New York for Game 5, they get full marks for the win. But you also know, we were a team that had just come out of a long and tough and tightly battled series as there has been in the Stanley Cup playoffs against the Devils. And I think for all of us we wanted to win the Stanley Cup and we wanted to win it as quickly as possible because we're all playing with some sort of injury or had fatigue and all those other things that play a role in the playoffs. But Vancouver was going through the same thing as we were. So you have to give them full marks for the Game 5 win."

Game 6 with their second chance to win the Cup wasn't a close affair. Bure wanted to set the tone on both ends of the ice. Early in the first period he delivered a hard check to Leetch. Message sent. Jeff Brown and Geoff Courtnall both added two goals and the trio lead Vancouver to an easy 4–1 win. That dominant performance had Vancouver one game away from the Cup, riding a two-game winning streak. After waiting fifty-four years to win the Stanley Cup, you just knew it wouldn't come easily for New York. There was just no way the Rangers were going to win the series in anything less than seven games. All of a sudden, the dreaded word *curse* was back in the lexicon of Rangers fans and the media. There were three long days between Game 6 and Game 7. It gave the Rangers a lot of time to think. But it also gave them a lot of time to rest their bodies. They were an older team that was built by Smith to win now. Could the rest help or would the pressure get to the Blueshirts?

Adam Graves shared his thoughts on the plane ride home after the Game 6 loss. "When you look back at some of the injuries that players were dealing with and traveling cross country, that extra day just gives you time to recharge and refocus. I think the biggest advantage for us not only was the extra day, but that Game 7 was on Garden ice, it was in New York, and for me that was a difference. Going to Vancouver I remember how loud the crowd was and just how ready Vancouver was, and they really took charge of that game. And it was a little bit lopsided and for us to be able to have those two days [to] regroup, get some rest, ice some of those injuries. And then at the same time, refocus and get ready to play on Garden ice. I think it was instrumental in us being able to win Game 7."

That set up a historic Game 7 at Madison Square Garden with everything on the line. The Rangers had swept the rival Islanders in the first round, four games to none. They took care of the Caps easily in the second round, four games to one. They barely survived the Devils in the Eastern Conference finals and were almost at the top of Mount Vancouver, there was 60 minutes of do-or-die Game 7 hockey standing between the Rangers and stacking their piece of history at the top of the NHL mountain and bringing Messier's guarantee to fruition.

FINALLY, NO MORE 19-40!

BY PETER BOTTE

Next year finally arrived for the Rangers on June 14, 1994.

Long the subject of derisive "19-40" chants by fans of the rival Islanders—who quickly rose from expansion team to four-time champions in the early 1980s—imported captain Mark Messier, coach Mike Keenan, and the Rangers won their first Stanley Cup in 54 years with a Game 7 victory over the Vancouver Canucks to send Madison Square Garden into pure euphoria.

"That was the best feeling ever, that was my only Stanley Cup win. We're still on a high from it and it's been 28 years," said Stephane Matteau, who scored the series-winning overtime goal in the previous round against the New Jersey Devils. "Myself and my teammates are still reminded every single day that we are in New York that we are Stanley Cup champions. I'm very grateful for that moment."

Emerging superstar defenseman Brian Leetch was named the Conn Smythe Trophy winner as postseason MVP, goalie Mike Richter was the team backbone, and several other imported role players from the Edmonton Oilers dynasty were key contributors. But it was Messier who delivered a hat trick after issuing a Joe Namath-esque victory guarantee before Game 6 of the semifinals, who finally fronted the long-suffering Blueshirts to the Promised Land.

"For us and for me personally, I had seen Mark play big in big games. So, in 1994 and being one of the biggest games in New York Rangers history, I knew that Mark was going to be leading the way," said Rangers winger Adam Graves, one of the former Oilers. "And then when you do see the guarantee, I think in many ways Mark just felt like we needed confidence. And as a group, it was a message that he wanted to send and wanted us to believe in ourselves.

"There was only ever one Mark Messier and he differentiated himself and was special in so many ways."

Leetch, Graves, and Messier scored and Richter made 28 saves for the Rangers in their 3–2 victory in Game 7, which finally was sealed on center Craig MacTavish's faceoff win with 1.8 seconds remaining to forever vanquish those pesky "19-40" chants.

"I think when people look back, they will see how close of a team we were, the closest team that I've ever been on," Graves said. "Each and every player played such an integral role . . . For all of us, it was an incredible feeling.

"Being a part of that group that first hoisted the Cup, you talk about Mark, and then Brian . . . and then everyone having that opportunity was just an incredible, humbling, privileged experience that we all will never forget. And quite frankly, it ties us all together for forever."

POSTGAME

1940, 1940, 1940

STAN FISCHLER (HOCKEY HISTORIAN AND ANNOUNCER/BESTSELLING AUTHOR): The history of the team since they won the Cup in 1940 is the reason that the 1994 Stanley Cup was so special. When Uncle Sam entered World War II in the beginning of 1942, the Rangers had a terrific team. They finished first in '42. Canada entered the war in 1939, the Canadian government wanted to shut down the NHL for the duration of the war, they were very serious about it. Lester Patrick, who was running the Rangers, thought that the league would be shut down. So, he let go his coach and basically let a lot of these guys enter the armed services teams. The Rangers ended up getting screwed because as it turned out the league played throughout the war. So, they were terrible throughout the war, that was one tremendous setback.

Now they're starting to rebuild in the spring of 1950 and they go to the Cup Final against Detroit. Now imagine this? They're in the Stanley Cup Final, the best-of-seven games and none of the games were home games. The Rangers had to play five games out of the seven in Detroit. Then they played the other two in Toronto because the circus was the big moneymaker in New York. Effectively, the elephants kicked the Rangers out.

So, the next season, everybody's all pumped up. They are training up in Lake Placid and the league had a rule that whenever a team went play an exhibition game, everybody had to go on a bus. The Rangers broke the rules and they went in different cars. One of the cars with five of their best players was in a terrible accident. They were snakebit again, because a lot of these guys were badly hurt.

Now listen to what happened to the Rangers next, the coach of the team that took them to the Finals, Lynn Patrick, walked out of New York and he took a job with the Bruins. So, the coach who took the Rangers to Game 7 of the Finals, goes to the Bruins. For the next five straight years the Rangers missed the playoffs because the Bruins got in ahead of them. Why, because they had Lynn Patrick as their coach. So, the Rangers can't catch a break.

So, it's always just one thing after another. It was always wait until next year, wait till next year. The scars from all of this were unbearable. Now finally, it's '94, and they had this wonderful team, but it wasn't the New York Rangers, it was the Edmonton Rangers for Crist's sake. They had all these guys Messier, Kevin Low, Glenn Anderson, and Adam Graves. So, for all this time, it wasn't wait for next year, it was always wait till the next decade for them and it finally came in 1994.

DON LA GRECA (RANGERS RADIO BROADCASTER): They made the finals in 1972 and 1979 but weren't close to winning the Cup when you consider how those two series went. They are an extremely devoted fan base and from 1940 to 1994 they didn't give the fans any championships, yet the loyalty and the passion they had for the team just continued to grow. And they really just loved that team so much.

MARK MESSIER (RANGERS CENTER): Of course, we had a great regular season [his first year in New York]. We won the Presidents' Trophy and then lost in the playoffs. It was a big disappointment. The next year we got a bunch of injuries, and the coach got fired. We missed the playoffs. You know we felt the depths of despair as an athlete playing in New York City. We felt that way all the way to the next year basically going start to finish in first place, winning the Presidents' Trophy than winning a Stanley Cup. Those three years, I really felt the roller coaster of emotions.

Building a Team & Team Building

STAN FISCHLER: The strange thing about the Rangers was that the coach hated the GM, and the GM hated the coach. It was unheard of, Neil Smith hated Mike Keenan. The only reason why they were able to get all those Edmonton guys was that Keenan kept *Hock mir nicht Kein Chinik* Smith. "You got to do it. You got to do it."

ADAM GRAVES (RANGERS LEFT WING): One of my favorite memories was we used to have what I called "ocean rides" on days off, or in between series. They would take our exercise bikes, move them outside, behind Playland Arena, overlooking the Long Island Sound. All twenty-five guys would be on bikes overlooking the Long Island Sound with music blaring and guys riding. People asked about memories and sometimes it's not always on the ice, in fact, so much of those great memories are off the ice and it's the human part of it. They are some my favorite times as a Ranger.

STÉPHANE MATTEAU (RANGERS LEFT WING): I remember those bike rides were awesome. They may not have always been fun because we had to ride the bike in the sun and it was 90 degrees outside, but they were special.

The Guarantee—Game 6 vs. Devils

GLENN ANDERSON (RANGER RIGHT WING): We were all in the limo with Brian Leech, Messier, and I think even Mike Richter might have been in there with us. We kind of chuckled, because it was the first we heard about it was in the newspaper. We're in the car with all the papers and we just said, "Way to put extra pressure on us." Mark was just trying to get the team going. The guys that hadn't won before, he wanted to build their confidence up and to not to be afraid of the task at hand.

ADAM GRAVES: I think in many ways Mark just felt like we needed confidence. And as a group, it was a message that he wanted to send and wanted us to believe in ourselves.

STAN FISCHLER: Being the captain, he was more effective in terms of winning that game in New Jersey than Keenan was. I was in the hallway, I worked that game, the Rangers were a mess. If you had seen them, at the end of the second period, they were still going to lose the game. You could see Messier rallying them. He didn't need the quote for motivation. The quote made him famous and became historic.

Backing Up the Guarantee—Third Period: Messier's Natural Hat Trick

ADAM GRAVES: There was only ever one Mark Messier. His long list of accomplishments came from how much he loved the game, and his respect for the game. It also came from his desire to be the best at the most important times. And that was one of the most important times in all of our hockey careers, and in Ranger history, and he came up with one of his biggest games of his career when we needed it most.

GLENN ANDERSON: That's what made Messier such a great force to be reckoned with and it was just kind of what he does. At this particular moment, he had to answer the call of what he said and put his best foot forward to produce what he did. We kind of basically followed suit as a team. We knew what his intentions were, and what it took to be successful and in those special moments.

STAN FISCHLER: Two things happen. I think that game turned on Alexei Kovalev's goal when it was 2-zip for the Devils. I interviewed [the Devils'] Bernie Nicholls at the end of the second period. I remember after I did that interview, I said to myself, the Devils are done.

Devils Send Game 7 to Overtime with 7.7 Seconds to Play

GLENN ANDERSON: What we said in the locker room was what a great opportunity for someone to come through in a clutch situation. And I love those clutch situations. And I always perform well when there's more pressure, and I love that kind of atmosphere. And I wasn't afraid of it. And neither were any of my former Oiler teammates. We took it on as a challenge.

STÉPHANE MATTEAU: Eddie Olczyk actually started it in Game 3 when I scored my first double overtime goal playoff goal in New Jersey. Eddie was not playing and the extra players need to be next to the locker room in overtime.

As I was getting ready to go out for the second overtime. I don't know if I wanted to make him feel better because he was not playing. He touched my stick and kissed it. I was very grateful for that, and sure enough, I scored my first double overtime goal.

And then Game 7, the same thing occurred. When I broke my lace, Eddie came out to go see the overtime by the benches and I said Eddie, can you do the same thing? And he did more than that and it that was a special moment. I remember it like it was yesterday. He kissed it. He danced with it. He hugged it. And it was a weird, funny, loose moment that I will remember forever. And then sure enough, I went there and scored my second overtime goal. So that's something that Eddie and I laugh about it today.

Matteau! Matteau! Matteau!

STÉPHANE MATTEAU: It was all in slow motion, I saw the puck going in the corner, very slowly. I had a very good jump and [Devils defenseman Scott] Niedermayer going into the corner. And because he was such a good skater, he was able to pivot and pretty much hooked me right from the get-go, from the near post. And I think the reason why I scored was because he hooked me and my body kind of turned towards the middle, towards the front of the net. And he kind of helped me to make my decision to put the puck towards the front of the net. And without having a plan, without knowing who was going in front of the net, to be honest I didn't have a clue that Tikkanen was there. And it's not something that I tried to do. It's something that I was almost forced to do when he hooked me from behind. To my surprise when I hit [goalie Martin] Brodeur's glove, it went between his legs, and I had the best seats in the house, I saw the puck going in very, very slowly. That was one of the weirdest goals. I think that's the only goal in my career that I scored like that from behind the net. I didn't have a plan whatsoever.

MARV ALBERT (HALL OF FAME BROADCASTER, FORMER VOICE OF THE RANGERS): Howie Rose called the Matteau goal, which was a great call. That was an overtime goal in Game 7 verse the Devils. I had been missing a lot of the playoff games because of conflicts with NBC in 1994 when the Knicks went to the Finals against Houston. I was doing those games for NBC.

STÉPHANE MATTEAU: The moment still gives me goosebumps. I still can't believe that it was me that was chosen for that moment. I feel very fortunate because we had so many great players on the team. I never considered myself as the best player on the team. But I was a good role player on the team. And I feel very blessed and fortunate, and I relive that moment every time I hear Howie Rose's call.

Stanley Cup Finals

ADAM GRAVES: You go on a long playoff run that is physical, including our series with the Devils that was about as physical and hard played series as there has been in the history of the National Hockey League. You were battling for every inch of ice, in every zone, and it was hard on the body. So, I think for all of us that extra couple of days in between Game 6 and 7 of the Finals gave us a chance. Especially going from the East Coast to the West Coast, back and forth, it gave us that much needed rest.

ADAM GRAVES: I think the loudest I've ever heard the Garden was when I couldn't hear John Amirante singing the national anthem at the beginning of Game 7 against Vancouver. But that particular night we couldn't hear him sing because it was that loud. And I'll never forget the Garden being full during warm-ups and chanting, "We Want the Cup" and having "New York, New York" playing just before the drop of the puck. The electricity and the energy of the Garden has never been, in my opinion, as loud as it was on June 14, 1994.

ADAM GRAVES: Going into Game 7, it didn't matter who scored or how it happened, we just wanted to make sure that we won. Quite frankly getting up by two goals and then up 3–1 and then Trevor Linden, answering with two goals of his own. Then the last couple of minutes of that game, were maybe the longest last couple minutes of my life with all the icings and everything else. But it was only appropriate because of our history dating back to 1940. And all those other things that were part of the Ranger history. It just made it that much more enjoyable. And we were up three games to one, they had tied it and brought it back to New York. So that was for many of us the biggest game of our lives.

No More "1940" Chants, EVER!

ADAM GRAVES: To be able to contribute and be a part of winning and then scoring was a privilege. But at that point, it didn't matter who scored it was just a matter of making sure that we won that hockey game and brought the Cup back to New York.

MARK MESSIER: It was an amazing journey for those three years. Coming to New York to begin with, starting with my first game in Montreal and the press conference and then coming home to an incredible introduction at Madison Square Garden with the former captains on the ice. I felt the passion of the fan base. At that moment, I felt a huge responsibility to try and bring the Stanley Cup to New York

I felt the passion of the fans. I felt the responsibility of trying to become a part of a team and of trying to bring a Stanley Cup here for the generations of fans that hadn't ever seen a Stanley Cup being given to the home team here in New York. It was a lot of emotion at that moment that came out from those three years. It was a lot of heartache, a lot of great times, a lot of blood, sweat, and tears that went into it as always. When Mr. Bettman [NHL commissioner] handed me the Cup that was basically an extension of all those emotions.

ADAM GRAVES: I'll never forget holding up the Stanley Cup because I handed it to Jay Wells [who was] such an integral part of that club.

DON LA GRECA: It meant everything to the Rangers fans to win the Stanley Cup in 1994 because you never thought it was gonna happen. The 1940 chant was a constant reminder from Islanders fans at the Coliseum. The Rangers fan base is so passionate, and they really didn't get anything back for their passion. To finally be able to do it in the fashion they did it by beating the Devils in seven games, and the Canucks in seven games, it was just like a weight had been lifted. And to finally get that championship. It just felt like the fans got that sense of closure and they finally got everything that they were looking for.

MARK MESSIER: I think the greatest part about the Stanley Cup is you could actually say it's the "people's cup" because so many people get to celebrate with it. They get to share that victory with the teams.

It's not easy winning a Stanley Cup. It's not easy being a fan, waiting to win a Stanley Cup and when it happens, there's an amazing celebration and we were part of one of the best ones.

Canyon of Heroes

GLENN ANDERSON: As far as winning in New York, there's no better place in the world to win. And the Canyon of Heroes and that parade is unforgettable. I just remember that everything was in slow motion. Great moments create great opportunities. And I think that was just the icing on the cake. Those two or three hours that we were on the float and then got the key to the city from Mayor Giuliani was absolutely one of those special moments in my lifetime.

STÉPHANE MATTEAU: It was surreal. It's lucky I had my jersey on, because at first, I wasn't moving much. And then people started to recognize my name, on the back of the jersey. I remember the left side start started to chant my name, and when I turned around to acknowledge them, the people on the right start screaming my name. The parade just went to a different level. And you could hear thousands of people cheering Matteau. On my float was the "Matteau, Matteau, Matteau" moment that Howie Rose made so famous. That was surreal listening to those thousands of people.

STAN FISCHLER: I mean it was surreal because so many fans didn't believe it was happening; it was like a dream. All hell broke loose because of that. Of course, they had the parade in the Canyon of Heroes, and they certainly made the most of it. Eddie Olczyk took the cup to Belmont racetrack and the horses were eating a meal out of the Cup. I would call that justifiable insanity.

If the Stanley Cup Could Talk

STÉPHANE MATTEAU: I don't know if I have ever read this story in a book. So, this is for you, the day that I had the Stanley Cup, in my hometown of Rouyn-Noranda, Quebec, I went to Éric Desjardins's bar, he was a former Flyer. And a fan took the Stanley Cup and raise it up to take a picture and the Stanley Cup snapped in half. The thinnest part of the Stanley Cup broke. And the fan actually took a picture with two pieces of the Stanley Cup. It didn't break because we were reckless. It's because the Stanley Cup came to my hometown in bad shape. And let's say I'm gonna call him "Bob," and he was in the bar and was a welder by trade. He took the Stanley Cup for about two or three hours came back and promised us that the Stanley Cup will never break again. And I don't know much about welding but was told one line of welding would have done the job. I think he did four lines of welding. About 10 years later, I found out that Bob had a party inside his own garage when he fixed the Cup. It was around one o'clock in the morning. So, I don't think I ever shared that story with anybody. But someone broke the Stanley Cup and Bob fixed the thing and I thought that was pretty funny.

GLENN ANDERSON: It took twenty-five years to find out about one of the stories, I didn't even know about this at the time but you find out these little nuggets down the road. One of our goalies brought the cup was into an establishment in the front door. It was crowded, the Cup was passed all the way to the back door and then it went out the back door. We did not know who had it (laughter). This happened on a regular basis with the Cup. Someone says, "Hey, Mess [Messier] do you have the Cup?" and he'll go, "No, I don't have it I gave it to Esa Tikkanen." And then he'd go, "Oh no, I don't have the Cup. I gave it to Anderson." And then they call me up and they go, "Anderson, where's the Cup?" and I will go, "Right where I left it, probably up in the room where I had it last." Sure enough, you know, it's right there (laughs).

I think that's why they've changed the rules and they have a guardian of the cup. Because of the time when we had it in Edmonton and in New York, that they made sure that there's a guardian now that stays with the cup.

Once a Champion, Always a Champion

ADAM GRAVES: In just one word: privileged. I always felt, and to this day, that wearing a New York Ranger jersey playing on Garden ice was a privilege. Having that opportunity was just an incredible, humbling, privileged experience that we all will never forget. And quite frankly, it ties us all together for forever. Whenever we run into each other, it seems like it was yesterday.

STÉPHANE MATTEAU: That was the best feeling ever, that was my only Stanley Cup win.

GLENN ANDERSON: Once a champion, you're always a champion. I think it was harder to win in New York, under the circumstances that were presented. I think it's much more difficult to win in New York than it is in a smaller town. But once you're a champion, there's not a better feeling in the world.

ADAM GRAVES: I've often said the special part for myself, and for all of us, was how much it meant to everyone. There're so many different stories about people on that particular night, June 14, they all stopped what they were doing, wherever they were in the world, to watch their team win. I think the feeling after we won was shared by everyone. You didn't have to be on the ice to share that feeling. The great part was it just brought so many people together. The energy and the joy were just terrific.

#7

1986 WORLD SERIES: NEW YORK METS vs. BOSTON RED SOX, GAMES 6 & 7

OCTOBER 25 & 27, 1986

THROUGH BILL BUCKNER'S LEGS AND INTO HISTORY

TIME CAPSULE

- Mayor of New York: Ed Koch
- Oscar, Best Picture: *Out of Africa*
- Oscar, Best Actor: William Hurt, *Kiss of the Spider Woman*
- Oscar, Best Actress: Geraldine Page, *The Trip to Bountiful*
- Grammy, Album of the Year: Phil Collins, *No Jacket Required*
- Grammy, Record of the Year: USA for Africa, "We Are the World," *We Are the World*
- President of the US: Ronald Reagan
- Price of Gas: $0.86/Gallon
- Heisman Trophy: Vinny Testaverde, quarterback, Miami

PREGAME

Right through the Five-Hole and into History

The Bronx Zoo was a book that detailed the 1978 Yankees and let me tell you that clubhouse had nothing on the 1986 Mets. The Mets spent their championship season gracing the front and back cover of the local tabloids. The Mets made news fighting with each other, with other teams, with the police, and fighting for a team-record 116 victories, including the postseason. It ended with their ace pitcher missing the ticker-tape parade.

"Meet the Mets, Greet the Mets." Their theme song took on a new meaning during the 1986 season as they brawled with the Reds, Dodgers, Braves, Pirates, and even themselves on occasion. A brawl with the Reds in July led to so many ejections that manager Davey Johnson used pitchers Jesse Orosco and Roger McDowell to play the outfield. Even a Mets celebration could lead to a fight. In Houston, four Mets went out to celebrate the birth of second baseman Tim Teufel's first child in a bar and ended the night behind bars. Ron Darling described the team as "a traveling rock show" in his autobiography, but the guys maybe took it a little too literal in recording their own song "Get Metsmerized." It did go triple platinum and landed them on MTV. They also graced the cover of magazines. You can add to their story a lack of grace, by the Red Sox, to one of the most unlikely errors in the history of the World Series.

There were characters in that clubhouse, for sure, but those characters would also become champions on the field.

The 1986 team did have a good mix of veteran leaders in Keith Hernandez and Gary Carter and young superstars in Doc Gooden and Darryl Strawberry. The entire traveling circus was led by the steady hand of former World Series champion Davey Johnson. Through it all the Mets won 108 games and the National League East by a whopping 21 1/2 games.

The New York Mets franchise didn't exactly have an auspicious beginning. They notched a mere 40 wins in their expansion year of 1962. The Mets never won more than 90 games between their expansion year and 1983 other than when they won 100 in 1969, the year the "Miracle Mets" won the World Series. They were known as the "lovable losers' and soon would just be loved. It took 17 long years, with only one more playoff appearance in 1973, before they would become the best team for a second time.

After thirteen years of bad baseball, it was a three-season climb to the top of the baseball mountain. The 1983 Mets team could only muster 68 wins but they 'won' a trade with the St. Louis Cardinals. Keith Hernandez was acquired from the Cards on June 15, and brought with him a championship pedigree. His Cardinals won the 1982 World Series. He was not happy about going from one of the best teams to one of the worst. Hernandez at his number retirement ceremony in 2022 said, "June 15, 1983, I have learned it was a joyous day in Mets Nation. Little old me in St. Louis wasn't very happy. What did I know? A life and career changing event. I remember Frank Cashen saying to me, welcome to the Mets, we have not squandered our draft picks and are ready to turn the corner. I was disbelieving. They finished in last place for the last seven years. But when I got to spring training in 1984 and I saw the group of talented athletes, all bright eyed and bushy tailed and looking up at me, I knew we had something special. And we did!"

They added another "kid" on December 10, 1984. The Mets traded with the Montreal Expos for veteran Gary Carter, nicknamed "The Kid" because of the enthusiasm in which he played the game. The Mets gave up Hubie Brooks, Mike Fitzgerald, Herm Winningham, and Floyd Youmans and maybe a bag of balls for the reigning NL RBI leader. Carter and Philadelphia's Mike Schmidt both drove in 106 runs. Carter brought with him three Gold Glove Awards to go along with a prodigious bat. The All-Star catcher with the Expos was now a Met in 1985. In his very first game on opening day, he hit a 10th-inning home run to beat the Cardinals, and bring joy to Hernandez's heart. This was just the beginning for Carter. He and Keith would become the cornerstone and leaders of the 1986 Mets.

Gooden and Strawberry were two of the draft picks Cashen was talking about to Hernandez when he traded to get him.

Strawberry became the third Mets player to win the NL Rookie of the Year Award in 1983. He powered his way to the award with 26 home runs, 74 RBIs, and 19 steals. Straw was the first position player to win the award for the Mets. In 1967, Tom Seaver won it and five years later Jon Matlack took home the honors. Seaver was the foundation of the first Mets world champion team. Seaver and Matlack were on the last Mets playoff team in 1973. That team landed in the World Series but lost in seven games to the Oakland A's. Could the award be an omen for future success?

Doc burst on the scene in 1984 as a 19-year-old phenom. He was throwing heat in major league ballparks before he was old enough to enjoy a hot towel and shave in a Queens barber shop. He won the NL Rookie of the Year award and was voted in as an All-Star. That was back-to-back years that the Mets had the NL Rookie of the Year. Doctor K went 17–9 with a 2.60 ERA and 276 strikeouts, earning his nickname and respect of the Mets fans and his peers.

The Mets looked to Davey Johnson to lead the ball club in 1984. Davey was elevated from the Mets' top farm club the Tidewater Tides, where he led them to the Triple-A World Series championship. Johnson seemed to have the Midas touch. He was a two-time world champion as a player with the Baltimore Orioles. Frank Cashen was in charge of baseball operations during Davey's time in Baltimore, so Cashen knew his character and leadership abilities. He turned out to be the perfect choice for these Mets. Johnson led the Mets to a 22-game improvement in 1984, leading them to 90 wins and a second-place finish in the NL East, 6 1/2 games behind the Cubs.

The next season the Mets won 98 games and finished second in the division again, this time behind the Cardinals, who won 101 games. Gooden took home the Cy Young Award, leading the majors with 24 wins, 1.53 ERA, and 268 strikeouts. Carter was feeling at home, belting 32 home runs and adding 100 RBIs. Strawberry hit 29 home runs. Hernandez added 91 RBIs and was the heart and soul of the team. Ron Darling was 16–6 behind Doc. Roger McDowell and Jesse Orosco both added 17 saves to secure the bullpen. Mookie Wilson was placed on the disabled list late in the season, so Cashen called up rookie Lenny Dykstra. He brought his hardnosed style and made an immediate impact. The Mets finished three games behind the St. Louis Cardinals who made it all the way to the I-70 World Series against the Kansas City Royals, who beat them. One thing was for sure at the end of the 1985 season: The Mets were staking a claim to New York City. They were second in attendance, not in the Big Apple, but in all of Major League Baseball. They drew 2.76 million fans to Shea Stadium.

Now the best was yet to come. The Mets won 188 games combined the previous two seasons without a division title to show for it. The '86 Mets were a well-constructed talented team on paper, even better on the field and built to win it all. In the offseason, Cashen traded with the Twins to bring in Teufel. Cashen wasn't done tinkering. He made an eight-player deal with Boston for left-handed pitcher Bob Ojeda to slot in behind Gooden and Darling.

Spring training in St. Petersburg, Florida, didn't get off the best start. Wilson was hit in the face with a ball as he was running between first and second base, in a rundown drill. In the aftermath, Carter was on his knees checking on Mookie as doctors rushed on the field. Wilson missed the start of the season but his vision returned and he clearly saw his now famous World Series Game 6 dribbler up the first-base line go through the legs of Bill Buckner to win the game and force a Game 7. But of course, we aren't there yet in the story.

The Mets were a confident bunch heading into the start of the 1986 season, but one that played in the pressure cooker of New York. When they started the season 2–3, some early doubt snuck into the clubhouse and the fans' minds. Order was restored with a sweep of the Phillies starting an 11-game winning streak and victories in 18 of the next 19 games. How's a 20–4 record in response to some early season controversy?

Ron Darling got the win to start the streak. Darling was part of one of the best staffs in baseball and won 15 games on the season with a 2.81 ERA. Doc Gooden won 17 games with 2.84 ERA. Bobby Ojeda led the staff in wins with 18. El Sid, Sid Fernandez, won 16 games. Their fifth starter, Rick Aguilera, won 10 games.

The bullpen was just as formable. They had a two-headed monster with Roger McDowell and Jesse Orosco. McDowell notched 22 saves and 14 wins, while Orosco saved 21 games and won eight.

The Mets were so loaded that they started looking at the magic number *in June*. They reached first place on April 22, in the tenth game, and stayed there the rest of the way. The players became celebrities in 1986, appearing on the cover of *Sports Illustrated, GQ, Time*, and *Esquire*. They also featured a power couple, Ray Knight married professional golfer Nancy Lopez and they had just welcomed a child into the world on May 26.

The Mets' 20–4 start to the season saw them coming back down to earth by going 5–6 on an 11-game road trip. They returned to Shea Stadium to take on the Dodgers on Tuesday, May 27, the night after Lopez and Knight welcomed in a nine-pound, 12-ounce bundle of joy named Arinn Shea. Becoming a father for the second time didn't soften Knight on the diamond. The Dodgers were on fire winning eight of their last eleven games. When Los Angeles pitcher Tom Niedenfuer hit Knight with a pitch, it was Knight who was on fire. Ray was no Sugar Ray Leonard but he could hold his own. He was a former Golden Glove boxer and stood 6-foot-1, weighing in at 185 pounds. The benches cleared as Knight slammed down his bat and charged Niedenfuer, who took Knight to the ground while Knight was landing punches. George Foster had hit a monster shot, a grand slam home run, off Niedenfuer in the previous at-bat, giving the Mets a 7–1 lead. So, when Ray was plunked on the forearm, he was sure it was intentional.

Knight wasn't done with all the 'fussing and fighting my friends' as the Beatles once sung in "We Can Work It Out." Dave Parker and Knight did work it out but it took 24 hours. Knight was in the middle of a second fight for the summer, on July 23. The Mets were in Cincinnati and Eric Davis stole third base and collided with Knight. Ray took exception to the hard slide and after some fussing, came the fighting. Knight connected first and the benches cleared. It took 20 minutes to restore order.

Knight was one tough ballplayer. He certainly wasn't alone on the 1986 Mets. John Harper asked Knight after the brawl in Cincinnati, *"We had a character and a mindset that was special,"* Knight told me. *"I'm telling you, if you wanted to pick any team in the history of baseball, I don't care who it is, the '27 Yankees, the Reds or Oakland in the '70s. Just the makeup of our team in '86, we weren't going to lose. Part of it was our toughness. Teams didn't want to mess with us because they knew we'd fight."*

* * *

Knight had no fear. Dave Parker was one of the most imposing players in baseball. He looked much more like a heavyweight boxing champion then an outfielder. His Roberto Duran, "Manos de Piedra" (Hands of Stone) impersonation may have inadvertently led to the brawl. He dropped an easy fly ball in the ninth inning and the game should have been over before the brawl started. Before the 30-year reunion of the 1986 team, Harper caught up with Knight and got his recollections on the brawl in Cincinnati.

"By then everybody knew I could handle myself," Knight said. "My dad had me start boxing when I was eight years old, and I was 17–0 in junior Golden Gloves until this southpaw broke my nose when I was sixteen years old, and I told my dad I was done fighting. So, we're out there in the middle of that melee, and Parker, big as he is, says to me, 'You really that tough?' And I said, 'There's one way to find out, big boy.' But at that point everything was broken up. So, after the game Parker tells a Cincinnati reporter that he was thinking about going to our hotel after the game, that if he knew what room I was in, he'd have going to drag me out and kicked my butt. Well, I get to the ballpark the next day and Bobby Ojeda and Doc Gooden run up to me and say, 'Did you see the paper?' They show me the story, and, man, I was steaming. I put on my pants and a T-shirt and go straight out to the field where the Reds are taking BP. Parker is on the other side of the cage and I walk over there, right past Eric Davis, and I said, 'Hey, Dave, I just read in the paper . . .' and he said, 'Ah, Ray, you know I've gotta say that stuff.' I said, 'I'm calling BS on that, Dave. If you've got a problem with me, let's get to it. Right now.' And he said, 'No, no, no, you're my man, you're my man.' And he shook hands with me and I said, 'Okay, fine. So, I turn to go back and I see about fifteen of our guys in the dugout. They had come out to watch the show.'"

Wally Backman confirmed the story to Harper and said, "Nobody wanted to mess with Ray. We had a lot of tough guys but Ray was the toughest. He didn't go around talking tough unless he had to, but just having him on the team gave us a sense that we were the baddest guys in baseball."

It wasn't just Knight. The Mets were a scrappy ballclub lead by the hard-nosed Dykstra and Backman. These two played the game as hard as anyone since Pete Rose. Dykstra's nickname was "Nails," as in tough as nails. They set the tone with hustle plays on the field.

By mid-June, the Mets lead was double digits. It was time to turn the tables on the Cardinals, who won the NL East the year before despite the

Mets' 98 wins. The Mets ended June with a three-game sweep of the Cards in St. Louis. The Mets lead Montreal by 10 1/2 games and St. Louis by an astounding 20 games.

They had served notice.

Whitey Herzog, the St. Louis manager, told the *Daily News* after the sweep, "The Mets are a shoo-in, there's not going to be any race." This was from the manager of the defending National League champions on the very first day of July, no less.

By the All-Star break the Mets' lead had blossomed to 13 1/2 games, the largest lead at the break since they added the divisions in 1969. All seemed right in Mets Nation, the Mets had five representatives in the All-Star Game: Gary Carter, Keith Hernandez, Darryl Strawberry, Doc Gooden, and Sid Fernandez.

The Astros took three of four from the Mets after the All-Star break. After Houston won their second straight game on July 19, 5–4, the group of Tim Teufel, Ron Darling, Rick Aguilera, and Bob Ojeda went out to celebrate the birth of Teufel's first child. Teufel left Cooter's Executive Games and Burgers with an open beer can. The suds were grabbed by a uniformed Houston police officer, hired by the bar to provide security. Darling rushed to Tim's defense and punched the officer. Teufel and Darling were arrested for aggravated assault and Aguilera and Ojeda were charged with hindering arrest. The four went to a bar to celebrate and ended up spending eleven hours behind bars. Upon their release and return to the Mets clubhouse, their lockers were decorated with stripes of black adhesive tape to mirror their surroundings for the prior eleven hours.

Jailhouse humor wasn't the only kind these fun-loving Mets doled out. Howard Johnson and Roger McDowell were the leaders in the clubhouse hijinks. They specialized in hot foot, rubber spiders, masks, wigs, and all sorts of rally caps.

Another sign of the Mets' exuberance was the curtain calls after a big home run. It may have annoyed opponents but at the same time endeared the players to the Shea Stadium faithful. An action photo of Gooden took up the entire height of a New York City building. The Mets constantly appeared in television commercials.

They weren't just ballplayers. They were A-list celebrities.

The Mets released George Foster on August 7, but not without controversy. The thirty-seven-year-old former World Series champion with the Reds was benched for 16 days due to "ineffective" play cited by the Mets. Foster said the benching was due to race, telling the Gannett Westchester-Rockland newspapers, "I'm not saying it's a racial thing. But that seems to be the case in sports these days. When a ballclub can, they replace a George Foster or a Mookie Wilson with a more popular white player." The Mets disagreed on his assessment. Both sides did agree that Foster's public comments on racism, hastened his release. According to the *New York Times*, both Foster and Davey Johnson used the same phrase when asked about it: "The comments probably were the straw that broke the camel's back."

Lee Mazzilli was brought up to replace Foster on August 7. Mazzilli was promoted from Tidewater and was a key down the stretch. He was popular in Queens from his first stint with the club from 1976 to 1981 before he was traded to the Texas Rangers in a deal that brought back Darling, as well as Walt Terrell.

Gary Carter was playing first base against Cardinals on August 16 and suffered a partial tear of the ligament in his thumb. He was placed on the disabled list. That left a void at catcher that was filled by Ed Hearn. Hernandez, already a leader, asserted himself even more in Carter's absence. It seemed like nothing could derail this magical season.

The Mets clinched the NL East on September 17 with Gooden firing a complete game. Here is what it sounded like on WWOR-TV (Channel 9):

"These Mets fans have waited for this for the better part of three seasons. Ever since the 1984 campaign when the Mets became a contender. And they are ready to bust loose in more ways than one. Thirteen years of waiting. Ground ball to second. Backman to Hernandez. The unbelievable season is not over but the championship is in New York. The inevitable has finally become a reality. And the adoring fans have swept onto the field. On September 17, the New York Mets became champions of the National League Eastern Division for 1986."

The Mets were in the playoffs for the first time since 1973. They were due to have home-field advantage but the Houston Oilers had a game scheduled to be played in the Astrodome so the Astros and Mets swapped home dates and the Astros ended up with home-field advantage. At the time the home field alternated between the NL East and NL West champions. It was not based on overall record. The Mets had 108 wins vs. the Astros' 96 wins, and Mets held that head-to-head matchup advantage as well. So, it was back to Houston, the scene of the crime, where you will remember on their last visit that four Mets were incarcerated in July. The series opened at the Astrodome for Games 1 and 2 and would go back to Houston for Games 6 and 7 if necessary. The only good news is that it seemed it was 'Houston who had a problem' because New York was almost as good on the road in 1986 as they were at home. Their record at Shea was 55–26 while they were 53–28 on the road.

Doc Gooden was magnificent in Game 1, giving up just a solo home run by Glenn Davis in the second inning over seven innings of work. It wasn't good enough as he was outdueled by former Met Mike Scott, who didn't allow a single run and scattered five hits and struck out a NLCS-record 14 in a 1–0 complete-game victory.

Next up for Houston was Nolan Ryan, who, like Scott, got his start with the Mets. This time it was New York's turn to enact some revenge by scoring five runs over the fourth and fifth innings. Bob Ojeda pitched a complete game and only gave up one run. The Mets won 5–1 and tied the series at one game apiece heading to New York.

Game 3 got off to a rough start for Darling. The Astros put up four runs in the first two innings capped by a Bill Doran two-run blast in the second. The Mets tied the score with four runs in the sixth inning. Darryl Strawberry high-lighted the inning with a three-run homer off of Bob Knepper. Houston took the lead back in the seventh and the Mets went into the ninth inning facing a one-run deficit with Houston's closer, Dave Smith, on the mound. Backman bunted his way on base. Then Dykstra won the game with a walk-off two-run shot over the right-field fence. The Mets were up 2–1 in games but this series was a long way from being over.

Houston gambled by throwing Scott in Game 4 on three days' rest. It paid off. Scott threw another complete game, this time only giving up three hits and won the game, 3–1. Carter had a chance to match Dykstra's-late game heroics in the ninth but flew out with a man on base. Now the series was even at 2–2, guaranteeing a return trip to Houston. If Carter got a chance again to come through in the clutch, there was the feeling he wouldn't come up short again.

Game 5 was postponed due to rain. That was not good for the Mets as it allowed Ryan to get full rest. The veteran took full advantage and pitched nine innings, giving up just two hits and one run while striking out 12. The old man was dominant. The Mets matched him with a younger version as Gooden pitched 10 innings and gave up only one run while striking out four. But that was only good enough to keep the Mets even. It was still 1–1 in the bottom of the 12th inning and Mets were looking for a hero. It turned out to be "The Kid." Carter singled in Backman and the Mets walked-off the Astros again at Shea, this time by the score of 2–1 and they took a series lead of 3–2 heading back to the Astrodome.

Game 6 felt like do-or-die for the Mets. They did not want to face the eventual NLCS MVP Mike Scott again. Scott had become a different pitcher after learning to throw the split-finger fastball after the 1984 season from Roger Craig, who was 10–24 as an original Met in 1962. Scott also had a good fastball, but it was his splitter, which had tremendous movement, that made him virtually unhittable. It's not a stretch to say the Mets were psyched out by Scott and their season was actually at stake on Game 6.

If the Mets won the NLCS, they would go to their first World Series since 1973 and have a chance to win their first title since 1969. If they lost the series, it would be a tremendous failure after they were an incredible 108–54 in the regular season and clearly the best—and most hated—team in baseball.

With all of that on the line and Bob Ojeda on the mound, Houston scored three runs in the first inning. Houston starter Bob Knepper kept the Mets off the scoreboard as Houston went into the ninth inning with a 3–0 lead.

In all likelihood: Scott could start warming up for his next day's start.

In reality: Not so fast.

The scrappy Mets lead off the ninth inning with a Dykstra triple. Wilson brought him home with a single. Hernandez doubled home Wilson and the lead was down to one. That knocked Knepper from the game. Knight tied it with a sacrifice fly off Dave Smith. Danny Heep had a chance to give the Mets the lead but struck out with bases loaded.

At least there would be a bottom of the ninth.

Johnson brought in Roger McDowell to face the Astros. There was no holding back. The Mets had Scott hanging over them and knew this was the game they had to win. McDowell tossed five scoreless innings, giving up just one hit. It was as clutch a pitching performance as the Mets had ever seen. Even if McDowell didn't get the win, he saved the season. Next up was Davey's other bullpen ace Jesse Orosco who tossed three innings behind McDowell. Davey was pulling out all the stops using McDowell and Orosco for a combined eight innings of work.

The tension was amazing in the Astrodome.

In the top of the 14th inning, Backman singled in Strawberry and the Mets had their first lead, but once again left the bases loaded when Wilson struck out to end the inning. Now it was the Mets who were just three outs away from the World Series. But Jesse Orosco, dominant all year, gave up a home run to Billy Hatcher off of the 'fair pole' in left. The game was tied at four. Bonus baseball continued. Fans across the country held their breath hanging on every pitch. Fans on the streets of Manhattan lined up at the windows of electronics stores to watch the game that had captivated the city.

Strawberry led off the 16th with a double off Aurelio Lopez and was brought home by Knight, who scored on Jeff Calhoun's second wild pitch after relieving Lopez.

Whew. The Mets had some breathing room.

Dykstra came up clutch again, singling home Backman. The Mets' lead was 7–4 going into the bottom of the 16th. It came down to this: The Mets needed three outs to get out of Houston.

The Astros scored two runs. They had two men on base and a full count. Jesse Orosco struck out Kevin Bass to end the threat, the inning, the game, and the series. Four hours and forty-two minutes of some of the best playoff baseball ever played had finally ended with the Mets punching their ticket to the World Series and Mets fans needing a drink.

Johnson had gambled and won using his two bullpen stars in Game 6. There would be no "Great Scott" to face in Game 7. Up next was the Boston Red Sox, the No. 1 rival of New York's other team. The Sox were still under the "Curse of the Bambino" for selling the best player in the history of baseball, Babe Ruth, to the Yankees. The Red Sox had not won the World Series since 1918. Was that enough punishment? Would the curse finally wear off?

After surviving Houston, the Mets entered the World Series as the favorites. They had home-field advantage and had won 13 more regular season games then the Red Sox.

* * *

Game 1: Shea Stadium was rocking but so was Red Sox pitcher Bruce Hurst. He allowed only four hits over eight innings and closer Calvin Schiraldi came in to lock down the shutout win. That wasted a dominant outing by Darling who gave up just one unearned run on a Teufel error when the ball went through his legs (remember that, by the way, because turnabout is fair play).

* * *

Game 2: A classic pitching matchup of Roger Clemens vs. Dwight Gooden. The two best young pitchers in the game. You would think it would be another pitching duel but it turned into a lopsided 9–3 Boston win. All of a sudden, the favored Mets were on the ropes. The dream season turned into a 0–2 series nightmare with the Mets now needing to win two of the three games coming up at Fenway Park to keep their season alive.

"Davey Johnson not only had a brilliant mind, but he also knew his team and knew his ballplayers. We had been through a grueling stretch against Houston in the National League Championship Series," Ron Darling said. "It took everything to barely beat those guys. Our first two games in the World Series we were flat, all you have to do is look at the results." He knew his team. Sometimes you have to go to the whip and sometimes you have to give your team a hug. That's kind of what he did, he gave a hug to twenty-five guys. He let them rest and be ready for Game 3. It was a critical decision made by a brilliant manager. It was one of the most underrated decisions ever made if you look at the little things that have transpired during the World Series.

* * *

Game 3: The Mets set the tone early, Lenny Dykstra with a home run to lead off the game. Heep drove in a couple of first-inning runs with a single and the lead ballooned to 4–0. Ojeda only gave up one run against his former team and the Mets won 7–1. So far, home teams were 0–3.

* * *

Game 4: Darling pitched well again, Boston didn't score until the eighth inning, but by that time it was too late. Carter cleared the Green Monster with a two-run home run in the fourth. Later in the inning Knight chipped in an RBI and Mets had a 3–0 lead. Dykstra hit a two-run homer in the seventh and Carter added his second round-tripper of the night an inning later, and the Mets won easily 6–2. The series was tied at two. No home team had won yet.

"It was emotional, and it was a combination of a lot of stuff that started when I was a kid." Ron Darling said. "When I played in my first high school All-Star Game, I remember a Red Sox scout telling me that he was really happy for me that I was going to Yale because professional baseball would never be in my future. So, I kind of carried that chip for a long time. My parents are blue-collar unbelievable folks that had very little and provided us with so much. I got a private high school education. I went to Yale as a collegian. You know, people from where I come from, don't have that story to tell. I do. It's all because of my parents. So, it meant a lot to be able to win Game 4 in Boston and pitch seven shutout innings. I'm sure they were on top of the moon, although they would never ever talk about it. We never talked about it. But I'm sure they are on top of the moon after that game."

* * *

Game 5: The Red Sox cruised behind a splendid effort by Bruce Hurst, who pitched 7 1/3 innings of shutout ball, won the game 4–2, the first victory by a home team in the series. The Mets, down 3–2, were heading home needing to win Games 6 and 7.

* * *

Game 6: This was an instant classic, and true to form with the '86 Mets season, was a wild night. It began with an uninvited parachuter skydive into Shea with a "Go Mets" banner trailing behind him. Trust me, that was just the tip of the iceberg. The game had a little bit of everything. The Red Sox trotted out Clemens, the American League MVP and Cy Young Award winner, to face Ojeda, who had won Game 3 in Boston. Ojeda, of course, had also kept the Mets in the crucial Game 6 of the NLCS. Boston jumped out to a 2–0 lead in the first two innings. Dwight Evans started the scoring with a double off the base of the wall. Marty Barrett's line drive to left made it 2–0 in the second. Ojeda went six full innings, giving up only those two runs. Clemens, who was selected in the 12th round of the 1981 draft by the Mets but did not sign with them, gave up two runs in the fifth to tie the game at 2–2.

Knight, who had one of the two RBIs in the fifth inning, committed a throwing error in the seventh that ultimately lead to the Red Sox taking the lead. Mookie Wilson kept the deficit at just one with a magnificent throw to the plate to nail Jim Rice, preventing another Red Sox run. Clemens had gone seven innings, giving up only four hits and two runs, only one of them earned, with eight strikeouts in a dominating performance.

In the top of the eighth, Red Sox manager John McNamara pinch-hit for the Rocket with the Red Sox leading 3–2. The Mets were happy to get him out of the game. McNamara sent up Mike Greenwell. The Mets countered with Roger McDowell, who stuck him out. The Red Sox loaded the bases but didn't score in that inning as Orosco got Bill Buckner to fly out on only one pitch. Bucker would stay in the game despite having two bad knees and being a defensive liability.

Watching Buckner run off the field between innings, even earlier in the game, was painful. It was first reported that Clemens was removed due to a blister. Then Clemens said he wanted to continue pitching while McNamara said Clemens requested to be taken out. The manager stood by his claim years later on an MLB Network special, saying Clemens entered the dugout at the end of the seventh inning and said, "That's all I can pitch." Either way, it was a bad decision but the Mets were not complaining.

Calvin Schiraldi, a former Met, had been warming up in the bullpen and came out for the eighth and was six outs away from a save and the first World Series championship for Boston since they traded the Babe. Mazzilli led off with a single. Dykstra reached on a bunt right back to Schiraldi, who threw the ball into the dirt at second. Everyone was safe. Backman moved them over with a bunt and that brought up Hernandez. He was intentionally walked and Shea Stadium was rocking in anticipation with Carter walking to the plate. The Kid lined the ball deep to left to Jim Rice. Mazzilli scored on the sac fly and as he crossed home plate, his arms were fully extended to the heavens. Strawberry flew out weakly to center fielder Dave Henderson but the game was tied going into the ninth. Rick Aguilera came in to pitch for the Mets and got the Red Sox easily. The bottom of the ninth started with Knight drawing a walk. Then Wilson bunted and catcher Rich Gedman's throw was high and pulled shortstop Spike Owen off the bag. The Red Sox argued but even the TV replay showed Knight was safe. The Mets couldn't capitalize against Schiraldi so Game 6 went to extra innings, just like Game 6 of the NLCS.

Henderson rocketed an Aguilera offering off the Newsday sign in left field for a home run that put the Red Sox up by one run and brought an eerie silence to Shea. Wade Boggs followed with a double and Barrett drove him home to stake the Red Sox to a two-run lead, 5–3. Buckner came to bat. McNamara had a chance to pinch-hit for him but decided against it. He also kept Buckner at first base in the bottom of the inning, which was a huge mistake. Schiraldi came out for his third inning of work and got the first two Mets. The Red Sox were one out away from winning the World Series, but back-to-back singles by Carter and Kevin Mitchell gave the Mets hope. Schiraldi got two strikes on

Ray Knight before he blooped a single to shallow center field to score Carter and move the tying run to third. Hernandez had retreated to watch the game on the television in Johnson's office in the clubhouse when it appeared the game was lost. Now that his team was rallying, Hernandez did not return to the dugout. He was hoping his seat had a couple more runs in it.

Bob Stanley came in for Schiraldi and delivered a wild pitch, just missing Wilson, who dove out of the way. Wilson was on his backside waiving Mitchell in to score the tying run. The 10-pitch at bat ended with Wilson hitting a weak ground ball to Buckner up the first-base line. It went through his legs, allowing Knight to score. The Mets' improbable 6–5 victory tied the series and sent the fans at Shea deliriously into the night with the series tied.

The decision to leave Buckner in the game at first base instead of putting in the more agile Dave Stapleton will forever haunt Red Sox Nation. McNamara, who passed away in 2020, defended his call by saying on the MLB Network show, "It was not any sentimental thing that I had for Billy Buck. If the ball was hit to either side of him and he couldn't get in front it, yeah, I would have questioned myself. But he got to the ball."

It wasn't just McNamara who made a mistake in the 10th. NBC Sports started setting up in the Red Sox clubhouse to capture the championship celebration. The Commissioner's Trophy was there and the champagne was on ice. But it was the Red Sox that needed to be put on ice and get ready for one more game and two more days after Game 7 was rained out.

If the Red Sox could win Game 7, and pick up McNamara, all would be forgiven in New England. But these wild, partying, fighting, rock star Mets had other ideas. The best two words in sports, *Game Seven* was coming up.

For the Mets, the next best two words in sports seemed inevitable: "World Champions."

LITTLE ROLLER UP ALONG FIRST...

BY PETER BOTTE

... Behind the bag, it gets through Buckner, here comes Knight and the Mets win it!"

The incomparable Vin Scully didn't say another word on the NBC broadcast for exactly 108 seconds after that declaration. That number fittingly was the hard-playing and harder-partying Mets' regular-season victory total before they stormed back to defeat the still-cursed-at-the-time Boston Red Sox in the 1986 World Series.

The clinching of the second and most recent championship in Mets history wouldn't have been possible without the insanity surrounding the Mets' comeback from two runs down in the 10th inning to steal a 6–5 victory in Game 6—culminated by Mookie Wilson's grounder that infamously squeezed through Bill Buckner's legs to spark sheer bedlam at Shea Stadium.

"If a picture is worth a thousand words, you have seen about million words," the great Scully finally returned to interject through the microphone as the celebration unfolded. "But more than that, you have seen an absolutely bizarre finish to Game 6 of the 1986 World Series. The Mets are not only alive, they are well. And they will play the Red Sox in Game 7 tomorrow."

A rainout the following night in New York actually pushed back the decisive seventh game until Monday, October 27, giving all involved a chance to recover from the wild finish they had witnessed or been a part of on Saturday night in Queens.

Up 3–2 in the series, the Red Sox had grabbed a 5–3 lead with two runs—including a Dave Henderson home run—against Mets righty Rick Aguilera in the top of the 10th inning.

The first two Mets were retired in the bottom half, before three straight singles against ex-Met Calvin Schiraldi by Gary Carter, Kevin Mitchell, and Ray Knight drew them back within one.

Boston reliever Bob Stanley's wild pitch with Wilson batting enabled the tying run to score, before Mookie's "little roller up along first" got through Buckner's hobbled legs into short right field to forever link them in history and to keep the Mets alive.

"Our attitude that year was we would never say die . . . It just showed the everlasting fight that we had inside of us," outfielder Darryl Strawberry said. "When the ball went through Buckner's legs I thought, we have got a chance, we've got another day to play. We got a chance to win Game 7 and to be champions."

Strawberry's eighth-inning home run put the finishing touches on the Mets' comeback from 3–0 down in Game 7.

As Straw alluded to the Mets fighting until the very end, they scored eight runs in their final three innings of the season to complete, dare I say, a second "miracle" championship in their history. The Wilson game winning hit in Game 6 was nothing short of miraculous.

POSTGAME

Championship Character

KEITH HERNANDEZ (METS FIRST BASEMAN/METS TV BROADCASTER): The trade turned into the best experience of my life because I had a talented group of guys, young players that were extraordinarily talented to be a part of and play with. The Mets did not, as Frank told me, squander their first-round draft picks, or any of their draft picks for that matter. So, the stars were aligned.

RON DARLING (METS PITCHER/METS TV BROADCASTER): I have never been on a team that not only wanted to beat you, but in some ways, maybe even embarrass you. That's kind of how that team was built, how those players were built, and where we were at in that calendar year.

KEITH HERNANDEZ: My mentor was Lou Brock. He was grooming me for future St. Louis teams but as it turned out, I stumbled right into a more perfect situation. The Mets were all young kids that were looking up to me. It was a whole different situation for me coming over with basically a bunch of twenty-two- and twenty-three-year-olds.

DARRYL STRAWBERRY (METS OUTFIELDER): It was just a great chemistry we had on that team. I am really thankful that I had the opportunity to play with such great guys, like Hernandez, Knight, and Carter. We were young.

MOOKIE WILSON (METS OUTFIELDER): That was just a fun team to be around. That team loved each other. I think that was part of our success.

The 1986 Season

DARRYL STRAWBERRY: When you have a good team that plays in New York City, everybody's going to hate you. We came to spring training in 1986 and we realized that this was the year that we needed to put all the pieces together. That's exactly what we did.

ANTHONY McCARRON (*NY DAILY NEWS* BASEBALL COLUMNIST/SNY CONTRIBUTOR): They were better than everybody else. They were tougher than everybody else. They could do anything on a baseball field and beat you in a hundred different ways. And they knew it.

DARRYL STRAWBERRY: I think our greatest moments were when we got into fights with other teams. I think those were the greatest moments because they showed the league that we weren't playing around. I don't think that was funny, but it was fun. We made a statement and let people know we were serious.

JOHN HARPER (*NY DAILY NEWS* BASEBALL COLUMNIST/SNY CONTRIBUTOR): From a baseball writer's perspective, those Mets' teams in the '80s were a dream to cover, before ballplayers came to live in fear of saying something that would haunt them on social media. The '86 Mets loved to talk, they weren't afraid to be colorful or controversial, all the more so because they had a manager in Davey Johnson who didn't mind stirring the pot himself, whether it was flat predicting the team would dominate that season or getting into occasional wars of words in the media with players in his own clubhouse.

ANTHONY McCARRON: It was clear early on that while there may be fiery disagreements, they might be mad at each other, but don't you mess with their guys. In addition to all the talent, they had great leadership with Keith Hernandez, Gary Carter, Ray Knight and a brilliant, cocky manager, Davey Johnson. Sure, they had their issues inside the team, but they partied and played together like few teams ever have.

KEN DAVIDOFF (FORMER *NY POST* BASEBALL COLUMNIST/PIX11 BASEBALL HISTORIAN): Those Mets were an all-time team of not only performers but personalities, personified by their fearless manager Davey Johnson, who told that group in spring training, "We're going to dominate." They did just that. Decades later, it's apparent that a high percentage of the roster enjoyed partying heartily. It explains, partially, why they had to settle for only one championship despite their massive talent.

ANTHONY McCARRON: Has there ever been a more outwardly cocky team in baseball history? And in their case, it's a compliment.

RON DARLING: I just think that there were so many personalities, big personalities, that was what I envisioned a rock and roll band traveling to be like. I felt we were like that.

Tough Team's Softer Side

DWIGHT "DOC" GOODEN (METS PITCHER): We were a wild bunch. You have probably heard it all. Roger McDowell was one of the guys that you didn't take your eyes off. Whether it was during the game, on the bus rides, or on the plane rides. He was quite a character and he kept everybody loose.

KEITH HERNANDEZ: Roger was probably the biggest prankster on the team. In Dodger Stadium during a day game, he put his uniform on upside down. He put one pant leg over his head, I don't know how the hell he did it. Then he put both arms in the pant legs with his face smushed against the rear side of the pants. He was standing in front of the dugout, and you could make out his face, because it was pressed tightly against his face. He looked like a science fiction monster or an alien. It was just the funniest thing—it made me laugh. It reminded me of the movie *The Thing*, and it was just hilarious.

JESSE OROSCO (METS RELIEF PITCHER): He was the best when it came to playing pranks and keeping everyone loose. One of the greatest moments was when we were at Dodger Stadium and Roger went in and got Tommy Lasorda's uniform. He put the uniform on upside down. So, it looked like Tommy was kind of floating around. I think it was good for baseball, when he did things like that. That was Roger McDowell.

The Mookie At-Bat

DARRYL STRAWBERRY: Our attitude that year was we would never say die. We were behind a lot of games but would never quit and we kept coming back and winning. So that was just a fight in us.

MOOKIE WILSON: Aw, man, it was a long at-bat.

RON DARLING: I was sent home by [pitching coach] Mel Stottlemyre after the last out in the bottom of the eighth inning. In those days, it took about two hours before we could leave the stadium after World Series games because there's 55,000 fans there and it was just impossible to move. Mel thought it would be a good idea if I just made it home and relaxed since I was slated to start Game 7. He told me before I left, we're gonna win this game. I don't think he knew how we're gonna win it. I got on Grand Central Parkway, and of course listened to [Mets broadcaster] Bob Murphy. I knew right away, after the Henderson home run, that I needed to come back. Whether you win or lose, you want to be with your mates. I ended up just getting [back] after Keith made his the second out. I watched the rest of the game from Charlie Samuels's office, he was our equipment manager.

KEITH HERNANDEZ: I made the second out of the inning and I certainly didn't want to see Boston having fun on our field, so I went up briefly to the clubhouse. Darrell Johnson was our advance scout, and ironically, a former manager of the Red Sox. Jay Horwitz was in Davey's office as well. I sat down in one of the chairs and everything started happening. I wasn't going to get off that chair because we were one out away from elimination. Superstitious as I am, we liked to say, "That chair had hits in it." So, I didn't move.

KEN DAVIDOFF: John McNamara's decision to leave Bill Buckner in the bottom of the 10th inning of Game 6 of the 1986 World Series ranks as one of the least defensible decisions in sports history. Everyone knew how banged up Buckner was. McNamara lifted Buckner for defensive replacement Dave Stapleton in each of the Red Sox's seven postseason victories that fall–and they might have picked up their eighth had McNamara done the same in Game 6. McNamara, defending the decision, claimed in a 2011 interview that Buckner was "the best first baseman I had," which of course begs the question why he lifted Buckner in all of the other games.

MOOKIE WILSON: It was the at-bat of my career, even though it may not be as flamboyant, as guys hitting home runs, the results were really, really big. I learned that you put your best foot forward every day and see what happens. I did nothing different. I've always run balls out. I mean, that's just the way I was raised. That's the way I was taught to play the game.

RON DARLING: When the ball went through Buckner's legs, like most people, I was in disbelief. I couldn't believe that happened. Those are the kinds of things that don't even happen in a college game. You very rarely would see that at the professional level.

DARRYL STRAWBERRY: When the ball went through Bucker's legs I thought, *We have got a chance, we've got another day to play. We got a chance to win Game 7 and to be champions.*

JOHN HARPER: It took a miracle to win Game 6 yet that was fitting in some ways for a team that believed it couldn't lose. They had bullied the National League from start to finish, winning 108 games and making enemies along the way with their big personalities, their boisterous home run celebrations, and their willingness to brawl any time an opponent pushed their buttons.

KEITH HERNANDEZ: I think it's the greatest single comeback in World Series history with the series on the line.

DARRYL STRAWBERRY: It just showed the everlasting fight that we had inside of us.

Game 7

KEITH HERNANDEZ: [On his sixth inning at-bat with the bases loaded] It was a situation where we needed a base hit not a sacrifice fly. We had to get in 2 runs and set up Carter for at least a chance to drive in a run behind me. So, a sacrifice fly wasn't gonna get it done and I was aware of that. I came through. I can also tell you that it was the same situation that I had in '82 with the Cardinals, which was kind of ironic. I was sitting there thinking this is my second World Series, and here I am coming up to bat in a situation that needs a base hit again. We're losing, we're behind and I just had to grit my teeth and do the best I can. And fortunately, I came through.

JESSE OROSCO: The game was like moving so fast. I had to try to keep my adrenaline at a certain spot to keep focus on pitching.

World Champions!

MOOKIE WILSON: At that moment, I was saying, "Thank God, we didn't have to go through the same thing we did in Houston." In Houston there were home runs, lead changes, taking the lead, then giving up the lead, and I think Jesse's expression kind of tells it all, "it's over, we finally did it, now let's go take some rest."

JESSE OROSCO: It was all a blur because everybody was going crazy. I threw my glove up in the air. I got champagne from my wife then went back in the clubhouse and celebrated. That was the greatest moment of my life. And then we all just jumped around all over New York City—it was our town. And I've got a ring to show for it.

DARRYL STRAWBERRY: It was just an incredible feeling. You know, after all the hard work and all that we went through that year. Then, having to come back in that series against the Astros, beating them, being down 0–2 in the World Series, and being able to come back and win that? It was just an incredible feeling for us.

RON DARLING: In '86 we were supposed to culminate that year with a World Series championship. So, when we did it, It was a combination of joy and relief all at the same time. Very few teams that are picked in the offseason to be the World Series champion win it.

KEITH HERNANDEZ: You start every spring training, and everybody has the goal to win the World Series. It doesn't happen very often. It was particularly fun to do it in the style that we did, where we just kind of dominated the league. the Mets were such a down team for so long. They were a last-place team and to have turned it around in three years was really remarkable and that's the difference. I am very proud that we won 108 games with a franchise that was a perennial last-place team after the Seaver trade. There are only a dozen teams that have won 108 games or more in the history of baseball. It's just a testament to the talent that we had. It wasn't just me; we turn that culture around, that culture of losing.

DWIGHT "DOC" GOODEN: It was incredible because I went from Rookie of the Year to winning the Cy Young Award to winning the World Series at twenty-one years old. I thought I was just going to win all the time. The group of guys were special guys. We all came up together as a young group. To win it in New York and to clinch it in New York and to share that moment with your team and your fans was definitely special. It's something that will always be close to my heart.

JESSE OROSCO: I think every player wants to be a champion. It's not easy to win a World Series. I just was so ecstatic about getting a chance to get in the play-offs. Then knowing we're getting closer. This '86 team played hard every day. We kept following through and progressing, and that's how things worked out with a championship.

Canyon of Heroes

RON DARLING: I think if they had ever put that into a little pill, we'd all be addicted. It's a combination of youth and feeling like you are at the top of your powers. You feel immortal. The sheer number of fans is incredible. We were told between the people on the parade route, the people in the buildings, and the fans at City Hall, it was 3 million people there for us. I was twenty-five years old, and I felt like I was five years old again.

DARRYL STRAWBERRY: That was a real plus. It was the biggest event of the year. Us winning was great, but the parade was even greater.

KEITH HERNANDEZ: The parade was really fantastic going down the Canyon of Heroes. You realize all the people that had a parade, teams or individuals, it was really fantastic. there was such a great outpouring of love from the fans. I think it was special because New York had been such a cellar dweller for so long. I think the town was just thrilled that the Mets had finally won it for the first time 1969. The Miracle Mets were a remarkable team and I think ours was just as remarkable.

RON DARLING: It was just unadulterated mayhem. It was beautiful.

DWIGHT "DOC" GOODEN: I missed the parade unfortunately. It was great, I watched it on TV. We still reminisce about it.

Looking Back

KEITH HERNANDEZ: I lived in Manhattan, so I couldn't [pay for] a meal for two months. Everywhere I went the owners would come over or their maître d's and they would buy the dinner, send over champagne on the house. It happened probably until the end of the year. It was just fantastic. People were so overjoyed and I felt that. I was glad that I was in the city after the World Series to be there and in the offseason, with all the fans who were just jubilant. It was wonderful.

RON DARLING: In those days, if you had someone staying with you in a small apartment, you would get a futon. For Game 1, I ordered a futon for my parents to sleep on in my tiny Manhattan apartment. It was delivered and put down and I gave a nice tip to the person that brought in the futon. I found out twenty years later, it was Ray Romano, the guy that did *Everybody Loves Raymond* that was the guy that delivered it (laughs). I did give him a nice tip, thank God. Because I think in some ways, the way TV works, if I had given him a bad tip, I probably would have been on the show.

KEITH HERNANDEZ: [On his *Seinfeld* appearance] They used my *Seinfeld* episode during sweeps week in 1992. At the time I had no idea the show was popular, I didn't watch prime-time. We're baseball players, we played night games, we couldn't watch prime-time. I had no idea what the show was about. It just basically opened me up to a whole new extension of life. Being a baseball player, we reach the sports segment of our society, but *Seinfeld* reached into every nook and cranny of American society as well as overseas. So, for people that didn't see me play, like young kids, they identify me to this day to that *Seinfeld* episode. So, it was one of the great things that happened to me.

RON DARLING: My life certainly was affected but I also think about how my teammates lives would have been affected is we didn't win that championship. It would be a great Off-Broadway play about what would happen to the '86 Mets if we hadn't won the World Series, that would be some psychological profile of what would have happened to the players on that team.

My entire life has been around baseball, my entire life. From the time I was a kid to now when I'm sixty-two years old. So maybe that is all taken away and I'm doing something different. The '86 World Series is a big reason why I'm where I am today doing Mets games on SNY. Ninety-nine percent of what has happened to me is the greatest thing that ever but then one percent is like I wonder what would have happened? Maybe I would have become an architect.

KEITH HERNANDEZ: To win the World Series and at the end of my career to have my number retired with the Mets organization is a great honor. I'm up there with one of six guys in sixty years of Mets history. I never dreamed that I would have my number retired. I'm up there with Gil Hodges and Casey Stengel, Mike Piazza, Tom Seaver and Jerry Koosman, I'm one of only four players that are up there. So, it's just terrific. (Author's Note: Willie Mays became the seventh person and fifth player to have his number retired by the Mets, in 2022.)

8

SUPER BOWL XXI:
NEW YORK GIANTS vs.
DENVER BRONCOS

JANUARY 25, 1987

SIMMS 22-FOR-25

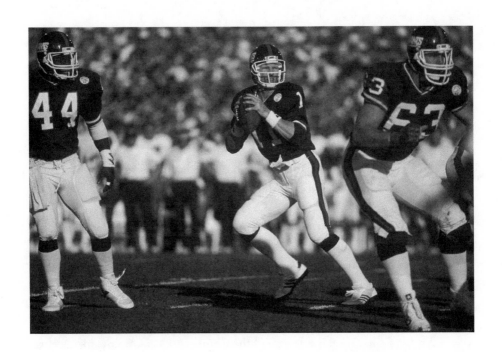

TIME CAPSULE

- Mayor of New York: Ed Koch
- Oscar, Best Picture: *Out of Africa*
- Oscar, Best Actor: William Hurt, *Kiss of the Spider Woman*
- Oscar, Best Actress: Geraldine Page, *The Trip to Bountiful*
- Grammy, Album of the Year: Phil Collins, *No Jacket Required*
- Grammy, Record of the Year: USA for Africa, "We Are the World," *We Are the World*
- President of the US: Ronald Reagan
- Price of Gas: $0.86/Gallon
- Heisman Award: Vinny Testaverde, quarterback, Miami

PREGAME

drought
noun \ ʹdraůt
- **a prolonged or chronic shortage or lack of something expected or desired**

An NFL championship is certainly something "desired" in football circles. A generation of New York Giants fans had been waiting since 1956. For them, the lack of a championship certainly fell into the category of a "prolonged or chronic shortage."

So what did it take to end the franchise's championship drought? Let's look back and trace the steps.

A day before New Year's Eve in 1956, Yankee Stadium filled up with fans looking for a celebration as big as the one the following night in Times Square. This celebration would not be automatic and set off at the stroke of midnight, but would instead need to be earned on the field. The "Monsters of the Midway" Chicago Bears stood in the way of the Giants and a championship celebration. The Bears were a slight favorite in the game, while the Giants were looking to end a decade of drought dating back to their last championship in 1946.

Halfback Frank Gifford, the NFL's Most Valuable Player—coupled with linebacker Sam Huff—were the dynamic duo that led New York. Huff was the first defensive player to glamorize the position. The Yankee Stadium field was icy, but wearing sneakers to gain better footing kept the Giants a step ahead of the Bears on every play. It worked better than all-weather tires, as the Giants ran over Chicago and to a title with a 47–7 blowout.

The win was followed by a thirty-one-year championship drought . . . but it wasn't for lack of effort, as they suffered losses in the title games of 1958, 1959, 1961, 1962, and 1963. Then the faucet turned off completely. Fans chanted "Good Bye, Allie" (Allie Sherman was the head coach of the Giants from 1961–68. His early success didn't save him from the being held accountable by the fans at the end of his run with the Giants). The franchise didn't get close to a championship game until George Young—Don Shula's right-hand man with the Dolphins—arrived in 1979 from Miami.

Having trouble agreeing on a general manager to guide the franchise's rebuild, Wellington Mara wanted George Young and asked the commissioner to help him out. So when Wellington and his nephew Tim Mara elicited the help of NFL Commissioner Pete Rozelle. Serving as a neutral party, Rozelle recommended Young.

Wellington's plan worked, and Young was named the franchise's new general manager, on Valentine's Day in 1979. The hire rekindled a love affair between the team and its fans. Big Blue had done little winning and had not made the playoffs for fifteen consecutive years when Young took over the GM's office at Giants Stadium.

It would not be an overnight process to return the team to championship contenders. Young's mantra was to build through the draft. And while he's now looked at fondly, the love affair that fans have for him today wasn't as much the case in the beginning. His first pick—the seventh overall in the 1979 draft—was Phil Simms out of little-known Morehead State. Locals couldn't believe that Young had taken this obscure player from a school they didn't know existed (especially with the seventh overall pick), and that the rebuild would be centered around Simms.

"I was down at Morehead, Kentucky, and I know all that stuff that was caught on video of the fan's reaction, I've seen it, I'm not sure that wasn't recreated," said Simms, joking around. "I've never had anybody verify that for me. But, you know, there is no way the fans were ready to boo. I'm sure they never heard my name before (laughing). It was just a different era. You know, we didn't have 770 people watching my tape and judging who I was and what round I would go in."

In fact, when Rozelle announced Simms's name to the draftniks at New York's Waldorf-Astoria Hotel on May 3, 1979, the reaction was so muted that NFL Films requested Rozelle make the announcement again. This time, when Rozelle said, "The New York Giants first-round selection, quarterback Phil Simms, Morehead State," the fans booed long and loud. Rozelle smiled. The moment was captured on film forever, but Simms wasn't upset by it at the time.

"I knew before the draft that the Giants were going to take me, at least they told me they were," said Simms. "I must say that at least seven teams told me they were going to take me in the first round. They openly told me, 'We're going to draft you.' And of course, back then they could do that because I wasn't going to get any calls from reporters. I knew it probably would be upsetting to everybody in New York when I was drafted, but I can say this with complete honesty, it did not bother me. On a scale of one to one hundred, it was a complete zero. It never even entered my mind ever. Even the first year when I played and got booed, or whatever you want to say, I just didn't care about it. I didn't expect the New York Giant fans to go, oh fantastic, we got him. Back then how many college players did you know? Maybe just a few quarterbacks in the country maximum."

The fans tune would dramatically change, but let's not get ahead of ourselves. Back to the building of the team and Young focusing on the draft. He now had his franchise quarterback and, just like the 1956 team, now went after a game-changing linebacker.

After a 4–12 season in 1980—their eighth consecutive losing season—the Giants had the second overall pick in the 1981 draft. With this pick, Young selected linebacker Lawrence Taylor out of the University of North Carolina. His eye for talent was further established when he took jockey-sized running back Joe Morris in the second round of the 1982 draft. Now with the quarterback, running back, and linebacker positions filled, the 1983 draft meant it was time for the team to focus on the offensive and defensive lines.

Young picked defensive end Leonard Marshall in the second round and offensive tackle Karl Nelson in the third. More pieces were added in the 1984 draft, when they got Carl Banks (linebacker, third overall), William Roberts (guard, 27th), Jeff Hostetler (quarterback, 59th), Gary Reasons (linebacker, 105th), and Lionel Manuel (wide receiver, 171st). The sure-handed tight end Mark Bavaro was added the following year. In the 1986 draft the team's championship defense was completed when Eric Dorsey (defensive end, 19th overall), Mark Collins (defensive back, 44th), Erik Howard (nose tackle, 46th), and Pepper Johnson (linebacker, 51st were added. This vaunted defense would become known as the "Big Blue Wrecking Crew."

In 1981, the Giants hired Bill Parcells as their defensive coordinator under head coach Ray Perkins. At the end of the 1982 season, Perkins decided to "roll" with the Tide and become the head coach and athletic director at the University of Alabama, to succeed the legendary Bear Bryant. Young's next move was to go fishing for a replacement, and he reeled in "The Big Tuna" to lead the Giants team starting in 1983.

When hired, Parcells was not yet, well, "Bill Parcells." And the ragtag team he took over had qualified for the playoffs only once in the decade leading up to his hire, and that was in 1981. His first year followed form with the Giants going 3–12–1.

In the meantime, Howard Schellenberger was building a college dynasty at "The U" in Miami. He won the national championship in 1983, beating Nebraska and making him the hot coaching prospect. He and Young worked together in Baltimore and Miami, and Young offered him Parcells's job after a loss to the St. Louis Cardinals in Week 14, but Schellenberger turned it down. That set the wheels in motion for Parcells to become a legend, and the Giants to become an NFL powerhouse . . . and it all happened under the watchful eye of Young.

The turnaround was swift. After a 9–7 record in 1984, the G-Men went to the playoffs and capped the year with a playoff win against the Rams. Though they would lose to the 49ers in the divisional round, the question going into the offseason was: could Parcells lead Big Blue to back-to-back playoff berths for the first time in over two decades?

The answer was a resounding yes. New York took two giant steps forward by not only making the playoffs again—with a 10–6 record—but also by avenging their second-round loss the year before to San Francisco. However, they would lose 21–0 to the Bears, who "shuffled" their way to a Super Bowl championship. That shutout loss would be the catalyst for the Giants to take their rightful place among the NFL elite the following season.

Leonard Marshall shared the impact of that loss to the Bears.

The agony of defeat in that case became a motivator, because we knew we were a much better football team than we played that day. Granted if we had an offense in Chicago, it might have been a much better football game. We flat our got our butts whipped, no ifs, ands, and butts about it. We got our butts whipped and got beat in all three phases of the game offense, defense, and special teams. I mean granted the Bears only scored two touchdowns on offence, but we got beat in every phase of the game. We made a commitment after that game. I think it started the night we boarded the flight to come home. All the players on that flight were pissed off, very disappointed and felt like crap, it was bad. I am not going to stand here and tell you it wasn't It was bad. We were in a bad way.

By the 1986 season, Young had completed his transformation of the team's roster. Parcells was now in his fourth season at the helm, with playoff experience under his belt. His team had learned to win, step-by-step.

In 1986, Taylor won the NFL MVP, becoming the first defensive player since Alan Page in 1971 to take home the honor. The Giants only lost two times in 1986 and won their first division title since the 1970 merger. Up first in the playoffs was a familiar foe in the San Francisco 49ers. It was the third year in a row they would face each other, and the fourth time in six years, with the Niners previously beating them in 1981 and 1984. The Giants got their revenge in 1985, and this would be their chance to even up this playoff rivalry—and they did just that. Led by LT, Big Blue completely shut down the high-powered San Fran offense. Simms and the offense were equally as dominant, and the Giants crushed San Francisco, 49–3.

Now with the 49ers out of the way, the last team in their way from appearing in their first Super Bowl would be a division rival: the Washington Redskins.

As divisional rivals, the two teams had already played twice during the regular season. On October 27, the Giants beat the Redskins in the Meadowlands, 27–20. That date might ring a bell . . . it was the night the Mets defeated the Red Sox in Game 7 of the World Series, across two rivers, at Shea Stadium. Many of the fans in attendance at the Meadowlands were also listening to the World Series game on the radio, and there were multiple spontaneous eruptions from the fans as the Mets were winning their championship. Their second match-up on the season would take place on December 7, in which the Giants were again victorious, this time 24–14.

Normally known for its swirling winds, Giants Stadium was the site of NFL Championship Game on January 11, 1987, had wind gusts measured at 33 miles an hour. Continuing their playoff momentum, New York played like they had the wind at their backs. In a rare move—especially back in those days—Parcells chose to take the wind instead of the ball when they won the coin flip. As a result, the Giants dominated the field position game on their way to a 17–0 victory, sending them to the Super Bowl.

When linebacker Gary Reasons was asked for his favorite Super Bowl memory, he paused and thought about it. "The euphoria of winning the NFC Championship Game. Knowing that you're going to the Super Bowl. It is really what every NFL player works for, from the end of the one season to the start of the next one. We accomplished and got to the Super Bowl. The success of your season is measured by getting to the Super Bowl. We did it at Giants Stadium and celebrated with our fans and the confetti raining down on us, it was just an indescribable feeling."

Just wait, Gary. It would get even better.

THE IMPERFECT QB WAS NEARLY PERFECT

BY PETER BOTTE

Joe Trimble, the longtime *New York Daily News* sportswriter, wrote of Don Larsen's World Series gem in 1956 that "the imperfect man threw a perfect game."

Trimble supposedly received an assist from the legendary Dick Young for the suggestion, but the writers covering the Giants' first trip to the Super Bowl on January 25, 1987, could have written something similar about Phil Simms's stellar performance in their 39–20 victory over the Denver Broncos in Super Bowl XXI.

Simms, who'd dealt with multiple injuries after the Giants drafted him with the seventh overall pick in 1979, completed 22 of 25 passes for 268 yards—for a Super Bowl record completion percentage of 88 percent and a nearly perfect quarterback rating of 150.9—with three touchdown passes and zero interceptions.

Indeed, Simms saved the best statistical game of his career for the biggest game of his career.

"Remembering the game, I never in the game thought, *Oh, wow, I really got it today, it's going really well.* Nothing like that," Simms said. "I was thinking about nothing but just doing my job, and thinking of the play, and never getting emotional.

"That's when you play your best, or at least when I did. My only regret is why didn't I have that mindset more often?"

The Giants hadn't won an NFL title since 1956, barely two months after Larsen had retired all 27 Brooklyn Dodgers he faced for the Yankees in Game 5 of the '56 Fall Classic. And they'd posted a combined record of 49–108–2 from 1973 to '83, with Simms ceding the starting QB job to Scott Brunner for the latter two of those seasons.

Giants coach Bill Parcells reinstalled Simms as the starter in 1984, although the team largely ascended to the top of the NFC behind a defense led by a coordinator named Bill Belichick and a revolutionary linebacker named Lawrence Taylor.

Still, the Super Bowl matchup against emerging Broncos star John Elway turned out to be Simms's time to shine, including TD tosses to Zeke Mowatt, Mark Bavaro, and Phil McConkey.

"I didn't let any outside influences affect my play," Simms said. "I think there's lots of reasons for that, I guess. One, we were a good team. We had a really good game plan for the day. We were a hot team going into the Super Bowl. And our offense was throwing the ball and we were making a lot of big plays towards the end of the year, everybody kind of got healthy.

"It just kind of all fell into place as we prepared for the Super Bowl. It wasn't good. It was off the charts, outstanding for those two weeks. And so fortunately, that doesn't always happen that way, but fortunately, it carried over into the game, kind of for our offense and for me."

And very nearly perfect.

POSTGAME

Feeling Blue No More

HARRY CARSON (GIANTS LINEBACKER): George Martin and I had gone through those years of bad football in the late seventies. Then we got to a point where we started playing a different caliber of football. It all started with George Young, Ray Perkins, and then Bill Parcells. We started to build a more formidable team. Any team that played us knew it was going to be tough. It was a different mindset.

LEONARD MARSHALL (GIANTS DEFENSIVE END): I was definitely the second piece of the defensive puzzle that the Giants were trying to build. In '81 we drafted Lawrence Taylor. In '83 they drafted me and Terry Kinard. In '84 we drafted Carl Banks. In '85 we drafted Gary Reasons. And then in '86 the rest of the crew came, Pepper, Mark Collins, Eric Dorsey, John Washington, Greg Lasker, a bunch of kids that contributed, we made some great acquisitions in the free agency market. One guy that stepped in and really became the quarterback of our secondary was Kenny Hill. He was bright, a Yale guy, a guy who bought an awful lot to those guys in the back.

The Big Blue Attitude

PHIL SIMMS (GIANTS QUARTERBACK): This was a guy that just was not afraid to take chances. And I think we all forget that with Bill Parcells, and I don't know if it's been talked about a lot.

LEONARD MARSHALL: The beauty of the '86 team was, that was the tightest group of men I've ever been around.

CARL BANKS: The concept of "making your opponent quit" was internal messaging that as a team we looked for who could be the possible weak link. Then what could we do as a group and as individuals to snatch their will. It was all part of our championship culture. it was more than just a saying it was a way of life.

Their eyes get big, they get nervous, if they gotta block you. That's when you know, because they've abandoned all of their techniques, and they're more concerned about not being embarrassed on the play.

In the game, we go back to our defensive huddle, and somebody would say hey, my guy is about to quit.

In 1986 we were playing the Redskins. Myself, Harry Carson, and Pepper Johnson walked through their pregame warmups and Harry walked up to

George Rogers and says, "Homeboy you're gonna drop this ball, you're gonna fumble twice."

He's standing in between all of their team and Harry turned around and we walked out. And wouldn't you know it, there was two fumbles that game by George Rogers.

Different Sides of the Tuna

PHIL SIMMS: Parcells kind of rallied behind me somewhat late in the year and when he rallied behind me, we started getting people back and the fortunes of our offense changed dramatically. He was behind us and trying to encourage us like I'd never really experienced before under him.

PHIL SIMMS: He wanted our team to be bullies. But think about the San Francisco 49ers playoff game in 1986, where we ran the fake field goal that led to a touchdown. That was huge in the game.

Think about the Washington championship game. We win the toss. And we chose to defend the goal instead of taking the ball. We kick off with the wind behind us because he wanted to score first and get on top. The wind was so vicious that he didn't think we would score going into the wind.

So those decisions I've never even thought of like this, I never even really told it to anyone in this framework. But those decisions changed our lives. I know they change mine. I know that it changed the way everybody looks at Bill Parcells and a lot of people on that team. Because those were game altering decisions. He made all of them.

SEAN LANDETA (GIANTS PUNTER): To give you an idea of how warm and fuzzy Bill Parcells could be, one Monday after a game, I was in the training room icing my leg. Parcells walks by the training room door looks in and says, with a growl, "What the hell happened to you?" I said, "I took a helmet to the ankle, no big deal." Five minutes later, he walks by the door again, stops and is glaring at me. As I'm thinking to myself, *What the heck does he want now?* He takes a drag from his cigarette and says, "Oh, I got it Landeta, next Monday night when we play in front of the whole country, and you punt like crap, I'll make sure to tell the announcers to let everybody know you hurt your ankle."

He then takes another drag of a cigarette and walks away. As I said to myself, *Great, Bill, thanks very much, you blankety blank blank.*

That's a nice story. That will make someone smile, right?

PHIL SIMMS: I think it really started in Minnesota. I'd really been struggling, and Parcells gave me a big speech. The week before we were playing in Philadelphia Bill Belichick walked by me one day, in the locker room, it was late, and no one was there but myself and a few coaches. I'm walking down the hallway and Belichik stopped me and said, listen, I just want you to know, I know what you're dealing with and you're a hell of a player.

I was much more aggressive when I threw the ball the next week, up in Minnesota, we played hard, and we made some plays at the end of the game that changed our fortune. And then, no matter what situation we're in, it seems like we never thought we were out of it, we never blinked, we knew we'll be alright, and we'd get it done.

L.T.

PHIL SIMMS: I mean I could write four books on Lawrence Taylor. I'll just say this, he was of course, a great player, bigger than life. He just wanted to win. He didn't care who got the sack or made a play, he was always hugging and grabbing whoever it was. He would always hug me, slap me, grab me, and most of the time he was the first guy I saw after a touchdown and he was like, "man we scored." Yeah, that's great. He was really into it. It's all about winning for him.

PHIL SIMMS: In practice some days he'd be tired, probably stayed out the night before too much. And I'd be walking to the practice field outside of the stadium and I'd look at him and say, "How are you doing, big boy?"

You know, kind of having a little smile and laugh.

He goes, "Man, Simms, there's only one thing to do."

And I said, "What's that?"

He goes, "I'm just gonna go crazy at practice today."

And he truly destroyed practice. Like, get him off the field so we can at least practice, he was that crazy and that good.

He was, besides Bill Parcells, the biggest reason we had success.

A Championship Omen

PHIL SIMMS: In practice on the Friday before the Super Bowl, you have your last practice run-through, the team was really practicing well, really well. I threw a pass to Lionel Manuel, it could have been the play we threw the first play of the game, and we were probably three quarters of the way through the offense that we were going to practice, and Bill Parcells goes, "Oh my God, men, okay, let's not leave it all on the field. All right, we're done." We were all like, oh, what is this? Bill had never done that before. Things were going so well in practice, I was throwing it well, and I think it actually made Bill a little nervous. And I think in the eight years I have played under him, that might have been the only time we ever did that. I guess looking back on it you could say it was all setting up for it to go well.

Undisclosed Location

GEORGE MARTIN (GIANTS DEFENSIVE END): The night before we were going to play the Super Bowl, Bill Parcells called a team meeting. He commanded everybody to go back to their rooms and pack their bags. I was thinking, *What's he talking about?* There were three buses out front, so we all boarded the buses and took off to undisclosed location. And this was totally unscripted. We knew nothing about it. He took us to an undisclosed location the night before the game, because Bill Parcells was astute enough to know that boys will be boys and girls will be girls. And you know that people would be looking for us for autographs and all manner of things. So, he took us to a secluded location. And I thought it was a stroke of genius because we didn't know where we were. We could not inform our relatives, friends of where we were. And I think it led to us being very, very relaxed, very restful and not being involved in all of what he calls "distractions" prior to the game. I said that was one of the shrewdest moves that I've ever seen by head coach prior to a game. It was a stroke of genius, and I think it contributed in a big way to our success.

A Super Good Omen

PHIL SIMMS: During warmups I'm throwing the ball and one of our coaches, Pat Hodgson, says to me, "Man, Blondie"—he always called me Blondie—"man, you are really throwing that ball!" I just kind of looked at him thinking, what's the difference today and every other day? I didn't even pay attention to it.

The Game Within the Game

GEORGE MARTIN (ON HIS SAFETY IN THE SUPER BOWL): I realized that it was a passing situation. So, I talked to my young tackle, Erik Howard, who was a rookie at that time, and I told him, no matter what I tell you, after we break the huddle, ignore it. And I repeated that about three times to make sure he heard me. When we broke the huddle, I yelled at him. I said, "Me game, me game" and the offensive tackle of the Broncos perked up and he thought we were going to run a game. So, when I got off on the ball, I faked inside, like I was coming inside, and he bit on it. And then I came on the outside and Elway was sitting there like a prize that I wrapped up.

It was one of the greatest moments of my life, on that stage, to be able to contribute to the victory. Some people say that it was a momentum swing, you know, it's just something that I will always cherish.

PHIL McCONKEY (GIANTS WIDE RECEIVER): But you know what play I think about more than any other? I think about the third and three play from our 40-yard line. I think it was the second play of the second quarter.

It's third-and-three, I'm in the slot. They just expect me to go hook up at six yards trying to pick up the first down. I stutter stepped the guy, and I took off. The two safeties vacated the middle and that's where I was going. The defensive back was so faked out he threw his legs into me, intentionally tripped me, and Simms threw the ball. It would have been a 60-yard touchdown. They didn't even call a penalty. I was outraged. So, I think about that more than I think about all the big plays and the touchdown in the Super Bowl. That was one of his three incomplete passes, the other two were drops. That's how perfect he was.

PHIL McCONKEY: When I was a little boy, I wanted two things. I wanted to score a touchdown in the Super Bowl, and I wanted to be a pilot. I loved football, but I was small, and nobody would give me a scholarship. So, I had to go to the Naval Academy. I figured I'd get one of those dreams, to be a pilot. I got that dream, but I couldn't let the other one go. I decided I needed to do something and take action to try to achieve the second dream. People laughed at me, but you know, there I was in Pasadena on January 25, 1987, and the second dream came true.

When the Clock Hit 00:00

PHIL McCONKEY: It was complete bedlam. It's kind of an out-of-body experience when you finally know that the game's over and you've won a Super Bowl and you've realized your dreams. You are on the field sharing this incredible moment with your teammates and you can't wait to see your loved ones and family afterwards to celebrate. I'm just delirious at that point. In the middle of all this, the most surreal experience of my life was looking down at the ground and seeing a .357 Magnum gun laying there in the middle of the field. My military training kicks in. I have my helmet in one hand and I grabbed the gun off the ground and safely pointed at the ground until the security guard came and took it from me. I guess what happened was the camera was following Simms because he was the MVP and somehow, I ended up on camera. The nation saw me picking up this gun, so I had a gun in my hand. The CBS switchboard was flooded with calls saying that McConkey had a gun in his helmet. At the postgame press conference, they asked me about that incident.

I said," Well, you know, I scored a touchdown in the Super Bowl to help my team win a championship and I saved some lives—all in a day's work."

HARRY CARSON: After the game, we're in the locker room and you expect that when you win a championship like a Super Bowl, there will be champagne flowing all over the place and guys are like spraying champagne over one another, that was not us. When we came in from the field, the way that we celebrated with Wellington Mara was I grabbed him, and we took him into the shower to get him wet. It wasn't champagne, wasn't beer or anything like that. It was just that we wanted to douse him with the water that came out of the shower, because he was one of us. We wanted him to feel like he was he was a part of us as well. This was actually prior to Wellington Mara receiving the Lombardi trophy.

Gatorade Bath

GEORGE MARTIN: That was exclusively a Harry Carson special, and Harry probably was one of only two or three guys that could do that without retaliation from Bill Parcells. It took a lot of gumption at first to dunk the head coach, one of the greatest head coaches ever, with Gatorade. But Harry made it a ritual. He was celebrating the moment of us winning and it became a tradition.

But Bill Parcells is very superstitious. So once Harry started, if Harry had quit it, I think he would've heard from Parcells to continue that tradition. So, it was something that's been monumental in Giant folklore.

HARRY CARSON: Well, actually, it wasn't created by me, it was Jim Burt, our nose tackle, who came up with the idea.

In 1985, Bill Parcells kind of made it known that Jeff Bostic was playing really well for Washington. We were about to play the Redskins, and during the week, Bill just kept riding Burt. Everybody thinks that it started in 1986, but it really started in 1985. Anyway, Parcells really got under Jim's skin. Jim got tired of hearing Parcells's mouth. Bill would say it in such a way that other guys in the locker room could hear it. That put Burt in a position where he felt challenged.

Jim played well in the game. The game was ending, he came over to me said, "That [expletive] Parcells is such a prick. He makes me angry sometimes. We ought to get him with something."

I said, "What do you mean we?"

He said, "Let's get him with the Gatorade."

I said, "What do you mean *we*, Jim?"

He said, "You're his guy; he won't do anything to you, but, you know, if I did something, he'd have my butt."

I said, "What do you propose to do, Jim?"

He said, "Let's get him with the Gatorade." That was Jim's idea.

I said, "Okay, we'll do it, but we have to wait until he takes his headphones off because I don't want him to be electrocuted or anything like that."

As the game was winding down, both Jim and I had a handle on the Gatorade bucket. Parcells took his headphones off, and we doused him.

That was really the first time that he was doused. It didn't happen again during the 1985–86 season. The next year we lost our first game against the Dallas Cowboys, it was a big game. Our next game was the San Diego Chargers and they had beaten the Miami Dolphins 50–28 so nobody really gave us a shot to beat the Chargers. Everybody's pissed because of the first loss against the Cowboys. As the game is winding down, we're leading, and we win the game. We were really happy about getting that loss off our back, beating a team that everybody thought was going to beat us. With our jubilation and everything, I decided to get Parcells with Gatorade. That was the first Gatorade shower of the 1986 season. Bill Parcells is very superstitious. If you do something one week, and if it works, you have to keep doing it. So, as we were winning during the course of the 1986 season, I continued to douse him with Gatorade. It wasn't that I wanted to do it. I felt like I had to do it because it's a superstitious thing. It really did become a symbol of the '86 season. As we were playing, and as we were winning, we continued to douse him and it got kind of comical. Whether it was me putting on a hat and overcoat—from the doctors on staff—to sort of sneak up on Bill Parcells, we had fun with it. He never objected to it. As long as we were winning, we're going to keep getting him with the Gatorade.

Super Bowl Gatorade Caper

HARRY CARSON: Everybody was expecting me to get Parcells with Gatorade, which I did. I had my uniform on and I got him as time was winding down, but it didn't show up on television. So, I thought I might as well get him with a second bucket. I asked the security guy if I can wear his jacket. I went and got a bucket of water. He would be expecting a number 53 jersey behind him, he would never suspect security guard wearing a yellow jacket behind him. I kind took my time; I splashed him with the Gatorade. He was not, in my opinion, thinking about a second dose of Gatorade, but that's what the whole deal was about.

Simms 22-for-25!

JIM NANTZ (CBS SPORTS ANNOUNCER): I had the honor of working with Phil for 13 years—side by side, I loved every single minute of it. His Super Bowl performance of going 22 of 25 was something that came up every single week of our journey around the NFL, and never by Phil, he's the humblest guy in the world. It's one of the legendary performances in the history of the game.

PHIL McCONKEY: Simms was absolutely flawless in the biggest game of his life against arguably one of the greatest quarterbacks in NFL history, Hall of Famer John Elway.

BART OATES (GIANTS CENTER): At the end of the game, if the quarterback's uniform is still as clean as when he just started the game, then we did a heck of a job. Phil had all day to throw the ball. He wasn't holding on to the ball long. He did a good job of just throwing the ball on rhythm. It was just one of those days. Since he wasn't getting touched, he should have been 100 percent.

KARL NELSON (GIANTS OFFENSIVE LINEMAN): As a matter of fact, every year when I watch the Super Bowl, I hope for a lot of incompletions in the first quarter so that I don't have to worry about anybody breaking Simms's record, because I think it's partly my record, too.

Looking Back

GEORGE MARTIN: I will always be proud of to be a member of that team that brought the first Super Bowl championship to the New York Football Giants.

LEONARD MARSHALL: Super Bowl XXI was one of the greatest thrills of my life as a twenty-five-year-old.

PHIL SIMMS: As Bill would always tell me, you know, Simms, when you're done playing, they're gonna appreciate you a lot more and that has really been true for my life, it's been great.

When I played, it was up and down and it was rough. I had to sit on that bench in Giants Stadium with those fans right behind me. I have lots of laughs with people [nowadays.] It used to be Phil, I loved you when you played. And then it turned into "Oh, Phil, my father loved you." And now I get this all the time, "My grandfather still talks about you," and I'm like, oh my God, to the grandfather group now so I have a good laugh over that. But there's never a week that goes by that I don't get comments about the Super Bowl.

GEORGE MARTIN: I think that on the face of it, people would say it's an honor and it was one that was immeasurable. And then when you realize that you're walking in the same footsteps of some of the immortal Giants of the past who just loom larger than life, it's surreal.

PHIL SIMMS: As time went on, being the MVP of the Super Bowl took on more importance in my life. It's an understatement, and I'm really happy it turned out well. But I think at the moment and probably for the rest of my career playing, it just didn't hit me that it meant as much as it does now.

Being the MVP and playing the way I did that Super Bowl, of course, has definitely changed my life and my family's as well.

I had TV offers, which I don't know if I would have gotten if it wasn't for the Super Bowl and the way I played.

KARL NELSON: I heard all of what the Giants' franchise and the Giants fans had been through. They were long suffering.

I was very happy for the fans that [we] were able to come through and win the Super Bowl. I was especially happy for the Mara family, as well, because they've been through quite a bit.

HARRY CARSON: Looking back, having gone through [the bad years], I had a much deeper appreciation for winning than the other guys on the team who never went through that stuff. It was very special for George Martin and me to weather the storm of bad football and see how the team evolved into a team that nobody wanted to play. I think Martin and I appreciated it more than everybody else on the team.

GEORGE MARTIN: I think it had such an impact because it ushered in a new era of winning. It bought us out of the dark ages of people always saying, "Yeah, the Giants were great back in the days of yore," but now we had modernized it. I'm so proud to be a part of the first Super Bowl championship team for the Giants, you know that your name is going to live on for forever because you've accomplished something that is so improbable because we used to be the doormat of the industry.

Revenge is Best Served Hot

PHIL McCONKEY: [Simms] was the greatest teammate of all time, but he was a joker - practical joker. He was always getting guys.

I told him, "My retribution is going to be greater, Simms!"

So, I waited for an ideal moment. We're in training camp. I think it was 1987 after the Super Bowl. We would throw our laundry into a mesh bag, and it would come back between practices.

I got to the locker early and I got his jockstrap and I put that icy-hot balm. I lined the interior of his jockstrap with the stuff. Then it dries so he puts it on, and he doesn't notice. It activates when he starts to sweat. So, I told Parcells and some of my teammates what I'd done. We get going in practice and he starts sweating and he's going up to take the snap and he's starting to wiggle and he's getting pretty hot down there.

Parcells knows what's going on and says, "Simms, what the hell's wrong with you? Why are you jumping around like that?"

Once it happened Simms yells out, "McConkey, you son of a bitch." He knew exactly who did it (laughing).

9

HEAVYWEIGHT CHAMPIONSHIP BOUT AT MSG: MUHAMMAD ALI vs. JOE FRAZIER

MARCH 8, 1971

THE FIGHT OF THE CENTURY

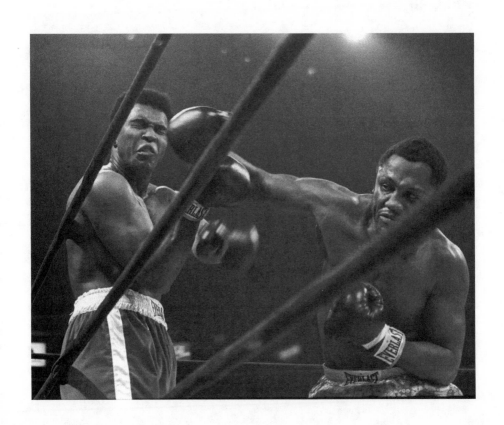

TIME CAPSULE

- Mayor of New York: John Lindsay
- Oscar, Best Picture: *Patton*
- Oscar, Best Actor: George C. Scott, *Patton*
- Oscar, Best Actress: Glenda Jackson, *Women in Love*
- Grammy, Album of the Year: Simon & Garfunkel, *Bridge over Troubled Water*
- Grammy, Record of the Year: Simon & Garfunkel, "Bridge over Troubled Water," *Bridge over Troubled Water*
- President of the US: Richard Nixon
- Price of Gas: $0.36/Gallon
- Heisman Trophy: Pat Sullivan, quarterback, Auburn

PREGAME

No Red Carpet Has Ever Been as Star Studded
The Fight of the Century
Smokin' Joe Frazier vs. The Greatest

Spectacular. Exhilarating. Intense. Unforgettable. New York has hosted just about every major sports event the world has to offer. The Miracle Mets beating the Orioles at Shea Stadium to win the World Series. The Knicks beating the Lakers in the seventh game of the NBA Finals at the Garden. The Rangers beating the Canucks in the seventh game of the Stanley Cup Finals—also at the Garden. The 1958 Colts-Giants overtime championship game ("The Greatest Game Ever Played") at Yankee Stadium. Secretariat's amazing run to finish off the Triple Crown in the Belmont Stakes. World Cup soccer games. Compelling finals at the US Open tennis tournament in Queens. Tiger Woods winning the US Open at Bethpage. The NCAA Sweet Sixteen.

Heck, even the Super Bowl (XLVIII) was held at MetLife Stadium, and even though only one team showed up in a lopsided championship game, the NFL wanted to give the New York area a shot at hosting the first cold-weather

Super Bowl. The weather gods cooperated with an unseasonably warm 49 degrees. Of course, there was a blizzard the next day.

All those games and events were vitally important to the passionate fan base of those teams and sports here in New York. But on an international stage, nothing before and nothing since before and nothing since Ali-Frazier matched the anticipation, social significance, electric atmosphere, and celebrity crowd generated at Madison Square Garden on March 8, 1971. It was a 45-minute death match, with Muhammad Ali and Joe Frazier beating the hell out of each other for 15 rounds. Frazier, the undefeated heavyweight champion, and Ali, the undefeated former champion who lost his title in the courtroom. Frazier finally knocked down Ali with a vicious left hook in the last round, but Ali's pride would not allow him to stay on the canvas. Even so, Frazier handed Ali the first defeat of his career with a unanimous decision to retain the undisputed heavyweight title.

It's one of the few instances where the performance exceeded the hype— and the hype was off the charts. Ringside tickets went for $150 and the blue seats at the top of the Garden went for $20. Imagine what the cost would be today. Second mortgages would be required to get into the building. You think big names populate celebrity row at Knicks games these days? For Ali-Frazier, realize that Frank Sinatra was unable to secure a ringside seat, he did find a way around that and got an up-close view by working as a photographer for *Life* magazine. Norman Mailer, Diana Ross, and Bob Dylan were all in attendance. Want more? How about Sammy Davis Jr., Hugh Hefner and Barbie Benton, Robert Redford, Miles Davis, Dustin Hoffman, Ted Kennedy, Hubert Humphrey, Diane Keaton, Woody Allen, and Dick Cavett. Burt Lancaster was doing commentary on the closed circuit broadcast with the legendary Don Dunphy providing the blow-by-blow. Adding to the buildup, the fight was not on live radio or home television in the United States. Instead, there was closed circuit television available in theaters and stadiums around the world, and 300 million people watched, in addition to a packed house of more than twenty thousand at MSG. In Pittsburgh, for example, tickets to watch the fight on closed circuit at Three Rivers Stadium had a top price of $15. These days, maybe, just maybe, that gets you one beer.

While Frazier was the defending champ, Ali, the former Cassius Clay and challenger, was the controversial main attraction.

Ali opposed the Vietnam War and refused induction into the military in 1967. His request to be excluded as a conscientious objector was denied.

He was arrested at his scheduled induction and found guilty at trial, fined $10,000, and sentenced to five years in prison. Although the case was overturned in 1971 before Ali would have been forced to serve any prison time, he lost his boxing license and was stripped of the heavyweight title. He lost more than three years of his prime athletic life.

"Why should they ask me to put on a uniform and go ten thousand miles from home and drop bombs and bullets on brown people in Vietnam, while so-called Negro people in Louisville are treated like dogs and denied simple human rights?" Ali said.

By 1970, one year before his case was overturned, Ali was granted a license to fight in Atlanta. He signed to fight journeyman Jerry Quarry on October 26, 1970. "The Greatest" was back. It had been 1,314 days since his last fight, when he defended his title with a seventh-round TKO over Zora Folley on March 22, 1967. Despite the layoff, Ali didn't have much of a problem with Quarry and the fight was stopped in the third round. It was a good tune-up. Six weeks later, Ali was back in the ring again—this time at Madison Square Garden—against Argentinian Oscar Bonavena. Bonavena agitated Ali before the fight by making chicken sounds to mock him for dodging the draft. He found a way, like few others, to annoy Ali.

Frazier had defeated Bonavena by decisions in 1966 and 1968, but could not knock him out. Ali surely wanted to shut Bonavena's mouth and put him away early, but it took 15 rounds to finally register a technical knockout. Ali put Bonavena on the canvas three times in the 15th round, but Oscar kept getting up. Ali was exhausted by the end of the fight, and it took a lot out of him. He was hit more in that fight than any of his previous battles.

But by winning, it set up the only fight people wanted to see.

Ali vs. Frazier.

They were friendly enough during Ali's exile that Frazier even loaned him money. But once the match was set, the promotion turned ugly. Ali is still, to this day, the single greatest trash talker in the history of sports. Not only were his words biting, but they often were funny and presented in a clever poem. Frazier was a real meat-and-potatoes guy who did not have the gift of gab. Ali crossed the line and insulted Frazier by calling him an "Uncle Tom," and a "gorilla," which led to Frazier's kids being picked on in school. Frazier was furious that Ali had made this personal, and was determined to whip him.

Ali countered with, "This may shock and amaze you, but I'm going to retire Joe Frazier."

If Ali was simply trying to sell tickets, he not only took it too far, but it also wasn't necessary. After all, the fight sold itself.

Ali billed himself as a pretty boy who was light on his feet in the ring. The Ali Shuffle, with the red tassels on his boxing shoes flopping to his every move, was mesmerizing. "Float like a butterfly, sting like a bee" was his motto.

Frazier's style, on the other hand, was strictly old school. He would bob and weave his way into an opponent's chest, unleashing frightening combinations. "You're not fighting Quarry. You're not fighting Oscar Bonavena. You're not fighting Sonny Liston," Frazier warned Ali. "You are fighting Joe Frazier."

Styles make fights. Could Ali dance his way away from Frazier? Could Frazier infiltrate Ali's comfort zone? Ali was 31–0. Frazier was 26–0. Something had to give.

In one of their pre-fight press conferences, Ali promised Frazier he would crawl across the ring if Frazier beat him. Frazier fired back and promised he, too, would crawl to his opponent if he lost. (Spoiler alert: Ali didn't have the energy to crawl to Frazier after losing a unanimous decision. The equally exhausted Frazier was out of gas, too.)

Ali was looking to regain all that was lost in more than three years away from the ring. Frazier was looking for respect. Frazier needed to beat Ali to achieve that once and for all time.

"I've achieved wealth and security for my family and there is only one thing more that I'd like to achieve," Frazier said in the days leading up to the fight. "That's to be the true champion. When I beat him Monday night, I'll be a true champion."

Monday night could not arrive soon enough for either of them. Ali was confident and brash before the fight, perhaps maybe a bit overly confident and overly brash. But that's how he motivated himself. "If Joe Frazier whups me, I'll take my hat off in front of the world and say he's the double greatest," he said. "If he whups me, he's a great, great fighter. But there ain't no way he will."

Later in life, Ali acknowledged that he regretted saying nasty things about Frazier and calling him names that he never should have called him. Frazier said he accepted the apology and that their battle had been going on far too long. If nothing else, they made each other an awful lot of money.

They would fight each other two more times after that incredible and unforgettable evening at Madison Square Garden. But with it, the trilogy sucked the life out of their boxing careers. All three were brutal fights, but there was only one Ali-Frazier I. If you close your eyes, you can hear longtime ring announcer Johnny Addie introduce two of the greatest fighters of all time to a delirious crowd at the Garden.

> For the main event of the evening, the battle of the champions, for the undisputed heavyweight championship in the world. From Louisville, Kentucky, weighing 212 pounds, recognized by boxing authorities as one of the greatest fighters to ever hold the heavyweight title, the former undefeated heavyweight champion, Muhammad Ali.
>
> And from Philadelphia, Pennsylvania, weighing 210 pounds, also undefeated in his brilliant career, with 26 consecutive victories, 23 by knockout, the heavyweight champion of the world, Joe Frazier.

The hype was over.

Ding. Ding.

It was time for The Fight of the Century.

FIGHT OF THE CENTURY? BELIEVE THE HYPE!

BY PETER BOTTE

In a sport in which promotion and publicity often aren't rooted in reality, the massive boxing spectacle that took place at Madison Square Garden on March 8, 1971, somehow managed to exceed expectations.

Widely regarded as the biggest match in boxing history in both athletic and political importance, and the first time two undefeated heavyweights squared off in the ring with the title on the line, the first of three fights between Muhammad Ali and Joe Frazier went the full 15 rounds, with Frazier retaining the belt in a unanimous decision.

"To have something called 'the Fight of the Century' and to have it live up to the billing is sort of unheard of," longtime boxing promoter Lou DiBella said. "It was as great in the ring as it was as a promotion."

It was one of the greatest heavyweight fights in history. It was the most star-studded crowd ever. It was a transcendent event outside the ring. . . . The fight in the ring was equally unforgettable."

The outspoken Ali, of course, had been stripped of the title in 1967 over his refusal to submit for the draft for the Vietnam War. Frazier, who ascended to the WBA and WBC crowns through elimination tournaments in Ali's absence with knockout victories over Buster Mathis and Jimmy Ellis, retained those titles before Ali won both the rematch in 1974—billed as Super Fight II (also at MSG)—and the classic "Thrilla in Manila" bout in the Philippines in 1975.

Beyond the social significance and the star-studded appeal in the crowd that night, the 1971 meeting turned out to be an absolute slugfest for the full 15 rounds. Frazier finally knocked down Ali in the final stanza before earning the unanimous decision from the judges to retain his title.

"The fight itself was back and forth. Simple: it was warfare. It was brutality. And yeah, it was tactical, but it was two men giving everything they had," DiBella said. "That's what made it so different. It was the two best heavyweights in the world, arguably the greatest heavyweight of all time, fighting.

"It was an epic athletic matchup. It captured the imagination of the entire country and the world. If you are looking at the most significant sports moments in New York, that's as significant as there ever has been in New York history."

POSTGAME

Who Was the *Real* Ali & Frazier?

LARRY HOLMES (FORMER BOXING HEAVYWEIGHT CHAMPION): Ali was quiet in private. I would go into his dressing room and stuff like that all the time. Ali was quiet but at the same time he wasn't quiet. As soon as he was around people he would let loose. That was the way that Ali was. He was a people person—he lit up in front of people.

LARRY HOLMES: Smokin' Joe Frazier was straight ahead. He would say if he was going to fight you, he would take you out, he would knock your brother out.

He would say, if his mama got in the ring with him, he'd knock her out. I didn't believe that (laughing). He was one of my heroes. He didn't let things get to him.

J RUSSELL PELTZ (HALL OF FAME BOXING PROMOTER/FRIEND OF JOE FRAZIER): Ali was the most famous person in the world. I don't think anybody would dispute that. In his time, he was the original trash talker with his poetry. Before every fight he would predict the round in which he would knock guys out. He was just a brand. He was a handsome, really a beautiful, man.

LARRY HOLMES: Joe Frazier was a tougher sparring partner because he was on top of you all the time. He didn't give you a break. He was relentless. So, he was really hard to spar with. Ali would dance and he would move around, laid on a rope and stuff like that. The same way he fought in Zaire Africa verse George Foreman. Ali did the same thing and let guys punch and lay on the ropes, but he was good at it.

J RUSSELL PELTZ: Ali was the first heavyweight with real speed. Most heavyweights before him were slow-moving shuffling guys who'd walk in and try and take your head off.

He was a conscientious objector to the war. The white establishment tried to destroy him with that, but to the young people, the kids, in the South and the colleges in the Northeast, Ali was their champion.

LOU DiBELLA (LEGENDARY BOXING PROMOTER): When you look at Ali's whole career, and the magnitude of it, you have to look at the man and the personality and the significance of the positions he took. At the time refusing to go to war in Vietnam was a very polarizing decision. Later, it's one that earned him a lot of respect. His changing of his name and adopting the Muslim faith, Islamic faith was another one. Look, he was better looking, better spoken, and more charismatic than almost any athlete regardless of color that ever preceded him. He rose to stardom at a time where blacks were still deprived the basic constitutional rights in this country, including the right to go to the same schools, and drink out of the same water fountains and go to the same restaurants as white people. So, I mean, for him to emerge as one of the most popular figures on the face of the earth as a Black man, as an athlete, who was the most outspoken, controversial, and edgy that there had ever been, is a testament to the magnitude of Muhammad Ali as a man, which was, in my mind, the greatest magnitude that I could ever ascribe to an athlete.

JOE HAND SR. (BOXING PROMOTER): I can tell you Joe was a good guy and everybody liked him. He was a giving guy.

LARRY HOLMES: Everybody loved Ali. Nobody had a bad thing to say about him. He was a good guy and that's what made him one of my favorites. He boxed and told jokes, said hi to people, and signed autographs. He made people happy.

Generous Joe

JOE HAND SR.: I remember being in New York with him right before the Ali fight.

I said, "Geez, look at the guy over there." There was a guy pushing a cart in the clothing district. I said, "That's Kid Gavilan, he was a champion boxer."

Joe didn't carry much money on him, so he asked me for $100 to give to him.

He ran over to Kid Gavilan and said, "Hey Champ, here."

He gave him the $100. That was the kind of person he was.

The Buildup

J RUSSELL PELTZ: In my opinion, it not only was the greatest sporting event of all time and may have been the greatest social event of all time.

LOU DiBELLA: It was the two best heavyweights in the world, arguably the greatest heavyweights of all time, fighting.

J RUSSELL PELTZ: In his time, Ali was probably the most famous man on earth. I don't think anybody in Sierra Leone or Zimbabwe cared about Willis Reed or Mickey Mantle, but everybody knew Ali.

It may have been the first time two undefeated heavyweight champions, although Ali was in exile, fought each other for the title.

LOU DiBELLA: Even though Joe Frazier was another proud Black man, Joe Frazier was the choice of a lot of white America in that fight. So, I think that's also one of the reasons why it captured so much attention and got so much fanfare. It was a significant fight in and outside the ring. A lot of factors—political and societal—played into that fight.

J RUSSELL PELTZ: Everybody who was anybody was at the fight, I mean, Frank Sinatra was there, as a photographer for *Life* magazine.

JOE HAND SR.: I had 1,200 tickets for the Ali- Frazier fight for the Frazier fans in Philadelphia. People came into the office to buy a ticket. They would ask if there was parking around Madison Square Garden.

I went to them and said I want to rent a train for the Frazier fight. I want it to go from 30th Street in Philadelphia to under Madison Square Garden.

Now people knew I had the tickets and the transportation, they bought all the tickets up right away. I told them that they must wear formal clothes. The wives had to wear dresses and the men tuxedos. If you didn't wear a tux, you couldn't go on the train. In those days to sit ringside you had to be in formal wear, or they wouldn't let you sit down.

I bought the tickets for 15 dollars apiece and sold them for 35 dollars each. It was a big payday for me. It became a big night for Joe Frazier, and I will say that train ride was a party car of all party cars!

The Fight of the Century

LARRY HOLMES: Muhammad Ali and Joe Frazier were two of the baddest guys to ever box. It was a great fight between Joe and Muhammad Ali.

J RUSSELL PELTZ: I never thought Ali had a chance to win because it was only the third fight of his comeback.

LOU DiBELLA: The fight was back and forth. Simply: it was warfare. It was brutality. And yeah, it was tactical, but it was two men giving everything they had. That's what made it so different.

LARRY HOLMES: Joe had no dog, no quit at all.

J RUSSELL PELTZ: Ali took tremendous shots from Frazier. He came back late in the fight after being hurt in the 11th round by Frazier.

J RUSSELL PELTZ: The knockdown was just perfect, and the fact that Ali got up showed guts and determination, and the fact that it was not stopped, only added to his legacy.

If the knockdown hadn't occurred in the 15th round, and Ali had won that round, there would have been some people who wrongly thought Ali won the fight.

Looking Back

LOU DiBELLA: It was one of the greatest heavyweight fights in history.

J RUSSELL PELTZ: Whether or not the Thrilla in Manila was a better fight, I don't know. Because going into that fight everybody figured Frazier was shot. So, it didn't have the same build up and did that didn't create the same magnitude that this fight had.

LOU DiBELLA: It captured the imagination of the entire country and the world. If you are looking at the most significant sports moments in New York, that's as significant as there ever has been in New York history.

LOU DiBELLA: I think Muhammad Ali had a great amount of affection for Joe Frazier. And I also think that they had that shared respect you have when you get in the ring with another man multiple times and go to war and almost kill each other.

I think Ali had a little bit of guilt about some of what went down in the promotion of the first fight. I think maybe he recognized that some of the comments were unfair. Yet I don't think Joe ever fully forgave Ali for questioning his blackness and his manhood.

#10

2000 WORLD SERIES: NEW YORK YANKEES vs. NEW YORK METS, GAME 5

OCTOBER 26, 2000

THE SUBWAY SERIES

TIME CAPSULE

- Mayor of New York: Rudy Giuliani
- Oscar, Best Picture: *American Beauty*
- Oscar, Best Actor: Kevin Spacey, *American Beauty*
- Oscar, Best Actress: Hilary Swank, *Boys Don't Cry*
- Grammy, Album of the Year: Santana, *Supernatural*
- Grammy, Record of the Year: Santana featuring Rob Thomas, "Smooth," *Supernatural*
- President of the US: Bill Clinton
- Price of Gas: $1.51
- Heisman Trophy: Chris Weinke, quarterback, Florida State

PREGAME

You Needed More than a Token
to Ride in this Subway Series

In October 2000, if you were standing in Grand Central Station, you could have taken the 7 train to Shea Stadium. Or you could have used your subway token to take the 4 train to Yankee Stadium. For the first time in forty-four years, there would be a Subway Series in New York. The teams were different, and the stadiums were different, but the excitement and energy in New York City was the same.

Frenetic.

Post–World War II, New York was a baseball town. It was the *Golden Age of Big Apple Baseball.* In a stretch of ten seasons (1947–56), there were seven Subway Series played between the New York Yankees and either the Brooklyn Dodgers or New York Giants. A New York team won nine of ten championships; the lone exception was the 1948 World Series, which won by the Cleveland Indians. The New York Yankees won six championships—including five in a row—from 1949 to 1953. They played in five World Series against Brooklyn.

In 1954, the Giants won their lone championship in that ten-year stretch. The Dodgers also won one World Series in that time frame, exacting revenge against the Yankees in 1955. So, all three Big Apple teams won at least one championship during that ten-year run.

The last Subway Series was played in 1956, and it offered one of the most memorable games in baseball history. That's when Don Larsen pitched a perfect game in Game 5 for the Yankees. It was the first-ever perfect game in the history of the World Series, and is still the only one. It was also the first perfect game in thirty-four years. This is the type of baseball that the Subway Series provided. Who will ever forget the image of Yogi Berra leaping into Larsen's arms to celebrate their perfection? The win helped the Bronx Bombers avenge their World Series loss the year before to the Dodgers, prevailing in seven games.

The Yankees had New York all to themselves when the Giants and Dodgers moved to California for the 1958 season. It was on May 28, 1957, when the National League owners voted unanimously to allow the moves. The Giants took up residence in San Francisco, while the Dodgers moved to Los Angeles. The golden age of New York baseball seemed to be over.

In 1962, the Mets replaced the Giants and Dodgers as New York's National League team, though it may not have been seen as major league baseball in those early years. Well, to say that the Mets were terrible would be an understatement. They lost 120 games and won only 40 in their expansion season. Then, in 1969, a "miracle" happened. Overnight, the Mets became not just a good team, but world champions.

It takes two to tango and two to play in a Subway Series. The Mets' dance partner, the Yankees, were also going through a period of bad baseball. By the time the Mets raised their championship flag at Shea Stadium, the Yankees had not won a World Series since 1962 or an American League pennant since 1964. They didn't make it back to the World Series until 1976, and were swept by Cincinnati's "Big Red Machine." But with the Bronx burning, they won back-to-back championships in 1977 and 1978. The Mets won the World Series in 1986, but the two teams didn't make the postseason together until 1999.

The Mets' last playoff appearance before 1999 was eleven years earlier, in 1988. After taking the wild-card series from the Arizona Diamondbacks, the Mets fell behind the heavily favored Braves, 3–0, in the 1999 NLCS. They showed heart by winning Games 4 and 5. The fifth game was a gut check that went 15 innings until Robin Ventura delivered the game-winning hit with his "Grand Slam Single." Shea Stadium erupted into a frenzied celebration. It saved the season for the Mets, for one game anyway. The Braves won Game 6 in 11 innings with a walk-off walk by Andruw Jones. Kenny Rogers's inability to throw strikes sent Atlanta to the World Series and the Mets home for the season.

The Yankees were back with a vengeance by the time the Mets were good again. The Bombers won the World Series in 1996 and again in 1998. That '98 team was a juggernaut, winning 114 games. Then, in 1999, the Yankees won 98 games and swept the Atlanta Braves in the World Series. By the time the 2000 season opened, the Bronx Bombers had won three of the last four World Series titles. Of course, the Yankees had legitimate World Series aspirations. But so too did the Mets.

The Yankees didn't match the 114-win total from 1998, or the 98 wins from 1999, but 87 were good enough to take the AL East by 2 1/2 games over the Red Sox. Across the Triboro Bridge in Queens, Bobby Valentine's Mets were on the rise, making the playoffs in back-to-back years for the first time in club history. Their lineup was filled with power hitters. Every starter hit double-digit home runs with the exception of shortstop Mike Bordick, a late-season acquisition. The Mets were led by Future Hall of Fame catcher Mike Piazza, who batted .324 with 38 HR and 113 RBIs. Infielder Edgardo Alfonzo also hit .324 with 25 HR and 94 RBIs. Third baseman Robin Ventura slugged 24 home runs of his own, while first baseman Todd Zeile chipped in with 22. The pitching staff had five starters who won between 11 and 16 games. Closer Armando Benitez saved 41 games.

The Mets finished with a 94–68 record, seven games better than the Yankees, but still one game behind the Braves in the competitive NL East. It was good enough to earn the wild-card spot and set up the potential of a Subway Series.

The core of the 2000 Yankees team was started by GM Gene "Stick" Michael, who found the "Core Four" (Derek Jeter, Andy Pettite, Jorge Posada, and Mariano Rivera). Then GM Bob Watson acquired Tino Martinez and relief pitcher Jeff Nelson. His successor, Brian Cashman, took over and constructed the rest of the powerhouse team. After the 1997 season, Watson resigned. He built the team that won the 1996 World Series and set the Yankees up for continued success. Watson was a trailblazer, becoming the first African American general manager to win a title. Some of Watson's most important acquisitions were getting Cecil Fielder from the Detroit Tigers, Graeme Lloyd from the Milwaukee Brewers, and third baseman Charlie Hayes from the Pittsburgh Pirates. All were key contributors to the 1996 champions, the franchise's first since 1978.

The Yankees couldn't win four out of five World Series titles without winning their first title. And the Yankees couldn't have won their first championship without Jim Leyritz. In Game 4 of the 1996 World Series, the Yankees were down to the Braves, two games to one. In the eighth inning, and with just five outs to go, they trailed Atlanta, 6–3. With a loss, the Yankees would have been in a three-games-to-one hole. Atlanta-Fulton County Stadium was up for grabs. Braves closer Mark Wohlers was on the mound with one out in the inning, the count was 2-2, when Jim Leyritz took an 86 MPH slider over the left-field wall for a three-run home run to tie the game at six apiece. The Yankees went on to win the game in 10 innings, 8–6. Jim Leyritz went on to hold a place in Yankees history, as they won the next two games to take the championship. That moment had similarities to another of the biggest home runs in Yankees history.

"It's very similar to the Bucky's historic home run in Fenway where Dent hit it with Mickey's River's bat." Said Jim Leyritz. "I'm in the dugout and I find out that I'm facing Mark Wohlers, he's throwing 100 miles an hour. And I only had two bats left for the next day against John Smoltz. I didn't want to use one of my bats and break it. Darryl Strawberry had a dozen new Mizuno bats sitting right next to the bat rack. And I looked at Straw and asked if I could barrow one of his bats. And he's like, yeah, go ahead. So, I took a brand new one out of the box. And as I went to the on-deck circle, Zim [bench coach Don Zimmer] said he throws 100, get it ready. When I hit the home run and got back to the dugout after getting a hug from everybody I reach over and I look at Straw and said, 'That was your bat.' I think that's a pretty funny story that a lot of people don't know about.

After taking over as Yankees GM, Cashman's first team in 1998 won a franchise-record 114 games, and are considered one of the best teams in the history of baseball. Cashman didn't rest on his laurels prior to the 1999 season: he traded for Roger Clemens. He had to give up David Wells, Homer Bush, and Graeme Lloyd to secure the Rocket. But, just like that, Cashman got his ace of the staff.

The 2000 Yankees were led by the Core Four: Derek Jeter, Andy Pettitte, Jorge Posada, and Mariano Rivera. The team would eventually win four World Series in five years. There were all in place on the Yankees roster by 1995.

"I got there in 1993. There was a lot of talk about some of the younger players that were going to become Yankees," said Paul O'Neill. "There was a foundation built before there by Gene Michael and Buck Showalter. Then when those guys came, that was a magical thing for our organization to be able to bring up homegrown players that came up from the minors and became the face of the Yankees through that championship run. Every one of those guys if you say their name, brings a smile to your face."

Jeter became the Yankees' all-time hit leader, reached the magical 3,000-hit plateau—with, what else, a home run—was the Yankees captain, and won a World Series MVP. His number 2 was retired on May 14, 2017, and he was voted into the Hall of Fame in 2020—his first year on the ballot.

Pettitte was one of the most clutch Yankees pitchers of all time, and retired holding the major-league record with 19 postseason victories. He is also second in wins for the franchise and second in strikeouts. His number 46 was retired on August 23, 2015.

Posada not only handled the staff, but he could also handle a bat. He had over 1,500 hits, 275 home runs, and exceeded 1,000 RBIs. His number 20 was retired on August 22, 2015.

Rivera retired as the career leader in saves in baseball history, with 652. The Yankees retired his number 42 on September 22, 2013. He was also the first player to be elected unanimously by the writers into the National Baseball Hall of Fame, when he was enshrined in 2019.

If you are going to have four players at the core of your team, that is a historically strong group.

By the end of the 2000 season, New York fans were praying to the baseball gods for a Subway Series. While the people were getting ready, the Mets and Yankees still had to win seven postseason games each to get there.

The Yankees took on the Western Division champion Oakland A's in the ALDS. The series started in the Bay Area. In Game 1, the A's beat the Rocket, 5–3. New York won Game 2 behind a strong outing from Pettitte and Rivera in Oakland, 4–0. Mariano got the save again in Game 3 in the Bronx, this time a 4–2 victory. Going into Game 4 at Yankee Stadium, the Bombers would advance to the ALCS with a win. But it wasn't meant to be that night, as the A's once again got to Clemens and won, 11–1. That set up a winner-take-all Game 5 in Oakland. Wanting to set the tone, New York put a six-spot on the board in the first inning. But Oakland wouldn't go away, cobbling together five runs in the second through fourth innings to close the gap to 7–5. But the A's couldn't get another run across the board, and a 7–5 final score meant that the Yankees were on their way to the ALCS.

With Oakland out of the way, they would now have to go through the wild-card Seattle Mariners. Similar to the start of the ALDS, New York lost the first game, getting shut out 2–0. However, similar to the previous series, the Yankees bounced back in Game 2, Behind a strong outing by Orlando "El Duque" Hernandez, they would take a 7–1 win to tie up the series. In Game 3, the Bombers bombed (if you will) the Mariners, 8–2, powered by back-to-back home runs by Bernie Williams and Tino Martinez. They then took a 3–1 lead in the series behind a shoutout by Clemens, winning 5–0. With the last game in Seattle, and hoping to ward off elimination at home, the Mariners responded with a five-run fifth, on their way to a 6–2 victory. Back in New York, the Yankees found themselves in a 4–0 hole heading into the bottom of the fourth. After scoring three runs that inning, they exploded for six runs in the seventh, including David Justice's three-run homer. Though the Mariners would add three runs in the eighth, it would not be enough as the Yankees took the 9–7 victory and punched their ticket to the World Series—their third straight. With his heroics, Justice would be named ALCS MVP.

For the Mets, they opened the NLDS in San Francisco. It was the first playoff game ever played at Pacific Bell Park, and the Giants sent their fans home happy after Game 1. After that, for the rest of the series, the Mets sent the Giants home . . . but not happy. In Game 2, despite Armando Benitez blowing a three-run lead in the ninth to send the game into extra innings, the Mets were able to prevail thanks to an RBI single by rookie outfielder Jay Payton. John Franco got the save by striking out Barry Bonds with the tying run on base.

Game 3 was eventful as well, also heading into extra innings—this time 13. In a game that would take more than five hours to complete, Benny Agbayani would be the hero with a walk-off home run, giving the Mets a 3–2 win and control of the series.

For Game 4, the Mets went to their fourth starter, Bobby Jones. He would go on to pitch one of the best games of his career, giving up just one hit and two walks on his way to a complete game shutout and a 4–0 victory—one that would send the Mets to the NLCS. Bob Murphy, the voice of Mets, said after the Mets secured the last out of the game and series,

A one hit shutout for Bobby Jones . . . the Mets have never had a better
ball game pitched in their thirty-nine-year history then this game pitched

by Bobby Jones. The Mets have never had a no-hitter and that is as close as you can get a one hit shutout, what a performance by Bobby Jones.

That was a big statement as there have been some pretty good arms in Queens, with Tom Seaver, Nolan Ryan, Jerry Koosman, and Doc Gooden.

Up next for New York were the St. Louis Cardinals. Sending Mike Hampton to the mound in Busch Stadium, the Mets would put six runs on the board—with three coming in the ninth—to win the first game of the series, 6–2. Hampton would go seven scoreless innings for the victory. In Game 2, Payton's ninth inning single was the game-winner for the Mets as they held on for a 6–5 win. Heading back to Queens, the Cards posted their first victory of the series in Game 3 with a dominant 8–2 finish. Game 4 would be the first of the series won by the home team, as the Mets put double digits on the board for a 10–6 win. The following night, Hampton went back to the mound and this time tossed a complete-game shutout as the Mets waltzed into the World Series with a 7–0 win.

New York had its coveted Subway Series.

New York Yankees vs. New York Mets.

Fans had their tokens ready.

Bragging rights were on the line.

The Yankees' domination of baseball was also on the line.

They had won two titles in a row and three of the last four. The Mets had a chance to end the Bombers' run. Daytime World Series games were a thing of the past. Network television dictated all World Series games needed to be played in primetime.

It wasn't just the fans; the players were also excited. "Yeah, it was an electric series," Clemens said. "I mean what a treat for New York fans, the Yankee fans, and the Mets fans. What a treat for the players as well, because we only had to go what 35 minutes across town to strap it on and get ready to play."

Game 1 of the 2000 Subway Series actually started on October 21, and ended after midnight on October 22. The Yankees won in 12 innings, 4–3, four hours and fifty-one minutes of nail-biting baseball.

The play of game came in the top of the sixth. With the game still scoreless, Todd Zeile came to the plate to face Andy Pettitte, with Timo Perez on first base. Zeile hit a long fly ball to left that *looked* like it was a home run, but the ball hit the top of the wall and bounced back onto the field. Perez may have been the fastest Met, but he didn't start running hard until he passed second base. Because of this, Derek Jeter was able to make an incredible, off-balance relay throw from behind third base to nail Perez at home. Zeile was able to offer some insight on the play.

I looked back on the Timo Pérez play a number of times. Mets fans bring it up a lot. I think quite honestly, I thought it was gone. Just like Timo thought it was gone. Just like a lot of people thought it was gone. I ran hard out of the box and was running into second, it didn't even cross my mind that he was not going to score. I mean, I thought that was a foregone conclusion. When I saw Justice pick up the ball and throw to Jeter I thought, *I better get on my horse and hustle into second, I don't want to get caught by them.* When Jeter threw it home, I remember I was turning and looking at home plate wondering, *Why are they throwing it home?* I was shocked like everybody else that the play was made, and he was out. I thought it was a foregone conclusion that he was scoring. I was running to first base figured he was running and scoring because he was the fastest guy on the on the field. I just saw a clip of it recently and I saw the look on my face when I rounded second, it was more shock, like, wait, how did that happen? Did he fall down? I couldn't compute it in that moment.

The Yankees won when ex-Met Jose Vizcaino singled in Tino Martinez off Turk Wendell. After a terrific start from ex-Yankee Al Leiter, Mets closer Armando Benitez blew a save opportunity in the ninth, as Chuck Knoblauch's sac fly scored Paul O'Neill to force extra innings. Would the Mets have won if Timo Perez ran hard as soon as Zeile hit the ball, no one can say for sure, but it sure could have made the difference.

As it turned out, it was the Yankees' thirteenth World Series victory in a row—a streak that began with Game 3 of the 1996 World Series.

Game 2 of the Subway Series will never be forgotten for, of all things, a broken bat foul ball. There was history for sure between Clemens and Piazza. During the season when they faced each other Clemens hit Piazza in the head with a pitch. So, the anticipation of his first World Series at-bat against Clemens had Yankee Stadium rocking. When the sawed-off bat went fair and landed near Clemens, he fielded it and curiously threw the bat into foul territory in Piazza's direction as he was running towards first base. The benches cleared but no punches were thrown.

More than two decades later, I asked Clemens about the incident with Piazza.

Well, everybody looks at the broken bat with Mike and they made the comment, "You threw the bat at him." I always respond, "No, I didn't. If I wanted to throw the bat at him, I could've hit him." I can tell you I had no idea he was running and when he shattered his bat and it ended up being in my lap, I fielded it like a ground ball. I took it and whistled it to the on-deck circle. I didn't think much of it at all. It was right back to business and trying to pitch a good game. Mike's a great hitter and there are a lot of great hitters on their team. That is the reason why they were in the World Series. Yeah. I mean, I think everybody knows that when you're out there, you got to be focused and locked in on what you're doing and especially in that series. There's so many emotions riding so high, and but it turned out well.

Clemens got Piazza to ground out on the next pitch to end the eventful first inning. Roger pitched eight scoreless innings allowing a mere two hits. In the bottom of the first, the Yankees got RBIs from Martinez and Posada to take a 2–0 lead. The Yankees looked like they were going to have an easy night, building a 6–0 lead heading into the ninth. Torre then took Clemens out and the Mets put five runs on the board. Rivera finally struck out Kurt Abbott to end the game, and the Yankees held on to win 6–5. The Yankees won their fourteenth consecutive World Series game and held a 2–0 series lead.

Game 3 shifted to Shea. There were no lengths the Boss wouldn't go to beat the crosstown rivals.

"I just remember, I think we were all on high alert because of Mr. Steinbrenner," Clemens said. "It was, you know, this was his deal and there's no way we can lose this series and not bring it home—a championship home for him—and let me give you some backstory. I remember going into the Mets [visiting] clubhouse. I've been in it before and it's run down, and it's been used up pretty good. One of the guys complained about the stools or something we're sitting on when Mr. Steinbrenner walked through the door and heard it. Within hours, he had recliners and couches and all kinds of things moved there. All of a sudden, it looked like the locker room was turned into your like living room at home. So, I remember that, and it was just a good hard-fought series."

The Game 3 starter for the Yankees was Orlando Hernandez. El Duque had never lost a postseason game. Robin Ventura put a perfect swing on the ball to lead off the second inning hitting a home run to put the Mets up 1–0. The game seesawed back and forth and entered the eighth tied at two. Yankees manager Joe Torre still had Hernandez in the game. But his 134th and last pitch was lined for an RBI double by Benny Agbayani to break the 2–2 tie. The Mets added another run and won, 4–2. The Yankees' Series lead was cut in half, 2–1. The loss also ended the Yankees World Series winning streak at fourteen games.

Could the Mets ride the momentum from the win the night before and tie the series up at two apiece? Could the Yankees bounce back after a tough Game 3 loss and take a commanding 3–1 lead?

The Mets were home in Game 4 and handed the ball to Bobby Jones. To try and stop the Mets momentum, Torre, taking his cue from the 1983 Tom Cruise movie *All the Right Moves*, replaced starting second baseman Jose Vizcaino with Luis Sojo. (Dating back to 1998 and during the 2000 season, starting second baseman Chuck Knoblauch had the "yips," developing a mental block when throwing to first base.) Torre also moved Derek Jeter to the top of the lineup.

The Mets' momentum lasted exactly one pitch, which Derek Jeter sent into the left-field stands for a 1–0 lead. Jeter was always clutch and extended his hitting streak in the World Series to 13 games. The Yankees never lost that early lead, building it to 3–0. But, not to be counted out, the Mets scored two runs in the bottom of the third. The plot thickened in the fifth inning when, with a 3–2 lead, Denny Neagle got Timo Perez and Edgardo Alfonzo to fly out to right. But with the power-hitting Piazza coming to bat and the Yankees nursing a one-run lead, Torre replaced Neagle with thirty-seven-year-old David Cone. It was Cone's first appearance in Shea since the Mets traded him to the Blue Jays in August 1992.

Cone was welcomed back by the crowd with a chorus of boos (no surprise there), and proceeded to get Piazza out on a popup to second to end the inning. Cone had only pitched one inning in the postseason, and that was eleven days before this appearance. Torre was managing with his gut, and it paid off. The Yankees didn't give up a run the rest of the way, and Jeff Nelson came in earn the win. Enter the Sandman to end the game, and Rivera got his fifth save of the postseason with two scoreless innings of work. The Yankees held on to win the game, 3–2, and were on the brink of their third straight World Series championship.

"It was special to get a win in the World Series. Joe Torre knew who was going to get his outs. It was [Mike] Stanton, [Ramiro] Mendoza, and me just trying to get to Rivera." Jeff Nelson said. "Everybody on the team knew their job. I can't speak for anyone else in the bullpen, but I hated just watching, I was always on the edge of my seat, because I didn't have any control. I wanted us to score right away, I wanted us get outs, I wanted the game to go fast. And it was like mentally exhausting just watching the game. I couldn't wait to get in there and pitch because at least it would settle me down. I would finally have a little bit of control over the game. I'm participating instead of watching. So, it's easier to go out and pitch and be a part of it and try to do my job and help my team win. I tried to throw up zeros and get outs. My whole time as a Yankee my job is to go out there in the sixth, seventh, or eighth inning and get outs and try to get the ball to the next guy. And I think that's what we did."

Yankee fans hoped to use two more subway tokens. One to ride the 7 train to Shea for Game 5, and then the next to ride the 6 train down to the Canyon of Heroes for the championship parade.

ALL ABOARD: THE SUBWAY SERIES RETURNS

BY PETER BOTTE

The at-bat most people recall from the 2000 World Series was Roger Clemens catching Mike Piazza's broken bat and hurtling it back in the direction of the Mets' catcher in the latest bizarre episode of their recurrent blood feud.

The Piazza plate appearance that always comes to my mind is the ball he smoked against Mariano Rivera, the legendary Yankees closer, which nestled into Bernie Williams' glove in center field for the final out of Game 5 to conclude the long-awaited first Subway Series in New York since 1956.

"It was a great moment for New York City, because the baseball world was all focused on us," Williams said. "Bragging rights were on the line, and it meant a lot to have the opportunity to play our crosstown rival for the championship. It was just a great moment for the game and for us, and I enjoyed every single moment of it."

Bobby Valentine's Mets made plenty of mistakes in losing that series, most notably a costly baserunning gaffe by Timo Perez in Game 1, and another amid the Piazza-Clemens kerfuffle in Game 2—at least according to Omar Minaya, the longtime general manager of the Mets who served as assistant GM that season.

"My take on Clemens throwing the bat at Piazza was I was just waiting for somebody, one of the lesser players, to go in and try to get into a fight with Clemens," Minaya said. "Then he would have been thrown out. I was watching the game and I was saying like one of our guys should just go at him because the moment you go out there, he's out of the game."

Derek Jeter eventually was named the series MVP as the Yankees copped their third consecutive title and their fourth in five seasons since Joe Torre took over as manager in 1996. The dynasty officially would end with losses in the 2001 World Series to the Arizona Diamondbacks and in 2003 to the Florida Marlins, and as of 2022, the Yanks only have added one more title in 2009 to their record list of 27 championships.

The 2000 Subway Series also held massive importance to Yankees owner George Steinbrenner, largely because of the crosstown opponents.

"We couldn't lose to our crosstown rivals under any circumstances," Williams added. "So, the stakes were really high in 2000, because that was the game of games and the series of series. I was so happy that we came out with the victory and championship."

POSTGAME

A Tale of One City But Two Very Different Teams

JEFF NELSON (YANKEES RELIEF PITCHER): We kind of backed into the playoffs that year.

We lost the last six games of the season; we got swept by Tampa and then we got swept by Baltimore. And I think the Red Sox wound up losing and that's why we won the division. We barely got past Oakland to start the playoff and they were saying, "The Yankees are old. It's our time to win."

The A's talked a little smack and we wound up beating them in five games.

Then, all of a sudden, the Mets did the same thing. The Mets started talking smack when we played them, they said, "we're gonna win this in five, the Yankees got lucky to even be here and we're the better team."

JEFF NELSON: The one thing was when you played for Joe Torre, we did our talking on the field. Nobody ever did their talking through the media.

TODD ZEILE (METS FIRST BASEMAN): Prior to the Subway Series during the regular season in 2000, when we were playing in Yankee Stadium for the in-season Subway Series, during a rain delay Robin [Ventura] dressed as Mike Piazza and did a whole tarp slide kind of routine on their tarp during the rain delay. Mike, Robin, Johnny Franco and myself we're kind of our own little group during those couple of years. We'd always try to find ways to kind of tease Mike because he was the big star.

Robin went in and put some pads under his jersey to make him look big and strong and strapped on a moustache and got Mike's helmet and put it on sideways and grabbed a bat and went to the plate and did his impersonation of Mike hitting a ball not knowing where it is. He then rounded the bases with a big slide into second base, big slide into third base and a slide into home on the wet tarp. The reason I bring it up is because it was significant from a team building standpoint. That was sort of a galvanizing moment.

I think from that point on our record was very good to the end of the season and into the playoffs and World Series.

The Buildup—A City Divided

ANTHONY McCARRON (*NY DAILY NEWS* BASEBALL COLUMNIST/SNY CONTRIBUTOR): To me, this one is unique because it's more than just "the first Subway Series since 1956": It's the first one ever between the Mets and the Yankees. While the nostalgia trip back to the days when NYC had three teams is nice—the Dodgers and Giants were long gone and the city's fandom had morphed over those forty-plus years. The Yankees were mid-dynasty when the teams met in the Fall Classic.

KEN DAVIDOFF (FORMER *NY POST* BASEBALL COLUMNIST/PIX11 BASEBALL HISTORIAN): The 2000 World Series capped a city—and area-wide baseball renaissance—reaffirming the city's identity as a baseball town—that began with the Yankees' title in 1996 and rose as Bobby Valentine lifted the Mets, with the advent of interleague play in 1997 giving us annual head-to-head series between the two compelling powers.

PAUL O'NEILL (YANKEES OUTFIELDER): Every newspaper, every TV station, every radio station was all over it, because it was all happening right there in New York. It was like going back to high school again, you're driving across town to face your rival. You add that it's the World Series, and it just made it that much more special.

JEFF NELSON: It was all over the news here. You would see that one house had Yankee fans and their next-door neighbor was full of Mets fans

OMAR MINAYA (FORMER METS GM): It was great to make it to the World Series, and it was not a normal World Series. It was a dream World Series.

MARTY APPEL (YANKEES HISTORIAN AND BESTSELLING AUTHOR): The World Series almost always has a "favorite" and an "underdog," but add to that the enormous pressure of George Steinbrenner knowing that a loss to the Mets would be unthinkable, as well as an embarrassment—meaning heads would roll!—and you have a sense of what a must-win it was in 2000.

OMAR MINAYA: Here you are in the World Series playing this game to own "the turf" of New York. If you grew up in New York, you understand turf.

JEFF NELSON: You go into restaurants and people would recognize you and say, "Okay, we got to beat the Mets." It was definitely an exciting time.

ROGER CLEMENS: You would leave Yankee Stadium, or Shea, and when you left the stadium to go out to dinner it was amazing, there were both Mets and Yankee fans asking for autographs.

GARY APPLE (SNY METS PRE AND POSTGAME HOST): It was unique. I remember being on the field in both ballparks and there was just something magical about it. I knew the guys on both teams, I knew how much it meant to not just the players, but how much it meant to the city.

JEFF NELSON: There was that pressure—we knew—anything that went wrong was always on the back page of the paper—we didn't want to be on the back page of the paper.

"The Boss" Effect

JEFF NELSON: Mr. Steinbrenner had three teams that you had to beat: Tampa, because he lived there; the Red Sox because of that rivalry; and the Subway Series because it was the Mets. It was of the utmost importance to win those games and win the World Series.

JEFF NELSON: The Boss went over to the clubhouse and once he saw that there were just some beat-up chairs in a locker room because Shea Stadium was old. So, he went over to Yankees Stadium, and he got every single person's chair, the couches, everything out of old Yankee Stadium out of our home locker room, and took it over to Shea Stadium and had all their stuff taken out and put our Yankee stuff in. He said I want these guys to feel as comfortable as possible.

PAUL O'NEILL: Mr. Steinbrenner redecorating the clubhouse at Shea Stadium was something that I won't ever forget from the Subway Series.

The Subway Series

Game 1: One of the Turning Points of the Subway Series came early. It was the sixth inning Timo Perez was on first base and thought Todd Zeile hit a home run. He didn't start running fast until he passed second base. He was thrown out at home by Derek Jeter. The Yankees needed 12 innings to win the game, 4–3. Could a Mets win have changed the outcome of the Subway Series?

TODD ZEILE: Sure, it was a turning point. There were no runs scored through six innings. That was going to be the first run not only of the game but of the World Series. It's a big momentum shift to see that turn from what a lot of people thought was a home run to not even being an RBI double.

Not to mention that had the run scored, I'd have been on second with Robin coming up. Who knows what would have happened? It was a huge shift from where we thought we were to the outcome of that game. And that was kind of a microcosm of the series, really.

JOHN STERLING: The Yankees were very fortunate to win the first game; the Mets really kind of kicked it away on a couple of different plays. Timo Perez didn't run on a ball that was hit off of the left-field wall. Derek Jeter caught the cut off throw. He was off balance and kind of in the air, and he threw the greatest strike home you'll ever see to get Perez. The Yankees were able to tie the game on the ninth inning sac fly by Knoblauch and obviously won the game on a little pop fly single by Jose Vizcaino.

ANTHONY McCARRON: The Timo Perez play—if he had scored, would the Mets have gone on to win Game 1 and the Series? The Derek Jeter home run to start Game 4 was huge because the Mets had, improbably, seized whatever momentum you can get in baseball by nearly coming back to win that zany Game 2 and then winning Game 3 at Shea.

KEN DAVIDOFF: While the Series went only five games, it was a terrific, ultra-competitive affair, with three of the games decided by one run and the other by two runs. The Yankees made fewer mistakes and benefited from some better luck.

GARY APPLE: The Mets felt like they had a real chance to win that series. I think they felt like that early in the series, but they let it get away and didn't recover. It was great for the city.

The Derek Jeter Effect

MICHAEL KAY (TV VOICE OF THE YANKEES): Jeter seemed as if he was designed in a lab to excel in pressure-packed moments. Joe Torre has told me that Jeter has a slow heartbeat. That makes sense when you consider he seems to slow things down when lesser players have the game speed up on them in big moments. That Subway Series was a can't-win proposition for the Yanks because if the Mets had won it, some would have invalidated the three previous titles the Yankees had won. Jeter said he would have had to move out of Manhattan if they lost. With all that pressure, all he did was win the MVP. That's Jeter.

SWEENY MURTI (YANKEES REPORTER): What he often said to me was that he treated every game the same, which meant that there were players who, in big moments, found themselves a little overwhelmed. Their performances showed that. Jeter never succumbed to that because of his mentality.

That is kind of an understatement on his part, because you can't really treat the high-pressure situations the same. It is different. It's bigger. There are more people watching and there are bigger stakes. His mindset was to welcome that. A mindset that not a lot of people have. He took that mentality and made it work for him by not being afraid to fail—that is another thing that he says quite often.

PAUL O'NEILL: His personality, his demeanor, his intensity, was all there before any of this stuff happened. Obviously when you think of the New York Yankees, Derek Jeter, number 2, is one of the guys that immediately comes to your mind. It was fun to see him come into the major leagues, become a Hall of Fame shortstop, and then watch the way that he became a leader of the Yankees.

SWEENY MURTI: Phil Hughes told me a story about losing Game 1 of the 2009 World Series.

There were a lot of young players that had never been to a World Series before. They were kind of down about losing Game 1.

Jeter was looking around the clubhouse, and he says, "So what? So what guys, it's one game, it's a seven-game series for a reason."

Phil said that "Okay, here's a guy who's been here that many times can is saying 'So what' after losing Game 1 of the World Series, then maybe it isn't as big a deal as we're thinking it is."

That just comes back to his mentality and his approach in pressure situations.

SWEENY MURTI: I still remember [former Yankees catcher and current broadcaster] John Flaherty telling me a story about one particular postseason game. Flaherty was sitting in the dugout, and Jeter took like a real awkward swing at a breaking ball just kind of fouled it off and he looked silly. He kind of stepped back in the box and chuckled and smiled. Like it was just some game in May. That's when it clicked for Flaherty.

He said he was nervous just sitting in the dugout for a playoff game. Here's the guy who can laugh at himself after taking a weird swing the batter's box, just like it's any other game. That's what Flaherty thought was the secret to Jeter success.

Wait, What, Did I Just See That?
Did Clemens Just Throw a Bat at Piazza?

ANTHONY McCARRON: Roger Clemens throwing the bat shard at Mike Piazza was one of the craziest things I've ever witnessed, not just on a baseball field, and a great bit of theater in the ongoing drama between the two. I still remember how Joe Torre's hands were shaking as he tried to defend Clemens in a post-game press conference. I think he knew he was defending the indefensible, but what else could the manager do?

JEFF NELSON: Clemens was a hyped guy when he pitched. He was always fired up would go into the trainer's room to get his red hot—a heat balm that that you can put on your arm. It gets in there and it loosens up the muscles. Clemens did the same thing, but he did it all over his body, and it gets into places that probably it shouldn't get into, so he gets fired up.

MARTY APPEL: As for Roger Clemens's "meltdown" against Mike Piazza, one must remember that Clemens had long been an enemy to Yankee fans. They came to accept him, albeit with some hesitation, when he donned the pin-stripes and proved to be formidable.

Now at age thirty-eight, seeing Clemens fire a bat at Piazza (claiming he thought it was a ball), made many fans remember why they didn't like him as an opponent. This was immature, unprofessional and certainly un-Yankee-like.

JEFF NELSON: Piazza didn't run until late because he didn't know where the ball went. Once he saw it going down the line, he didn't know it was foul, and he started running. Clemens grabbed the bat and threw it, but in my opinion, I don't think he knew that Piazza was running at that time. He just threw it in that direction. I don't think he threw it at him.

OMAR MINAYA: I just think Clemens was full of adrenaline at that moment. I think it's just as hard to put yourself in his shoes. With the player that he is, I don't actually think he was throwing it at Mike, he just threw it in the area. I think he just got caught in the emotion but didn't specifically throw it at him personally.

GARY APPLE: It was just strange. I always thought Clemens's explanation was bizarre. I have heard the explanation that he thought the bat was a baseball. I'm not buying it, it just never made sense to me.

DWIGHT "DOC" GOODEN (YANKEES PITCHER/FORMER METS PITCHER): I mean, when you are pitching a game with that type of magnitude, everybody's fired up, but I'm sure he wasn't throwing the bat at him. He is not that type of guy.

He's a fiery guy. He likes to go but I don't think he was doing that.

JEFF NELSON: That year Clemens showed everybody why he's Roger Clemens. He would intimidate the best hitter on the team, he would knock him down.

He did the same thing with Piazza. When he knocked him down, he owned the rest of the Mets team. They're thinking if he's going to knock down our best player, then I'm not digging in at the plate. He was great in that way. I learned a lot from how he intimidated hitters and how if you don't intimidate hitters, you're not going to stay in this league. But I just think that he just didn't know Piazza was there. It was kind of funny when you read his lips, and he says, "Oh, I thought it was the ball," which was obvious it wasn't.

I just don't think he would have intentionally thrown it at him.

New York, New York

BERNIE WILLIAMS (YANKEES OUTFIELDER): It was a great moment for New York City.

JOHN STERLING: The city was so terribly involved. It was all in New York like the old days like when I was a kid in the fifties and every game was really close.

Looking Back

PAUL O'NEILL: Obviously, every world championship means a lot, and they all have their separate stories. When I look back, I probably had more fun than any other time during the Subway Series.

JEFF NELSON: When you go and win four World Series, you experience a lot but my favorite was the 2000 World Series.

ANTHONY McCARRON: I think folks have forgotten how close it really was, even if the Yanks won in five games.

TODD ZEILE: I mean, we lost in five games, but they were one-run games the whole way. Seesaw battles that the Yankees just prevailed.

OMAR MINAYA: We put that team together. So, myself, as a as an evaluator of talent, I just kind of enjoyed the moment. I enjoyed the fans, enjoyed the energy. I was a little brokenhearted because we should have won that first game. We were up going into the ninth but didn't win it.

I was a proud New Yorker. I mean, it doesn't get better than that.

The Last Yankees Dynasty

JEFF NELSON: New York is a tough place to play and win. You had more media then anywhere, you had Mr. Steinbrenner, and you had the fans who at old Yankee Stadium expected 100 percent effort all the time. And we just we never got complacent. You know, we never felt, "Okay, hey, we win one, we're good." I think the expectations as a Yankee are greater than anywhere else.

BERNIE WILLIAMS: I think it just kind of sets us apart from other Yankee teams when you look at the championship tradition of the Yankees organization over the years. You can look back at the 1950s. You know when they had Joe DiMaggio. You can also look at the 1960s when they had Mickey Mantle. Every generation of Yankees teams had a great group of players that were part of winning teams for this organization. I'm just so proud to be a part of that tradition

JEFF NELSON: In 2016, we had our twenty-year anniversary for the '96 team, and we went out on the field. Everybody went to their position, you look around, and you're like, "Wow, we have a really good team." You look at those players and, and it's like, "No wonder we won."

Both the Mets Dreams and the Yankees Pipes Burst

OMAR MINAYA: I don't know if you knew about this but there was a pipe that burst in the Yankees clubhouse after Game 4 of the World Series. A game they won 3–2. It flooded the Yankees clubhouse (laughing). I don't think that ever got out. Of course, the Yankees blamed the Mets for breaking the pipe and flooding their entire clubhouse.

JEFF NELSON: Yeah, we had a pipe burst in our locker room. the Boss was in there and participated in cleaning this stuff up with all the workers. I mean he got his gloves on and he started cleaning everything up along with all the workers. He said, "You know what, I want my guys to feel as comfortable as possible so they can go out and be the best they can be." He also said, there's some kind of conspiracy going on here. We get over here, and all of a sudden, the pipe bursts (laughing).

PAUL O'NEILL: There was a big ruckus in the locker room and George Steinbrenner had a fire hat on, and was directing the firemen, on how to get things taken care of. That is certainly one of the stories that I remember from the Subway Series.

A Cautionary Tale from Charm City

JEFF NELSON: One night we were in Baltimore during the 2000 season, we flew in, we were a bus ride from the airport to a downtown hotel, and it was late. Our team bus broke down and we had to pull alongside the road, and we were only like 15-20 minutes outside the city. All of a sudden, the air conditioning stopped so we all got off the bus. Some of the Latin players would really dress up. Rubén Sierra was on our team, and he had this canary-yellow suit. Everybody told him, "Hey Ruben, to go stand behind the bus so you could be like a caution cone and make sure nobody hits us." Everybody was laughing.

11

2001 MLB REGULAR SEASON: NEW YORK METS vs. ATLANTA BRAVES

SEPTEMBER 21, 2001

PIAZZA'S 9/11 HOME RUN

TIME CAPSULE

- Mayor of New York: Rudy Giuliani
- Oscar, Best Picture: *Gladiator*
- Oscar, Best Actor: Russell Crowe, *Gladiator*
- Oscar, Best Actress: Julie Roberts, *Erin Brockovich*
- Grammy, Album of the Year: Steely Dan, *Two Against Nature*
- Grammy, Record of the Year: U2, "Beautiful Day," *All That You Can't Leave Behind*
- President of the US: George W. Bush
- Price of Gas: $1.46/Gallon
- Heisman Trophy: Eric Crouch, quarterback, Nebraska

PREGAME

Playing Away the Blues Even for
Just a Brief Moment in Time

It was the perfect end-of-summer morning in New York City. The bright blue sky was full of sunshine and promise. The greatest city in the world had a refreshing feel to it in the days after Labor Day. After a June, July, and August filled with beach parties and barbeques, New Yorkers left for work knowing the next lengthy break wouldn't come until Christmas. They hustled to catch trains or grew impatient with traffic crossing the rivers into Manhattan, or just moved swiftly with their heads down walking with a purpose toward their offices when getting there on time is the first victory of the day.

It was Tuesday, September 11, 2001.

Men and women kissed their spouses and kids goodbye, wishing each other a good day, perhaps planning what was on the menu when they reconvened for dinner. Kids put on their backpacks and jumped on the school bus unaware how their lives and the world was about to change.

The early water cooler sports talk in the matching 110-floor North and South Towers of the World Trade Center in lower Manhattan was all about commiserating about the New York Giants losing their Monday night season opener in Denver to the Broncos. The previous season ended with a one-sided Super Bowl loss to the Baltimore Ravens and the new season was already off to a rough start. As the team plane landed at Newark Airport after an overnight flight from Denver, it was parked next to United Flight 93 to San Francisco. It was not even worth noting, especially with their bodies still aching from the loss and nothing usual about seeing aircraft ready to head into the skies in the early morning hours.

The Giants players were only thinking about loading up on the team bus for the ride back to their cars parked at Giants Stadium, and then driving home to hit the sack. Some of the team officials, who had parked at the airport, exited through the terminal and walked right past the gate for Flight 93 with no earthly idea that the passengers waiting to board would soon be victims in the greatest tragedy to ever take place in America.

Meanwhile, the Jets were on their third coach in three years, the Yankees were destined for another trip to the World Series after beating the crosstown Mets in the 2000 Subway Series, and the Mets were struggling through a disappointing season and striving to simply reach .500. All those situations were as to be expected.

The plaza in front of the Twin Towers was in rush hour form. It was just another day in New York City.

Then it happened.

American Airlines Flight 11 left Boston's Logan Airport for Los Angeles. But terrorists stormed the cockpit and hijacked the flight, redirecting it toward New York City. At 8:46 a.m., the Boeing 767 crashed into the North Tower between the 93rd and 99th floors. It was traveling at 466 miles per hour and carrying 10,000 gallons of fuel. Initial reports speculated that it was a small aircraft that lost control and collided with the tower.

That was soon dispelled.

This was no accident: this was a terrorist attack.

Soon, the tower turned into a fireball.

United Flight 175 from Boston to Los Angeles crashed into the South Tower at 9:03 a.m. By then, it was clear the United States was under attack. This was not Pearl Harbor—it was much worse. The South Tower came crashing to the ground at 9:59 a.m., while the North Tower collapsed at 10:28 a.m.

American Airlines Flight 77 took off from Dulles in Virginia to Los Angeles, but was hijacked and hit the Pentagon in Washington at 9:37 a.m. The target of United 93, the plane parked at Newark right near the Giants charter flight, was later thought to be either the White House or the Capitol. By then, passengers on Flight 93 became aware of the three previous hijacked planes. When they realized their flight was hijacked as well, they stormed the cockpit and the hijackers sent the plane crashing into a field in Shanksville, Pennsylvania. Everyone on board died, but there's no telling how many lives were saved by them not letting the plane reach Washington.

The final death toll was 2,976, with more than twenty thousand people injured. One day after New York was resplendent as it approached the fall season, the air all the way from downtown to midtown reeked of smoke and gasoline. The sight of the collapsed towers will be forever etched in the minds of all Americans—especially New Yorkers. Missing person posters were taped to street signs around Manhattan. Hospital emergency rooms were flooded with people looking for loved ones. It was surreal . . . and heartbreaking.

How could the country ever recover? Would New York ever be the same?

Walking around the city in the days after 9/11 brought a sense of fear. Was it safe to ride the subways? Or go to work in a skyscraper? Ride the elevators to a high floor of an apartment building? It was impossible to walk the streets and not constantly look over your shoulder. It was unrealistic that New York could snap out of this state of depression any time soon. There were no distractions. The Mets, Yankees, Giants, and Jets had games postponed, as MLB and the NFL temporarily shut down all games. And, no matter what sport, the games always provided a few hours to put problems aside. This situation was unprecedented and at the time New Yorkers were all dealing with the fallout individually one minute, one hour, and one day at a time. It was overwhelming.

When the Giants returned to their practice field—which was carved out in the middle of the Giants Stadium parking lot—they looked south and to the east just a handful of miles away and could easily see the black smoke still hanging over lower Manhattan. There was a hole in the Manhattan skyline where the towers had stood. One of the eeriest sites was the park and ride at Giants Stadium, where many New Jersey commuters would leave their cars and takes buses into Manhattan. So many cars remained in the aftermath of 9/11, clearly belonging to people who left for work that morning and never made it back across the Hudson River.

The Giants and Jets each visited the site of the attacks as the search transitioned from looking for survivors to attempts recovering the remains of the deceased. Jets quarterback and Long Island native Vinny Testaverde lost one of his high school wide receivers. He found out just before kickoff when the Jets returned to play for their first post-9/11 game, on September 23 in Foxborough, against the Patriots. A poster was taped to a wall near his locker with the pictures of missing firefighters and police officers, and that's how he learned about his fallen teammate.

Eight days before the game in New England, Testaverde visited lower Manhattan.

"I was down at Ground Zero talking with the rescue workers, the firemen, the police officer, the steel workers," Testaverde said. "I think all of them pretty much wanted us to go back to playing football because it's hard just to think about what happened twenty-four hours a day. So they need something to take their mind off it for a while, especially now to start some of that healing process and getting back to our normal way of life."

The Mets were in Pittsburgh on the morning of 9/11. When the games were cancelled, they took a bus back to Shea Stadium. As they crossed the George Washington Bridge, the team looked to their right and saw the black smoke downtown. They had watched the events unfold on the televisions in hotel rooms in Pittsburgh, but it became even more real once they returned home.

In the ensuing days, the Mets worked out at Shea and then congregated in the parking lot, which had become a staging area to drop off donations for the workers at Ground Zero. Manager Bobby Valentine, a native of Stamford, Connecticut, practically lived in the parking lot helping out. He was proud that his players were by his side.

"A goose bump moment, the first time they all came out of the stadium together," Valentine told the *Daily News* nearly two decades later. "They spent hours away from their families, precious time when people were still wondering what might happen next."

Giants general manager Ernie Accorsi received a compelling voicemail from a longtime fan saying, "My love of the Giants saved my life." He explained that he went to the game in Denver and as a result did not make it back the next day for his job at Cantor Fitzgerald, which was located on the 104th floor of the North Tower. "My kids have a father today because of my love for the Giants," he said. Accorsi played the voicemail for the team. Cantor Fitzgerald was decimated by the attacks.

The NFL postponed its games for the weekend after 9/11. Testaverde of the Jets and Michael Strahan of the Giants were outspoken that their teams would not play even if commissioner Paul Tagliabue did not call off the games. The Jets were scheduled to play in Oakland and the Giants had a home game against Green Bay. It took two days for Tagliabue to announce the games were off.

"This is America," Testaverde said. "We mourn, we comfort and we come together. After a period of time, we get back to a normal way of life. It would be hard for us to fly out of LaGuardia and look at that smoke and rubble as we take off, knowing there's people buried in there and people dead in there."

Baseball didn't resume until September 17. Shea was being used as a police command center, so the games against the Pirates were moved from Shea to Pittsburgh, where they summoned the strength to win three in a row. The Yankees were back in action on September 18 in Chicago. That meant the first game in New York would be Friday, September 21, with the Mets hosting the Atlanta Braves.

It was the first high-profile sporting event held in New York after the attacks. It was in a small way an attempt to show that America would not be intimidated, and the first attempt in New York to return to normal, even if just for a few hours, in the wake of the tears and fears that were left from the terror attacks. But, of course, there was the concern that it might still be too soon to play a baseball game just ten miles from the attacks. Was it insensitive? Was it safe? Or did New York need this night?

"It's going to be a difficult night in some way and in some ways it's something we're looking forward to," Mike Piazza said leading up to the game. "We want to get back home and see our fans, but it's going to be tough from an emotional standpoint."

Piazza is from Norristown, Pennsylvania. He played for the Dodgers from 1992 until they traded him to the Marlins early in the 1998 season. The Marlins quickly traded him to the Mets and he endeared himself to Mets fans by signing a new contract at the end of the season and, two years later, leading them to their first World Series since 1986.

On September 18, one week after the attacks, the Mets met with New York city officials, the police, and Shea Stadium executives and decided the stadium could be secured and made safe for the fans. Mets players elected to donate their pay from one game, which came to $450,000, to benefit the New York Police and Fire Widows and Children's Benefit Fund, which was founded in 1985 by Rusty Staub, a former player for the Mets.

It was a night for many tears and cheers at Shea, which was nearly packed to capacity with 41,235 fans. Diana Ross sang a stirring rendition of "God Bless America" before the game. Chants of "USA! USA! USA!" nearly shook the place. Liza Minnelli belted out a heartfelt performance of "New York,

New York," with NYPD and FDNY officers (players defied MLB regulations and wore NYPD and FDNY caps) performing an impromptu kick line. During each of the songs, the Mets and Braves players and the fans were wrapped up in the incredible display of patriotism.

Entering the game with a record of 74–73, the Met were third in the NL East and on the outside looking in for a potential postseason berth. But at this moment, their game on September 21 was so much bigger than the playoffs, and baseball as a whole. "Our purpose is to try to show people we're giving our best in a scenario that is less than fortunate and there a lot of people in an unfortunate situation who may be able to gain some strength from us," Valentine said.

It was a quieter than usual crowd at Shea for most of the evening. The fans were happy to have a slight degree of normalcy back in their lives, but didn't quite know how to act. The Mets trailed 2–1 heading into the bottom of the eighth. After a groundout by Matt Lawton, Edgardo Alfonzo drew a walk to bring up Piazza, who had already doubled twice.

As part of the Mets one-game salary donation, Piazza contributed a team-high $68,000. What he was about to give the fans was worth so much more.

THE HOME RUN THAT HELPED START THE HEALING

BY PETER BOTTE

Mike Piazza never has been comfortable being depicted in heroic terms for hitting home runs, especially the euphoric one he blasted on September 21, 2001, at Shea Stadium.

In the first professional sporting event in New York in the aftermath of the 9/11 terrorist attacks, Piazza's go-ahead home run in the eighth inning lifted the Mets to a 3–2 victory over the rival Atlanta Braves and uplifted, even for a brief moment, a devastated city desperately in need of a reason to cheer again.

But heroic? No, insisted Piazza on that chilly and chilling night in Queens more than two decades later. Those labels, the Hall of Fame catcher often has said, were reserved for those who never made it out of the two World Trade Center towers ten days earlier and those sifting through the debris and carnage at the site in the ensuing days, weeks and months.

"Number one, I was just happy to come through in a big moment. The fact that a lot of people have made it a very significant moment in their lives is an honor for me. I just try to honor it as best I can," Piazza said. "I was just blessed to be in the right place at the right time and have teammates supporting me and fans supporting me.

"Honestly, it was just my faith in God that helped me get through a tough moment emotionally, as we all did that week. It really comes down to the love I felt from the team, the fans, and the city."

The Mets had been in Pittsburgh on September 11, and bused back to New York before providing assistance in whatever small way they could, primarily led by manager Bobby Valentine while the Shea parking lot was used as a staging area for Ground Zero relief efforts.

They donned hats honoring first responders when returning to the field on September 21, but the Mets trailed 2–1 in the eighth when Piazza came up to face Braves reliever Steve Karsay, a product of Christ the King High School in Queens, after Edgardo Alfonzo had drawn a one-out walk.

After taking a fastball down the middle, Piazza cranked another fastball an estimated 425 feet and over the wall to center, leading to a jubilant release from the home crowd and ultimately resulting in a 3–2 Mets victory that even Braves Hall of Famers and longtime Mets nemeses Chipper Jones and Greg Maddux conceded was a fitting result on this incredibly emotional night in Flushing.

"If you watch the crowd reaction shots to Mike Piazza's homer that night, you see people who seem surprised by their own reactions. Who weren't sure, in the wake of the horrors the New York area had experienced, if they'd ever be able to feel joy over a baseball game again," Ken Davidoff said. "The baseball drama of that night, set against the backdrop of the pain of the terrorist attacks, enabled folks to find solace in the ballgame while not forgetting what had transpired."

POSTGAME

Returning to New York

TODD ZEILE (METS FIRST BASEMAN): We were in Pittsburgh on 9/11, we got evacuated from the hotel because the hotel was connected to the federal building in Pittsburgh. As Flight 93 went off course, in an abundance of caution, they evacuated us. Obviously, we couldn't fly. We chartered a bus and made our way back to New York City.

On the way back, in the middle of the night, guys were talking about the day's events and how the world had changed. We got to the GW Bridge about two in the morning, there was very little traffic on the road, I think we had to be escorted over the bridge. We went very slowly over the bridge. Everybody gathered to the right side of the bus to look downtown, Where the towers stood, were floodlights shining in the air. There were silhouettes of smoke billowing from the buildings that had been destroyed. It was a powerful sight. There was also a smell of an electrical fire all the way up town as high as the GW Bridge. We just kind of paused for a minute and there was not a sound on the bus. The only sounds were from some of the guys that had direct ties to New York City and the fire department and feared that they had been directly impacted and lost loved ones, or friends. There was a lot of emotion there. We slowly completed our way over the bridge, and for the next thirty minutes it took for us to get to the parking lot of Shea, there was literally silence. Everybody was just deep in their own reflection of what had happened, what it looked like and then it just became real. What we were watching on TV didn't seem real, and in that minute, it became real.

To Play, or Not to Play? That is the Question

JIM DUQUETTE (FORMER METS GM): Here's what was going on behind the scenes before the Piazza game after 9/11. We almost didn't play that game. We had considerable pushback from certain players in the clubhouse that were concerned about the security at Shea. Understandably so. They were very concerned about playing the game. I was the assistant GM at the time and as a group, we had to talk it out.

It was in the players' hands, guys like John Franco and Al Leiter were a big part of it. Franco, in particular, knew what it would mean to New Yorkers— being a New Yorker himself. It wasn't until we got assurances from the NYPD that the security would be really tight that our players felt comfortable to play that game. We did play and obviously, because of all of that was going on in the aftermath of 9/11, we had the most iconic game in the history of the Mets organization. Well outside of Game 6 of the World Series '86. That's iconic for other reasons, obviously. But us playing the game in which that moment happened with Piazza was in question up until that day that we played it.

JAY PAYTON (METS OUTFIELDER): There was a lot of controversy about whether we should have played or whether we shouldn't have played. I think once you got to the stadium and just saw all the energy, love, all the fans—how it brought everybody together—it was the beginning to the healing. Then how it ended with Piazza hitting a home run and us winning that game, and it being able to get back to a feeling of normal. So, in hindsight, it ended up that the best thing we could have done was playing that game.

Play Ball

TODD ZEILE: I remember getting to the ballpark, the amount of security was different. Just the feeling there was different. I think there was still a question in the players' minds—was this the right time? We had waited but was this the right time, was anybody going to show up? Did anybody want to use baseball, to take a little break from the trauma?

OMAR MINAYA: I was at the game and was able to watch it with a friend of mine who was at the World Trade Center on 9/11. He just happened to be on the last elevator in the second building and it really affected him. He was still shaken by the whole event as was the whole city. Shea Stadium historically is known for planes going over it so that had an impact the night: we we're gonna play baseball, we were gonna get through this, and we're gonna move on.

TODD ZEILE: The things that I remember most about that day is I had a lot of pride in wearing the NYPS and FDNY hats. I had an instrumental role in getting those hats. In one of our visits to ground zero. I traded a Mets hat and got an NYPD hat in return. I then said that I would wear it and then some of the other guys liked the idea of wearing the hats in recognition of the first responders. We got hats brought to Pittsburgh and we wore them there. We were told by the league and the commissioner that it was a violation of the uniform policy, and we were not allowed to wear them, we were given a memo to cease and desist.

Because I was the player rep, I was the one quoted, but I was really just quoting the sentiment to the team, which was, essentially, we're going to wear them and if they think we are not going to wear them, they can try to come down here and take them off our heads. When we took the field that day, wearing the hats, I remember the families and the first responders just lining the field. That was one thing that was powerful.

ANTHONY McCARRON (*NY DAILY NEWS* BASEBALL COLUMNIST/SNY CONTRIBUTOR): It was a great way to think of something else for a few hours, a distraction from horror and grief. I think much of the city was just happy to have a ballgame to watch, a slice of normalcy in an unimaginable time.

TODD ZEILE: I remember hearing the bagpipes. Robin has jokes that he can never hear bagpipes again without breaking into tears because of that moment. And then yeah, I remember hearing Diana Ross, Mark Anthony during the anthem, and then the one that stuck out to me more than anything was Liza Minnelli. I remember her coming up the tunnel, she's such an iconic New Yorker. She brought the place to its feet singing "New York, New York," and that is when you saw a change in everybody at that moment when she sung "New York, New York." There was such a sense of pride for the forty thousand people that were there.

JAY PAYTON: I got my own special moment because after Liza sang, I got my big hug from her. I happened to be standing right there because I was first guy up that inning. She came over and gave me a big hug and my mom actually sent that picture off and got an autographed from Liza. She signed it and sent it back to me.

TODD ZEILE: It felt like it set the stage for the home run to come. It felt destined for something good to happen. And you know, it couldn't have been scripted any better.

Piazza's Home Run

TODD ZEILE: I almost feel like I wasn't surprised. It almost felt like it was what was supposed to happen. I wasn't jumping up and down. I don't think I felt surprised by it. I don't know how to describe it, except, yeah, this is what was supposed to happen.

JAY PAYTON: It was electric. It was almost as if you could just sense it. I think everybody felt we were going to find a way to win that game. And with Piazza up in that situation and all the big hits he's had in his career. You just kind of knew that he was going to make it special. And sure enough, he did.

EDGARDO ALFONZO (METS SECOND BASEMAN): His home run meant a lot; I mean it really meant a lot after what the city went through. I think it did something really nice for the fans and that's why he's one of their favorites here in New York.

KEN DAVIDOFF (FORMER *NY POST* BASEBALL COLUMNIST/PIX11 BASEBALL HISTORIAN): I don't like to overstate the importance of this night or the Yankees' subsequent postseason success that fall, because it didn't magically erase people's pain or fix their problems. But there's a reason that night remains so cherished. It offered hope that, even if we could never "go back to normal," we could still find joy in such simple matters as a ballgame.

GARY APPLE (SNY METS PRE AND POSTGAME HOST): It helped the healing process. I don't know anybody, in my circle, that didn't know somebody who was touched by 9/11 or lost someone in 9/11. It was just still so raw even ten days later. I think that was the first time since 9/11, that there was a moment where we all collectively felt a little better. To this day the awfulness is still so apparent, but that night gave us all a moment to feel good collectively as a city.

GARY APPLE: I have talked to Piazza and this guy is in the Hall of Fame. He's done a lot of great things. He's the greatest hitting catcher in history. Yet that specific moment is probably the one moment he is known for. So, when you think about the career that he had, that's the moment—a regular season game between the Mets and the Braves I think that sort of encapsulates the magnitude of that moment. And it wasn't just the city; it was the whole country got caught up in that particular moment.

The Healing Process Begins

BOBBY VALENTINE (METS MANAGER): It was a real scary time. No one knew how to react or what would come of it. But with Mike's home run, with the crowd being so emotional and with all the pregame and events during the game. I feel that it was a major moment in the healing process for many people, not only in New York, but around the world. It was it was a real spectacular event.

JAY PAYTON: It was great that we played. It was kind of like showing them that, "Hey, we are strong. We're not going to run and hide and stay sheltered because that happened." Despite the controversies of whether the game should have been played or not, it showed that it was the right decision. It gave everybody a minute to forget, and that's what they needed.

OMAR MINAYA: It was a moment that allowed everyone to exhale and almost get back to normal. We were still in mourning. We were all still in shock and afraid. But also, as New Yorkers you always feel like no matter what happens you got to bounce back. I think Piazza's home run said it was all right to cheer and start moving forward.

JAY PAYTON: Of course, you'll never forget what happened, but everyone needed a little reprieve from it.

#12

SUPER BOWL XXV: NEW YORK GIANTS vs. BUFFALO BILLS

JANUARY 27, 1991

WIDE RIGHT!

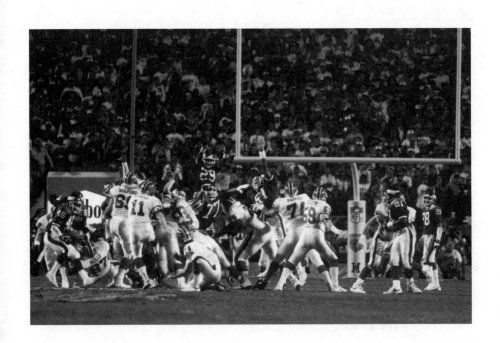

TIME CAPSULE

- Mayor of New York: David Dinkins
- Oscar, Best Picture: *Driving Miss Daisy*
- Oscar, Best Actor: Daniel Day-Lewis, *My Left Foot*
- Oscar, Best Actress: Jessica Tandy, *Driving Miss Daisy*
- Grammy, Best Album: Bonnie Raitt, *Nick of Time*
- Grammy, Best Record: Bette Midler, "Wind Beneath My Wings," *Beaches: The Motion Picture Soundtrack*
- President of the US: George H. W. Bush
- Price of Gas: $1.15/Gallon
- Heisman Trophy: Ty Detmer, quarterback, BYU

PREGAME

**The rocket's red glare, the bombs bursting in air,
Gave proof through the night that our flag was
still there.
Oh, say does that star-spangled banner yet wave,
O'er the land of the free and the home of the brave?
—Francis Scott Key, "The Star-Spangled Banner"**

Those words may have never held as much meaning—nor had hearing them meant so much to so many—as it did on January 27, 1991. Whitney Houston captivated the entire country with her rendition of the National Anthem prior to Super Bowl XXV, just days after the country entered the Persian Gulf War. As a backdrop to the performance, 73,813 fans in Tampa Stadium stood and waved tiny American flags as Whitney's voice washed over them, filling the stadium and country with national pride. For two minutes and one second, Houston's rendition helped unify the country and fill countless Americans with great patriotism. Still, more than thirty years later, it is known as the most poignant and inspiring performance of "The Star-Spangled Banner" ever sung before a sporting event.

Giants running back Ottis "O.J." Anderson remembers how he felt listening to Whitney's performance. "For me to be a part of history, since we had the Gulf War going on, meant a lot. The game wasn't supposed to be played but the President said it was good for the country," Anderson said. "So, I thought let's just do it. My connection to having the greatest performance of the national anthem ever by Whitney Houston, and we will forever be connected to it. So, I feel proud of that."

The anthem was one of the many highlights that exceeded expectations from the beginning to the end of Super Bowl XXV. The championship was still on the line when Bills kicker Scott Norwood lined up for a field goal with just eight seconds left in regulation. In between the anthem and the last-second field goal attempt was the heroics of a backup quarterback and previously thought-to-be washed-up running back. It was one of the most memorable Super Bowls of all-time.

Anderson resurrected his career by the time the Super Bowl rolled around and believed his destiny was to be a star on that field in Tampa. He was born in West Palm Beach, Florida, and was an outstanding player at the University of Miami, leaving as their all-time leading rusher. He was the eighth overall selection of the St. Louis Cardinals (where he spent eight seasons) in the 1979 draft—one spot after the Giants drafted Phil Simms. He topped the 1,000-yard mark in five of his first six seasons in St. Louis, and it took a players' strike in 1982 to hold O.J. under 1,000 yards. Going back to 1979, he topped 1,600 yards in 16 games, collected the Offensive Rookie of the Year Award, and was named to the Pro Bowl. After another Pro Bowl season in 1980, and four more successful seasons, injuries seemed to derail his career in 1985. His game seemed to be in decline when the Giants traded for him in 1986.

At the time of the trade, the Cardinals were 1–5 and the Giants were 5–1. When asked about his feelings at the time, O.J. said, "I felt I went from the outhouse to the penthouse. No other way to look at it."

The year he was traded, Anderson played eight games for the Giants and rushed for a total of 81 yards. But he was still a big powerful back and scored a touchdown for the Giants in Super Bowl XXI. Little did anyone know at the time that O.J. would become one of the keys to their second Super Bowl title.

"It was a parting gift from Parcells," O.J. said, when asked about his touchdown run in Super Bowl XXI. "Bill pulled me to the side and said, 'Hey kid, I'm gonna send you in. Hopefully you score. In case you never get here again, you can say you scored a touchdown in a Super Bowl. You know, at least you experienced what it's like to try and make a touchdown in the Super Bowl and be part of that elite group of backs who played and scored in the Super Bowl.'"

His first two years in New York, O.J. totaled just 214 rushing yards. Compare that to his rookie season, when he rushed for 193 yards in his very first game. In 1989—this third full year with the G-Men—he became the bell cow for coach Parcells, totaling a career high 14 rushing touchdowns (topping his previous three years combined by three). He also surpassed the 1,000-yard mark for the first time since 1984.

O.J. washed-up? No way.

Recognized as the Comeback Player of the Year, O.J. would look to put the finishing touches on his comeback with a second Super Bowl title. This time he would be counted on to shoulder the load for Big Blue. "I felt that I never left the game," said he said. "When Joe Morris got hurt, I was ready for it. I had practiced hard to do all the things I needed to do in order to reap the benefits of playing with called upon. I was able to execute, and it meant a lot to be recognized with the Comeback Player of the Year Award."

But before we get to how he took full advantage of his opportunity, we need to examine the rest of the Giants return to glory.

It took four long years—from their Super Bowl XXI win—for the Giants to make it back to the Super Bowl. The following season, the '87 Giants couldn't overcome the players' strike and finished a disappointing 6–9. It was the second time in six seasons the NFL players went on strike.

The players went out on strike on September 22, wiping out both the third week of the NFL season and the team's hopes for back-to-back titles. The players were looking to gain the right to free agency, better pension benefits, and the elimination of playing on artificial turf. The 1987 players' strike may have been credited with creating the modern era in the NFL. What it also did was extinguish the Giants chance at a second title in two years. New York was 0–2 before the strike, then its replacement players went 0–3, handing the baton back to the real team after the 24-day walkout at 0–5. The Giants never recovered and finished 6–9.

The following season, Lawrence Taylor was suspended for thirty days for violating the NFL's substance-abuse policy, missing the first four games of the season. The Giants split those four games and were a mediocre 3–3 after six games. They won seven of their next nine games and improved by four wins over the previous season, but their 10–6 record was not good enough to qualify for the playoffs. Their loss to the Jets, of all teams, in the final game of the season kept them out of the postseason.

Giants linebacker Gary Reasons shares the impact of losing LT for violating the NFL drug policy:

We knew we had a very good football team in 1988. We still had the nucleus of what was there from 1984. But when you take a big piece out of a football team, and what Lawrence Taylor was capable of doing, it hurt. Other teams had to game plan around how to deal with Lawrence Taylor. And when they didn't have to deal with that, it gives an offense a lot more flexibility on how they're going to call their games and play their style of football. So, Lawrence was sorely missed. Obviously if he's in the lineup we're going to have an opportunity to be a little bit better and we might've gone 4–0 in that stretch instead of 2–2. He definitely could have changed that and the shape of any football game with his presence.

The Giants started to return to form in 1989, rolling off four wins to start the season. After falling to the Eagles in Philly, they won another four in a row to get to 8–1. They won the NFC East and made the playoffs for the first time since their Super Bowl championship season.

Entering the playoffs, they hosted Jim Everett and the L.A. Rams in the divisional round. The Giants took a 6–0 first quarter lead, but Everett found Flipper Anderson with just 17 seconds to go in the half and the Rams got on the board and took a 7–6 lead at the half.

In the third quarter, O.J. Anderson punched it in from two yards out and the G-Men took the lead back, 13–7. But Mike Lansford tied the game with two fourth-quarter field goals, the last one with just over three minutes to go. That led to one of the most memorable playoff exits in Giants history.

Former Giant and legendary broadcaster Pat Summerall takes over from there:

Pat Summerall: First-and-15 for the Rams at the Giants 30, Everett going deep, touchdown to Willie Anderson and he doesn't even stop, he is heading for the locker room, the Rams win it . . . this place got very quiet very quickly.

John Madden: Flipper Anderson is from here, he is from New Jersey, I think he ran and caught that pass and is going to run home.

Flipper may not have run to his childhood home in Paulsboro, but he sure sent the Giants Stadium fans home in disbelief and feeling blue. Even so, the team was trending up and heading in the right direction going into the 1990 season.

And they did just that, starting a perfect 10–0. Though there were still six games left, the thought must have creeped into the mind of the players (as it did of the fans) that they may be able to match the record of the great '72 Miami Dolphins.

Thanksgiving weekend against the Eagles in Philadelphia saw the home team holding a one-point lead at halftime, 14–13. Unfortunately the second half was no contest, as the Eagles beat the stuffing out of the Giants by scoring 17 points and knocking New York from the ranks of the unbeaten with a dominant 31–13 victory. Hoping to avenge their loss, they then traveled to San Francisco to take on an old rival. The 49ers' perfect season had also ended the week before in a loss to the Rams. The Niners were the successful ones in getting their season back on track, shutting down the Giants offense and winning the game, 7–3. It had now been six straight quarters without a touchdown, and only three points total over that span. But it became the turning point for this championship team, as Giants defensive end Leonard Marshall explains. "Our team started 10–0 and lost to the Eagles. The next game we went out to San Francisco and lost 7–3. That's when you saw our team's transformation, where we took on a whole new identity. Guys became convinced we could play with anybody. We knew we were good, but we didn't think we could play with everybody. It was the losing of that game in San Francisco that changed the mindset of our football team."

The fans didn't know what Marshall knew at the time about the team's confidence. Their nerves were briefly quieted the following week with a victory over Minnesota, 23–15. That set up what was thought, at the time, to be a possible Super Bowl preview against the Buffalo Bills, also 11–2.

The date was December 15. Early in the game, Bills quarterback Jim Kelly went down with a knee injury (replaced by backup Frank Reich), and he would miss the rest of the regular season. But that was not all.

Phil Simms already had a Super Bowl win under his belt and was hoping to lead the Giants on the path to another title. But Simms, the Super Bowl

XXI MVP, was brought down by Leon Seals after a scramble late in the second quarter, and was slow getting back up, then limping off the field. A gamer, Simms was under center to begin the third quarter. On the fifth play of the quarter, after stepping back for a pass to Dave Meggett, Simms immediately dropped to the ground. He walked off the field and was later diagnosed with a broken foot. His season was over, and with that the hopes of a second Super Bowl title for the Giants seemed to be slipping away. The four-point loss, 17–13, was the least of the Giants worries.

The next man up was veteran backup quarterback Jeff Hostetler. Hoss was a third-round selection of the Giants in the 1984 draft who had played sparingly in his first seven seasons. He wanted to play, but there was no way he'd be replacing a healthy Simms. But his drive to play was more than just at quarterback, as he even volunteered to play special teams, which led to a blocked punt by Hoss in a 1986 game against the Eagles. By the 1990 season, he knew he was a good quarterback and showed it when he had his few opportunities, including leading the Giants to a win against the Phoenix Cardinals earlier that season. But as long as Simms was healthy, a good game here and there would not be enough for him to stay on the field. So, he decided that at the end of the season he was going to hang it up . . . but as with O.J., fate would not allow it. When Simms went down, the Giants were Hostetler's team. The chance to lead a championship caliber club to a title was his, and destiny would soon be his, as well.

"By that time, I had waited six and a half years for my chance." Hostetler said. "I had some opportunities, played really well against the Cardinals. With five minutes to go, came from nine down, and won that game.

"I felt really good about things but never saw the field for, I don't know how many games in a row. I remember going home and talking to my wife and I just had it.

"I said, 'After six and a half years, I can't do this anymore.' I told her at the end of the season, we were heading back to Morgantown. I was going to retire. I would figure something else to do. I just couldn't do it anymore. And six weeks later, I was standing on the podium, having just won the Super Bowl."

Gary Reasons shared his thoughts on Hostetler finally getting his chance to run the Giants.

I came in 1984 with Jeff Hostetler as part of our draft class. Jeff was a very athletic, gifted quarterback guy. He could run the ball, throw the ball. He's not going to run it at a ton of times, but he certainly had enough speed and could be very elusive. Jeff sat behind Phil Simms for seven seasons and didn't really take any meaningful snaps. And then in 1990, when Phil went down with an injury, I think all of us felt that Jeff Hostetler had the goods and he could play. He showed that from day one of the first game he played. We didn't really miss a beat. Sure, we were disappointed that Phil wasn't leading our team, but we had a lot of confidence in Jeff and he certainly stood tall. He took some beatings. There were some times when he was asked to stand in the pocket and throw the ball down the field and when that happens, the quarterback is going to take some hits and he did. He didn't point a finger, just got up dusted himself off, got back in the huddle and went to work again. And that showed that he's made of tough stuff that we didn't have the ability to see with him over the first seven seasons with the Giants, because he was just sitting there and only played cleanup duty. His toughness really came out in latter part of 1990 in that season. And I was very happy for Jeff and glad that he was on our team to finish out the season for us.

The Giants would not lose again with Hoss at the helm. His first start was against the Cardinals, whom he beat for the second time that season. They finished the year by beating New England by three and headed to playoffs with a 13–3 record.

Up next was the divisional round, facing off against the Chicago Bears. It was a dominant performance by all the key performers: O.J. rushed for 80 yards, Hostetler threw for two touchdowns, and defensive coordinator Bill Belichick's defense confused the Bears. The Giants breezed to an easy 31–3 victory, their first postseason win since the Super Bowl.

Now in the NFC Championship Game, the Giants would again face off with the defending champion 49ers, who had knocked them out of the playoffs the previous year. Looking for three straight NFC championships and a chance to become the first team to three-peat in the Super Bowl, the 49ers were at home and expected to win. All that stood in their way was Big Blue. It was the fifth time the Giants and Niners met in the playoffs in ten years, yet the first time without Bill Walsh, who had retired after the 1988 season and was replaced by defensive coordinator George Seifert. They split the first four, with each team winning on its home field.

The Giants hoped that their Week 12 loss on the gold coast wouldn't serve as foreshadowing for this game, even though the championship game was also held in Candlestick Park.

With the game even at 6–6 going into the half, it was anyone's game. The Niners struck first in the third quarter, when John Taylor caught a 61-yard touchdown pass from Joe Montana—one of the few explosive plays in the game—to give San Francisco a 13–6 lead. The Giants cut the lead to four with a field goal at the end of the quarter. That is when Leonard Marshall cut down Montana, sacking him and knocking him out of the game with just under 10 minutes to play. The momentum was short-lived, as the Giants got the ball back but could not move it to take the lead. On fourth down, they set up to punt. Knowing that his team needed to keep their momentum and not give the ball back, Bill Parcells gambled and ran a fake. Gary Reasons made the move pay off as he ran up the middle—catching the 49ers off guard—picking up the first down. That set up a field goal, cutting the lead to one with only 5:47 left.

Reasons gave his reasons for running the fake punt.

We have a fake punt in our playbook typically every week if the situation is right. Well, this situation called for it in the championship game. As I ran onto the field past Parcells, he said use it if it's there. So, that is something that I audible to out on the field. Of course, we are normally just going to punt the ball away, but I noticed that the 49ers were in the setup and the formation that we had expected and our game plan would certainly allow us to run that play. And it worked out great. Also, to our benefit they only had ten players on the field on that play. The individual who was missing was supposed to be lined up right where I was going to be running the fake. It was a real good opportunity for us to make a successful play and the end result was it put us in position to score and which was paramount to winning that game. It was a good opportunity for me to create a play and a very lasting memory for myself, my teammates, and the fans.

The Giants needed a defensive stop or a turnover, and with Steve Young now in at quarterback, the 49ers moved from their own 20 to the Giants' 40. The clock was rolling toward two minutes, and Parcells was going to have to start thinking about using his timeouts (he had all three remaining), as the 49ers were trying to play keep-away and run out the clock. But the game turned when LT was in the right place at the right time. Erik Howard forced a Roger Craig fumble that Taylor snatched out of the air, and the Giants had life and the ball at their own 43-yard line with 2:36 remaining. Hostetler drove them into field goal range, and Matt Bahr kicked the Giants into the Super Bowl with a 42-yard field goal with zeros on the clock for a 15–13 victory. They had won a conference title game without scoring a touchdown against one of the best and most dominant teams in the Super Bowl era.

"I have to echo Parcells, he always said, great players make great plays when the opportunity presents itself. Great players shine and they execute," Reasons said when asked about LT's fumble recovery. "And, you know, in certain situations, me, with the fake punt, the defense causing that fumble and Lawrence being in the position to recover it, we had the tenacity on defense to get the job done. Our mantra was that we were going to do anything and everything we could to win football games together. It was a relentless pursuit to the football; relentless pursuit is just how we play defensively. We just grew together as a team over the years and came to understand that big players need to make great plays in big moments and Lawrence certainly made them."

George Martin elaborated on what LT meant to the New York Giants over the years.

Well, if you're going to write about LT, you gonna need a few more volumes of books in order to capture what Lawrence, not only meant to the team, but to the whole community here in New York. Lawrence was an entity unto himself. He was a Superman in red, white, and blue. He was an impact player. He played with reckless abandon. He was leader without ever uttering a word. And Lawrence will be the first to tell you, he didn't go out there with that rah-rah stuff. He just went out there with the passion and commitment to win, and he played his heart out and he always did that. I always tell him that the greatest compliment I can give him is that I'll be able to tell my grandchildren that I played with the great Lawrence Taylor, and that is without any hype.

O.J. Anderson had predicted his destiny when he was a star back at The U. "When I came out of the University of Miami, I said, if I ever play in the Super Bowl, in the state of Florida, there would be no doubt, that as the featured running back, I'll win the MVP. That was 1979. Now twelve years later, I had an opportunity to play, but what really was more exciting in 1989, it was at the Hard Rock Stadium, which is where the Dolphins play, and the Super Bowl was there. I was the featured running back for the Giants. In the playoffs the following season, we got beat by Flipper Anderson in the last minute. So, I thought my dream, and prediction was over and then, finally, I had a chance to come to Tampa and I was able to fulfill it."

Americans were unified in their pride in their country; all were inspired by Whitney Houston, now all that stood in the way of O.J. and destiny was sixty minutes of football.

GIANTS HAVE THE (WIDE) RIGHT STUFF

BY PETER BOTTE

The Giants essentially executed their game plan to perfection, even if they still needed a 47-yard field goal attempt to sail wide right to earn their second NFL championship in five seasons in Super Bowl XXV.

Buffalo Bills placekicker Scott Norwood pushed his kick with four seconds remaining to preserve the Giants' 20–19 victory in Tampa on January 27, 1991.

With backup quarterback Jeff Hostetler running the offense following a late-season injury to Super Bowl XXI MVP Phil Simms, veteran running back Ottis Anderson ran for 102 yards and a touchdown and earned the MVP trophy as the Giants dominated the time of possession. They controlled the ball for a whopping 40 minutes and 33 seconds to keep the high-powered Bills offense—led by future Hall of Famers Jim Kelly, Thurman Thomas and Andre Reed—off the field.

"When I looked at the other Super Bowl MVPs, I felt I was in an elite group." Anderson said. "I know that everyone can't win an MVP award. You know, you could be a Hall of Famer and not be part of our MVP family. It's such a small family, I feel so honored be a part of it."

"There are only about 40 people who have ever won the Super Bowl MVP. It's so unique when you look at how many Super Bowls have been played and you have some two-time and three-time winners, which changed the number tremendously as far as honorees in a that special elite group."

Added linebacker Gary Reasons: "Ottis became a great teammate for us throughout his time in New York and was very instrumental in our championship season and what he meant to us. Everybody remembers that flipper that he threw to Mark Kelso in the Super Bowl, as he came around that left side and right around the corner, the big right-hand flipper, and that was right in front of our bench. That was an amazing thing to see. Because it excited all of us and it reminded us of what kind of a player he was."

The game was played with the backdrop of United States' involvement in the Gulf War and opened with Whitney Houston's goosebumps-inducing version of the national anthem.

Hostetler outgained Kelly in passing yardage (222–212), including a second-quarter scoring strike to wide receiver Stephen Baker, a.k.a., "The Touchdown Maker."

Defensively, Lawrence Taylor registered only one tackle and Leonard Marshall had the Giants' lone sack of Kelly, with Thomas accounting for 190 yards (135 rushing) from scrimmage for the Bills. But Buffalo would go on to lose four consecutive Super Bowls, beginning with Norwood's miss at the end of regulation.

"We were running around all over the place. The sheer unadulterated joy of everybody was amazing to me," linebacker and long snapper Steve DeOssie said of their reaction to Norwood's miss. "We were like a bunch of kids. That's the only thing I can compare it to. We looked like a bunch of kids that just won a little league championship. We were hugging and smiling and laughing and crying and looking for our families. The impression I got was a lot of guys were like, 'What the hell what just happened? What is going on?' It was joy with disbelief with the desire to share it with each other."

POSTGAME

The Team Makeup

LEONARD MARSHALLL (GIANTS DEFENSIVE END): This team was built of character. It was built with guys who were sound minded. They were tough. They were physical. They were men of character. They were very disciplined. It was an amazing group of guys.

JEFF HOSTETLER (GIANTS QUARTERBACK): You don't get into the NFL by just being complacent and standing on the sidelines. I just wanted the opportunity to contribute and play. I think I am the only Super Bowl–winning quarterback that ran the ball, caught a pass, and blocked a kick before I ever threw a pass.

When the opportunity came, I think guys were really happy for me, not the circumstance, but happy for me to get the opportunity. I felt they had a lot of confidence in what I could bring to the table.

People don't realize, we lost three out of four games when Phil went down, and two of those games were against two teams that we played in the playoffs. For me to come into that circumstance, when everybody had already jumped off the bandwagon, being a backup quarterback, people were saying I was going to be the weak link.

Then we won five in a row against teams that were the cream of the crop and against two teams that we lost to earlier.

BART OATES (GIANTS CENTER): Bill Parcells was always on edge. He always put pressure on you. He was a guy that wanted to know that you could handle pressure in practice. He'd be vocal, he would be calling you out. He held you accountable. He just coached us hard.

LEONARD MARSHALL: The '91 team just had swagger. It had a quiet confidence that the '86 team didn't have. The '86 team was overconfident. The '86 team knew we were the best thing since sliced bread. In training camp, we knew we were going to be the team to beat. We knew we were going to dominate NFC East. The '91 team didn't know that.

NFC Championship Game vs. San Francisco 49ers

LEONARD MARSHALL: I can remember Parcells walking in the locker room in the old Giant Stadium and talking to the guys. He said, "In the week of the preparation to play the 49ers in the championship game, we've got a few more days to get our stuff together. I don't know about you guys, but this is what I plan to do. I'm planning to pack for two weeks. Here's the deal we can either pack for one week, which means to go to San Francisco and lay an egg and we come back home. Or we can pack for two weeks, because there's not going to be a bye week and we go straight to Tampa Bay. So, what's it going to be, guys?"

He walked out of the room and left us to talk about it among ourselves. It became the chatter in the locker room. It became a motivating factor. And that's how the guys viewed it. Personally, I packed for two weeks.

LEONARD MARSHALL: The 1991 team had swagger. Because of that swagger, we played our asses off every opportunity we had. It showed in the championship game against San Francisco—probably the greatest fist fights I've ever been in. I thought It was actually a better game than the Super Bowl. Many of my teammates will tell you that, too. That it was one of the greatest fist fights that two teams could ever get into. It was physical, it was tough. It was a test of will. It was a test of character in men. It took relentlessness to win that game to be able to go on and play in the Super Bowl.

LEONARD MARSHALL: If you recall, to honor the troops, we wore armbands in the NFC Championship Game against the Niners. Our field goal kicker Matt Bahr was very intricate in our expressing gratitude for the military. Our military give us the opportunity to play a game like football and because we are free.

Bahr beat San Francisco with a last-second field goal and the one thing that was caught on video was him saying that this win was for the troops—for the United States military services. That allowed us a chance, a bunch of kids, to go out and play a kid's game, have a celebratory day, and to go on to play for the world championship.

JEFF HOSTETLER: After the game, Parcells normally got on the bus and that was it, the buses were leaving. If you weren't on it nobody was waiting around. I came out after the game after doing a bunch of interviews, and they wanted me to go down and speak with John Madden.

Parcells was down there at that point, and I said, "Listen, the only way I'm going down there for the interview is if you hold the bus. I know Bill, and he's not going to wait around for me. If I'm doing an interview, and I don't care who it is for."

They all laughed, and they said, "Oh no, it'll be fine. We'll make sure you get a bus, and everything will be good."

So I go down, I do the interview, and I tell Madden the same thing. I said, "Well, I'm really worried because if I don't get back up there, I know Bill's taking off."

Sure enough, I do the interview, I come back up, I think we had six buses, and all six buses were gone. There wasn't anything there.

I walk around and I'm thinking, "Okay, now what am I going to do?"

It's during the Gulf War and we're not going into the airport, they're going right down out onto the tarmac. There is no way for me to be able to get on that plane. And I just didn't know what to do.

Madden came up and he just started laughing. He said, "Well, you're right. He did it, didn't he? Hey, don't worry about it, I'll get you there."

I'm thinking, how in the world is that going to happen? Well, I didn't realize the influence that John Madden had. So, I jumped on his bus. We're talking about the game and different things. The next thing I know, we pull up to this back gate.

I'm thinking, *Where is this*?

Somebody comes out, the gate opens, we pull in, and we come in the back of the airport, or right out onto the tarmac, right at the front of the of the plane. Everybody's loaded (laughing). I thanked him. You know, he just laughed, and I go up the stairs, and right there in the front is Bill.

He just looks at me, kind of nods his head as if to say, "Well done."

We're off to Tampa (laughing).

How to Beat Buffalo

LEONARD MARSHALL: I recall when we got to Tampa, the first conversation we had amongst the players was how the hell are we were going to stop these guys who scored 91 points in two weeks against two different teams. I heard one of the guys talking and saying he saw the game plan that Bill Belichick was working on while flying from California to Tampa.

It deployed two defensive linemen and occasionally play five defensive backs and four linebackers. According to the plan, the only linebacker who wouldn't come out of the game was Lawrence Taylor. The two defensive linemen that weren't coming out of the game were Erik Howard and myself. We thought he was crazy.

The day we implemented the game plan, he said, "I'm going to use this scheme to invite them to run the football. I don't care if Thurman Thomas gets 180, 190, or 200 yards in the game. We are going to stop them from getting deep passes, and each and every time they come across the middle, we will make them pay a price for it. We should fare well."

BART OATES: We only had one week; we just beat the Niners as a double-digit underdog, playing the Buffalo Bills and their high-scoring offense as the Gulf War was going on. I mean, there was this calmness about us as a team that started with Parcells. I think because of the way Parcells approached the game ultimately, we were able to be calm throughout the game and played well.

O.J. ANDERSON (GIANTS RUNNING BACK): Well, you know what I like Parcells and the whole coaching staff, they came to me the night before the Super Bowl. And they asked me about plays that I felt comfortable running. And I said to him, coach [Parcells], keep it between the tackles. If you keep it between the tackles, I think I can do a lot of damage. Parcells said, just to keep them honest, we got to take it to the outside every once in a while. Only two plays went outside. One I lost maybe a yard or two, and other was down by the goal line and the next one I turned the corner on Mark Kelso. It was strategy because we knew how powerful Buffalo was. They had just beat the Raiders in the playoff game, 51 to whatever it was, to pretty much nothing (51–3). So we knew we had to try to somehow slow down Jim Kelly and their high-scoring offense.

STEVE DeOSSIE (GIANTS LINEBACKER): When we got to Tampa from San Fran one of the first things I did was buy a camera. I didn't happen to have one with me.

I started carrying it with me everywhere. I had it with me for the entire Super Bowl week and took it to all sorts of different events. On Saturday, I figured I'd bring it to the walkthrough and check out the stadium and get some interviews from the guys.

Playing in the Shadow of the Gulf War

HOWARD CROSS (GIANTS TIGHT END): We were in a hotel, and they're armed military guards walking around with M-16s checking people in and out of the hotel. They took the film out of my camera as I walked into the stadium because they wanted everything to be a certain way. It was just a little overwhelming to be in that scenario at that time in history. It was the first time in my life that the world was more like it is today.

LEONARD MARSHALL: At that time, football wasn't as significant as the Gulf War, that's when I decided: this is the new American game. America is going to engage in this game more than other games. It was a big deal to a bunch of my teammates.

HOWARD CROSS: It was extraordinary. Seeing gunships flying around, both teams wearing red, white, and blue, singing in the national anthem in unison.

BART OATES: I'd say that I was in a patriotic mood.

Whitney Houston Sets the Stage

HOWARD CROSS: It was one of those moments I will never forget. It was the first time in my lifetime that I had to live through our country in a conflict with another country. I don't think there was a dry eye on the sidelines, in the stands, or from people watching around the world.

LEONARD MARSHALL: To be standing and having a hometown girl like Whitney Houston, a girl who grew up in East Orange and Newark, performing the national anthem.

It was a big deal to America to have had a performer of that magnitude, a Black female, born in Newark, New Jersey, performing the national anthem in front of some 20-plus million viewers on television, and certainly over one hundred thousand people in that stadium. It was just an honor, and a blessing, man.

Wide Right!

BART OATES: Two series before we took it all the way down to the three-yard line and ended up settling for a field goal. We had a chance to actually go ahead on a sweep play where Ottis Anderson ran to the left side. I missed a block on Jeff Wright. O.J. was a little old and not as quick as he once was and was tracked down by Jeff Wright. We didn't execute on that on that play. A lot of that had to do with me I was thinking, man, if we scored a touchdown, Scott Norwood wouldn't be trying to field goal here. My mindset was if he kicks that field goal and we lose, they're gonna go back and start analyzing why we lost, and I am going to be the goat because we didn't score the touchdown. The play was called "Right 39," and it would have been one of the pivotal plays and the reason why we didn't win.

So here is how it would go, Tuesday it would have come out in the papers. Wednesday, I'd get cut, and we'd put our house on the market because I'd be playing somewhere else the following year. But all because of one field goal that goes wide to the right I was saved.

HOWARD CROSS: The scouting report said he [Scott Norwood] wasn't very dependable over 43 yards off grass. I think he was kicking it from 46 or 47 yards. So, watching the kick then when he missed it, we were like, Oh my God, they missed—those scouting reports were right (laughing). It was kind of a relief.

LEONARD MARSHALL: When that kick sailed off, wide to the right, I'll never forget, I turned to my father, who was in the stands. I don't know if he could hear me or not, but I said, "You're going to have one hell of a weekend."

O.J. ANDERSON: Finally, like Joe Namath, I made a prediction, and it did come true. So, watching that ball sail wide right I was thinking it happened. I fulfilled my prediction that I would win Most Valuable Player in a Super Bowl played in the state of Florida.

STEVE DeOSSIE: I actually thought to myself, *What if we win? It'd be kind of cool to capture it on camera.*

I just wrapped it in a towel and put it in my locker. At halftime, I don't know what came over me, but I just put it in a towel and tucked it away on the on the sideline under a bench. When we got ready for the Scott Norwood field goal attempt, I grabbed it and just started filming and didn't realize the gravity of it. I just had it there and my sort of sneaky plan came to fruition, and I was able to document a lot of good stuff on the field. The thing that stood out the most was standing next to Matt Bahr who told me that he's going to miss it. He knew that Norwood wasn't that good on grass from over 45 yards he was so calm, and I was losing it. Obviously, he was right. The whole thing was just a surreal experience. Then to watch it sail wide right, was just amazing. *Far right.*

I got a lot of good stuff in the locker room and some more great stuff later that night. So, it was it just kind of came together step by step where I didn't take it there on Saturday thinking that I would want it after the game. I just took it there Saturday to get Saturday stuff, and then like why not get even more?

At halftime, it was like, *Oh my god, I cannot get caught doing this. But I can't not do it.* So that's how I ended up having it on the field for the final attempt of Norwood's field goal.

BART OATES: I had a feeling of elation when he missed but sheer panic prior to the kick. We won one Super Bowl before four years earlier and the majority of the guys on the Super Bowl XXV team were guys that played in Super Bowl XXI. We were an experienced group. We also understood how monumentally difficult it is to get to a championship game. You know that if you lose the odds of actually making it back are so slim regardless of how good of a team you have. I'm sure the 1985 Chicago Bears that won the championship thought they were going to win a lot more and never even went back to Super Bowl, much less won another one.

STEVE DeOSSIE: I got to relive it three weeks later. I've never been around anything like it. It was just phenomenal. The best thing about it was the sharing of it. It was everyone—the coaching staff, the trainers, the owners, and the equipment guys. I've never seen anything like it before and have never seen anything like it since. And that to me was the best part of it, the hours of video I took for the whole week.

Super Bowl Champions!

HOWARD CROSS: It was phenomenal, Man. Guys play their entire careers and never get a chance to go to a Super Bowl much less win one.

LEONARD MARSHALL: [Bill Belichick] was right. I mean this cat was right. At the end of the day, Thurman had a big day on the ground, but they couldn't score points. They couldn't get to a red zone. They barely crossed the 20-yard line in the game. We felt that our plan worked and worked in our favor. At the end of the day, we were shocked, but we were more shocked that he had the courage to make the decision to deploy the scheme. We defeated probably their best team, that was probably the best chance Buffalo had to win the Super Bowl was in 1991 against us.

JEFF HOSTETLER: Obviously Ottis had a great game, and our offensive line did a great job. We had a great game plan, and we kept Buffalo completely off kilter.

We moved the pocket around, threw the football, ran the football—it was a simple game plan. I think, as a team, everybody focused and did their jobs. That's why we came out at the end with the W.

O.J. ANDERSON: Disney offered the opportunity for me and other players to change what we said [if we won the Super Bowl, and were named MVP, instead of the standard "I'm going to Disneyland!"]. I felt committed to dedicating the win to our troops.

I said, "I want to dedicate the win to our troops."

Because of the significance of what they were doing for us, and also the troops set aside one day and watched our game.

LEONARD MARSHALL: I was elated, elated, elated. You know enthusiastic about it. Happy for our coaching staff and our owner. Happy for the entire Giants family. All the people that put in the time, the energy, and the effort. From training camp throughout the season, everything that went into the culmination of the 1991 New York Giants, all that crossed my mind.

JEFF HOSTETLER: I'm proud of the job that we did and proud of the fact that I'm one of those very few that can say that they are a starting and winning quarterback in a Super Bowl.

LEONARD MARSHALL: Guys asked me if I had a lot of confidence in Hostetler. I said you better believe I did, he practiced against arguably the top, second, or third-best defenses in the league every week. How could he not be game ready?

O.J. ANDERSON: The first Super Bowl, I didn't have a whole lot to do with the win. When you look back at Super Bowl XXV where I was very much a part of it. It felt like I had a lot to do with everyone else's destiny and had control of it. It was such an honor to be able to perform at a high level at an event of such magnitude.

JEFF HOSTETLER: Being a Super Bowl winning quarterback is pretty special company to be in. I had to wait for six and a half years for the opportunity to play and then to take advantage of that, is pretty special. I think the circumstances around it are pretty special, too. We were a team that started off the season on fire. Then before I took over, we lost three of our last four games, and everybody jumped off the bandwagon. Two of the teams that we lost to, we ended up facing in the playoffs, and we ended up winning both of those games to win a Super Bowl. It's obviously great company to be in. I'm just proud to have had the opportunity to compete like we did.

HOWARD CROSS: It meant everything. When you are a kid growing up you dream of playing in the Super Bowl and making plays and being part of something that big. It was so different because it of where our country was as a whole. It just meant so much more to be a part of it.

LEONARD MARSHALL: After the game my father and I sat and ate, and we talked. As I promised, we ended up having a hell of a weekend! We ended up spending some real quality time together in Tampa, and some real quality time in Orlando, at Disney World, after the game was over. It was just a memory I'll never forget.

An Early Omen

O.J. ANDERSON: We are getting ready to play the Bears (in the first round of the playoffs) and normally we have our equipment attendants who load the pads in our pants and make sure everything is in order. That particular Sunday, I came in early; they hadn't put the pads in my pants so I decided I might as well do it myself, I was not paying attention to the color of the pants I just put the pads in the first pair of pants that I saw. Both my practice and game pants were in my locker. I grabbed my practice pants by mistake and put the pads in there. I went into the training room and had them tape my ankles and take my shoes, so that I had support. When I realized what happened, I knew I didn't have enough time to change. I would have missed the kickoff.

I figured I wasn't going to play so it wasn't important—nobody would notice. Then [Rodney Hampton] got hurt, and it changed my whole life.

What was unique was I practice every day in those practice pants like I did before I made that mistake. Every Friday they sent my pants out the cleaners to get clean for Sunday and, you're right, I kept wearing them on Sunday.

Bill Parcells said, "You better wear those freaking pants every day like you've been wearing and do not do anything different. I will pay your fine to the league for not being up to code and in the official uniform."

I was fined, he paid it, and we kept winning.

13

1978 AL EAST TIEBREAKER: NEW YORK YANKEES vs. BOSTON RED SOX

OCTOBER 2, 1978

BUCKY "BLEEPING" DENT

TIME CAPSULE

- Mayor of New York: Ed Koch
- Oscar, Best Picture: *Annie Hall*
- Oscar, Best Actor: Richard Dreyfuss, *The Goodbye Girl*
- Oscar, Best Actress: Diane Keaton, *Annie Hall*
- Grammy, Album of the Year: Bee Gees, *Saturday Night Fever: The Motion Picture Soundtrack*
- Grammy, Record of the Year: Billy Joel, "Just the Way You Are," *The Stranger*
- President of the US: Jimmy Carter
- Price of Gas: $0.63/Gallon
- Heisman Trophy: Billy Sims, running back, Oklahoma

PREGAME

Shakespeare once asked, "What's in a Name?" Well, William, if it's a brand-new middle name, the answer is a lot!

Three years in a row one team delivered three of the greatest sports moments in New York sports history.

October 14, 1976: Chris Chambliss sent the Bronx Bombers back to the World Series in dramatic walk-off fashion.

October 18, 1977: Reggie Jackson delivered three home runs on three swings of the bat and delivered a World Series championship to the Yankees.

October 2, 1978: Who would be the Yankees' hero?

If asked that question on Opening Day, fans would have gone through most of the Yankees roster before coming up with the right answer. They could have chosen Chambliss or Jackson, who were both still on the team. They could have selected Thurman Munson, Graig Nettles, Willie Randolph, Lou Piniella, Mickey Rivers—and that was just on the offensive side. How about the pitchers who included Ron Guidry, Catfish Hunter, Goose Gossage, and Sparky Lyle?

You get the idea. The light-hitting Bucky Dent would be way down the list. He hit a grand total of 40 home runs in his entire career, with a .247 batting average. But the answer was indeed Dent, who blasted his way into the pantheon of New York sports legends one Monday afternoon during the 1978 tiebreaker playoff game to decide the AL East between the Yankees and Red Sox at Fenway Park.

You can't ask for much higher stakes: one game against your archrival, where the winner advances and the loser goes home.

Dent grew up in Georgia and Florida, and was a good enough high school player to be selected as the sixth overall pick in the 1970 MLB draft. He was off to the Windy City to play shortstop for the White Sox at the tender age of twenty-one. By 1975, he was selected to play in his first All-Star game. He hit .264, but his fielding percentage led the American League. This was before Cal Ripken, built like a third baseman, changed the offensive expectations for shortstops. They were mainly relied upon to secure the defense up the middle, and Bucky did that as well as anyone. After four years in Chicago, Dent's life changed forever on April 5, 1977, when he was traded to the Yankees for Oscar Gamble and LaMarr Hoyt. He took over the hallowed ground at shortstop at Yankee Stadium from Fred "Chicken" Stanley and would bat in the nine hole.

So how did this light-hitting, bottom of the order batter—without his own bat no less—end up being the hero of one of the most dramatic games in this rivalry's history? Well, the fact that the Yankees even made it to the play-in game is a big part of the answer and why it was such a historic home run.

So, let's take a look at how the defending champion Yankees got to the one-game playoff in Fenway.

It took the Yankees fifteen long years to battle back to become the 1977 champions of baseball. When 1978 started—and Don Zimmer's Boston Red Sox stormed out of the gate and built a massive lead in the division—it served notice that repeating as champs was not going to be easy. Heck, by July, it looked as if it were not going to be possible.

Boston was on cruise control while the world champs were on life support, at one point training them by 14 games. The '78 Red Sox were being compared to some of the best teams in Boston history. Their lineup was stacked with future Hall of Famers Jim Rice, Carl Yastrzemski, and Carlton Fisk, as well as stars in Fred Lynn, George Scott, Rick Burleson, and Dwight Evans. There was no relief from top to bottom. Moreover, they played in a bandbox at Fenway Park with friendly dimensions, the Green Monster, and unfriendly fans if you were an opposing player.

Boston's record on July 19 was 62–28, while the Yanks were 48–42. The triangle between Billy Martin, Reggie Jackson, and George Steinbrenner was unsustainable. George protected Jackson—his star acquisition—while Billy tried to manage him. The year before, Fenway hosted one of the most talked-about skirmishes in memory. It aired live on NBC in front of a national TV audience, as well as locally on WPIX in New York. The whole country watched the Jackson vs. Martin feud as it boiled over in the Yankees dugout—in full view of the cameras. Martin was angry that Jackson didn't hustle in the outfield, which allowed Rice to turn a shallow fly ball into a double. That prompted Martin to pull him for Paul Blair. To say Jackson didn't appreciate the embarrassment of being taken out of the game in the middle of an inning was an understatement. The two had to be separated in the dugout with all-time Yankee greats Elston Howard and Yogi Berra having to physically restrain an irate Martin.

Here is how it sounded on WPIX-TV (as described by Phil Rizzuto and Bill White):

> Look at Billy, he is hot. Reggie has done that on several balls hit to right field. Look at Elston [Howard] getting between them, he wants to make sure there are no blows being struck down there. That may be the first time I have ever seen that happen in a dugout with a manager and player . . . and in full view of the crowd on the right side and certainly in full view of our cameras and we would presume the [NBC] *Game of the Week* cameras as well. Someone just put a towel on the NBC camera. One of the Yankees ballplayers they didn't want it shown but of course it was shown.

This eruption prompted Steinbrenner to threaten to fire Billy. [Backup catcher] Fran Healy, a Jackson confidant, played the part of Henry Kissinger and brokered a truce between the two, but bad blood was already flowing. The relationship between the three dominated the back pages of the New York tabloids, as the Yankees went on to win a championship in 1977 despite the constant internal battling. Of course, it was Reggie who hit three dramatic home runs on three swings in the decisive World Series game against the Dodgers. All three were stars in New York City. All three demanded the spotlight and respect. As big as New York is, it wasn't big enough to contain all three egos.

The '78 Red Sox were soaring, while injuries were holding back the champions from the Bronx. Rumors of Martin's firing were a constant in the papers. The Red Sox kept pulling away, and that is when the Jackson and Martin situation blew up. Billy put on the bunt sign for the first pitch, then took it off. But Reggie kept bunting in the 10th inning of a game against the Royals. When Reggie popped out, Martin went out of his mind and wanted to suspend him for the remainder of the season. They had finally reached a breaking point. Martin was convinced to reduce it to a five-game suspension. But upon Reggie's return, Martin heard rumors that Steinbrenner was trying to trade him to the White Sox.

At O'Hare International Airport in Chicago, Martin told reporters—in reference to Jackson's return from being suspended and Steinbrenner's illegal political contributions to impeached President Richard Nixon—"the two of them deserve each other. One's a born liar, the other's convicted." That was the final straw. The manager of the reigning world champions would quit the next day, on July 24, 1978. Martin cited health reasons for resigning, forcing The Boss to financially honor his contract. It was Billy's dream job, and his resignation announcement at Kansas City's Crown Center Hotel wasn't without tears from the fiery manager.

> I don't want to hurt this team's chances for the pennant with this undue publicity. The team has a shot at the pennant and I hope they win it. I owe it to my health and my mental well-being to resign. At this time, I'm also sorry about these things that were written about George Steinbrenner. He does not deserve them nor did I say them. I've had my differences with George, but we've been able to resolve them. I would like to thank the Yankee management . . . the press, the news media, my coaches, my players . . . and most of all, the fans.

Martin would remain a fan favorite in the Bronx, as he had won five World Series as a player with the Yankees in 1950, '51, '52, '53, and '56. He didn't play in 1950, but was on the roster and got his ring. Then, of course, he won the 1977 World Series as the pinstripes' manager. Who would they get to replace him?

On June 30, 1978, Bill Veeck had fired Bob Lemon as the White Sox manager. Lemon, the Hall of Fame pitcher, had turned Chicago around. In 1976, they finished in last place. In 1977, after Lemon took over as skipper, they finished with 90 wins and improved by 26 games. The Boss took notice and, on July 25, Lemon was hired to replace Martin.

Lemon had the pedigree to immediately command respect inside the Yankees clubhouse. He was a seven-time All-Star, a World Series champion, and a Hall of Famer. But the most important thing he brought to the clubhouse was his calm demeanor. Martin, remember, was the perfect person for the Yankees to replace the calm Bill Virdon late in the 1975 season. And the low-key Lemon was perfect to replace Martin, a startling contrast to the combative Billy.

Things looked bleak in the Bronx when Lemon took over. What's ironic is that, even with all the turmoil surrounding Yankees, they had managed to win six of seven, including a five-game winning streak. The low point was on July 19, when the Yankees were a staggering 14 games behind the Red Sox. Nobody knew it at the time, but things were pointing up in the Bronx.

There were not yet wild-card teams in the playoffs, so the Yankees could continue to play better, get their injured stars back, and still not catch Boston. It was a big hill to climb, for sure. Plus, with the way the Red Sox were playing, it would take one of the greatest comebacks in baseball history for them to even have a chance.

The Yankees were decimated by injuries to key players. They had lost Mickey Rivers, Willie Randolph, Dent, and starting pitchers Don Gullett, Catfish Hunter, and Ed Figueroa at some point during the season.

What helped them stay afloat was that "Louisiana Lightning," Ron Guidry, had stayed healthy throughout the summer. Guidry was the best pitcher in baseball, and was having one of the greatest seasons any pitcher has ever had. He finished the season with a 25–3 record, 1.74 ERA, 35 starts (16 complete games), nine shutouts, and 273 2/3 innings pitched, while giving up only 187 hits. He also struck out 248 batters, including one memorable game in which he set an AL record by a left-handed pitcher with 18 Ks. There are only 27 possible outs in any nine-inning game, and Guidry recorded 18 on strikeouts. In fact, outside of Nolan Ryan, no other AL pitcher had more than 183 that season. "Gator" also led the majors in ERA and wins.

In Guidry's last eight starts, he was 7–1. He pitched 57 2/3 pressure-packed innings after July 25, and gave up just 33 hits. He came in second to Jim Rice in the AL MVP voting that year. Rice did hit 46 home runs with 139 RBIs and a .315 batting average, but should Guidry have won the MVP? Maybe. But he did win the Cy Young.

When some of his teammates began to come back from injuries, the Yankees started to pick up steam. Hunter, for one, came back in July to go 6–0 in the month and 3–2 in August as the Yanks made their furious march toward first place.

The entire New England region was on edge. There was no way the hated Yankees could come back and do it to their beloved Sox again, could they?

The rivalry is one of the best in all of sports, not just baseball. It seems as if the two teams face each other almost yearly for the AL pennant. And this wasn't a new thing: just over a century ago, in 1919, the Red Sox sold the best player in the history of the game to their rivals. The Yankees got Babe Ruth and the Red Sox got a curse. New York became the winningest team in baseball history, while Boston suffered "the curse of the Bambino." The Sox didn't win a single World Series championship for eighty-six years. In 1978, Boston fielded one of the best teams they had ever assembled. It wouldn't happen again. It couldn't happen again. And certainly not to those Damn Yankees.

Going into the game on the night of September 6, 1978, the Yankees had cut the Red Sox lead to just four games, with seven of their next ten games against their hated rivals. The first was a four-game showdown in Fenway. A sweep would put the Yankees in a first-place tie for the division lead with the Red Sox and send a strong message. It would officially wipe out the entire 14-game lead Boston once owned. Losing the series would effectively end the season for New York. The pressure was immense. And as any fans of either team can tell you the series will forever be known as the "Boston Massacre."

The Yankees won the Thursday night game, 15–3. Then they won the Friday night game, 13–2. Then, on Saturday, Guidry pitched a two-hit shutout to win 7–0. And on Sunday, when they beat the Red Sox 7–4 behind a strong outing from Figueroa and Gossage, they had officially tied the Sox for first place in the AL East. The massacre consisted of 42 runs over the four games to complete the climb to the top of the division.

The Yankees then went to Detroit and took two of three, before returning home for a weekend series with Boston. On Friday night, Guidry threw another two-hit shutout and defeated the Sox, 4–0. On Saturday, Catfish pitched a complete-game victory, 3–2. The Yankees had now won six games in a row against the Sox in the month of September. Boston finally won on Sunday, 3–2, cutting the Yankee led to 2.5 games.

New York lost consecutive games in Cleveland on September 22 and 23. After the emotional two weekend series against the Red Sox, it was no wonder they had a letdown. But it was a short-lived two-game skid. When they woke up on the morning of September 23, they still had a one-game lead over Boston with eight games to go. The Yankees went 6–1 down the stretch. You would think that would have been good enough to win the division, but you would be wrong. It wasn't good enough, as Boston won its final eight games to catch New York and send the season into a one-game tiebreaker for the division and the right to advance to the ALCS.

In game 162, the final game of the regular season, the Yankee lost to the Tribe, 9–2, as Indians pitcher Rick Waits threw a complete game, giving up only five hits. He could have run for mayor in Boston that day and won in a landslide. The Fenway Park scoreboard flashed "Thank You, Rick Waits." Boston tied the Yankees on top the division and forced the one-game playoff.

The Red Sox were cursed, but thought it may have been lifted as they won a coin toss to host Game 163 at Fenway. The Yankees had won the season series with Boston, had just won four straight at Fenway, but the toss of the coin determined who had home field. So soon after the "Boston Massacre," the Yankees were not at all intimidated going back to Beantown.

What makes a moment special?

The stakes—so now it came down to nine innings of baseball for the pennant.

The match-up—maybe the best rivalry in all of sports, Red Sox vs. Yankees.

And a surprise protagonist.

In one of the most memorable games ever played in historic Fenway, the Red Sox and their fans attempted to erase the memory of the 14-game lead they held over the Yankees in July and the sixty years of not winning a World Series.

Then, in the seventh inning, up steps Bucky Dent with the Sox up 2–0. With Roy White on first and Chambliss on second, it was Bucky Dent—not Reggie Jackson or one of the team's other sluggers—at the plate. All seemed well in Red Sox Nation until Dent borrowed Mickey Rivers's bat and hit one of the most famous home runs in the Yankees' glorious history. The three-run blast gave the Yankees a 3–2 lead, and a Munson RBI double increased that to 4–2. Even so, the Sox still had three more innings to prevent Dent's blast from crushing the dreams of an entire city.

So, for the third year in a row, the Yankees were about to supply one of the greatest moments in New York sports history, and this one was provided by the least likely of the three. The hero of this moment was going to leave Fenway Park with a place in the history books—and this book for that matter—with a brand-new middle name that starts with an "F," ends with a "G," and you can figure out the rest.

BUCKY "BLEEPING" DENT GOES DEEP

BY PETER BOTTE

For the record, Bucky Dent's real first name is Russell, and his actual middle name is Earl.

Dent forever earned a far saltier middle name—let's call it "Bleeping," rather the actual word used by those in Boston—after the light-hitting short-stop's seventh-inning home run over the Green Monster vaulted the Yankees to a 5–4 victory in a one-game tiebreaker playoff to win the American League East on October 2, 1978, en route to their second consecutive World Series title.

"I have always said sports is a game of moments. Big moments," Dent said. "I remember as a kid Bill Mazeroski breaking my heart when he hit his home run and beat the Yankees in the 1960 World Series. You always dream of those kinds of things.

"I remember being in the backyard pretending to be Mickey Mantle. He was my hero. I was playing stickball and saying, "The bases are loaded, two outs in the ninth inning," and I'm up. You always kind of dream of those things as a kid, I always wanted to grow up and be a Yankee and play in the World Series. I was lucky to do that the year before and we won. Now we're in one of the biggest games ever.

"I never realized how big the home run was going to be until it was kind of all over with. I was home one day right after we won the World Series and one of my dearest friends called me and told me, 'That home run is going to change your life.'" The Yankees trailed the Red Sox by 14 games on July 19, before closing the season under new manager Bob Lemon—who'd taken over after Billy Martin was fired—with a 52–21 mark over the final 73 games to tie Boston with 99–63 records.

Game 163 pitted former Yanks righty Mike Torrez against 1978 AL Cy Young winner Ron Guidry, who'd improve to 25–3 that day with 6 1/3 innings of two-run ball.

Still, the Yanks trailed 2–0 before singles by Chris Chambliss and Roy White set the stage for Dent, who'd hit four home runs in 412 previous plate appearances that season. After fouling a ball off his ankle, Dent exchanged his cracked bat for one he borrowed from Mickey Rivers. He promptly lifted Torrez's 1-1 fastball into the screen above the Green Monster for a three-run homer and a 3–2 lead, en route to a 5–4 win to advance to the ALCS against the Kansas City Royals.

"I knew I hit the ball pretty good, but I didn't know if it was gonna get out. I didn't know if it was gonna be high enough," said Dent, who went on to be named World Series MVP in the Yankees' title defense against the Dodgers. "I do remember rounding the bases and coming around third, how quiet Fenway Park was. It went dead silent."

And he'd forever be known as Bucky "Bleeping" Dent.

POSTGAME

The Addition of Bucky Dent

MARTY APPEL (YANKEES HISTORIAN AND BESTSELLING AUTHOR): When Bucky first arrived on the scene, one would estimate that 15 to 20 percent of fans at the game were female. A lot of the increase—today it might be more like 45 to 50 percent—was due to his sex appeal and the poster of him with the bat behind his back. Teams did go on to market their product better to women fans, but a lot of that started with Russell Earl Dent.

SPARKLY LYLE (YANKEES PITCHER): I got to tell you when we got Bucky Dent, I think the whole team was very happy.

The First 162 Games

BUCKY DENT (YANKEES SHORTSTOP): We started out slow because we had some injuries. Meanwhile the Red Sox were playing .750 baseball.

As the season started to go on, we started to get healthy. Gator was spectacular that year. We knew every fifth day we were going to win because he was on the mound. Then what happened is we started to get healthy, just as that started to happen the Red Sox got a little nicked up. That's when we started to pick up a game here and pick up the game there.

We then kind of said to ourselves, if we get to September, and we're close, we play the Red Sox seven times, we got a chance to beat them.

BUCKY DENT: The other big factor was that the press went on strike and then Billy stepped down as the manager. I think with the press not writing negative things, and Billy stepping down and Bob Lemon coming in, it kind of relaxed everybody.

I remember Bob coming in and saying, "Hey, you guys were world champions last year, just relax and play the game and go out and win this thing."

It's almost like you could feel the air lighten. Everybody kind of like relaxed and nothing negative was being written so you could concentrate on playing the game of baseball.

MICKEY RIVERS (YANKEES OUTFIELDER): We had fought that whole season from behind with Boston. We played great the entire year and caught them. We finally went ahead of them but then they won their last eight games and tied it up with us. They just kept fighting, fighting, fighting and forced the one game playoff.

RON GUIDRY (YANKEES PITCHER): It was a special year for all of us. Because, you know, a lot of people forget that we were 14 games behind Boston at one time, they conceded everything to Boston, and we took it away.

BUCKY DENT: We got close in September, we got to within seven. We then we went up there first part of September and we killed the Sox four straight and then we went back to New York and beat them two of three games.

It came all the way down to the last game. You gotta give the Red Sox credit. They won the last eight games. We won six in a row then wound up losing on the last day. I'll never forget that and after the game we were walking up the tunnel and they told us that we lost the coin flip and we had to go to Boston the next day and play in Fenway.

Game 163

KEN DAVIDOFF (FORMER *NY POST* BASEBALL COLUMNIST/PIX11 BASEBALL HISTORIAN): Ron Guidry started Game 163 on three days' rest, his third straight start on short rest after not doing so at all for the first 32 starts of what proved to be his Cy Young Award–winning season. With the tension sky-high at Fenway Park, Guidry yearned to lay low before he took the mound. So, he positioned himself underneath the trainer's table in the visitors' clubhouse and instructed Gene Monahan, the Yankees' head trainer, to keep his whereabouts unknown.

That code of silence extended to bombastic Yankees owner George Steinbrenner, who wanted to check in with his ace before the huge game. Monahan told The Boss that he thought he saw Guidry in right field, getting his thoughts together. So, Steinbrenner headed that way, and Guidry slept soundly, his focus not disrupted by his employer. The misdirection paid off brilliantly and historically.

BUCKY DENT: Gator came in early, and everybody has their own little routine to get ready to play.

Gator told Gene Monahan, "I'm gonna go under the table and take a nap," and pulled the thing down so he couldn't be seen. He said, "Don't let anybody bother me, I'm just gonna go ahead and take a nap."

I don't think anybody really knew he was under there.

He went under there and he wanted to kind of hide from George Steinbrenner. Plus, he was coming back on short days' rest, so he was just going under there to relax.

RON GUIDRY: I'd need a lot more time to tell you that story because it's too long, but I was taking a nap underneath the trainer's table before the playoff game. And the trainer woke me up thirty minutes before the game.

BUCKY DENT: That game was the most pressure-packed game I ever played in in my life. I think every player that played in that game would tell you the exact same thing. You could feel the electricity in the crowd even before the game. As the game went on, you could tell that game was something different.

Our team was always loose and the night before we went out had some beers as a group. When we came to the ballpark, they were loose and joking around, but you could feel that little more seriousness about the way they went about their business. As the game went on you could feel the pressure start to build.

RON GUIDRY: When you play 162 games and then you wind up tied, and you got to play another one, that's a big game. You can play all of the regular season games. It's not like a playoff game. It's really different.

The Bat Has a Home Run in It!

BUCKY DENT: I came up in the seventh but what had happened is that before the game, I was struggling a little bit, and Mickey Rivers was standing during batting practice, I said, "Hey, homie, let me try your bat."

So, Rivers said, "Yeah, go ahead."

I took some swings with it and in my second round of batting practice I hit a ball at the end of it and it kind of got a little hairline crack right under the tape.

I didn't think anything of it.

MICKEY RIVERS: Bucky is my homie. He asked me before I got to the game to use my bat. You know, I'm on the on-deck circle with my bat sitting down on my knees. And I thought about it after he fouled one off his foot and said, "Oh homie, you got the wrong bat." I then told him to use my bat and that "it had a home run in it."

BUCKY DENT: Mickey's hilarious. He was always saying funny things.

He told me when I was going back up to the plate, he said, "You know, this one has a home run in it."

I said, I was worried more about my leg and playing three more innings. So, I just grabbed the bat and went up there and he was right, you know, it did have a home run in it.

Over the Green Monster into History!

SPARKLY LYLE: I think Bucky was averaging three or four home runs a year at that point in time. I don't know if you know this or not, but his leg was purple. From like, his ankle, halfway up his calf, from hitting balls off his leg all the time. You know, they didn't have those protectors or anything like that. When Torrez went in there and hit that ball off his leg, we all went oh my God, he's not coming back because he was in such pain. What Bucky said was, "I know he's coming back in there again; I am taking him into the net." And you know what, he did just that!

BUCKY DENT: When I came up in the seventh inning, Mike Torrez tried to run some fast balls in to me earlier in the game, and I popped up a couple of them; I just missed them. When I came up, he threw me a sinker down and in and I fouled it off my ankle.

I went, "Oh, my God." I didn't wear my shin guard that day, I wore my guard all year because I had a blood clot that I had cut out. I said, it's just one game. I'm not going to wear it. You know it was hurting. I was trying to walk it off, you know, because we didn't have any more infielders—we only had 24 guys that day—because Willie Randolph was hurt. I'm walking around and they are spraying it.

In the meantime, I found out by talking to Torrez years later, he told me that he didn't think it was gonna take me that long to get back in the box. That's why he just stood on the mound didn't throw any warm-up pitches. Well, it took a little bit longer than he expected.

Mickey came up to me and said, "Hey, Homie, that's the wrong bat. It's cracked."

I really wasn't paying attention. So, as I started to walk towards home plate the bat boy came up and said, "Hey, you know, Mickey said use this bat, that one is cracked," so I just grabbed it, put it in my hands walked up to the batter's box and I kind of had a feeling Mike might try and throw a fastball back in on me. So, I was looking for something kind of in and he threw a fastball down and I hit it pretty good. I was really running hard to get the second in case the ball hit off the wall. I wanted to make sure I was on second base. I didn't realize it was gone until I rounded first base, and I saw the umpire signaled that it was a home run. I looked and I saw Yastrzemski who was buckled at the wall. I was just like, wow, we're ahead, okay, we're up 3–2. And then as I started towards home, I could hear a sprinkling of the Yankee fans cheering and then I touched home and started towards the dugout, and all the guys came out. I could see Mr. Steinbrenner, and everyone, was standing and all excited.

MICKEY RIVERS: I thought it was a great thing that it was Bucky who hit the big home run. Remember he fouled a ball off of his foot a couple of times, and that kept the pitcher, Mike Torrez. out there awhile. That hurt Torrez by forcing him to stay on the mound that long. He didn't even try to loosen up. Bucky took eight minutes to ten minutes to put stuff on his feet and stuff like that.

CHRIS CHAMBLISS (YANKEES FIRST BASEMAN): What a thrill and I had a perfect view because I was at second base. Both Roy White and I were on base. I had a perfect vantage point form second base. I watched that pitch go right in. And Roy and I met Bucky at home plate. That was such a thrill. Those are just great memories, and those years are special to all of us. Bucky came through for us that day.

MICKEY RIVERS: It just so happened that he did hit a home run. It was just a lucky thing. I just wanted to see him get a hit. I just got lucky that there was a home run in the bat, and it was a historic home run.

BUCKY DENT: After the home run, Mickey jokingly said, "I told you it had one in it."

RON GUIDRY: We were losing 2–0 when Bucky hit the three-run homer and it changes the whole completion of the game. You go on to win 5–4, you'd beat Kansas City in the playoff, you beat the Dodgers in the World Series.

BUCKY DENT: My buddy Mike and I tried to get the ball out of the net over the Green Monster. There were so many balls up in the net from batting practice. So, when they got them all down, we didn't know which one it was.

The Last Out!

BUCKY DENT: Nettles and Gossage always talk about the last out of that game in Boston and I do too.

Nettles always talks about how it came down to Goose and Yastrzemski for the final out. Gossage always talks about the fact that he had a vision the night before that it was going to come down to him and Yastrzemski.

So, when it did come down to that, I'm standing shortstop, and I'm thinking, "Okay, Goose, this is it, it's you against him."

Nettles is over at third base and he's saying, "Pop him up, pop him up."

Goose then does just that, he popped the ball up to Graig. Nettles goes, "Not to me" because he didn't like to catch popups. I didn't go over to catch that popup because when it was hit all of a sudden, I feel something go down my arm. I looked up and I saw Nettles catch it; I looked down I thought a bug was in my shirt. But my [St. Christopher] medal I wore around my neck had broken. I'm trying to pull my medal out of my shirt, I didn't find it. I started looking down on the ground to find it while everybody's jumping up in the air, celebrating, over on the mound. So, I said, "What the heck," and I'll go and celebrate and come back later to look for it. I went inside and everybody's jumping up and down. In the meantime, I go back on the field and look for my medal and I couldn't find it.

I go back in, I take my shirt off and everybody's yelling and screaming, and my medal had fallen down in my cup. And I was like, "Oh my God, thank God, I didn't lose it."

The way the last out played out between the three of us, you know, just the vision of Nettles saying, "Pop it up, pop it up."

Then Goose in his brain going, *Okay, if I don't get him out, what's the worst thing that can happen? I'll be back in Colorado tomorrow, hunting.*

Everybody in their mind had their own things going on. Those are some of the funny things that happens in baseball.

An Unlikely Hero

MARTY APPEL: There really wasn't a more unlikely hero than Bucky Dent. In a lineup of sluggers, the defending world champions boasted superstars, while Dent was an ordinary player. He'd hit five home runs all season.

But here was his moment, and he conquered it. It would not have gone out of Yankee Stadium, but the Yankees had lost the coin toss and the playoff game was in Fenway Park. There, it made it.

ANTHONY McCARRON (*NY DAILY NEWS* BASEBALL COLUMNIST/SNY CONTRIBU-TOR): Obviously, Dent was no power hitter, with 40 home runs in a career that lasted twelve years.

But every time someone does something like this, you admire it for their ability to seize the moment and deliver. Not everyone does, not just in baseball, but in life. So, he will always have a significant place in the history of what's been an intense rivalry for years. It probably helps longevity that his name begins with "Buck"—I'll let you think of the rhymes that Red Sox fans make with that syllable. Might not have the same oomph if he went by Russell, his actual first name.

RON GUIDRY: It was one of those great moments in sports. I keep laughing at Bucky. I tell him that they're gonna show that film so often that one of these days that balls gonna hit the top of the wall.

JOHN STERLING (RADIO VOICE OF THE YANKEES): To be honest, the World Series or the big playoff games are many times won by someone you don't know about, there was Dusty Rhodes for the Giants in the 1954 World Series against Cleveland. The Yankees had a backup infielder, Brian Doyle, who also became an unlikely playoff hero in 1978.

Bucky "Bleeping" Dent!

BUCKY DENT: I heard the story after it was all over with. Zim (Don Zimmer) and his wife Soot, who I loved, were driving and they got to the mountains in Carolina. He just pulled over and got out and just walked over and screamed, "Bucky F-cking Dent" at the top of his lungs!!!

I guess he told the story to somebody and that's how it kind of started and gave me my middle name.

I wear it with honor, I love it. I still feel honored that we got to play in one of the greatest games ever—and we won.

It topped off an incredible year—1978—coming back in the division against Boston, then we beat Kansas City. We were then down two games in the World Series to the Dodgers, then we came back and won the World Series, it was one of the greatest seasons ever.

Dent Keeps Rolling and Becomes the World Series MVP

BUCKY DENT: I was the MVP of the World Series and I think people forget that because of the home run in Boston. That is a tremendous honor being named the most valuable player in the World Series.

There were some other guys that had a great Series. Nettles played great at third. Brian Doyle played great at second base. I think Munson had a pretty good series. I was just honored that I was named the Most Valuable Player in the World Series.

I think what happened was I hit the home run and in baseball streaks follow streaks. I hit the home run and then we go to Kansas City, and I started to get locked in again. I started to focus more and then I was in the World Series and it's a different thing. We had won it the year before, and we didn't want to lose to the Dodgers. So I just kind of got locked in.

MARTY APPEL: The circumstances of the big moment in the big game by the least intimidating Yankee made it all storybook. And then, he went on to win the World Series MVP Award, getting 10 hits and batting .417 against the Dodgers as the Yankees retained the world championship trophy.

Coming up Big in the Biggest Moments

BUCKY DENT: You always kind of dream of those things as a kid,

My friend to me, "the home run is gonna change your life."

It did because I played in one of the greatest games ever played. And I hit a three-run home run.

SPARKY LYLE: It meant a ton because you got to remember that when we went into that World Series that put us back-to-back-to-back World Series which I thought was very big at the time. We were in three straight World Series; I think we definitely had a spot in history.

KEN DAVIDOFF: Bucky Dent played in an era when most shortstops didn't hit. Ninth hitters in 1978 simply didn't come up with big hits very often. Now throw in the context—a rare, tiebreaking 163rd game against the rival Red Sox, at Fenway Park, after the Yankees had erased a 14-game deficit, with ace Ron Guidry falling into a two-run hole, with two outs and two on in the seventh inning. That's some serious drama. So, when Bucky sent one over the Green Monster to give the Yankees a lead they wouldn't relinquish, and the Yankees proceeded to win it all, it ensured that Bucky would never again have to pay for a meal in New York.

BUCKY DENT: We weren't picked to win the division. then we weren't picked to beat Kansas City, then we weren't picked to beat the Dodgers. We overcame all those odds and did it, it was just a great feeling.

#14

MARIS HITS 61st HOME RUN: NEW YORK YANKEES vs. BOSTON RED SOX

OCTOBER 2, 1961

---

61 IN '61

TIME CAPSULE

- Mayor of New York: Robert F. Wagner Jr.
- Oscar, Best Picture: *The Apartment*
- Oscar, Best Actor: Burt Lancaster, *Elmer Gantry*
- Oscar, Best Actress: Elizabeth Taylor, *Butterfield 8*
- Grammy, Album of the Year: Bob Newhart, *The Button-Down Mind of Bob Newhart*
- Grammy, Record of the Year: Percy Faith, "Theme from *A Summer Place*," *A Summer Place: The Motion Picture Soundtrack*
- President of the US: John F. Kennedy
- Price of Gas: $0.31/Gallon
- Heisman Trophy: Ernie Davis, running back, Syracuse

PREGAME

Everyone's Favorite Color of M&Ms in the Summer of 1961 was Pinstripe and Trust Me, They Didn't Melt in the Summer Heat.

"The Babe," "The Great Bambino," "The Sultan of Swat." All were nicknames for the Yankees' power-hitting star, George Herman Ruth. He was arguably the best player in the history of baseball, and his single-season record of 60 home runs was seen as an untouchable standard when he set it in 1927. Get this: the Babe, by himself in '27, had more home runs than any other American League team. The Philadelphia A's were a close second to Ruth with 56. As a team, the Yankees had 158.

In the clubhouse after hitting his 60th home run, Ruth famously said, "Sixty! Count 'em, 60! Let's see some other [player] match that!"

At the time, it seemed unimaginable. Between 1918 and 1932, there was only one year that Ruth *didn't* hit more homers than at least one team in the AL, and that was 1925. So, if I am doing the math right, Babe out-homered at least one team in the American League team in fourteen of fifteen seasons.

In 1999, Nike made a commercial featuring Cy Young Award–winning pitchers Tom Glavine and Greg Maddux, with the tag line "Chicks Dig the

Long Ball," referring to Mark McGwire's power hitting. This was a sentiment not lost on fans of Babe Ruth. In fact, that may have been where the concept started. Babe was the biggest star in all of baseball, so maybe "dudes" also dug the long ball as well.

The Bronx Bombers won 17 titles between Ruth's record year of 1927 and the summer of 1961. That summer featured a torrid pace of home runs hit by Roger Maris and Mickey Mantle. Now, how did Maris fit into this group? That's a good question. Mickey Mantle took over as the face of the franchise from Joe DiMaggio, who had taken the mantle from Lou Gehrig, who had taken it from Babe Ruth.

In the summer of 1951, at nineteen years old, Mantle made the Yankees roster and was given the number 6. Even that early in his career, Mantle carried the weight of great expectations. Ruth wore number 3. Gehrig wore number 4. DiMaggio wore number 5. So the expectations were that Mantle would be the next great Yankee superstar. However, he was sent back down to Kansas City after slumping in the beginning of the season. Maris, by the way, would also come from Kansas City, but not until the end of the decade.

Mickey flirted with the idea of quitting baseball after his demotion, only to be talked out of it by his father. Luckily for Yankee fans, he kept going. Later that season, Mantle was called back up—this time wearing the now famous number 7. In the 1951 World Series, Mantle injured his knee after being waved off catching a fly ball by DiMaggio. His knees would never be the same. Even so, the Yankees won the Subway Series over the New York Giants, four games to two.

In 1952, Mantle started in center field, replacing the recently retired DiMaggio. By 1956, he had fulfilled his expectations by delivering a Triple Crown season, batting .353 with 52 home runs and 130 RBIs. At the time, it was the second most home runs hit by a Yankee in a season to the Babe. He was eight short or Ruth's record. Mantle hit 536 home runs during his career and was named to 13 All-Star teams and played in 12 World Series, winning seven titles.

The Mick was the toast of the town.

Heck in 1956 he and Teresa Brewer released a single, "I Love Mickey." The lyrics went like this:

I love Mickey (Mickey who?)
You know who, the fella
With the celebrated swing

Oh, I love Mickey (Mickey who?)
You know who, the one who
Drives me batty every spring

The Yankees weren't playing like the Bronx Bombers any more. Their home run totals were down by 1957. They were led by Mantle's 34 home runs. Yogi Berra was the only other Yankee to hit over 20 homers, slugging 24. Mantle and Yogi combined were still short of Ruth's record. It was more of the same in 1958, with Mantle and Berra leading the way with 42 and 22, respectfully. No other Yankee hit as many as 15.

The Yankees attempted to solve their power outage on December 11, 1959. They sent Hank Bauer, Norm Siebern, Marv Throneberry, and Don Larsen to the Kansas City A's for Roger Maris, Kent Hadley, and Joe DeMaestri. The goal was that adding Maris would infuse some much-needed power into their lineup. New York was stuck in the middle of the pack in home runs, finishing fourth in an eight-team American League. In 1958, Maris had hit 28 homers for the Indians and A's. In 1959, he hit another 16 round-trippers for the A's. The Yankees, who had dominated baseball for decades, finished in third place in the AL standings. Something had to be done. This was just not up to the Yankees standard. Trading for Maris turned out to be something special.

In the trade were a couple of notable Yankees. Don Larsen had authored his perfect game in the World Series in 1956. In 1957, he was 10–4, though his numbers dropped in '58 (9–6) and '59 (6–7). Larsen was a player in decline—as was Bauer, who played right field to start the 1958 season. He was an All-Star in 1952, '53, and '54, but that was five long seasons ago by the time the trade occurred. At thirty-six years old, his power numbers were coming down. In 1956, he had hit a personal best 26 round trippers. But that number dropped to 18 in 1957 and 12 in '58. Hank finished the 1959 season with just nine home runs and 31 RBIs. It was the first time since his first full season in 1949 that he had hit less than double digits in homers. To add to their desperation, the Yankees missed the World Series in 1959. It was only the second time in thirteen years that happened. It was time for some young blood.

On Opening Day in 1960, as he ran out to his spot in right field, Maris was in his prime at twenty-six years old.

Make no mistake: Roger Maris was no Mickey Mantle. He was a soft-spoken midwestern boy, born in Hibbing, Minnesota. By the time he was twelve, the family moved to Fargo, North Dakota. He had Midwestern values and sensibilities. He didn't crave the spotlight like Mantle. He was a family man who didn't enjoy all the trappings of the New York City nightlife either. He didn't come up in the Yankees' farm system. So the fans favored Mantle, their homegrown superstar who fit better in the white-hot spotlight of New York, which was not the case with Maris, who just wanted to blend in and play baseball.

The 1960 Yankees won the pennant with a 97–57 record, which was an 18-win improvement from the previous season. Maris was an All-Star and hit 39 home runs, 112 RBIs, and batted .283. Mantle also was an All-Star with 40 home runs, 94 RBIs, while batting .275. The voting for MVP was won by a razor-thin margin, as Maris received 225 points and Mantle got 222 points. Maris may have taken home the MVP, but Mantle took home the hearts of Yankee fans.

The Yankees won the American League again in 1961, with a 109–53 record (in 162 games). Back in 1927, they had won the pennant and World Series with a team-record 110 victories (in 154 games). Trust me when I tell you that those eight games will be very important as this story unfolds.

The power-hitting duo had just scratched the surface in 1960 of what they were capable of and what was yet to come.

Could one of them hit 61 in '61?

This season shaped up to be a battle between the M&M Boys and Ruth. Maris had not hit a home run in his first 10 games and was off to a slow start. By the end of April, the reigning MVP had hit just one homer, compared to Mantle's seven. It matched the number on his back, but gave no indication to what was to come.

May was an entirely different story, as Maris's home run swing flowed, bashing 11 in the month. Mantle hit seven again and had a 14–12 lead on Maris. On May 19, the 30th game of the season, manager Ralph Houk slotted Maris in the three-hole in front of Mantle, who batted cleanup against Cleveland. The summer started to heat up in June—and so did Roger, slugging 15 round-trippers in the month. That put Maris's total at 27. Mantle was still red hot and finished the month with 11 home runs for a total of 25.

There were two All-Star games in 1961. And why not? If one is good, two has got to be better! By the second All-Star break, on July 10, both were All-Stars and Maris had a 33–29 edge on Mantle.

On July 17, the commissioner of baseball, Ford Frick, made a ruling that to be considered the official single-season record in baseball, any accomplishment had to be completed in the same 154-game season as when Ruth hit his 60. The season was expanded by eight games in 1961 with the addition of two new expansion teams, the Los Angeles Angels and the Washington Senators. That was a controversial decision. At the time, both Maris and Mantle were on pace to beat the record in the 154 games allotted by Frick, but now the pressure was intensified.

Was there a "Ghost of Ruth" tipping the scales? You make the call. In the city of Ruth's birth, Baltimore, Maryland, on that very same day, Mantle and Maris each had a home run taken away when the game was rained out. The Yankees were leading 4–1 in the top of the fifth when it was called—a half-inning short of an official game.

By the end of July, Maris's lead was down to 40–39. Either, neither, or both could, in fact, catch the Bambino.

There were daily totals featuring the three of them in each day's newspapers. After 112 games, the chart listed: Ruth 36, Maris 41, Mantle 43. It really was possible for these guys to eclipse Ruth. On August 11, Mantle had 44 bombs and Maris 42. By August 13 the two were tied at 45. It was all anyone could talk about in baseball that summer—especially in New York City. Mantle and Maris were on the back page of all the tabloids, on the cover of *Life* magazine, *Sports Illustrated*, and on the minds of sports fans everywhere.

All the pressure from the media, fans, and Maris himself was taking its toll. He was shy and didn't want the added attention. Yankees fans were rooting for "The Mick" to break the record and his lack of being a quote machine didn't endear him to beat writers and columnists, either. On the other side of the spectrum, Mantle was a media darling. At that time, way before social media, the press was the main conduit to the fans.

Whitey Ford's son, Ed, told me when asked about the rooting interest between the two players in the Ford household, "I remember we were all rooting for Mickey. We'd liked Roger, but Mickey was a little closer to our family than Roger was. It was just a great year. You know, my father won 25 games that year. Nobody even remembers that (laugh). All you hear about is Mantle and Maris."

Whitey did in fact win 25 games and took home the Cy Young Award as the best pitcher in baseball. In those days, there was not a separate winner in the American League and the National League.

Now back to Mickey and Roger. Maris didn't seem to care as much about the record as he did about winning. His on-field demeanor also didn't show off the joy of playing a kid's game for a king's ransom. All of this had the fans and even the supposedly impartial media rooting for Mantle as the season came down the home stretch. What didn't work for Mantle was his body. He pulled muscles in his forearm and battled leg and knee injuries. The worse affliction may have been an abscess on his hip. The Mick was also battling a respiratory and eye infection. Mel Allen, the voice of the Yankees, told him that Dr. Max Jacobson might be able to help. The doctor famously treated President Kennedy, Truman Capote, and other celebrities. He was known as "Dr. Feelgood." To say that Mantle didn't feel good after the shot he received is an understatement. He ended up in Lenox Hill Hospital, on the Upper East Side of New York City, to have the wound on his hip lanced.

Mantle's regular season was over after the game against the Orioles on September 26. He finished with 54 home runs, six short of the Babe. If it wasn't for his injuries, Mickey may have also topped Ruth. He hit two homers against the Tigers on September 3, with the second being his 50th of the season. Over the next 19 games, while battling infections and injures, he hit only four. He would be forced to watch Maris go for the record from a hospital bed.

Maris also hit two home runs off of the Tigers in one game during that September series. The day before Mantle hit his 49th and 50th home runs, Maris hit numbers 52 and 53. All nine of his September home runs were hit under the most intense pressure imaginable. He was battling opposing pitchers, the fans—at home and away—the media, the ghost of the Babe, and hair loss due to stress. After the pair of dingers versus Detroit, he got number 54 against the Washington Senators. That was game number 140 of the season. He then went on a tear, slamming number 55 on September 7 against Cleveland. Two days later he got one off of Cleveland's Mudcat Grant for number 56. There were just 11 games to go to top the Babe in Frick's 154 game mandate, and he still needed five more for the record.

It would be seven long days between homers. He victimized the Tigers again for home run numbers 57 and 58 on September 16 and 17. Now it was off to Charm City and the birthplace of the Babe to face the Orioles.

Games 153 and 154 would be played on September 19, 1961, in a doubleheader. Maris was stuck on 58. In order to surpass the Babe in 154 games, and satisfy Frick's edict, he would need to hit two dingers to tie Ruth and three to pass him over those two games. Maris went 0-for-3 in the first game (153) and 1-for-5 in the second (154). Per Frick's ruling, Ruth's record was safe.

The next day, Maris got number 59 off Milt Pappas. Then, on September 26, he tied Ruth with a home run to right field in the third inning.

Here is how it sounded on WPIX-TV, Mel Allen with the call:

This is what people have come to see . . . there it is, there it is, if it stays fair and it is, number 60. How about that, there is a standing ovation, a standing ovation for Roger Maris who got number 60. And they are calling him out of the dugout, this is most unusual, they are asking him to come out of the dugout, this is something, they are standing and asking Roger to come out, how about that, come on out of there, there he is.

The rival Red Sox were coming to town for a three-game set to finish the season. The last game of the 1961 season was October 1. Could Maris hit 61 in '61? It would all come down to this day. The Red Sox's Tracy Stallard was all that stood in the way of history. Only 23,154 fans showed up to Yankee Stadium to see Maris chase history and the team prepare for the upcoming World Series. They had won the pennant; the Cincinnati Reds were up next. Game 1 of the World Series was just two days away. But a home run in the World Series did Roger no good in chasing the regular season home run record. Up first was a date with destiny in the final game of the season. Could Maris do it? Could he defeat all who seemed to be against him and break the unbreakable record?

ROGER THAT: *61 IN '61!

BY PETER BOTTE

Two teammates spent the Bronx summer of 1961 chasing a Yankees legend and the most hallowed record in sports.

In the end, after months of debate about asterisks and whether Roger Maris or Mickey Mantle was the preferred choice to eclipse Babe Ruth's total of 60 home runs in 1927, it was the reserved Maris who emerged as the pinstriped star to break the mark. The lefty slugger finally belted No. 61 in '61 off Boston's Tracy Stallard at Yankee Stadium on October 1, the Bombers' 162nd and final game of the season.

"Baby Boomers, like me, enjoyed the summer of '61 because let's face it, there were no bills to pay, no dates to fret over . . . just the joy of seeing the M&M boys chasing the Babe," author and former Yankees PR man Marty Appel said. "We learned the word *antihero* which was how Maris was painted, with most of the public favoring Mantle, who had been a 10-year veteran of the team and by now, the game's hero. He was baseball's first television star.

"This newcomer, Maris, who always seemed to have a chip on his shoulder and a surly look, was not going to be the fan favorite. But as people turned from him and cheered on Mick, it appeared that Roger, who stayed healthy, would be 'The One.' There were a lot of people still living who grew up idolizing Babe Ruth. This was a bitter pill. But Roger overcame all of that to prevail."

Maris had ripped 39 homers and won the AL MVP award in 1960, his first season with the Yanks following a trade from the Kansas City A's. But that couldn't prepare the mild-mannered North Dakotan for the onslaught of attention he'd receive when he and Mantle, who finished the '61 season with 54 homers, waged their assault on Ruth's record in the first season of expansion and an extended schedule from 154 games to 162.

Even baseball commissioner Ford Frick ruled that breaking Ruth's record would have to be achieved in 154 games to count as the official mark.

Thus, there only were 23,154 fans at the Stadium when Maris took Stallard deep to the right-field seats with one out in the fourth inning for the Yanks' lone run in a 1–0 victory in Game 162.

Maris's mark stood until MLB's steroids era, PED-tainted sluggers Mark McGwire and Sammy Sosa belted 70 and 66 home runs, respectively, in 1998, before Barry Bonds, also tainted by suspected PED use, surpassed them all with 73 in 2001.

Another Yankees outfielder, Aaron Judge, captivated the game in breaking Maris's franchise and American League mark, with 62 home runs in 2022.

POSTGAME

The Summer of '61

BILLY CRYSTAL (AWARD-WINNING ACTOR AND LIFELONG YANKEES FAN): I was thirteen that summer, and the ghost of the Babe was mythical. So, when Mantle and Maris started hitting homer after homer in the same Yankee Stadium Babe played in, to this thirteen-year-old it was otherworldly.

I was still recuperating from the heartbreaking loss to the Pirates in the World Series of 1960 so when my hero Mickey Mantle and the newcomer Roger Maris went wild, so did I . . . . with joy. On top of the chase there was a pennant race which wasn't decided until September. Two teammates in the house that Ruth built going after his seemingly impossible to break record. Never been a season like it.

MARTY APPEL (YANKEES HISTORIAN AND BESTSELLING AUTHOR): Ruth's mark was hallowed. No one had ever seen power like his and he set baseball on a different course than the hit-and-run, pitching-dominated game it had been. Home runs were sexy, they were fun, they put fannies in the seats. Ruth was the biggest baseball star who ever lived, so if someone was going for that record, which none had conquered in thirty-four years of swinging for the fences, it was a big deal. Add in the fact that Roger Maris was competing with Mickey Mantle, everyone's boyhood hero, to take down Ruth's record, and there's no wonder all eyes were on the chase.

JOHN STERLING (RADIO VOICE OF THE YANKEES): That was a phenomenal summer. Maris and Mantle were great. It was so much fun and so were the other home-run hitters like Johnny Blanchard, Yogi Berra, Moose Skowron, and Elston Howard.

I was just beginning radio; I was on a station in Long Island. So, I was I really felt part of it. I was listening and watching every game and it was just a great joy.

Finally, towards the end of the year the Yankees played the Tigers and beat them all three games at the Stadium and that kind of opened it up and the Yankees went on to win the pennant. It was incredible summer watching Mantle and Maris duel night after night. The media made out that Maris and Mantle didn't like each other, which was total nonsense. They were living with each other in Queens. Mantle got an injury on his upper hip and he went to Doctor Feelgood, the guy's name was Jacobson, who had worked on a lot of big stars and he gave these magic shots, that were shots of speed. Mantle development infection and he couldn't play the whole World Series, but the other Yankees beat the Reds in five games.

BOB COSTAS (LEGENDARY SPORTS BROADCASTER): The setting of Yankee Stadium had something to do with it and Yankee history. All three guys—now four if you count Aaron Judge—are connected to the Yankees. They all wore pinstripes. In 1961, you have to keep in mind, there are many people very much alive, who saw Babe Ruth play. So, he's not just a mythical figure, he's a real person, to a lot of people—fans, members of the press, and other people around the Yankees.

Maris and Mantle

JOAN FORD (WIDOW OF WHITEY FORD): I loved Maris. He was a very nice person, as was his whole family. Roger was serious, while Mickey was funny, very funny.

MARTY APPEL: Mantle was baseball's first television star. This newcomer, Maris, who always seemed to have a chip on his shoulder and a surly look, was not going to be the fan favorite.

KEN DAVIDOFF (FORMER *NY POST* BASEBALL COLUMNIST/PIX11 BASEBALL HISTO-RIAN): One Yankees legend held the single-season home run record. Another legend chased it. And then a third guy served as an interloper of sorts. Poor Roger Maris. The stoic North Dakota native, in only his second season as a Yankee following a trade from Kansas City, had no chance to win a popularity contest with the homegrown, beloved Mantle, who already had five World Series rings and two AL MVP trophies by '61. Throw in the nuance that the AL played its very first 162-game schedule that season, compelling commissioner Ford Frick to issue a directive that the Babe's record would hold as the "154-game season mark," and it all made for a very thick plot.

BOB COSTAS: Mel Allen presided over the ceremony at Yankee Stadium when Ruth came out there, leaning on a bat as a cane and made his final speech. Now there's a lot of overlap there. And in Mickey Mantle, you have arguably the most popular player of his time. He was already a certified Hall of Famer, if he had retired after that year, he would have still gone to the Hall of Fame. So, he was perhaps the popular choice, and the greater player in the larger view. But Maris had won the MVP the year before. And the Yankees are the Yankees, they win the pennant that year, they go to the World Series and win it. So, you've got all these factors that that are like a 10 out of 10 scale in terms of interest and historical significance. So, I think that was part of it. And the fact that these two guys on the same team, it wasn't like it was Roger Maris and Rocky Colavito or something. They're, they're on the same team Maris was hitting third and Mantle was hitting forth. And for a very long period of time, until September, they're neck and neck. So, it's a real race. It's even different than McGwire and Sosa, we know that McGwire and Sosa are different now, because we see it through the rearview mirror through the prism of steroids. But Maris and Mantle playing in the same game. They're in the same batting order. It's neck and neck. Plus, it made for good headlines that it's a marathon so that the M&M boys had all the elements.

ANTHONY McCARRON (*NY DAILY NEWS* BASEBALL COLUMNIST/SNY CONTRIBUTOR): Mantle was the big star, the best player and the next man up in the Yankees' incredible run of iconic players. I think the world rooted for him because he was such a star. Maris had been the MVP the year before, but he was a much quieter man, didn't bask in the spotlight and was uncomfortable with the attention, especially when it was obvious that few wanted him to be the one who broke the record. It makes it all the more amazing that he had the season he did.

Maris Hits No. 61

ED FORD (SON OF WHITEY FORD): I watched it. I was eight years old that summer. And I just I remember Phil Rizzuto's call. And then the scramble for the baseball in the stands. The stadium wasn't sold out, but in the right-field section, it was packed because everyone wanted to get the baseball.

JOAN FORD: It was great to be able to watch it. And I had a great seat, being Whitey's wife. What made it extra fun was that I loved both of them. It was a very, very beautiful part of my life when I saw it.

I was so happy when Maris broke the record. The fans in Yankee Stadium were happy, very happy, we loved him for breaking the record.

BOB COSTAS: He was a big-time team player. He was a stoic guy from North Dakota, a product of his time and place. They practically had to push him out of the dugout to get him to waive his cap after he hit 60 and then 61. He was so reluctant to call attention to himself. Now guys take a curtain call. There was that element in him.

BILL LEIDERMAN (PARTNER/CO-OWNER OF MICKEY MANTLE'S RESTAURANT): Mickey was always happy for Roger. He was always proud of Roger. He said Roger was a great guy.

Mickey would say, "You know, if I hadn't gone to the hospital, maybe I would have done it. If I hadn't gotten injured."

He took a shot and got a bad reaction to it. He missed 12 games. I think it was one of those shots of B-12 that Kennedy used to get, the shot of speed. But you know, he was fine with all of that and was never bitter about it.

61*

MARTY APPEL: When I think of 1961 from the perspective of having become the Yankees PR man, the ruling by Commissioner Ford Frick to cut off Maris at 154 games was about as stupid a marketing decision as the head of any industry could make. Faced with the most exciting story in sports in years, he completed derailed the last eight games, rendered them meaningless, lost the opportunity to celebrate today's game, today's players. Who does that?

It would take some thirty years before another commissioner, Fay Vincent, made it right.

Looking Back (and Forward in the Summer of 2022)

ED FORD: I was talking to my son yesterday as we were watching the Yankee game and Judge hit the two home runs and I said he could hit 60 home runs. My son asked me, "What's the record?" I told him, well there's three guys who took steroids that beat Roger. But no, Judge may be the first guy not on steroids to beat Roger. I think that's a big deal.

JON HEYMAN (BASEBALL COLUMNIST FOR *NY NEWSDAY* AND *NY POST*): Everyone loves the long ball, it's not just "chicks who dig the long ball," as the commercial said. Home runs are the ultimate in baseball, and Roger Maris's record 61 home runs was one of the most cherished records in baseball. There was a bit of extra magic to it, as the 61 home runs came, symmetrically, in 1961. But more importantly, it was the biggest single-season record in sports, it was two Yankees (one beloved and one not as beloved) chasing the vaunted record of

Babe Ruth, the greatest Yankee of them all. I still believe it remained the real home run record, as the three National League sluggers who hit more homers in a single season are all linked to steroids. And it remained the record—officially, at least the American League record—for exactly sixty-one years until Aaron Judge topped it by one.

#15

JUDGE HITS 62nd HOME RUN: NEW YORK YANKEES vs. TEXAS RANGERS

OCTOBER 4, 2022

JUDGE BREAKS MARIS'S RECORD

TIME CAPSULE

- Mayor of New York: Eric Adams
- Oscar, Best Picture: *Coda*
- Oscar, Best Actor: Will Smith, *King Richard*
- Oscar, Best Actress: Jessica Chastain, *The Eyes of Tammy Faye*
- Grammy, Album of the Year: Jon Batiste, *We Are*
- Grammy, Record of the Year: Silk Sonic, "Leave the Door Open," *An Evening with Silk Sonic*
- President of the US: Joe Biden
- Price of Gas: $3.95/Gallon
- Heisman Trophy: Caleb Williams, quarterback, USC

PREGAME

All Rise for the New AL Home Run King

Is there a better bet than betting on yourself? Apparently, Aaron Judge doesn't think there is. Kenny Rogers may have been looking ahead to the summer of 2022 when he inked his Grammy Award–winning song, "The Gambler."

> *If you're gonna play the game, boy*
> *You gotta learn to play it right*
> *You've got to know when to hold 'em*
> *Know when to fold 'em*
> *Know when to walk away*
> *And know when to run*
> *You never count your money*
> *When you're sittin' at the table*
> *There'll be time enough for countin'*
> *When the dealin's done*

Aaron Judge must be a big Kenny Rogers fan, and his gamble sure did pay off. Judge was entering his walk year in the summer of 2022. Sports talk radio and the internet were on fire with talk of little else than Judge's contract situation.

The slugger set Opening Day as the deadline to get a deal done with the Yankees, or he was going to head into the offseason as a free agent. On Opening Day, Brian Cashman announced that Judge had turned down a contract for $213.5 million dollars, paid over seven years. The Yankees added that they would up Judge's salary for the 2022 season, an eighth season, to be between $17 million and $21 million, and they would let an arbitrator determine the exact number.

Cashman, who rarely talks about contract negotiations in the media, may have done so to try to save face with Yankee fans. At an Opening Day press conference, where he shared the details "for transparency purposes," Cashman said that he made a fair offer and said the following: "We were unsuccessful in concluding a multiyear pact. Obviously, our intent is to have Aaron Judge stay as a New York Yankee as we move forward, and I know that is his intent as well, which is a good thing. We're going to be entering those efforts in a new arena, which would be at the end of the season when free agency starts, and maybe that will determine what the real market value would be, because we certainly couldn't agree at this stage on a contract extension." Cashman gambled by sharing the contract numbers that he and the Yankees would win in the court of public opinion. Just before the noon deadline on Friday, June 24, the Yankees and Aaron Judge agreed to a $19 million contract for 2022, avoiding an arbitration hearing.

Just to set the record straight, before we get to the home run record, Cashman gambled and lost. Judge gambled and won.

Now that's out of the way, let's get to why we are here: the American League home run record chase that dominated the headlines during the summer of 2022. Babe Ruth hammered 60 home runs in 1927. Roger Maris hit one more than the "Sultan of Swat" by slugging 61 in 1961. Now sixty-one years later, Aaron Judge hit one more than Maris and set the AL home run record with 62. The moniker of "Home Run King" has been passed from one Yankees right fielder to another to another in just under a century. Now that is a pretty cool coincidence.

They all played right field for the Yankees and they all set the record in dominating fashion. Each of them had a completely different style. The bombastic Babe Ruth famously said after hitting his 60th home run, "Sixty! Count 'em, 60! Let's see some other son of a bitch match that!"

Roger Maris was far less bombastic, and didn't seek, nor enjoy, the spotlight the way the Babe did. According to Jack Orr, in his book *My Greatest*

Day in Baseball, Maris said, "I never wanted all this hoopla. All I wanted is to be a good ball player and hit twenty-five or thirty homers, drive in a hundred runs, hit .280 and help my club win pennants. I just wanted to be one of the guys, an average player having a good season."

Aaron Judge's approach was somewhere between Ruth and Maris, saying after his 62nd home run, "I tried to enjoy every single moment. I didn't think about, 'Hey, they're all on their feet to see you hit a home run.' I tried to think about, 'Hey, they're here to see an exciting ballgame and see something special.' Having that mindset helped me stay pretty calm, but there was definitely a little pressure in there."

His manager, Aaron Boone, had a front row seat all summer and summed up the record-breaking season this way, "Just an all-time great season. He's been the leader of this team, for a division-winning team, one for which he's gotten big hit after big hit. I think it's a historically great season, and one they'll talk about when we're long gone."

The family of Roger Maris followed the Yankees around as Judge tied and passed him. They spent a lot of time getting to know Judge and his family. After Judge finally passed his father and set the home run record, Roger Maris Jr. tweeted, "Congratulations to Aaron Judge and his family on Aaron's historic home run number 62! It has definitely been a baseball season to remember. You are all class and someone who should be revered. For the MAJORITY of the fans, we can now celebrate a new CLEAN HOME RUN KING!!"

That was a not-so-subtle shot at Barry Bonds, Mark McGwire, and Sammy Sosa, who all hit more home runs than Roger Maris but were also connected to performance-enhancing drugs. Barry Bonds may have hit 73 home runs, but he may one day have an asterisk for a more unsavory reason then Maris's asterisk for playing more games than The Babe. Hence, Maris Jr. called Judge the "Clean Home Run King" in his tweet. It's a sentiment with which many agree.

In response to the Maris family being there for the record, Judge said, "I know it's a tough situation; it's your dad's legacy and you want to uphold that. Getting a chance to meet their family, they're wonderful people. Having my name next to someone who's as great as Roger Maris, Babe Ruth, and those guys, it's incredible."

Aaron Judge was the AL Rookie of the Year in 2017 and mashed 52 home runs. Since then, he hit 27 in both 2018 and 2019, and 39 in 2021. So he had power, but he also had injury issues—thus missed a lot of games. He turned thirty on April 26, 2022, which may have been the reason Cashman was concerned about going above seven years for Judge. After all, Aaron played in 112 games in 2018, 102 games in 2019, 148 games in 2021, and even during the COVID-shorten season of 2020, he was injury prone, playing in 28 of the Yankees' 60 games.

Judge played in 157 games in 2022, so he proved he could stay healthy. When Judge is healthy, he proved he could consistently hit the long ball. In April, the Yankees played 20 games and he hit six homers. April showers lead to May flowers and a doubling of his home run total. He then hit 12 dingers in 27 games in May. June only saw him hitting one less, with 11 in 28 games. In July, Judge was consistent, hitting 13 in 25 games. He cooled off a little in August by delivering nine balls over the fence. The pressure really dialed up in September, where he delivered 10 balls into the seats and then the final tiebreaking home run in Texas for his only—but most important—dinger in October.

Get this: Judge not only set a home run record, but almost won the Triple Crown. To go along with his 62 home runs, he paced the American League with 131 RBIs. His .311 batting average was just behind Luis Arraez (.316). The Twins' second baseman trailed Judge as late as September 28, but went 5-for-13 down the stretch to take home the batting title and denying Judge of the exclusive group that includes only one player between 2022 and Carl Yastrzemski in 1967. That would be Miguel Cabrera, who won the Triple Crown in 2012. That should give you an idea of how historic Judge's season was.

It wasn't easy at the end of the season. Aaron hit his 60th home run on September 20 versus Pittsburgh. He finished the series the next day, and played four games against the Red Sox, where the home fans hoped he would set the record. The Maris family joined the traveling circus as well. It would be eight longs games where every at bat was met with huge crowds collectively holding their breaths and pointing their cameras, hoping to capture history.

Sadly for Judge, the Maris family, and the home fans, he wouldn't tie the record at home. It came north of the border in Toronto, on September 28. Michael Kay was on the call when it happened.

And the 3-2, drilled deep to left field! This could be it! See ya! He's done it! No. 61! He's been chasing history and now he makes it! He and Roger Maris are tied with 61 home runs, the most anybody has ever hit in a single season in American League history!"

John Sterling on the radio called it this way:

> And the payoff. There it goes. It is high! It is far! It is gone! No. 61! He ties Roger Maris for the American League single-season record with 61 home runs! It's a two-run Judge-ian blast! Here comes the Judge! A two-run blast and the Yankees take a 5–3 lead on No. 61 for Judge.

It would be another six games before Judge would set the record, on October 4 in Texas. That is two home runs in 14 games, wherein Judge had to endure questions about his "home run slump." His response was to pause, look at the reporter, and asked if indeed he was in a slump. There was laughter in the clubhouse, but the pressure sure did build during that time.

"I can't lie," Judge said. "The past couple of games, I looked up in the seventh inning and I'm like, 'Dang, I've only got one more at-bat. We'd better figure this out.'"

Figure it out he did and, on October 4, the wait was over for Judge, Yankees fans, baseball fans, and even the Maris family. Michael Kay was lucky to again be able to make the historic call.

> There it goes, soaring into history! He's done it, he has done it, 62! Aaron Judge is the American League single-season home run leader. The AL king, case closed!

John Sterling, who has been calling Yankee games since 1989, memorialized the moment in his own way:

> It is high, it is far, it is gone! Number 62 to set the new American League record! Aaron Judge hits his 62nd. All the Yankees out of the dugout to greet him. Just think of it, three Yankee right fielders—The Babe, hitting 60 in '27, the Jolly Roger, hitting 61 in '61, and now Aaron Judge hits his 62nd home run—the most home runs any American Leaguer has hit in a single season. And the American League has been alive for 120 years. This is Judgment Day. Case Closed."

The case was indeed closed, and that is the way these two longtime, popular Yankees broadcasters ended their calls. As fans watching on television or listening on the radio took it all in, Aaron Judge was living the moment and shared what he was thinking as he circled the bases. "I was thinking of my wife, thinking of my family, my teammates, the fans. All of that was running, kind of running, through my head, just the constant support I've gotten through this whole process."

Even the Captain, Derek Jeter, tweeted, "Congrats @TheJudge on 62! Postseason Next!!!

Joe Biden, the President of the United States of America, said, "History made, more history to make." He seemed to be on the same page as Jeter.

One thing is for sure: after the postseason, it's a trip to the bank for Judge to, as Rogers once sung, "count his money, because the deal was done." Judge gambled on himself and won. Kenny Rogers, Roger Maris, and The Babe are all looking down on Aaron Judge with pride and certainly humming the tune to "The Gambler."

ALL RISE FOR THE NEW YANKEE HR KING

BY PETER BOTTE

The numerical symmetry was astonishing.

Sixty-one years after Roger Maris had blasted 61 home runs in 1961, modern Yankees slugger Aaron Judge finally equaled the franchise mark—with Maris' son Roger Jr. in attendance—in Toronto, on September 28, 2022.

Judge still needed one more, however, to claim the record alone, and it took him six more games to accomplish the feat by going deep for No. 62 against Texas righty Jesus Tinoco on October 4 as the first batter in the Yanks' penultimate game of the regular season.

"I had a good feeling off the bat. I just didn't know where it was going to land or what it was going to hit. There was a good sense of relief once I saw it in that fan's glove," Judge said that night. "I tried to enjoy every single moment.

Judge's historic campaign was only made more remarkable by his status as a pending free agent after turning down the Yankees' offer before the season started of a seven-year contract extension worth $213.5 million. Talk about betting on yourself. Judge parlayed his historic season into a nine-year

$360 million contract to remain in pinstripes after receiving a comparable offer in free agency from his hometown San Francisco Giants, and even more money to play in San Diego for the Padres.

Judge was unanimously named the American League's Most Valuable Player in a season in which Angels two-way star Shohei Ohtani registered 34 home runs, 95 RBIs *and* a 2.33 ERA with 219 strikeouts over 166 innings pitched.

"Judge handled the pressure as well as anybody I've ever seen," former Yankees pitcher and current YES Network analyst David Cone said. "I mean, he never let anything bother him . . . It was just remarkable. He was so confident in himself. He never wavered the whole year. He literally carried this team to the playoffs. There's got to be enormous pressure down the stretch too, because the whole world was watching. That's a lot of pressure.

"I wasn't around for Maris and I didn't see Babe Ruth play. But I certainly saw Aaron Judge this year. It was the best thing I've ever seen."

POSTGAME

Betting on Himself

JIM DUQUETTE (MLB NETWORK ANALYST): There's the pressure to kind of bet on yourself, he always had that ultra-confidence that, as a player, he was going to perform at a very high level during his free agent year. Yet not everybody does it, right? You add in the fact that you're on the most recognizable team, not just in MLB, but in the world with all the expectations that comes with that.

ED RANDALL (LEGENDARY NEW YORK BASEBALL WRITER AND BROADCASTER): They were hoping to tie him up. I think he had every reason to turn it down. Of course, a lot of eyebrows were raised at the time because he's had an injury history. How could he possibly do this? He should err on the side of safety, then he could say, "I'm signed and I'm done."

MEREDITH MARAKOVITS (YANKEES REPORTER, YES NETWORK): It shows the amount of confidence he has in himself and his ability. The only question about him has been, can he stay healthy? If he's healthy, I don't think there's ever been a dispute that he is one of the best players in baseball.

BRENDAN KUTY (YANKEES BEAT REPORTER, *STAR-LEDGER* AND *THE ATHLETIC*): It was having the balls to turn down nine figures and say, I want more. I'm going to show you why I deserve more.

IAN O'CONNOR (COLUMNIST AND BESTSELLING AUTHOR): What was really impressive to me was the way he handled that pressure. He made it almost like it wasn't even there. It was very genuine. He just went out and played baseball. I do think he was angry that Brian Cashman announced the terms. He made that pretty clear, but it's not like he played with anger because of that. I think he just stayed within himself. He made a very big moment, very small, which is what you have to do at the plate in baseball.

PETE CALDERA (YANKEES BEAT REPORTER, *BERGEN RECORD*): That's exactly what he has: intestinal fortitude. He had an innate belief in himself and his ability. Not only that, but his ability to perform on the biggest stage under the most intense pressure in a free agent walk year was impressive. I think if we are being honest, most of us were pretty surprised that he turned down the contract at the time.

JIM DUQUETTE: He found a way to handle and manage all the pressure and still perform like he did and that is exceptional.

The Chase

TODD EHRLICH: How did you handle the unbelievable amount of pressure that surrounded you during the home run chase? Maris famously talked about how much the presume affected him. I've been covering games since the 1980s and have been in this Yankees clubhouse many times during the chase, and no one I have covered has carried themselves with more class, grace, and patience than you. How did you do it?

AARON JUDGE (YANKEES OUTFIELDER): For me, it was it was simply, it was out of my hands. Things were going to work out the way they were supposed to, and that would be great. If they didn't, they didn't. Getting a chance to show up and have the teammates I did and be in the chase for the division throughout the whole season just made it easy. My focus was to go out there and win. If I just focused on being myself and help my team win,

then I'm probably going to hit a couple of homers. So, just having that in the back of my mind really made it easy for me to go out there and just have fun with it and, you know, just kind of enjoy the race.

BOB COSTAS (LEGENDARY SPORTS BROADCASTER): I think the fact Aaron Judge is not only obviously one of the best players of his time, but he carries himself with kind of an old school sort of dignity and grace. So, you can see him as part of that lineage.

PETE CALDERA: Maris was under enormous pressure because he was chasing the ghost of Babe Ruth and what he meant to the franchise. People may have been rooting against Maris, but I don't think anyone was rooting against Judge. It was the complete opposite that people were hoping that he would achieve this record.

BRENDAN KUTY: I've been impressed with how Aaron has handled himself for as long as I've known him, and that goes back to 2014. He's always a stand-up guy. It didn't change during his push to get to 62 home runs. He understood his media obligations. He understood his fan obligations. You still saw him signing autographs and taking selfies and playing catch with fans in the stands and throwing baseballs out there. You didn't see a change in his public persona and that's got to be really hard for anybody to do, especially in his circumstances.

JIM DUQUETTE: We're in New York and we are used to Derek Jeter as the kind of example. I will say he was Jeter-esque. I think it's deeper than just having a role model. A lot of it has to do with how you're raised. Just my experience of being in baseball guys who handle those situations with the same type of class and grace and dignity are usually someone that had an upbringing that kind of showed them what is right, what is wrong, and what humility means. I give his parents a ton of credit for how they raised him as an individual, and for the fact that it seems like he never forgot where he came from.

SWEENY MURTI (YANKEES REPORTER): I think in the way Jeter treating every game the same no matter the importance of the game. I think you saw some of that with from Judge. Even as the home run chase was coming down the stretch, you could see it in his interactions with fans, with kids especially. Those are things that he took very seriously. He told me himself, how he remembers being a young fan, and trying to get an autograph from player and what that moment meant to him.

He said, "It might only be thirty seconds in my day, it doesn't have to be a whole lot of time for me, but it can make a difference in in that fan's life."

ISIAH KINER-FALEFA (YANKEES SHORTSTOP): Just understanding that it might not ever happen again. You know, with the juiced balls a couple of years ago, everybody was hitting a lot of homers. There was a close second place to lead the league in homers. This year, I think the second-place guy in AL (Mike Trout) was at like 40, which is like 22 under Aaron Judge's total. I mean, that's a huge gap. So, I think just looking at that, people need to understand that it might not ever happen again.

MEREDITH MARAKOVITS: I think one of the things that was so remarkable about it was just how steady Judge stayed throughout. He really, truly did seem unfazed as if no moment has ever been too big for him. That was not just during the home run chase, that seemed to be the way he's conducted himself throughout his professional career. That's the thing that stands out. You're watching one of the most unbelievable feats happen, and you wouldn't even know it, because while he shows emotion, he's the same guy every day.

SWEENY MURTI: You could see the fun he was having playing the game and in the way he treated people. That's just a testament to him and how he how he plays the game.

PETE CALDERA: What was most impressive I think about Judge's season was that he got better as the team got worse. When the injuries hit their lineup and when they began losing games, they became essentially a .500 ballclub after the All-Star break, that is when he elevated his game. That's hard to do when you're the central figure in a lineup. When the opposing teams have a scouting report and hold their pitchers meeting before the game, the first item on the docket is don't let Judge beat you. He still found a way and that makes Judge's season even more impressive.

ISIAH KINER-FALEFA: He enjoys the big stage. He's meant for it. He's the captain. He's humble. I think that's the biggest thing, you know, anyone else that hit 62 home runs would be blowing up everywhere and acting like a piece of crap, honestly. It didn't change who he is. He still has time for the rookies. He still has time for the media. He still has time for everybody. I think people just need to understand that it's going to be a long time before people find a guy like that. He could be all over the billboards and whatnot, and still put his team first. He wants to put his team teammates up there with him on the billboard, not just himself, even though he's the only guy that deserves to be up there. I'm just happy I got to be a part of it.

PETE CALDERA: Basically, the last three to four weeks of the season, every time he came up to the plate the entire ballpark was expecting him to do one thing.

ED RANDALL: I think the fact that Judge has been able to have the season he's had is just an incredible achievement.

SWEENY MURTI: Judge made it look as easy. At some point, you recognize that it's not that easy. It took a little bit of time to finally get to 61 and 62, I think we all understood that. Just getting to that moment was really special to watch.

IAN O'CONNOR: I was there in Toronto after he hit the 61st home run. Judge's mom and Roger Maris Jr. were waiting for him outside the Yankees clubhouse. He gave his mother this warm hug, and then he talked to Roger Maris Jr. You could see the respect that Judge was showing Maris's son. I think he got it. I think he understood what it meant to be the home run champion of the New York Yankees. It's different from any other franchise in the sport. Afterwards in the press conference he talked about what it meant to be linked to Babe Ruth and Maris. He got it.

PETE CALDERA: I'll say it was very interesting that Roger Maris Jr. had very strong feelings. He let it be known pretty early in the process that he believed if Aaron Judge surpassed his father's record, he would have a "legitimate" home run record in baseball. That's a matter of opinion and debate, but he made those feelings very clear.

MEREDITH MARAKOVITS: Early in the year when it looked like he was on this historic home run chase, I asked, "What would 60 mean to you, what would 61 mean to you?"

He would continue to say, "I'll let you know when I get there. I'll let you know when I get there."

He finally got to 61, and I said, "All right, now you go to let me know."

He held true to his word. He told me that it was meaningful. I think playing in New York, he understood the way fans felt about it—the importance of it. I think it was a special moment for him even though, maybe at times, it was hard for him to admit it.

The Ride to the Record

MICHAEL KAY (TV VOICE OF THE YANKEES): It was amazing to be along for the ride, especially when it got to August, and you realized he had a chance to do it and put together a season for the ages. When he got closer, the tension and the pressure mounted because each at bat was under such scrutiny with national networks showing it live each time he came up.

For me personally, I felt a lot of pressure and not because of ego and wanting to be connected to the call but for Judge and his family. That call is for him, connected to his moment to paint the picture for him and his family.

BRENDAN KUTY: The pressure was enormous. Every at-bat people were standing when Judge was at the plate. They were living and dying with every single pitch. I just couldn't imagine being under that kind of pressure to do what people say is the hardest thing in sports, to hit a round ball with a round bat. The hardest thing in baseball is to hit a home run. So, they're expecting Judge to do the hardest thing in professional sports, on every single pitch.

DAVID CONE (FORMER YANKEES PITCHER/YANKEES TV BROADCASTER): It's one of the most impressive things I've ever seen.

JIM DUQUETTE: We saw down the stretch that every time he comes to the plate, the fans are on their feet in Yankee Stadium. He goes on the road and in Texas, they're selling out the place because they're there to see him only because that's the only thing that that's really worth watching with the Rangers. All those things are huge pressures.

IAN O'CONNOR: To see a guy handle something like that with great dignity and grace, was one of the more impressive parts of the entire feat.

62!

MICHAEL KAY: Being the Yankees announcer for thirty-one years I've had so many great moments to witness and call and numbers 60, 61, 62 rank right up there with any one of them.

BRENDAN KUTY: They're watching for it every time he was up. Holy crap. So, I think getting the 62nd home run was such a huge weight off his shoulders. Judge did it, he walked through it.

IAN O'CONNOR: I think Aaron Judge took an incredible journey that was very, very big—the magnitude of it was off the charts—and turned it into a small moment for him at the plate. That's why he was able to get to 62.

MARTY APPEL (YANKEE HISTORIAN AND BESTSELLING AUTHOR): What a coincidence it is that the most glamorous record in American sports has been held by three Yankee right fielders, going back over a century. Yes, even with football and basketball possibly having surpassed baseball in popularity, there is no record like the majesty of the home run record that all sports fans follow.

MICHAEL KAY: Judge, without argument, had the greatest season of any player since MLB started testing for PEDs. For Judge to reach a number that had only been touched two times in AL history speaks for itself. You can make the argument that the totality of the season ranks up there with any season in baseball history when you consider the distance between Judge and the second-place finisher in all the damage numbers. And to hit over .300 in an era when sluggers are allowed to hit .220 if they hit 40 home runs, that makes it all the more remarkable.

JON HEYMAN (BASEBALL COLUMNIST FOR *NY NEWSDAY* AND *NY POST*): The most impressive thing about Judge was his performance got even better in the second half while the rest of the Yankees lineup was falling apart around him. Almost every other Yankees hitter either suffered from injury or a stark drop in performance in the second half—yet Judge kept doing his thing. And he did it even better. With other teams so obviously pitching around him, he managed to put together one of the best second halves in baseball history. He took his walks—many, many walks—but when he got a pitch to hit, he didn't miss it.

It was reminiscent of the latter-day Barry Bonds. This was comparably amazing. Only difference was, this was 100 percent legitimate.

ISIAH KINER-FALEFA: To have seen all that firsthand is special. So, for the rest of my life, I was his teammate in the greatest season of Yankee history so that's pretty awesome.

IAN O'CONNOR: I mean it was very impressive to do it in a time when it's very difficult to hit the baseball for one, never mind hitting it over the wall. Aaron Judge was doing everything, he was playing great defense, he was not only hitting home runs, but he was also hitting for average again in a very difficult time to do that.

MARTY APPEL: What Aaron Judge did in 2022 was remarkable in that it was so "Ruthian," that is, so far ahead of the everyone else. It was as though he was playing a different game. Kyle Schwarber of Philadelphia was 16 behind Judge for the major league lead, while Mike Trout of the Los Angeles Angels was 22 behind for the American League lead. And while one could say Babe Ruth was "pushed" by Lou Gehrig, always happy to one-up his teammate, and Roger Maris was certainly "pushed" by Mickey Mantle during the great M&M home run race of 1961, there was no pace horse, no teammate or league opponent who "pushed" Judge to his heights. He was Secretariat—alone in the field.

ED RANDALL: The idea was that they were going to have a modern-day Maris and Mantle with Judge and Stanton. That didn't materialize.

IAN O'CONNOR: I grew up a Yankees fan and to me, it wasn't so much the American League record it was the Yankees record. To me the storied record of what was Babe Ruth's 60, then Roger Maris's 61, that was a bigger deal to me. Frankly, I didn't really care about the American League record. The Yankees are associated as a franchise with the home run more than any other team in the sport. The Yankees made the home run a storied aspect of the game obviously, via Babe Ruth. I just saw a tremendous athlete, the best athlete in New York, probably have the best individual season I've ever seen a New York athlete have.

ED RANDALL: It's a singular achievement. The thing that warms my heart is that, if you will, he played alone out there when he hit 62 home runs. Roger Maris hit 61 home runs sixty-one years ago, how crazy is that that it was sixty-one homers and 61 years ago, then Aaron Judge hits 62. They took away from Maris because they said it was an expansion year and he played in more games. However, Maris was playing in huge ballparks at the time.

SWEENY MURTI: It's one of the most impressive seasons that you're ever going to see by a New York Yankee. Not just for the home runs. In September, he was chasing down the batting title, which would have given him a shot at the Triple Crown.

In Yankees history, there are a few iconic seasons; one of them is Roger Maris hitting 61 homers in 1961. Another is Mickey Mantle winning the Triple Crown in 1956, the last Yankee to do so. Aaron Judge in September was in position to try to take down both of those seasons at once. So that in itself was just amazing to consider.

ISIAH KINER-FALEFA: Maybe in twenty or thirty years, we're going to be doing a documentary on it or maybe a movie too. It's going to be pretty insane when they do the movie, I was the guy playing shortstop when it was going on. It's going to be a story that is passed down forever.

IAN O'CONNOR: I would even go back to Lawrence Taylor in 1986 and still say Judge's season is better than LT's and the best season I've ever seen a New York athlete have.

PETE CALDERA: It absolutely should go down as one of the most impressive individual baseball seasons we've ever seen.

#16

1968 US OPEN TENNIS

SEPTEMBER 9, 1968

ASHE MAKES TENNIS HISTORY

TIME CAPSULE

- Mayor of New York: John Lindsay
- Oscar, Best Picture: *In the Heat of the Night*
- Oscar, Best Actor: Ron Steiger, *In the Heat of the Night*
- Oscar, Best Actress: Katharine Hepburn, *Guess Who's Coming to Dinner*
- Grammy, Album of the Year: The Beatles, *Sgt. Pepper's Lonely Hearts Club Band*
- Grammy, Record of the Year: The 5th Dimension, "Up, Up and Away," *Up, Up and Away*
- President of the US: Lyndon B. Johnson
- Price of Gas: $0.34/Gallon
- Heisman Trophy: O. J. Simpson, running back, USC

PREGAME

Youth Was Served at the 1968 US Open

Arthur Ashe was an amateur tennis player in 1968. That makes his accomplishment at the US Open Tennis Championship at Forest Hills Stadium in Queens one for the record books.

This was the first year the Open was *truly* open. Professional players were now allowed to play in what had previously been an amateur-only event. And even with a murderer's row of Australian players—led by Wimbledon champion Rod Laver—in the field, Ashe emerged with the trophy.

The total purse for the event was $100,000—the most in the history of tennis at that time. As a result of his amateur status, the twenty-five-year-old Ashe was not allowed to pick up the winner's check of $14,000. That went to runner-up Tom Okker. Ashe was paid only a per diem to cover his expenses, which came to the grand total of $280. "It was twenty dollars a day for fourteen days," he said. "It used to be fifteen dollars, but New York expenses are high."

No kidding.

What made Ashe's victory memorable was certainly not the money or that he was an amateur talented enough to beat a field comprised of a who's who of his sport. Or even that he was the first American to win the event since Tony Trabert in 1955.

He was the first African American to win a Grand Slam event, which helped tennis become a more diverse game.

"The triumph is the most notable achievement made in the sport by a Negro male athlete," wrote Pulitzer Prize–winning journalist Dave Anderson in the *New York Times*.

Ashe was, essentially, the Jackie Robinson of tennis.

Robinson, of course, famously and regretfully, had to endure endless racial slurs when he broke the color barrier in baseball with the Brooklyn Dodgers in 1947. Many of his teammates had his back, notably Pee Wee Reese, and Robinson's ability to overcome racist taunts from fans and opposing players to become a Hall of Fame ballplayer made it just a bit less troublesome for those who followed his lead in baseball and for breakthrough players in other sports.

The United States was in the middle of the civil rights movement in the sixties, and it was a turbulent time in America. All you had to do was turn on the evening news and you would see a racial disturbance in different cities from coast to coast. Birmingham in 1963, New York in 1964, Watts in 1965, Chicago in 1966, seven cities in 1967—including Detroit, Newark, Atlanta, Cincinnati, and Tampa. Then on the night Dr. Martin Luther King Jr. was assassinated in Memphis, on April 4, 1968, it was reported that riots broke out in more than a hundred cities around the country.

"I'm no Negro militant, no crusader," Ashe told the *New York Times*. "I want to do something for my race, but I figure I can do it best by example, by showing Negro boys the way. That's what Jackie Robinson and Willie Mays have done."

The *Times* reported in January 1968 that Dr. King wrote Ashe a letter of encouragement before he made his first political speech at a church in Washington, D.C. "Your eminence in the world of sports and athletics gives you an added measure of authority and responsibility. It is heartening indeed when you bring these attributes to the movement."

Five months after King was assassinated, Ashe enjoyed the signature moment of his career. Consider the first paragraph from the Associated Press story reporting on Ashe's victory over Okker: "Arthur Ashe Jr., a scrawny Negro amateur once barred from playing on the courts of his native Richmond, Virginia, reached the pinnacle of tennis yesterday when he won a slam-bang, scoot and scramble duel from young Tom Okker of the Netherlands for the US Open championship."

Ashe was discriminated against growing up, but rose above the turbulence with dignity and grace. As Filip Bondy, who covered tennis for the *New York Daily News*, wrote:

> There were no blacks playing tennis or virtually no blacks playing tennis back then. Times have changed, you do see people of color, men and women of color out on these courts. It's a very international and a very diverse ethnic presentation when you go to a tennis tournament. But back then that was not the case, it was more like golf, frankly. And here comes this kid almost, this young man, out of nowhere and an amateur. The tennis world was changing so rapidly, this tournament had just become an open.
>
> But beyond that, Ashe also represented a whole new culture that was coming around. And, he was embraced, he did not face the kind of opposition that say Jackie Robinson faced when he broke the color barrier. I don't know of any opposition to his playing or anything like that. And he was a well-spoken man and actually had some conservative views. So, he was deemed, quote, safe in many ways. I don't want to compare his breakthrough to Jackie Robinson in terms of the racial issue. But at the same time, it was a white sport, and here comes a black player out of nowhere. And so, in that way, it is it was a major pioneering effort and, and others followed. So, he was an inspiration. I don't want to say that he wasn't.

Ashe was known for his calm demeanor, but had fire on the court that made him a true champion. "Arthur is 6-1 ½, weighs 147 pounds and moves like a motorized swizzle stick," legendary *Boston Globe* tennis writer Bud Collins wrote at the 1968 Open. "He can run and hit for hours."

Even so, his experiences off the court shaped him as an adult and how he viewed the world.

"I feel more at ease in Europe that I do here. And this is the country I live in," he said at that US Open, then speaking about his plans to turn pro early in 1969. "I know what's going to happen in February. There will be places here in New York where I can't rent an apartment—even if I had a million dollars."

Two weeks before the US Open, Ashe defeated Bob Lutz in Boston for the National Amateur Title. By the time he defeated Okker, he had won 26 consecutive matches.

Ashe came into the US Open red-hot. He was seeded fifth in the field because of an incredibly strong group of Australians led by top seed Rod Laver followed by Tony Roche, Ken Rosewall, and John Newcombe. If Ashe was going to win the tournament, he was likely going to have to beat at least two—and possibly three—of them. As the highest-seeded American, he was also carrying the banner of his country in its national open.

Ashe had a bye into the second round and made quick work of fellow American Frank Parker, followed by Paul Hutchins of Great Britain, in straight sets. He lost a total of just 15 games in the six sets as he cruised into the fourth round against No. 14 seed Roy Emerson. Of the eight players in Ashe's part of the bracket, Emerson was the only other one seeded, and was going to present his first real test.

Ashe initially struggled, but tennis is a game of endurance and he was able to advance, eliminating Emerson 6–4, 9–7, 6–2 to reach the quarterfinals. He found the field had opened up like traffic never does on the Long Island Expressway. It may have required a double take, but the top two seeds were missing. Laver, the reigning Wimbledon champion and unquestioned best player in the world, was stunned by No. 16 seed Cliff Drysdale in five sets. Laver was ousted by losing the last two sets 6–1, 6–1.

"Rod never played well, but I think I contributed to that," said Drysdale, who was facing Laver for the first time.

The combination of Laver's sore left wrist—he was a lefty—and Drysdale's two-handed backhand and savvy play set him up to play Ashe. American Pancho Gonzales pulled off the other big upset in the fourth round, eliminating No. 2 seeded Roche in straight sets. Ashe couldn't have planned this better if tournament officials had let him make up the draw.

Instead of having to go through Laver in the quarters, he was now facing Drysdale, a far less intimidating opponent. "He wins more garbage points than anyone I know," Ashe said before the match. "He gets a lot of points on miss-hits, drop shots and half volleys. He's never hit a hard volley in his life."

In the late sixties, that qualified as trash talk. The sports world was still four months away from Joe Namath's guarantee. Ashe wasn't necessarily being critical of Drysdale, who just played a different game than the hard hitters. "The trouble is you don't know where the ball is going," Ashe said. "It's like a pitcher facing a batter. He never knows when the ball might be hit down his throat."

Along with the racial aspect, there was a political backdrop to the Ashe-Drysdale match. Drysdale's South African heritage was not lost on Ashe. South Africa had a system of apartheid, which denied basic human rights—as well as the right for blacks to vote. "Sure, it entered my mind that Cliff is from South Africa," Ashe said. "I couldn't help but think of it."

Ashe took care of Drysdale . . . but barely. He dropped the first set, 8–10, but then won the next three 6–3, 9–7, 6–4. "The amazing thing is I feel I've been playing badly and still winning. That's something," Ashe said. "What would happen if I played as well as I think I should? I guess that proves that I've improved in the last year."

He now awaited the winner of Newcombe, the No. 4 seed, vs. Clark Graebner of the US, the No. 7 seed. Ashe and Graebner were buddies. Ashe left little doubt where his heart was at for that match. "I hope Clark makes it," he said. "I want Clark because that will mean the United States will be guaranteed one man in the final—him or me. That's really important to the powers that be. An all-foreign final isn't much box office."

Ashe got his wish. Graebner upset Newcombe 5–7, 11–9, 6–1, 6–4 to set up an all-USA semifinal, which also continued the trend of amateurs dominating the pros in the tournament.

In the Ashe-Graebner semis, the first set went to Graebner, 6–4, but then Ashe stormed back to win the last three 8–6, 7–5, 6–2. "Arthur's serve was just too strong," Graeber said.

Indeed, as it had been measured at 115 mph.

On the other side of the bracket, it was the No. 8 seed Okker against the No. 3 seed Rosewall. Once Laver was eliminated, Ashe picked Rosewall to win the tournament.

He was wrong, as Rosewall didn't even make it to the finals. Okker took care of him 8–6, 4–6, 6–8, 6–1, setting up an unlikely final between the No. 5–seeded Ashe and the No. 8 seeded Okker. Facing Okker was a better matchup for Ashe than the more experienced and tournament-tested Rosewall. Both players were on a roll, so it had the look of a match that would go the five-set distance.

The greats of the game lined up in different corners picking a winner.

"I lose only to the champion—I have to pick Okker," Rosewall said. "He's not only fast but he is capable of making some of the most fantastic shots I have ever seen."

Even Bill Talbert, the former US Davis Cup captain, lined up on Okker's side. "Okker's all-around strength will beat Arthur," he said. "It's true that Ashe serves harder, but Okker is quicker and has more shots."

But Gonzalez, a forty-year-old grandfather who was a tough out for Okker in the quarters, sided with Ashe in the final. "I think I would have to pick Ashe because of his powerful service," he said. "Ashe serves as hard as any man in tennis. He has too much power for Okker."

After reaching the semifinals at Wimbledon and winning the US Amateur, Ashe was now in position to win the US Open and emerge as one of the greats in the game. Rarified air in the sports world for an Army lieutenant.

ARTHUR ASHE POSTS HISTORIC US OPEN VICTORY

BY PETER BOTTE

Barely two decades after Jackie Robinson broke baseball's color barrier in Brooklyn, Arthur Ashe became the first African American male to win tennis' US Open in Queens on September 9, 1968.

In the first year the Open permitted professional players to participate, the amateur Ashe posted a five-set victory over Tom Okker of the Netherlands at Forest Hills Stadium to earn the first of his three career Grand Slam titles.

"Arthur Ashe was a class act, on and off the court. He handled all the adversity that crossed his path with incredible grace and dignity," said tennis journalist Ann Liguori. "The racism that Ashe had to endure, growing up in segregated Richmond, Virginia, and throughout his career, would have derailed most."

"But Ashe carried the hopes and dreams of African Americans, in a white person's world, becoming the first Black male to win the US Open in 1968 and the only Black man to win the Wimbledon, US Open, and Australian Open titles."

The twenty-five-year-old Ashe used 25 aces in his five-set victory over Okker, including a 14–12 decision in the opening set.

Due to his amateur status before turning pro the following year, however, Ashe was ineligible to accept the US Open first prize winnings, instead receiving just his daily expenses for his historic victory.

The former West Point lieutenant further made his mark later in his career and in retirement through various humanitarian efforts, including working to educate others about HIV and AIDS. He was believed to have contracted HIV from a blood transfusion during heart bypass surgery in 1983 and he died from AIDS-related pneumonia at forty-nine in 1993.

"Ashe's legacy as a civil rights activist is as important, if not more important, than his illustrious tennis career," Liguori added. "He remains one of the most important figures in sports history and I was honored to interview him for my *Sports Interview* cable series, in which I spent an hour talking to him about his career, his life, his legacy, and important topics of the day in 1990, just a few years before his death.

"The interview took place at the 21 Club in midtown Manhattan and I remember how very honest, scholarly and classy Ashe was. It's the interview I cherish most, to this day."

POSTGAME

Ashe Opened Up the US Open

JAMES BLAKE (FOMER TENNIS CHAMPION AND OLYMPIAN): The importance of Arthur Ashe winning the US Open was not only symbolic in winning what is supposed to be the most open tournament possible. Before him, it had not been truly open. The opportunities for African Americans was not the same and they were nonexistent in the world of tennis. He made it possible and was inspirational for generations to follow as there was recognition for the hurdles (often seemingly insurmountable) that he was forced to clear to achieve this goal. It made so many feel like there was hope. That opened the door to a sport that seemed to be closed before he accomplished what he accomplished and that led to numerous people entering the sport that may never have been involved, including myself.

FILIP BONDY (*NY DAILY NEWS* COLUMNIST): Professionals had been banished from the Open. And now professionals were welcome to play for the national title. They were expected to win easily. It is like when the US hockey team won the Olympics with a bunch of amateurs in 1980. Ashe was embraced at the time.

MARK CANNIZZARO (*NY POST* COLUMNIST): This obviously was a powerful time in our society and what Ashe did was eye-opening. Even in the face of the racism, Ashe always did everything with such grace, as if not letting the challenges he had in front of him bother him at all.

Arthur Ashe the Man

JAMES BLAKE: Arthur's efforts off the court was a shining example of what could be done with a voice thanks to success on the court. He was committed to using his voice in any situation he was in to help others that were in more trying situations. When he was on top of the world as the Wimbledon champion, he fought to end apartheid. But even when he was struggling and stricken with HIV/AIDS he did all he could to help others that had the same fate and were alone and underfunded. What he did off the court is the biggest reason he is a legend in my opinion. He used his voice and made a lasting difference to help the world. That is what every athlete, in my opinion, should strive for.

FILIP BONDY: Just his presence first as an athlete playing tennis in a very white sport opened a lot of eyes and a lot of opportunity for others. But what he did then was he became something of a spokesperson and worked with all sorts of organizations. He was, as I mentioned before, not a radical, he was not like Muhammad Ali, he was accepted by the white establishment with much more open arms than a Muhammad Ali was at the same time, in the same era.

MARK CANNIZZARO: Ashe was so graceful as a man and as an athlete, and you could not help but respect him. I personally found him inspiring not only because I was a tennis junkie growing up but because of the way he conducted himself with such grace in the face of adversity.

17

1983 STANLEY CUP FINALS: NEW YORK ISLANDERS vs. EDMONTON OILERS, GAME 4

MAY 17, 1983

FOUR IN A ROW!

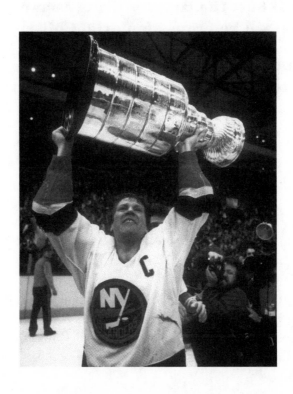

TIME CAPSULE

- Mayor of New York: Ed Koch
- Oscar, Best Picture: *Gandhi*
- Oscar, Best Actor: Ben Kingsley, *Gandhi*
- Oscar Best Actress: Meryl Streep, *Sophie's Choice*
- Grammy, Album of the Year: Toto, *Toto IV*
- Grammy, Record of the Year: Toto, "Rosanna," *Toto IV*
- President of the US: Ronald Reagan
- Price of Gas: $1.16/Gallon
- Heisman Trophy: Mike Rozier, running back, Nebraska

PREGAME

Home is where the heart is.

In the 1980s, the Heart of Long Island was the Nassau Veterans Memorial Coliseum.

The home address for the Stanley Cup from 1980 to 1983 was 1255 Hempstead Turnpike in Uniondale, New York.

The Islanders were a family on and off the ice. Their extended family were the people of Long Island that stretched from the Queens border to the tip of the Hamptons.

"We were the loudest of any building, if we were down, they'd be just cheering us on. But more than anything else, they just brought us into their family." Bobby Nystrom said about Islanders fans. "We would be out at a restaurant they'd buy you dinner. We played softball together to raise money for youth hockey. I bet I knew 25 percent of the crowd. I'd see them walking in and it was like, Oh, there's Jerry, there's Phyllis, it was just such a close relationship with the fans. And you know, there was no mystique about us. The fact is that we are mostly country boys and Long

Island just loved us. And we love Long Island back because we had similar personalities. It was great."

"When we first got to Long Island, the team was very young," said Denis Potvin. "There was never a time when any of us who were single guys coming into Long Island, and New York, a big expansive place, were ever left alone. There was always a family willing to have us over for any kind of holiday, the fans would have us as part of their family gathering. To me, that was huge in getting our team close to the fan base."

"The Islanders were Long Island. We used to refer to it as hockey's Fantasy Island," said Jiggs McDonald, their play-by-play announcer during the eighties. "That was their identity. However, if you grew up an Islanders fan, if you've been around that team since their inception in '72, then you knew just how tough things were. Their record the first year was horrendous. The number of players they lost to the World Hockey Association (WHA) was devastating. [The amount of] goals scored against them was inconceivable. Any fan had to be a very proud and happy individual as the team grew into a success."

Jiggs went on to say, "The relationship with the fans in the confines of the Coliseum was one thing. Fans had access to the players and the practices. The players had to come out of the Coliseum after games. They weren't able to sneak out get in their cars and drive up the tunnel and disappear. They had to come out that door and walk through a maze of people to get to their vehicles. Also, the team frequented three favorite watering holes where the fans had access to them. There wasn't the social media and the selfies with cell phones, the way there is today. It was just a very, very special time."

"You know everyone mocked the fact that we went down Hempstead Turnpike when we won the first Cup, Bobby Nystrom said. "To us, it was the greatest thrill to see those fans there. They were throwing us beers into the back of trucks. I mean, it was just a really, really close relationship."

The Islanders family started with their expansion birth in 1972. They were the first hockey team in the tri-state area to challenge the stranglehold the Rangers had in New York, as one of the original six National Hockey League teams. The NHL had just a half a dozen teams for a quarter of a century, between 1942 and 1967. The Original Six—or *Six Équipes* in French—were the New York Rangers, Boston Bruins, Chicago Black Hawks, Detroit Red Wings, and Montreal Canadians.

The Rangers franchise has been playing in New York since 1926. They had won their last Stanley Cup in 1940. The "1940" chant would become a favorite of Islanders fans to get under the skin of their rivals. Rangers fans would retaliate with the chant of "Potvin Sucks." I gotta say, from an Islanders fans standpoint, factually speaking, it had been 1940 since the Rangers hoisted the Stanley Cup, and Denis was a pretty darn good player. He was the very first pick in the 1973 draft. Point to Islanders fans, but I digress.

"Right from day one, the 'Potvin Sucks' chant was a little scary, because it seemed to be an angry chant," said Potvin. "Of course, what led to it, is the fact that after the Rangers beat us in '79, we turned around, played the Rangers in each of the next four years and beat them in the playoffs and then went on to win a Cup. So, I think that had a lot to do with the chant getting angrier and angrier. Then as time went on it just kept going. People sometimes would say, 'Well, I'm not sure who Potvin is but the chat is great.' And they kept it going." (A quick side note from the Rangers perspective: the "Potvin Sucks" chat emanated from a questionable hit by Potvin on February 25, 1979, where he sent Ulf Nilsson violently into the boards, leaving him injured and impacted his career.)

It was a meager start for the Islanders, who set a record for losses and goals allowed in their inaugural season. Late in that season, the franchise brought up Bobby Nystrom. Losing lead to winning. The Hall of Fame brain trust of general manager Bill Torrey and head coach Al Arbour added five Hall of Famers through the draft to build the dynasty.

In the 1972 expansion draft, they added Billy Smith, who was the goalie for the four championships. In 1974 they drafted Clark Gillies in the first round and added Bryan Trottier in the second. The previous year, they had selected Denis Potvin with the first overall pick and, as we established earlier, he certainly "didn't suck!" Then, in 1977, the braintrust brought in Mike Bossy with the 15th overall pick. That is five homegrown Hall of Famers selected and nurtured by Torrey and Arbour. The hockey world would soon find out that the nucleus of a second proud franchise was going to inhabit the New York market. And the Islanders trajectory was like a rocket ship: straight up and fast!

Jiggs McDonald explains the key to their quick rise from expansion to champion:

The depth of their roster was key. Everybody bought into the program, everybody. There was no backbiting. Guys accepted their roles and played their roles. There was nobody that I know of complaining about ice time or who they were playing with. I'm not going to say it was a big happy family. I'm sure there were some guys that thought they should be doing other things but didn't get the opportunity. Al Arbor just had a way of selling each individual on what their role was and what the responsibilities were and the guys accepted it. I think it comes right down to discipline, knowing what your job is, and going out and doing it.

The Islanders went from a paltry 12 wins in their first year and added seven in year two to 19. Then took a big step forward in year three with 33 wins and another leap to 42 the next season. Then another jump to 47, then 48, and finally finished the 1978–79 season with an impressive 51 wins. It took seven years to improve their total by an incredible 39 wins. That was enough to go from the worst record in the NHL in their expansion season to leading the NHL with 116 points. The Islanders were ready to win . . . and win . . . and win . . . and win.

And that is exactly what happened.

Just like that, a dynasty was born.

STANLEY CUP #1: 1979–80 ISLANDERS (39–28–13)

Starting in the 1979–80 season, the Islanders owned the NHL for four straight seasons. This had been building for years, but if you had to pick a single date, it may be fair to say that the dynasty began on May 24, 1980. That evening, Bobby Nystrom scored an overtime goal to give the Islanders their first Stanley Cup.

It only took the Islanders eight seasons to go from an expansion team to Cup champions. They topped the 100-point mark in only their fourth year in existence. They went over the century mark for four straight seasons, and then in 1979–80 dipped below the 100-point mark, accumulating 91. Before the playoffs started, they acquired what would turn out to be the missing piece to their championship run, and a man who is still with the Islanders today as a part of their broadcast team: Butch Goring. Butch went from the Kings of LA to become a king in Long Island. It was not easy for Bill Torrey to make the deal at the time. He had to give up fan favorites Dave Lewis and Billy Harris. Corralling Goring from the Kings was a tough call, but one that unlocked a dynasty.

"When we got Butch, that's what really enabled us to win the Stanley Cup." Bobby Nystrom said. "He was an absolutely fantastic second line centerman, and also just an awesome penalty killer. And he was a calming factor on the bench, I used to get frustrated and come in, slammed my stick, and break it. And he'd be rubbing my back, and say, don't worry about it focus on the next shift and the next shift. So, he was a great, great part of the Islanders and helping us win the Stanley Cup."

Goring added some offensive firepower to the Islanders second line. Butch scored 19 points in 21 playoff games, and with the spark that Butch added to the team they soared through the first two rounds of the playoffs, disposing of his former team from LA, in the first round. It was off to Boston to take on the Big Bad Bruins next in the semifinals.

"Clark and I were roommates and we're just watching the sports, on the news, in a Boston hotel room and the sportscaster says, 'The Islanders play the Bruins tomorrow night, and the Islanders are gonna lose in five games, because they're going to be intimidated by the Boston Bruins,'" Nystrom recalls. "So, I had a little bit of a fit and I said, 'Clarky, that's nonsense.' I said, 'we're gonna go after these guys. I say you take [Terry] O'Reilly. I'll take [John] Wensink,' and that's exactly what we did. Thank God I didn't lose the fight (laughing). But Clark and I set the tone there. Needless to say, Clark fought O'Reilly, I think, three times. But that's exactly what transpired. We were both pissed off."

"Of course, to win the first Cup they had to beat Boston, and Clark Gillies had to beat up Terry O'Reilly at least twice, maybe three times," said Stan Fischler. "Gillies said that the Cup wasn't satisfying to him, because he had to do what he didn't like to do and that is beat guys up. And of course, Terry O'Reilly was the heavyweight champ of the Bruins, and Clark had to take care of him and many of the guys will say they never would have beaten the Bruins, if it wasn't for Gillies. Gillies said that the second Cup where they beat Minnesota, he found that very satisfying, because it was clean hockey. Which was interesting. Very interesting indeed."

Before we get to the second Cup, the Islanders still needed to get their first. They did beat—and beat up—the Bruins in five tough games behind the leadership of Nystrom and Gillies. That set up a series with the high-flying Sabres, with a berth in their first Stanley Cup Finals on the line. But it wouldn't be easy, as Buffalo had won the Prince of Wales Trophy with the best record in the conference. The Islanders, eyeing their first Stanley Cup Finals berth, took Game 1, 4–1. In Game 2, on May Day, Nystrom netted the game-winning goal in double overtime to give the Islanders a second straight road win and a two-games-to-none lead in the series. In Game 3, the Islanders blew out Buffalo 7–4 to take a commanding three-games-to-none lead.

The Sabres would not give up that easily, and took the next two games (7–4 in Game 4 and 2–0 in Game 5), but Game 6 would be played on Long Island; a loss would have meant heading back to Western New York for a Game 7 in Buffalo. The Isles fell behind 2–0, but that wasn't enough to deter them from their date with destiny. They went on to score the next five goals, on their way to a 5–2 victory, setting off a celebration that nearly tore the roof off the Nassau Coliseum, and punching their very first ticket to the Finals. It took eight seasons, but the Islanders were heading to the Stanley Cup Finals.

After disposing of the second-best team in the NHL, they faced the Philadelphia Flyers, who had the best record in the league. A daunting task, but one that the young Islanders relished.

"Do you believe in miracles?" Al Michaels famously asked as the clock ran out on the Russians in the Olympics, a little less than three months earlier. The Americans went on to win the gold medal by defeating Finland, and the "Miracle on Ice" was born. It was then that Islanders fans thought "We do believe in miracles again" after they inked Olympic hero Ken Morrow.

Morrow brought his championship pedigree to the young franchise. Could a miracle happen twice in a row? Could Morrow become the first player to win a gold medal and a Stanley Cup in the same year? Nystrom said, Morrow, a defenseman, wasn't the goal scorer that Mike Bossy, Brian Trottier, and Clark Gillies were, but he was a champion who scored key goals when his team needed them the most. "He had quite a year. He was very quiet and unassuming. He added a whole dimension to the team." The game-winning goal for their fourth straight Stanley Cup was scored by none other than Ken Morrow—but we are getting way ahead of ourselves. Now it was the Philadelphia Flyers who stood in the way of Ken Morrow and his place alone in the history books.

As the Islanders were newbies, the Broad Street Bullies were making their fourth trip to the Finals. The had won back-to-back championships in 1974 and '75, followed by Montreal winning four straight Cups. Only two teams had won the Cup in six seasons, but neither had the golden touch of a gold medal winner on their side.

The moment was never too big for this Isles team. As the pressure built, the team got better. There were four blowout games, and two games that went into overtime. The Islanders win in Game 1 was an indication of how they played when the pressure was at its height. The game was tied at three going into overtime, where Denis Potvin beat Pete Peeters at the 4:07 mark of overtime, to give New York a 4–3 win and notch the franchise's first Cup Finals victory. (Fun Fact: Denis Potvin became the first player to win a game for his team in the Stanley Cup Finals on a power play goal in overtime.)

Games 2 through 5 were all won by the home team in convincing fashion. Philly won Game 2 in a laugher, 8–3. The series went back to Uniondale, and the advantage went to the Islanders, who won both games in convincing fashion—6–2 and 5–2—taking a commanding 3–1 series lead. The Flyers held serve in their building with a 6–3 win, cutting into the Isles lead. It was on to Game 6 at the Coliseum. The Islanders got goals from the usual suspects Denis Potvin, Duane Sutter, Mike Bossy, and Bobby Nystrom during regulation, and, don't you know it, the game went into overtime once again, tied at four apiece. New York needed a goal for a championship and Philadelphia needed a goal to send the series back to the Spectrum for a winner-take-all Game 7.

That is where John Tonelli found Bobby Nystrom with a perfect pass and Nystrom unknotted it with a deflection and inked their names in New York sports folklore forever, securing the first ever Stanley Cup for the Islanders, with his goal at the lucky 7:11 mark of overtime. Here's how it sounded on CBC:

> Henning pass right on the stick of Tonelli, coming in with Nystrom, Tonelli to Nystrom, Bob Nystrom scores the goal, The Islanders win the Stanley Cup!

It was his fourth overtime goal, which was second only to Rocket Richard. The Coliseum exploded. Trottier was voted the playoffs' Most Valuable Player, and Queen's "We are the Champions" blared on the loudspeakers.

"You know, it's so funny, every time there was an overtime, I always had a feeling that I could score the goal," Nystrom said when asked about the Cup-winning goal. "And that whole mindset came from something that Al Arbour said to all of us. He said, 'Never fear losing, love winning. If you can look in the mirror and say that you did your best, then that's fine, but you just got to improve.' The thing that he taught to us, which I still carry with me today is, 'Who would you rather be, the guy that's on his heels, backing up, backing up, being afraid that he's gonna get scored on or make a mistake? Wouldn't you want to be the guy that's on his toes and skating hard and going at it and attacking, attacking, and knowing he's going to score the winning goal?' I mean, that was that was the best lesson I ever got from Al and I got plenty of them."

"Well, the goal that won the Islanders their first Cup had some very interesting elements to it," said hockey maven Stan Fischler. "First off, the guy who was supposed to be sent to the "Banana Line," Wayne Merrick, was hurt [John Tonelli, Wayne Merrick, and Bob Nystrom made up the Banana Line which was named that because they wore yellow jerseys during practice]. Arbour replaced Wayne Merrick with Lorne Henning, who was basically a penalty killer and the fourth forward. Henning was the guy who set up Tonelli who then of course passed it to Nystrom. The interesting thing on that play was that Tonelli was on his wrong wing. He was on the right side; he should have been on the left. And Nystrom was on the left side, he should have been on the right so it was like a comedy of errors. And the funny thing is that Nystrom really did not shoot the puck. He deflected it. He had his stick in a certain way that there was no way Pete Peeters could stop it, it was just a phenomenal play. But Henning, who was there instead of Merrick, Tonelli on the wrong wing. Nystrom on the wrong wing, but of course they won the Cup with that play."

Wrong wing, right wing, it worked and the Islanders had their first Stanley Cup! The Islanders had supplanted the Montreal Canadiens as champions. And, by the way, the Rangers still hadn't won a Cup since 1940. The hockey world—and all of New York—was focused on Long Island and the newly crowned champs.

Nystrom explains how the Islanders only took eight seasons to go from an expansion team to a dynasty, "I'll give you two words, Al Arbour. Wait, I'll give you four words, Al Arbour and Bill Torrey. If you look back at Al's resume, look at how many Cups he won. Every time he went somewhere, for some reason they won the Stanley Cup. Bill and Al worked so closely together because it's not necessarily all about talent. It's about guys that get along. You know, we had guys come into the team and if the players didn't really like them, there would be evidence on the ice. Bill and Al knew that there was something wrong, and he would get rid of that person. So, we weaned or filtered guys that were hotshots and they were the ones that executed the deal, the transfer, or the trade because they could see it. And they had an eye for talent and character."

STANLEY CUP #2: 1980–81 ISLANDERS (48-18-14)

Now that the Islanders had one Stanley Cup under their belt, it was time to double up. They cruised through the regular season by winning the Patrick Division, amassing 110 points. Mike Bossy led the team in points and goals, becoming only the second player in NHL history to score 50 goals in 50 games. Bossy led the team in goals with 68, Bryan Trottier led the team in assists (with 72), and Denis Potvin led the team as their captain. If they were going to become a dynasty, they would need to rely on those three players along with their coach, Al Arbour, and the great goaltender, Billy Smith, who would have to stand on his head in the playoffs.

The Islanders had served notice the season before—and during the regular season—that they were here to stay and weren't a one-hit wonder. Their barnstorming of the 1981 playoffs served notice that they were here to dominate. They more than doubled their opponents' scoring in the playoffs with 97 goals while giving up only 48, and set a playoff record with 31 power-play goals. Bryan Trottier set a record for longest point scoring streak, from April 8 to May 21 in 1981, by scoring 11 goals and adding 18 assists in 18 straight playoff games.

"Obviously it reflects on the linemates I had, our power play, and the team in general," said Trottier, when asked about his playoff streak. "We just had an overall feeling and purpose that all of us should contribute, and everybody wanted to contribute, and no one more than I did. So, for me to be able to put that string of games together where all of a sudden it's eighteen games. Wow, that's kind of cool.

"I think eighteen straight games in one playoff season, just reflects probably the most on Mike Bossy. Then it reflects on the power play because it was just red hot in the playoffs. I think when you're looking at Clark Gillies, Bobby Nystrom, Bob Bourne, and Butch Goring—they go out there, they put the fear into everybody, they put people on their heels, and all of a sudden, we come out there with a second wave of attack and boom. Things happened offensively, and it was really kind of fun to be able to contribute to that success and put that string of games together."

The Islanders took their second Cup by blowing out the Minnesota North Stars in four of the five games by scores of 6–3 in Games 1 and 2, 7–5 in Game 3, and then winning their second straight Stanley Cup in dominant fashion in the clinching game, 5–1. Bossy finished with a playoff record 35 points.

Trottier set a record by scoring a point in all 18 playoff games, which was a part of his record 27 straight playoff games with a point from 1979–80 through 1981–82. Potvin set a record for defenseman by adding 25 points. But it was Butch Goring—the key acquisition from the season before—who was named the MVP of the playoffs, taking home the Conn Smythe Trophy. The young franchise had served notice the Stanley Cup would go through Long Island for the foreseeable future.

STANLEY CUP #3: 1981–82 ISLANDERS (54–16–10)

Three's a charm, but it wouldn't be easy to gather their third straight Cup. Led by Mike Bossy—who paced the team in goals (64), assists (83), and points (147)—the Isles won the Patrick Division, as well as the Prince of Wales Conference, winning 54 games en route to 118 regular season points. Their offense and defense were both elite, as they finished second in goals and second in points allowed in the NHL. They started the playoffs by crushing the Penguins, outscoring them by a football score of 15–3 in the first two games. Pittsburgh wasn't going to go quietly, as Jiggs McDonald explains.

> You knew that the Islanders were vulnerable, they could be beaten, and Pittsburgh almost had them. When you go back to Cup number three, in that opening round, they breezed through Pittsburgh. It was the best-of-five series, they won the first two home games, and went to Pittsburgh. They lost Game 3 on a Saturday night. Maybe they were overconfident; maybe not.
>
> The team is walking across the street from the hotel to the arena. Everybody has their overnight bag with him because they we're going back to New York after the game. There's no question they were going to beat Pittsburgh three straight games. They lost. Now they have to go back to the hotel and hope they get their rooms back to stay over.
>
> They got beat again on the Sunday night in Game 4. They were down by a couple of goals in the third period in Game 5. That I think was the huge kick in the butt. I mean they could have been finished after two Cups. After the Islanders breezed through the first two games at home, Pittsburgh seemed to have their number. It was a huge message to the team, 'Yeah, we're not invincible.'

Game 5 was won with a John Tonelli goal in overtime, and the Islanders escaped and advanced!

"When they managed to beat Pittsburgh, there was no looking back," Jiggs continued to say. "I don't think they took the foot off the pedal from there on until they were eliminated by Edmonton."

But before we jump ahead to the fourth Stanley Cup and the drive for five that was stopped by Edmonton, the Islanders first needed to lift their third straight Cup. Next up after Pittsburgh was the hated rivals from "the city that never sleeps." The Rangers were not going to be intimidated, and took Game 1 by a score of 5–4. The Blueshirts weren't going to go easily. That was the Islanders first home loss of the year, and it came in April no less. They won Game 2 at home (7–2), but Game 3 went into overtime. In the NHL playoffs, a bad bounce of the puck and the Islanders would have been down two games to one, but Bryan Trottier wouldn't have any of it, scoring the game winner at the 3:00 mark of the first overtime with the assist going to Kenny Morrow. The Islanders knocked the Rangers out of the playoffs in six games at Madison Square Garden by a score of 5–3, and set up the Wales Conference finals against the Nordiques. By this time, they had regained home ice dominance, winning the first two games easily, taking Game 1, 4–1 and Game 2, 5–2. Game 3 was played north of the boarder, and this time it took an overtime goal by Wayne Merrick to seal the victory. The Isles had a commanding three-games-to-none lead in the series. They went on to sweep Quebec and that brought on the second straight team from Canada, Vancouver.

Game 1 was another overtime thriller, and as he did all season, Mike Bossy led the Islanders. The Canucks looked to serve notice that they wouldn't be a pushover in the Stanley Cup Finals. They took the lead with seven minutes to play, and that is when Bossy tied it up with a heads-up play to force overtime. As we know by now, that is where the Islanders were at their best. Mike showed Vancouver who was "Boss" by winning the game at the 19:58 mark of the first overtime, completing the hat trick and sending a dagger into the hearts of the team from the Pacific Northwest. The Islanders went on to sweep the series for their third straight Stanley Cup championship. Mike Bossy was awarded the Conn Smythe Trophy. Once again, Lord Stanley's Cup called Long Island home!

Jiggs McDonald pulls back the curtain on what made the Islanders so good in the playoffs.

Discipline extended to off ice conditioning as well as accepting on ice roles. I don't know that there was another team in the league that stretched the way the Islanders did before games. There were three different occasions on which body fat and conditioning were measured. The one in March was the most important. You probably had a week to two weeks if you weren't where they wanted you to be, to get there before the playoffs started. It came from the top down from Torrey and Arbour down to the trainer. Some of the players didn't like it, but they did it and that's what I mean when I say discipline.

They were a fun group of guys to be around. They enjoyed the local bars, Doctor Generosity's, the Salty Dog. They were all over the place, but on the first of March, everything came to a to a halt. There were no team functions. There were very, very few times that you saw anybody postgame anywhere from March on. It was all geared to the start of the playoffs and winning. Geared to going as far as you could possibly go.

STANLEY CUP #4: 1983 ISLANDERS (42–26–12)

Fourscore and many years ago, the New York Islanders set out on the 1982–83 season with their eyes firmly set on winning their fourth straight Stanley Cup. They did show signs of vulnerability, winning only 42 games and dipping under the magic 100-point mark with 96. They scored just 302 goals, which was good for 15th out of the 21 teams in the NHL. They finished second in the Patrick Division and fourth in the Prince of Wales Conference. There was a ton of hardware added that season, with Billy Smith winning the Conn Smythe Trophy (and MVP of the playoffs), the architect Bill Torrey scooping up the Lester Patrick Trophy, and Mike Bossy won the Lady Byng Memorial Trophy. Now there was just one more little piece of hardware for them to collectively hoist up: the Stanley Cup.

Up first in the playoffs were the pesky Washington Capitals. The Caps finished the regular season just two points behind New York, but this was the playoffs and the Islanders dispensed of them in four games, with the 3–1 series win. That was their incredible thirteenth straight playoff series win! Then they toppled the hated Rangers, four games to two, for their fourteenth consecutive playoff series win. The Bruins topped the NHL with 110 points and were next on the Isles dance card. But, again, it was the playoffs, and the Islanders beat them with relative ease, four games to two, for their fifteenth playoff series victory. No other NHL team had won fifteen straight playoff series. Only the "Great One," Wayne Gretzky and the Edmonton Oilers stood in their way.

Edmonton was attempting to win their first ever Cup. If the Islanders were going to win their sweet sixteenth straight playoff series and their fourth straight Cup, they had a great team in front of them. Edmonton posted the second-best record in the regular NHL season and were the only team to surpass 350 goals, scoring an incredible 424. Gretzky scored 71 goals and had 125 assists on the season, winning his fourth Hart Trophy. Edmonton had just joined the NHL during the 1979 NHL-WHA merger just four years before. The World Hockey Association upstarts had stunned the NHL with their early success, and would continue to do so after this season. They put out on the ice along with Gretzky the likes of Mark Messier, Jari Kurri, Paul Coffey, Glenn Anderson, and between the pipes was the duo of Andy Moog and Grant Fuhr. They were young, hungry, and supremely talented and swept their way through the playoffs, with a 11–1 mark. The Islanders countered by sending out five future hockey Hall of Famers: Mike Bossy, Denis Potvin, Billy Smith, Bryan Trottier, and Clark Gillies. They were led by Hall of Fame coach Al Arbour and Hall of Fame general manager Bill Torrey. That was the backdrop for the Stanley Cup Finals.

The first three games were won by the Islanders behind the goaltending of Billy Smith, who pitched a shutout in Game 1, 2–0, stonewalling Gretzky and company with 35 saves. His suburb goaltending extended the rest of the series, as the Isles won Game 2 (6–3) and Game 3 (5–1) with relative ease. Great teams stand up to great challenges. The Islanders did what seems impossible in retrospect and held the high-powered Oilers to six total goals in the Finals. They shut out the Great One altogether. The trade for Butch Goring was on full display with his defensive know-how. Billy Smith stood on his head the entire series. Tasting a fourth Cup, the Islanders came out flying in the first period of Game 4 with goals by Bryan Trottier, John Tonelli, and Mike Bossy. They were up 3–0 and cruising, but the Oilers bounced back with two goals in the second period. That is when the gold-medal winner put the game and Stanley Cup out of reach with an unassisted goal at the 18:51 mark of the third period, and the rest is history. Once again, Queen's classic "We Are the Champions" blared on the loudspeakers. The Islanders were indeed elite.

They had won sixteen straight playoff series. They won the hearts and minds of all Long Islanders and the home of the Stanley Cup for the fourth consecutive year was indeed 1255 Hempstead Turnpike in Uniondale, New York.

WILL THERE EVER BE ANOTHER 4-PEAT?

BY PETER BOTTE

The Islanders of the early 1980s aren't mentioned enough among the greatest dynasties in professional sports history.

Since the Bill Torrey—assembled, Al Arbour—coached Isles captured their fourth consecutive Stanley Cup title with a sweep of Wayne Gretzky and the Edmonton Oilers in the 1983 Finals, no other team in the NHL, NFL, NBA, or MLB has won four straight championships.

In fact, only the Chicago Bulls (1991–93 and 1996–98), Yankees (1998–2000), and the Lakers (2000–02) have won three consecutive titles over that span. The Houston Comets did win the first four WNBA titles from 1997 to 2000.

"Beating Edmonton, that was our most satisfying series. Because they were a hotshot goal-scoring machine. And I think we held them to six goals in that series," said Bobby Nystrom, who'd scored the overtime winner against the Philadelphia Flyers to clinch the Isles' first Cup in 1980. "When we beat them and they only scored six goals, that was probably the most awesome memory, because we shut down the Oilers."

Gretzky often has said that the takeaway that stood out the most to the emerging Oilers from that series was walking past the Islanders' locker room and seeing an exhausted team barely celebrating its fourth consecutive championship. Gretzky, Mark Messier, and the Oilers would begin a string of five Stanley Cup crowns over the next seven seasons in Edmonton the following year, easily defeating the Isles in five games in the '84 Finals.

"That was one of the great memories for our entire hockey team. Because we really felt like they could give us a heck of a battle," former Isles center Butch Goring said. "Nobody had really challenged us when we won our second Cup [against the Minnesota North Stars in 1981] or our third Cup [against the Vancouver Canucks in 1982]. "We knew Edmonton had some tremendous talent. So, we were very much on high alert."

The Islanders of that era certainly had plenty of their own star power, featuring five eventual Hall of Fame players: goal hound Mike Bossy, two-way center Bryan Trottier, defenseman Denis Potvin, swashbuckling goalie Billy Smith, and power forward Clark Gillies.

The Isles advanced as far as the league semifinals in 1993, 2020, and 2021, but they haven't returned to the Finals since 1984. Their string of nineteen consecutive playoff series wins also may never be approached again in any sport.

"I have to say that it's one hell of an accomplishment," Nystrom said. "We were not the kind of guys that bragged. But it's a real tribute to the type of team we had and the coaches and the general manager.

"Each year our whole thought process was we're gonna get another one."

POSTGAME

The Keys to a Dynasty

BRYAN TROTTIER (ISLANDERS CENTER): I think the foundations of our success was work ethic and the willingness to pay the price. They're huge; you need those things in order to be successful.

BRYAN TROTTIER: We learned from Montreal Canadiens how to practice, how to conduct ourselves, how to play with purpose, and play together with unity.

STAN FISCHLER (HOCKEY HISTORIAN AND ANNOUNCER/BESTSELLING AUTHOR): The Islanders were strong at every position. Billy Smith was one of the greatest clutch goalies of all time. What a defense—Kenny Morrow should be in the Hall of Fame. He was a tremendous, tremendous, tough defenseman who scored big goals in the playoffs. Denny Potvin was arguably the greatest defenseman of all time. Denny did it both ways and he was a great, great captain.

You go down the line you got Bossy, arguably the greatest goal scorer of all time. You had Trots, probably one of the greatest two-way centers of all time. You had Gillies on the left side alternating with Tonelli, who should be in the Hall of Fame. Then you have a second line with Butch Goring who was a great, great, penalty killer. He was the missing piece. They had a phenomenal power play with Trots, Bossy, and Potvin. They had traffic penalty killers with Butch Goring and Lorne Henning. They had one of the all-time coaches—you couldn't pick a better coach. Al Arbour was perfect for that team. Bill Torrey was a great GM, I mean, he was the guy who found Trots. The stupid Rangers passed on Bossy twice . . . insane.

So, in every particular position, the box was checked. It was unbelievable. And of course, they were upset by Toronto in 1978. And they were upset by the Rangers in 1979. And then it wasn't just that they got Goring. This is the brilliance of Torrey, he got Butch, but he also got Gord Lane, who was one of the most intimidating defensemen of that time. Gord would take off his mother's head if she tried to go around him. And in addition to Gord Lane, they got Kenny Morrow right after the 1980 Olympics.

What can I say, unbelievable moves—just terrific stuff.

DENIS POTVIN (ISLANDERS DEFENSEMAN): There are sixteen players who have our names on all four Stanley Cups. Back in those days, you only had seventeen skaters and two goaltenders. So, it means that every year there was maybe one or two players that were added to our roster. We started developing as a very young team. For instance, I sat next to Bryan Trottier for fifteen years. All sixteen guys knew each other inside and out on the ice.

BRYAN TROTTIER: You can't win it with one or two or even five players, you need twenty guys.

I think fifteen or sixteen of us were on all four Cup-winning teams. So that's a pretty strong nucleus to have. So, yeah, to be in the same conversation as one of the all-time greatest dynasties is a wonderful compliment. We always just take it and run.

If we're like, oh yeah, for sure, we're number one, there's nobody better, it's like we're pounding our own chests. That's not the way the hockey guys are.

It just makes for a great conversation and I think it's just a fantastic to be considered one of the all-time great dynasties in sports.

JIGGS MCDONALD (FORMER VOICE OF THE ISLANDERS): They weren't concerned about making as much as they possibly could; they just wanted to win. They wanted to get their name on the Stanley Cup, that was more important than anything to majority of these guys.

BRYAN TROTTIER: Al was motivating us on a daily basis and making sure that we don't get complacent. You need that brain trust to keep it all together,

DENIS POTVIN: You have to understand the pain of losing before you can actually cherish how much it takes to win. So, there's several factors in why we did what we did, how we did it, and how I don't think it's going to be replicated.

BRYAN TROTTIER: I think all of us to a man appreciated each other. Al, as coach, Bill, as general manager, and the team that was put together as a group, had great chemistry.

JIGGS MCDONALD: It wasn't a job; just to have a seat at every game, and a good seat at that, was great. To be around those players, that was a key part of it too. I know I had the players' trust. there were nights that I would drive a player to a game or home from a game. Depending on if the wife needed the car or his car was in for service. Clark Gillies and I used to drive back and forth from the games from time to time, and other players as well. My kids, my two girls babysat for Butchy and both babysat for the Sutters's children at one time or another.

There was camaraderie. I was accepted from the moment I arrived.

DENIS POTVIN: There was one training camp in the early seventies where Al Arbour wanted us to increase our focus. We of course had the same coach year after year. He went and got Maharishi Mahesh Yogi, put him in a room in one of the hotels where we had our training camp, and then each one of us had to go to this particular room and have a session with the Maharishi (laughs). So, we all learned Transcendental Meditation, which the purpose is to focus, get in line with your body, all of those things. That was another way that Al would get the message across. Now we look back on and I think it's funny, the way he went about it, but he was meticulous, every training camp, there was something different, because in his belief, even though we'd won a Stanley Cup, a game in October was just as important as a game in April. He didn't like to lose, nor did we.

BRYAN TROTTIER: You want to battle? We'll battle. You want to play hockey? We'll play hockey.

That's what makes for championship teams is just the confidence we have in ourselves each other.

DENIS POTVIN: Al Arbour was such a good judge of character that, one time, we were not playing very physical—and he wasn't happy with that, because we had a very physical team.

So, one day before the game, the two trainers are following him with a couple of dozen boxes of eggs. Al walks in, comes right over to Bryan Trottier and me, and then goes to each and every player. He hands us a raw egg. He says you guys can put the raw egg in your hockey pants. I know you'll never break it. So, he handed an egg to every one of the players all around the room and then just walked out. He got his message across.

But his point was, you guys are not hitting anybody. You're not physical enough. So, I'll give you the raw egg you put in your pants. And I can tell you, you're not going to break the egg because you're not playing physical. That was his message.

BRYAN TROTTIER: There's a whole bunch of ingredients I thought worked and that's how you learn to win.

Four in a Row!

BUTCH GORING (ISLANDERS CENTER): For us, that was a tremendous accomplishment to beat them four straight games and to shut Gretzky down.

BOBBY NYSTROM (ISLANDERS RIGHT WING): That was a tribute to Al because he constantly preached to us about goals against. That was probably the most awesome memory, because we shut down the Oilers.

What Gretzky and the Oilers Learned from the Champs

JIGGS MCDONALD: I've heard it right from Wayne's mouth to me personally, that they learned so much from the Islanders. He personally and the rest of the Oilers team took note of that moment, when they saw just how banged up the Islanders were after beating them in the Cup finals. Edmonton was definitely very, very talented, maybe more talented than the Islanders, but not as disciplined.

Wayne has as openly talked about the fact that the Islanders were very calm in their celebration in the Islanders dressing room after they won the Cup as they walked by spoke volumes as to what it took to win and what the commitment had to be in order to win the Cup.

BRYAN TROTTIER: Yeah, we went crazy. We had a stick boy outside of the locker room and we didn't want to rub salt in the wound. So, we just said, "Hey, if there's a couple guys from the Oilers coming just give us a heads up."

There were one two or three or four guys walking by, he's said, "Hey guys are coming."

We just kind of tone it down a little bit, and then as soon as they went around the corner, woo-hoo, we went crazy again. So, it might have worked against us, we don't know, we thought we were just being a little bit respectful to them. Their story makes for great headlines. Our story is—hey we're just humble little hockey players that don't want to rub salt in the wound and make them feel any worse. It may have come back to haunt us to a degree but it's no big deal.

BOBBY NYSTROM: I think that that's absolutely true. We actually went out to Edmonton one time, a few of us to play in this charity softball tournament, and so we met them. A lot of their guys were pretty hard living, partying guys. I think they thought that they could just blow us away. But you know, we were a little bit older and more mature than they were, and we knew exactly what it took to win a Stanley Cup.

Looking Back at 19 Straight Playoff Series and 4 Cups

STAN FISCHLER: No other team has come close to this fact. They won nineteen straight playoff series. Do you hear that? Nineteen straight playoff series. Now when the Canadiens won five straight Cups there were only two rounds. So, they won ten straight series. Okay? When Scotty Bowman's Canadiens won four straight Cups. But it was thirteen straight playoff series. The Islanders won nineteen straight. The attrition of that amount of playoff hockey kills guys. But they had the depth. They were motivated. And that's it.

BUTCH GORING: We just went out and played our game and we really didn't think about being a dominant hockey club. We felt if we played our best game, we were probably going to win. We didn't think much about dominating the NHL, but I'll tell you one thing, It sure was a fun time.

BOBBY NYSTROM: I think that the reason that we were able to win four straight Cups was that after we won the first one, we weren't just patting ourselves on our backs. But it was such an exhilarating feeling that we wanted to do it again and again and again. But I think more than anything else it was the leadership that Al provided. Just the way that he treated us, and the character of the players on the team.

JIGGS MCDONALD: How you compare winning four consecutive and going to the Stanley Cup final for the fifth consecutive year and winning nineteen consecutive playoff series? I can't. I can't think of anything that would compare to the Islanders dynasty run.

STAN FISCHLER: That's why I said all along no one is going to win three straight cups, because you can't deal with that attrition that comes with the grind of playoff hockey. How the hell the Islanders did that, I can't tell you because it was just astonishing, astonishing.

BOBBY NYSTROM: I have to say that it's one hell of an accomplishment to win nineteen straight playoff series. But you know, we were not the kind of guys that bragged. We had a fantastic group of guys. Each year our whole thought process was: we're gonna get another one; we're gonna get another one.

BRYAN TROTTIER: I think it reflects on a team that was built on determination and structure. Everybody had ahold of the rope. We are sure proud of our accomplishments. Whether it's up to us to say, that I don't know, but at the at that time, we felt we were unbeatable. I think that's a wonderful feeling of confidence. It's a wonderful feeling of accomplishment.

BOBBY NYSTROM: When we get together it's like a family reunion. We laugh at the same old jokes and we laugh at the same old stories. You know what? They are just the best guys, I loved them. They are just awesome.

DENIS POTVIN: I don't think winning nineteen consecutive playoff series will ever be done again.

JIGGS MCDONALD: Here's a cute story that hasn't gotten publicity or hasn't been talked about. In '83–'84 when the Islanders were going for the fifth cup, in Edmonton, the home team provided the coffee for the visiting team. There were big urns of coffee. Would you believe [Oilers coach] Glen

Sather dictated that the Islanders get decaffeinated coffee. The training staff has admitted it, and I asked Sather about it.

He just laughed and then he came back and said, "Yep, that's a true story." That isn't the reason the Islanders didn't win a fifth straight Stanley Cup Final in '83–'84 but it's just one of the little things that go on in one-upmanship and playoff hockey.

BOBBY NYSTROM: I want to share some of my acceptance speech. I haven't given it yet but want to read it to you for your book.

> I'm accepting the nomination to go into the New York Hockey Hall of Fame. Needless to say, I truly appreciate the award. But we all know that hockey is a team sport. I wouldn't be here if it wasn't for my incredible teammates. They were the best guys in the world. The guys that every mother would love. They were kind, polite, caring and considered right up until game time. And then they were a whole lot different. If you met any one of those guys on the street. You'd be absolutely amazed at how nice and pleasant they were. But when it came time to play, they were a different animal. There's a bond between us. And to this day when we get together it was like we were never apart. We are telling the same stories and jokes and are laughing as if we've never heard it before. I want to accept this award, but I also accepted for on behalf of my teammates because without them I would have been nothing.

That's how I feel, and now I want to cry. That's hard to admit.

Boys Will Be Boys

BRYAN TROTTIER: Butch bought a Ferrari with his playoff bonus after the first Stanley Cup.

He said, "I am going to treat myself to a Ferrari."

I'm like, "All right, Butchy."

He came back with this tiny little Ferrari. It looked like it was like a go-kart. We took the car—seven or eight of us just picked it up and set it on a cement ledge so he couldn't drive it away. The wheels were like six to eight inches off the ground. It was pretty funny. I don't know how he got it off. Probably had to call some tow truck. I have no clue. I'd love to hear Butchy's side of the story because I've never asked him because I didn't want him to know that I was a part of it.

What makes it so funny was Butch saying, "Who put my car up there? Who put my car up there?"

I said, "I don't know, I don't know (laughing), but when we find out who did it. Boy, he's going to be in big trouble."

You know, it was a pretty comical sight.

Potvin Socks???

DENIS POTVIN: When I made the decision to try and offer the olive branch and do something fun with the chant forty-three years later, I came up with a sock idea with the slogan. You've been chanting it for forty-three years—now you could wear it. I think it's great. And it's been great it's going exceptionally well. I'm okay with it now. I got to add this—in all forty-three years. I can say with absolute certainty, I've never met a Ranger fan who was disrespectful, never. So, it's great. I want them to keep chanting it now and now hopefully they are chanting Potvin socks, not sucks (laughs).

#18

1976 ALCS: NEW YORK YANKEES vs. KANSAS CITY ROYALS, GAME 5

OCTOBER 14, 1976

CHAMBLISS WALKS OFF THE ROYALS

TIME CAPSULE

- Mayor of New York: Abraham Beame
- Oscar, Best Picture: *One Flew Over the Cuckoo's Nest*
- Oscar, Best Actor: Jack Nicholson, *One Flew Over the Cuckoo's Nest*
- Oscar, Best Actress: Louise Fletcher, *One Flew Over the Cuckoo's Nest*
- Grammy, Album of the Year: Paul Simon, *Still Crazy After All These Years*
- Grammy Record of the Year: Captain & Tennille, "Love Will Keep Us Together," *Love Will Keep Us Together*
- President of the US: Gerald Ford
- Price of Gas: $0.61/Gallon
- Heisman Trophy: Tony Dorsett, running back, Pittsburgh

PREGAME

Chambliss's Blast Sent Him and the Yankees Walking Off into the World Series

It took less than six seconds to undo a dozen years of misery in the Bronx. That's how long it took—in Game 5 of the 1976 American League Championship Series—for the baseball hit by Chris Chambliss to leave Yankee Stadium and send the Bronx Bombers to the World Series.

The New York Yankees set the standard for winners in all of sports. Winning their first World Series in 1923 and, decade after decade, have not stopped winning. Over the next thirty-nine years they won nineteen World Series championships. That gave them twenty rings entering 1976. For the record, it did take the Yankees two World Series losses to the New York Giants in 1921 and 1922 before breaking through with a championship in 1923. To go along with all those World Series victories, they also collected a total of nine pennants between 1921 and 1964, making another nine World Series appearances. Seeing their team play in October seemed like a birthright to Yankee fans.

Well, the dozen years between losing to the St. Louis Cardinals in 1964 and Chris Chambliss's heroics took its toll even on the most loyal fans. In 1972, the Yankees drew under one million fans—their lowest attendance since 1945. The Mets drew more than double that number to Shea Stadium.

The Mets, who didn't have the championship pedigree, winning a lone World Series in 1969, taking over New York from the Yankees?

What could the Yankees do to take back their city and take back their rightful place at the top of the baseball standings? Often, when tough times come, tough people show up to rectify matters. "The Boss," George Steinbrenner, was that man. He bought the proud franchise for $10 million on January 3, 1973. Steinbrenner, as the Yankee's principal owner, forever changed the fate of the franchise.

The Boss was not going to be outspent or outworked in his pursuit of a title. He would use free agency, trades, and cold hard cash to acquire the best players, managers, and front office personnel.

Steinbrenner was from Cleveland, and he brought some home cooking with him to the Bronx. He selected former Cleveland Indians (now Guardians) executive Gabe Paul to be the president of the Yankees. A month before Steinbrenner took over the Yankees, on November 27, 1972, the Yankees acquired third baseman Graig Nettles from the Indians. Cleveland would have its imprint all over New York as the Yankees rebuilt. On April 26, 1974, they acquired first baseman Chris Chambliss and reliever Dick Tidrow from Cleveland.

Chambliss would restore the glory to the Yankees two years later with one swing of the bat. Did the Yankees' brain trust know he would win the pennant in one of the most famous home runs in the history of the Bronx Bombers? Maybe not, but they didn't just bring in Chambliss's bat to restore former glory. It was emblematic of the foresight and bottomless budget they employed in their pursuit of former glory.

Expectations were nothing new for Chambliss. He was the first overall selection of the Indians in the 1970 January draft. He stormed into the league and scooped up the AL Rookie of the Year Award in 1971. So the Yankees had a big bat, but that was just the tip of the iceberg for a team looking for their first pennant since 1964.

They also built through free agency. One of the best pitchers in baseball, Catfish Hunter, was made a free agent after the 1974 season, when Oakland A's owner Charles Finley breached his contract. Hunter was coming off a Cy Young Award season, winning 25 games with an AL-best 2.49 ERA. He also tossed 19 complete games, something unheard of in today's game.

Hunter brought with him a championship pedigree. The Swingin' A's won three championships in a row, in 1972, '73, and '74. Getting a player of his stature to come to the Bronx was exactly what Steinbrenner would become famous for doing. Not about to miss an opportunity, The Boss made Hunter the highest-paid player in baseball heading into the 1975 season, giving him a five-year, $3.35 million deal.

As almost every team in baseball went after the star pitcher, the Yankees sent a clear message to the rest of the league that they would be major players in any player movement from that point forward. Catfish had a terrific season in 1975, winning 23 games—completing 21—and throwing a league-leading 328 innings. He finished second in the Cy Young voting to Orioles great Jim Palmer. His Yankees still finished 12 games behind the dreaded Boston Red Sox in the AL East.

That meant The Boss was not done.

The Texas Rangers finished the 1975 season a ghastly 19 games out of first place. Their manager, Billy Martin, wouldn't be there to see the end of the season. He only managed 95 games for the Rangers before being informed that his services were no longer required. He who hesitates is lost. In Steinbrenner's mind, he who hesitates loses baseball games. So, on August 1, the Yankees acted quickly and hired Martin to become their manager. The former Yankees second baseman wasn't the only one with ties to the glory days, as Martin's coaching staff included Yogi Berra, Elston Howard, and Whitey Ford.

Martin inherited a talented Yankee squad. The team had added Nettles, Chambliss, and Hunter to a pretty decent core. They had their clubhouse leader in catcher Thurman Munson, the 1970 Rookie of the Year. In 1975, he drove in over 100 runs, batted .318, and won a Gold Glove. Munson became the ninth captain of the Yankees in 1976. The 1977 team featured Munson and newly acquired Reggie Jackson butting heads, but that is for another chapter of this book. For this team, he was the undisputed leader.

The 1975 Yankees finished strong with Martin, winning 16 games in September. The team was targeting 1976 to return to glory, as '76 was the first year of the "new" Yankee Stadium, a multi-million-dollar project in the Bronx. The mighty Yankees played their home games at Shea Stadium for two years while waiting for Yankee Stadium's facelift to be completed (*gasp*).

The new stadium made its debut in 1976, at the same time the facelift of the Yankees roster was completed as well. On Opening Day, April 15, 1976, a crowd of 54,010 packed the stadium to watch an 11–4 victory over the Minnesota Twins. The team also opened Monument Park that day. The way they played against Minnesota, that team sent notice that they would need to make room a few more monuments.

The makeover of the roster had a key transaction on December 11, 1975, when the Yankees fleeced the Pittsburgh Pirates in a trade. They acquired starting pitcher Dock Ellis and second baseman Willie Randolph for starter Doc Medich. Paul and Steinbrenner also pulled of a blockbuster by trading Bobby Bonds to the Angels for centerfielder Mickey Rivers and starter Ed Figueroa. Bonds had a spectacular season for the Yankees in 1975, hitting .270 and adding 32 home runs, 85 RBIs, and 30 steals. But it wasn't enough to bring a pennant to New York.

These trades were the building blocks to a pennant and championship, but at the time were initially scoffed at. Figueroa and Rivers lacked the star power of a Bonds. Rivers had speed and was a plus outfielder who had stolen 70 bases the season before, leading the American League. The Yanks wanted frontline starter Frank Tanana to go along with Rivers, but Gabe Paul "accepted" Figueroa, based on his success against the Red Sox. He was 3–0 against the Yankees' archrivals. Figueroa didn't have the reputation of Tanana, but had won 16 games and his 2.91 ERA was fifth best in the AL—not a bad player to accept in a deal.

The duo of Steinbrenner and Paul were astute at bringing in personnel, and were equally astute at retaining the pieces that were in place when they took over. When the 1976 season started, there were only five holdovers from the pre–Steinbrenner/Paul era: Munson, Nettles, left fielder Roy White, reliever Sparky Lyle, and shortstop Fred "Chicken" Stanley. There was also a new attitude and new rules, as losing was simply not to be tolerated. Steinbrenner was ruthless. As was his manager, Billy Martin. There were two new sheriffs in town.

New leadership and new players equaled different results. The team was in control from the first week of the season, jumping out to a 10–3 start through April. At the trade deadline, they acquired starting pitchers Ken Holtzman and Doyle Alexander in a massive 9-player deal with the Baltimore Orioles. Holtzman was a three-time champion with the A's and teammates with Hunter. He also was an All-Star in 1972 and '73. Alexander went 10–5 the rest of the season for the Yankees.

Munson led the Yankees on and off the field. He also led George Brett in the AL MVP voting, collecting the hardware as the league's best player.

Munson had a great year, batting .302, with 17 home runs and 105 RBIs. (Spoiler alert, they would face each other in the ALCS.) Munson and the Yankees would once again get the better of Brett and the Royals. But it's the how that made it so historic and memorable.

Rivers paid immediate dividends, finishing third in the AL MVP voting with a .312 average, eight home runs, 67 RBIs, 95 runs, and 43 steals. Chambliss was solid as well, batting .293 with 17 homers and 96 RBIs. Nettles led the American League with 32 home runs. Oakland's Sal Bando and future Yankee Reggie Jackson finished behind Nettles, tied with 27 homers.

The pitching aquations all paid off as well. Hunter won 17 games with a 3.53 ERA. Figueroa led the team with 19 wins and a 3.02 ERA. Ellis was 17–8 with a 3.19 ERA as the third starter. Lyle was the closer, saving a league-leading 23 games while winning seven others. He would go on to win the Cy Young Award a year later.

Yankees baseball was back with vengeance—as were their fans. The Yankees drew more than two million for the first time since 1950. They drew over 2.3 million fans, while the Mets drew under 1.5 million. The Bombers won 97 games and the American League East division by 10 1/2 games over the Baltimore Orioles, and 15 1/2 games over their rivals from Bostin.

But winning the division no longer got you a one-way ticket to the World Series. Since 1969, the two division winners faced off in the American League and National League Championship Series. The AL was dominated by two teams since 1969. Either the AL East Baltimore Orioles or the AL West Oakland A's played in every ALCS since its inception. This was the Yankees' first-ever trip to the ALCS. Their opponent was the Kansas City Royals. Both the A's and O's were out of the Yankees' path back to the World Series.

The Royals limped into the playoffs, winning just two of their last eleven games. But it was enough to hold off the A's and win the AL West by 2 1/2 games.

It was a best-of-five series. The Yankees had won 97 games and the Royals had won 90. The ALCS would start in Kansas City for the first two games, and then move to New York for the final three, setting up a potential dramatic walk-off scenario for New York.

The Royals had former Yankee Larry Gura take the ball in Game 1. He went up against Hunter, the Yankees' ace. The Yankees put up a two-spot in the first frame behind two throwing errors by Royals star George Brett. Catfish pitched a complete game, allowing just one run and five hits. Brett tried to make up for his defensive lapse by contributing three of the five KC hits, but it wasn't enough, as the Yankees won 4–1.

In Game 2, the Yanks were looking to deliver a near knockout punch by heading back to Yankee Stadium with a 2–0 series lead . . . but the Royals had other ideas. The game was the polar opposite of Game 1, as it was the Royals who got out to the early first-inning lead by scoring twice. And they got solid pitching from Paul Splittorff and Dennis Leonard. The Yankees were beyond sloppy, with five errors, and lost 7–3. The series was knotted at one apiece heading back to christen the newly refashioned Yankee Stadium, which was hosting a postseason game for the first time since 1964.

In Game 3, Kansas City did it again—this time scoring three runs in the first inning off Ellis, who blanked the Royals from there on out and pitched eight strong innings. Chris Chambliss blasted a two-run homer in the fourth. Foreshadowing, well yes, with the benefit of 20/20 hindsight. The Yankees added three runs in the sixth inning and Lyle shut the door with a scoreless ninth for the save. New York was on the doorstep of the pennant, leading 2–1, needing just one win in the next two home games to go to the World Series for the first time in a dozen years.

The Yankees could almost taste the champagne. Would Martin start his No. 4 starter Ken Holtzman, or pitch Catfish on just three days' rest? Or does he save Hunter for a possible Game 5, where he would be pitching on a more comfortable four days' rest?

The answer was Billy wanted to close the door on the Royals as quickly as possible. So, Martin went with Hunter, even though he had pitched a complete game in Game 1. Whitey Herzog did the same and brought back Larry Gura on short rest to try and extend the series to a winner-take-all Game 5.

Catfish was knocked out in the fourth inning, giving up five runs. Hunter told the *New York Times,* "I think my arm would've been a little stronger with another day's rest. I didn't think that I'd pitch until the fifth game, but he said pitch so I pitched. When he says here's the ball, I'll take it. If he says here's the ball tomorrow, I'll take it. I'll be in the bullpen tomorrow. I'll volunteer."

Nettles tried to pick up Catfish and the Yankees with a couple of home runs and three RBIs, but it wasn't enough, and the Royals took Game 4, 7–4. The gamble didn't pay off. So, it was down to a do-or-die single-game elimination in front of 56,821 fans at Yankee Stadium. The winner would face the Big Red Machine, the defending World Series champion Cincinnati Reds.

Six magical seconds from contact to clearing the fence would unleash the wildest celebration that the new Yankee Stadium had seen. For that matter, it was maybe the most bedlam any Yankee Stadium of any era had experienced.

Chris Chambliss cemented his place in Yankees history with one majestic swing of the bat.

CHAMBLISS'S BLAST SENDS YANKS BACK TO WS

BY PETER BOTTE

Chris Chambliss had to rely on his days as a football running back just to get around the bases.

The lefty-swinging first baseman had just propelled the Yankees back into the World Series for the first time in a dozen years on October 14, 1976, with a walk-off home run against Kansas City Royals reliever Mark Littell in the ninth inning of a 7–6 win in Game 5 of the AL Championship Series.

Chambliss had to navigate through hundreds of jubilant fans who stormed the field while he made his way around the bases, even trucking one fan like Jim Brown lowering his shoulder into an oncoming linebacker. (Honestly, search for the video on YouTube.)

"That was a scary trip. The scariest part was hitting second base, about two steps after that I tripped and went down to one knee and all I could think of was everybody pounding on top of me and burying me in the dirt or something," Chambliss said.

"But I quickly got up and from then on I didn't worry about touching all the bases. I couldn't wait to take a left turn and get into the dugout."

Indeed, Chambliss didn't even touch home plate amid the chaos—and he technically still hasn't to this day.

"That is a good story. I didn't touch it on my first trip around the bases," Chambliss added. "I went directly into the clubhouse from [third] base. I then took a couple of cops with me, put a jacket on, we went back out to the field.

"When we looked at home plate, there was nothing but people around us, but of course the plate was gone when I got back out there. The fans had taken the plate. So, I put my foot on that area and then we walked away."

Chambliss's blast, which came after KC's George Brett had tied the score with a three-run home run off Grant Jackson in the eighth, ended an unheard-of dozen-year championship drout for the Yankees. They hadn't reached the Fall Classic since losing to the St. Louis Cardinals in 1964 and hadn't won a World Series title since defeating the San Francisco Giants two years earlier.

The '76 Yanks actually were swept in the World Series by Pete Rose, Johnny Bench, Joe Morgan and Cincinnati's Big Red Machine, but the Chambliss homer helped set the stage for the championships in 1977 and 1978 following the free-agent addition of Reggie Jackson and others.

"That home run by Chambliss and getting us to the World Series gave you a prelude to how those next several years would be for the Yankees," Ron Guidry said. "Because we were building a great team."

POSTGAME

The Buildup

SPARKLY LYLE (YANKEES PITCHER): I was traded there in 1972 and I had a hell of a year there and we only missed the playoffs by one game. I think that's when we started looking around that clubhouse and saying, hey, you know what, I think we're gonna be pretty good here in a couple of years. Of course, with the addition of Chambliss and Nettles and [Dick] Tidrow it was just something that I think we all started talking about, but never knew it was going to happen that quick.

CHRIS CHAMBLISS (YANKEES FIRST BASEMAN): Remember that '76 was the first year that we went back into the refurbished Yankee Stadium. Billy Martin was our manager. It was just some kind of a special year. We won the division by 10 1/2 games and we were really a good club. They had made those great trades for Willie Randolph and Mickey Rivers, and the Graig Nettles trade and my trade. Then all of a sudden, we were winning and then we went to the World Series. It was just an exciting time.

THE 20 GREATEST MOMENTS IN NEW YORK SPORTS HISTORY

Chambliss Walk-Off!

SPARKLY LYLE: Oh, man, it was absolutely mind-boggling for me. I mean, not only for myself, but everybody else in that ballpark. As soon as we heard the sound of that ball coming off of Chambliss's bat, we knew it was gone.

ANTHONY McCARRON (*NY DAILY NEWS* BASEBALL COLUMNIST/SNY CONTRIBUTOR): You can see how much it meant from the television clips where the fans flood the field in a joyous, if a little dangerous, celebration. I think some of the great photos of him raising his arms as he knows it's going out and Thurman Munson leaping in joy in the background add to the feeling, too.

SPARKY LYLE: I remember Dick Tidrow and I just looked each other in the eye and just started screaming. I also remember the fans closing in on us and I kept thinking if I don't make a hard left turn here and head for the clubhouse, I'm not gonna get there.

CHRIS CHAMBLISS: That was a scary trip. I didn't worry about bases. I couldn't wait to take a left turn and get into the dugout.

JOHN STERLING (RADIO VOICE OF THE YANKEES): It was euphoria and the euphoria spread onto the field. Chambliss had to fight his way through the crowd, like a running back. They weren't even sure if he touched the plate. So, he came out later and touched the plate.

CHRIS CHAMBLISS: When did I hit home plate? I didn't touch it on my first trip around the bases. I then took a couple of cops with me, The fans had taken the plate. So, I put my foot on that area and then we walked away.

CHRIS CHAMBLISS: After I hit the home run, I dropped the bat. Well, Graig Nettles, who was the quickest thinker on our team, ran out there and picked up my bat and brought it back to the dugout. He was protecting all of our equipment because our gloves and stuff were on the top step. Graig used my bat to protect all that equipment. I still have that bat.

MARTY APPEL (YANKEES HISTORIAN AND BESTSELLING AUTHOR): This was as big a home run as Bobby Thomson's 1951 "Shot Heard 'Round the World." With one swing, his team was going to the World Series. Before the term *walk-off homer,* Thomson and Chambliss both did it.

The two of them shared something else in common—they were very likable guys, well suited for their moments and the glory that came with it.

JOHN STERLING: That was a tremendous moment in New York sports and the atmosphere was as euphoric as you can imagine.

MICKEY RIVERS (YANKEES OUTFIELDER): I think Chris Chambliss was amazing to get that home run it in that situation like that and helping us win the pennant. We always seemed to have things go our way, because we played as a unit, and that was what was great about that moment.

CHRIS CHAMBLISS: It was a thrill of a lifetime. The series versus Kansas City was so tight. Then it came down to the last inning and we're tied. It's the bottom of the ninth, it was just a thrilling time when I hit it there were so many people in the stands, throwing stuff all over the field. It was really an exciting time.

One Swing End Yankee Drought

CHRIS CHAMBLISS: I'll just give you two real quick stories, my walk-off home run ball was hit not into the stands but into an area where a lot of cops were. So, one of the cops brought the ball into the clubhouse and gave it to me.

KEN DAVIDOFF (FORMER *NY POST* BASEBALL COLUMNIST/PIX11 BASEBALL HISTORIAN): It's all about the drought. The '76 Yankees hadn't won a championship since 1962 and hadn't even qualified for the World Series since 1964. Not since the start of their existence had the Yankees, the sport's most successful franchise by a mile, experienced such a dry run. They endured a highly competitive series with the upstart Royals, who erased a three-run deficit in the eighth inning of Game 5. When Chambliss, one of general manager Gabe Paul's many excellent acquisitions, led off the bottom of the ninth inning with the pennant-winning, walk-off homer, the Yankees' "long" journey through the baseball desert had ended.

ANTHONY McCARRON: Pre-Chambliss, there hadn't been that many home runs like this, so it will always stand out. Off the top of my head, we had Mazeroski and Bobby Thomson, so to see a sudden dagger like this, at home, for a team that hadn't been there in a while (for that franchise, anyway), was movie-script stuff in real life.

#19

2002 US OPEN GOLF

JUNE 16, 2002

TIGER DESTROYS BETHPAGE

TIME CAPSULE

- Mayor of New York: Michael Bloomberg
- Oscar, Best Picture: *A Beautiful Mind*
- Oscar, Best Actor: Denzel Washington, *Training Day*
- Oscar, Best Actress: Halle Berry, *Monster's Ball*
- Grammy, Album of the Year: *O Brother, Where Art Thou?: The Motion Picture Soundtrack*
- Grammy, Record of the Year: U2, "Walk On," *All That You Can't Leave Behind*
- President of the US: George W. Bush
- Price of Gas: $1.36/Gallon
- Heisman Trophy: Carson Palmer, quarterback, USC

PREGAME

Bethpage Can't Tame Tiger

Tiger Woods was ferocious and feared like no golfer since Jack Nicklaus, but despite his long list of incredible accomplishments, the calendar insisted he was just a mere cub when he arrived at Bethpage Black in Farmingdale, New York, for the 2002 United States Open.

Woods had already won seven major golf championships, including three Masters titles and his first US Open in 2000. In fact, a little more than two months earlier, he won his second straight Masters, and a victory at Bethpage would keep his dream of the first Grand Slam in the same calendar year very much alive.

He was the only golfer to hold the titles of all four majors at the same time, although his victories in the US Open, British Open, and PGA Championship came in 2000 and he won the green jacket at the Masters in 2001. It was called the "Tiger Slam." He won the US Open by an astounding 15 strokes.

Woods was only twenty-six years old when he arrived at the very difficult Bethpage Black.

What made this US Open so unique is that it was the first being played at a true public course, where everyday hackers showed up for tee times and then went around the course spraying divots all over the place. Back in 2002, it cost $31 to play during the week and $39 on the weekend. Pebble Beach, also a public course, had previously held the US Open, but at that time it cost $350 to play a single round.

Now Bethpage was awaiting millionaire golfers. The course was made US Open–ready with a $3 million update by the USGA. Now it was to be the home for one week to the greatest golfers in the world. And one of them stood out among the rest.

"Growing up on a muni, that's where I really learned to play the game," Woods said. "I wasn't able to play at country clubs. We didn't have the money, so I played in Long Beach."

Eldrick "Tiger" Woods was a child prodigy. He played his first hole on a regular golf course—not pitch and putt—at eighteen months old. He was a regular on the course with his father when he was just three years old. Fast forward a bit and he joined the PGA tour as a professional in 1996, when he was just twenty. He won the Masters in 1997 by 12 strokes. *Twelve strokes!* Two months later, he was ranked No. 1 in the world for the first time. It was a position he pretty much held for all but short periods until his life went off the tracks in 2010.

US Open courses are the most challenging with their narrow fairways, tough rough and fast greens. The par-70 7,214-yard Bethpage layout was the longest in US Open history. Six of the par 4s exceeded 450 yards. The 499-yard 12th hole was the longest par four in US Open history. Woods, by the way, had never won a major championship on a par-70 course in eight attempts.

"You tell him that, it's going to become one-for-nine," said Nick Faldo, who tied for fifth at Bethpage.

Faldo, who by then had won six majors, expressed the pros' lament going into the US Open. These courses are killers. "It's an absolute monster," Faldo said. "They have managed to get everything. We have got length, accuracy, mega-thick rough, and you've got bunkers that are eight feet deep and you've got superfast greens and it's blowing. Apart from that, it's dead easy. If Tiger shoots 12-under this week, I'm quitting."

Woods was still building his legacy. The nasty car crash in 2009 after his wife caught him cheating, the major injuries he sustained in a one-car accident in California in 2021, the back surgeries, knee surgeries, all of that was years away. It seemed impossible that with victories in seven of the first 21 major championships he played that he wouldn't break Nicklaus's record of 18. That record stands today with Woods stuck on 15 following his Masters victory in 2019.

Woods was a rock star at Bethpage. He was young, personable, and the first African American superstar on the PGA Tour. He was the Michael Jordan of golf. He now had a chance to add a major championship in the media capital of the world. His popularity had no limits. He just had to keep hitting the ball better than anybody else and stay out of trouble.

"The US Open is more than a golf tournament," Davis Love III said. "It's a test of mettle, your patience, your guts. If the scoring is easy, it would be like any other week. But the US Open is a test of everything you have. That's why it's hard to win and why we want to win so bad."

Woods didn't tee it up at the start of the first round thinking about anything but winning. He didn't focus on how it was one down and three to go to become the first golfer to win the Grand Slam in the same year. One hole at a time. One round at a time. One tournament at a time. He couldn't be thinking about the British Open and PGA when the national championship was at stake.

But he sure was asked about winning four in a row before round one.

"Anything is possible. I've won four in a row before. I don't see why I can't do it again," Woods said. "But the key is making sure you don't look at winning four in a row. You have to take it one step at a time. You put so much energy into that one week and leading up to that week that I don't think most of the people appreciate how much it takes out of you."

Even for the best in the world, the US Open courses are a struggle. That probably came as a relief to the golfers who played Bethpage on a regular basis.

"There is no room for error when you play a US Open," Woods said. "You know if you make a mistake you have to go ahead and take your punishment and move on. And everyone in the field has got to deal with it. It's just probably one of the most brutal mental tests there is in our sport."

The golf media world descended on Farmingdale, about thirty-five miles from Manhattan, on the south shore of Long Island. Of course, with traffic that can easily be a ninety-minute trip. The press group included Hank Gola, one of the best golf writers in the country, who was covering for the *New York*

Daily News. He had been writing about Woods's incredible rise to the top of the golf world, and Woods was the Pied Piper of Bethpage. Huge crowds followed him all week.

"It was just a reaffirmation of his general popularity. He had already kind of transcended the game by bringing in people who didn't even have to like golf in order to like Tiger Woods," Gola remembered. "And that was probably the biggest stage that he ever won on. The place was crazy that week. And I think it just furthered his popularity and probably brought some people in from the New York area as well."

Woods had a little-known connection to New York, which Gola once wrote about.

"I remember doing a story about Earl Woods, his dad, who actually learned the game while he was stationed at Fort Hamilton, in Brooklyn. So if it wasn't for New York, there will be no Tiger Woods, because Earl wouldn't have ever caught the golf bug," Gola said. "So, I think he probably just brought more people in and I don't think it was like a big explosion because it was already there. It was already on the way to critical mass. But in the New York area, probably just some more eyeballs on him. It probably influenced some more kids as well, but I think it was already well underway."

Bethpage lived up to the standards the US Open sets to bring the world's best to its knees. The crowds were typical New York. Massive and enthusiastic. The fans circled around the greens in incredible numbers, making it feel as if the players were performing in an amphitheater. Truth is Phil Mickelson was a New York favorite even though, like Woods, he's from California. There was something about Mickelson, his fearlessness, his go-for-it attitude, that endeared him to New Yorkers long before the Open. But as the weekend progressed, the fans adopted Woods as one of their own, realizing there were witnessing greatness, and cheered as he came down the stretch with the outcome never in doubt.

By the time late Sunday afternoon arrived, that warning about the difficulty of the course was not hyperbole, it was prophetic. Woods shot 67, 68, and 70 in the first three rounds, putting him at five under par and with a four-shot lead over Sergio Garcia and five shots over Mickelson. That left room for a little drama early in the fourth round when Woods three-putted each of the first two holes, allowing Garcia and Mickelson to close within two shots. But neither could get any closer the rest of the round. Woods shot a final-round 72 to finish at 277, three under par. He was the only golfer in the field to finish under par.

When Woods won his first Open at Pebble Beach in 2000, he was also the only golfer to finish under par. It's virtually impossible to comprehend that Woods was 12-under par in 2000 and the next closest golfers to him—Ernie Els and Miguel Angel Jimenez—were three-over par. Woods held an unheard-of 10-stroke lead after three rounds.

At Bethpage Black in 2002, Mickelson was still in search of his first major championship and he was the only other golfer not to be finish over par. He shot even-par 280, three shots back. Jeff Maggert was third at two over and Garcia was fourth at three over.

Jim Nantz, who anchors CBS golf coverage, said Woods's emergence at the Masters in 1997 "really opened up the game of golf. Suddenly, there was a whole new legion of fans, more people were watching and more people were interested. More people wanted to get into the game and that spawned a commitment by the golf community to give people a chance to participate in the sport. With Tiger's help along comes the First Tee Program, which has expanded internationally and involves literally hundreds of courses around the country. For kids who otherwise would have never had a chance, nor the financial wherewithal to get involved in the game, suddenly had a chance to not only go learn how to play, but also be taught nine core life lessons as part of the program. It was an amazing undertaking. And all this was really triggered by Tiger's quick rise to the top of the game of golf."

Woods had plenty of support from the fans at Bethpage, but Mickelson was a big crowd favorite. And being able to hold off Mickelson in the final round increased Woods's popularity and added to his legacy.

"Now, he didn't come to Bethpage having never won at a public golf course. He did that at the 2000 US Open at Pebble Beach," Nantz said. "The difference is Pebble Beach is a lot more expensive as a public golf course than Bethpage. And then when you factor in that it's New York and he's bringing the Tiger Woods show, which at the time, it's the greatest show in golf, to a public golf course. It was the perfect confluence of the rise of the game, the rise of Tiger Woods and the increase in the popularity and participation of the sport by minorities. And it was a really important trigger point in the game for Tiger to come to New York, perform to the height of his powers and to win. It was another statement victory for him."

TIGER TAMES BETHPAGE BLACK

BY PETER BOTTE

There is a warning sign just ahead of the first tee box at the public course known as Bethpage Black on Long Island.

It reads: "The Black course is an extremely difficult course which we recommend only for highly skilled golfers."

Tiger Woods certainly qualifies under that heading, and he tamed the vaunted track to win the 2002 US Open at Bethpage State Park with a 3-under finish for a three-stroke victory over Phil Mickelson—and his eighth of 15 career Grand Slam titles through 2022.

"That was at one of the heights of Tiger's power and, despite that, everyone who was familiar with Bethpage Black knew how difficult that golf course was, not to mention when you combine its difficulty with the treacherous US Open setup," *New York Post* golf columnist Mark Cannizzaro said. "Woods being the only player under par on such a diabolical course only added to his legend."

The wire-to-wire win at Bethpage marked Woods's sixth win in nine majors since the start of the 2000 campaign, although he didn't capture another Grand Slam title until the 2005 Masters.

Tiger once seemed destined to shatter Jack Nicklaus's record of 18 major crowns, but after winning the US Open for the third time in 2008 at Torrey Pines, he went more than a decade without adding another—due to various injuries and off-the-course problems—until finally notching No. 15 at the Masters in 2019.

But he'll always have that week at Bethpage in 2002 in which he sent the Long Island throngs into Tiger-chasing delirium.

"Tiger Woods, for all of his dominance, was never a country club kid," Cannizzaro recalled twenty years later. "He grew up in California playing whatever golf course his father, Earl, could get him onto and he broke course records at a lot of those courses. Bethpage Black also was a place that Earl had played several times when he was younger.

"People are and have always been fascinated with the things Tiger was able to do on the golf course, because so many of those things were unprecedented . . . and things that those mortals amongst us could never fathom doing ourselves. On top of that, we on the East Coast didn't get a lot of chances to see Woods up close with not a lot of PGA Tour events in the area. So, getting the chance to see that greatness in our area on a public golf course that we all play added to the drama of what he accomplished."

POSTGAME

Bethpage's "Black Course"

PADRAIG HARRINGTON (THREE-TIME MAJOR CHAMPION): Back then the golf courses were set up to be really difficult with heavy rough. So going to this great course by all accounts, where they hadn't been before, it turned out it really was a great golf course—they set it up brutely difficult that week which very much suited the best player in the field, Tiger Woods.

JUSTIN LEONARD (FORMER BRITISH OPEN CHAMPION): That was a brutal one. The golf course was brutal, If I remember correctly the weather was pretty bad which made it even tougher. The fans were very boisterous, typical New York crowds. It was a fun week, but it was a hard one.

ANN LIGUORI (TENNIS AND GOLF BROADCASTER): Bethpage Black, becoming the first truly public course to host a US Open, was a huge story in the years leading up to that 2002 US Open. Known as the "People's Open," Bethpage Black, the top municipal course in the country, and probably the toughest. People slept in their cars at Bethpage, waiting to play the course!

PADRAIG HARRINGTON: The 2002 US Open was the first time we visited Bethpage Black, and there was an extreme amount of hype. A big deal was made of the fact that it was a public golf course but coming from Europe, that made no sense to us because all golf courses have public access—certainly in Ireland you can turn up and pay a green fee at private courses. But I did get the fact that it was the people's golf course of New York.

Tiger's Dominance

JIM NANTZ (CBS SPORTS ANNOUNCER): It was just a year removed from Tiger's completion of what we called the Tiger Slam. It was a point in his career where he accomplished something that had never happened in the modern era, for one player to hold all four major championship trophies at once.

So, when he came to Bethpage '02, his stature in the game was his peak. And so was his talent as a player. I mean he was bigger than life.

PADRAIG HARRINGTON: It was one of those tournaments where you would love to think that you could challenge Tiger. I was in the last group with him on Saturday, but the reality is that he had the measure of everybody on a golf course like that. I think the crowds probably helped him—Tiger is not from New York, but the crowds really did love him there. The crowds were large and boisterous, but very appreciative—maybe because I'm Irish I feel at home everywhere in the States, but certainly at Bethpage I got a good welcome myself.

PADRAIG HARRINGTON: The tougher the challenge the better for Tiger, in the sense that some of the swashbuckling nature of his game was replaced by a more conservative and steady game, so putting him on a tough golf course was what he liked and wanted. He was the only guy to finish under par and he won by three shots, but the reality is that if he was pushed a bit more he would have finished 4, 5, or more under par—whatever was required he would have done.

JUSTIN LEONARD: He was a great competitor, and not only did he want to win, but he wanted to win by as many strokes as possible. That's why he won so big so often.

HANK GOLA (*NY DAILY NEWS* AND *NY POST* COLUMNIST): It was remarkable. Tiger in his prime had more skill than any other golfer in history. Now, that doesn't mean that I'm gonna put him over Jack Nicklaus as the best ever, because of longevity. But for those few years where he was dominating golf, I don't think anybody else played as well. And to do that on a course, like Bethpage, which was just kicking everybody's rear ends was quite impressive.

PADRAIG HARRINGTON: It was a pretty easy win for him to be honest. Three under par was well within him that week, whilst the rest of us probably deceived ourselves in many ways when it came to the challenge. That was Tiger during his peak!

JUSTIN LEONARD: I don't know if it meant more to him to win on a public golf course. I think it meant a lot to the people from New York to see him win on Bethpage Black. I would imagine a lot of people that were there that week had played the golf course quite often. I think seeing Tiger Woods win on their golf course made it so special for the golf fans up there.

HANK GOLA: He actually won a couple of times on public golf courses. I think that was a great symbolic victory for him. He did the same thing at Pebble Beach when he ran away with the US Open there at another public golf course, by the way, even though it cost the public three hundred dollars to play there at the time. But yeah, he just was far and away the best. You knew that anytime there was a major it was easy. It was Tiger and then everybody else.

JIM NANTZ: What comes to mind for me from Bethpage in '02 was that Tiger was able to hold off Phil and win at Bethpage before a boisterous crowd of golf enthusiasts.

ANN LIGUORI: As dominant and as universally appealing as Tiger was, fans were rooting for Phil Mickelson to win. They were in awe of Tiger but wanted Phil to become the "People's Champion."

Phil was celebrating his thirty-second birthday that final Sunday and I remember fans serenading him, singing "Happy Birthday" on his every hole. New Yorkers love Phil! Phil was the underdog and New Yorkers and most sports fans love rooting for the underdog.

Back then, Tiger was in his prime, physically strong, prior to all the back surgeries and other injuries. He had won six of the last nine majors at that time. He was so focused and fierce. He didn't like Phil. Tiger wasn't friendly back then, to his fellow competitors, to the fans, or to the media.

Tiger's Legacy and Effect on the Sport

JIM NANTZ: Tiger came in as a professional in the fall of 1996 and he turned professional after arguably the most successful amateur career we had seen since Bobby Jones. And in '97 he played his first major as a professional and he won at Augusta. And that day, April 13, 1997, really opened up the game of golf.

MARK CANNIZZARO (*NY POST* COLUMNIST): Tiger has a memory like an elephant. He never forgets and holds grudges quite well. I was highly critical of him in 2002 during the Martha Burk protesting of Augusta National not having any women members.

Years later, after Augusta finally admitted a couple of women members, including Condoleezza Rice, Woods came up to me and said in a snide way, "you must be really happy about this." This was some eight or nine years later and he still remembered.

ANN LIGUORI: What's most amazing to me is how he has transformed as a person—from a fiercely, private, inaccessible, unfriendly person and player, to a much more accommodating, warmer, seemingly joyful guy, relishing his status and place in history and seemingly enjoying parenting and being a good father.

FILIP BONDY (*NY DAILY NEWS* COLUMNIST): I think that there's a valid comparison between Tiger and Arthur Ashe: a young Black man comes up in a very white sport, and shows everybody that this can be done, despite all the obstacles. In golf there's probably more obstacles than tennis, in terms of finance, and just opportunity. Tiger also like Ashe, was not a radical by any means. He was embraced by the white spectators; he was not viewed as a threat to them whatsoever. Again, we go back to Jackie Robinson and what he meant, that was a different era and just his presence, even though he was not a radical by any means.

They were viewed as deserving superstars who kind of were different and because they were different, they were fascinating and they created a whole new audience.

MARK CANNIZZARO: I have a difficult time saying Tiger is *the* greatest of all time, because of Jack Nicklaus, who owns the most major championships, at 18 to Tiger's 15. An argument can be made, though, that Tiger is the most influential player of all time, a player who changed the game more than any other player.

JIM NANTZ: Tiger has gone through so many operations to his knees, back, and neck, and then he had the car crash. Somehow this guy has been stitched back together and is still competing. The Tiger story has so many chapters and layers to it. There were several points along the way where you would have thought that might be it for him. That he's never going to bounce back. Most recently was 2019 when he fought his way back to winning the Masters. Most people thought that was impossible for Tiger to ever be at that level again.

20

1973 BELMONT STAKES

JUNE 9, 1973

FROM SECRETARIAT
TO AMERICAN PHAROAH

TIME CAPSULE

- Mayor of New York: John Lindsay
- Oscar, Best Picture: *The Godfather*
- Oscar, Best Actor: Marlon Brando, *The Godfather*
- Oscar, Best Actress: Liza Minnelli, *Cabaret*
- Grammy, Album of the Year: George Harrison & Friends, *The Concert for Bangladesh*
- Grammy, Record of the Year: Roberta Flack, "The First Time Ever I Saw Your Face," *First Take*
- President of the US: Richard Nixon
- Price of Gas: $0.39/Gallon
- Heisman Trophy: John Cappelletti, running back, Penn State

PREGAME

Passing "The Test of the Champion" from Secretariat to American Pharoah

"The Waiting is the Hardest Part"—Tom Petty

Secretariat won the Belmont Stakes in record time, and in doing so made a quarter-century of waiting just a little bit easier. Charles "Chic" Anderson was on the call for CBS Sports and shared this memorable description of Secretariat that day, "moving like a tremendous machine." That call and that horse is etched into the memory of race fans forever. Secretariat motored to a memorable 31 lengths to win the Belmont Stakes and the Triple Crown of horse racing.

"The Sport of Kings" crowns only its most royal champions, in one place, and one place only—Belmont Park in New York.

The last Triple Crown winner before Secretariat was Citation in 1948, leaving a gaping twenty-five-year wait between champions. In 1948, World War II had ended three years earlier, and the Triple Crown victory was just the tonic the country needed to divert their attention.

Team sports provide a singular champion every year, but in horse racing to hold that distinction you need to capture all three jewels of the Triple Crown. This is indeed the rarest and most difficult to win of all the championships. Nobody knew at the time when Citation was crowned that a generation would pass before another Triple Crown would be won. That is what makes the Triple Crown one of the toughest feats in sports to accomplish.

First, a horse must be in top form as a three-year-old. That is the only age they can compete in each of the Triple Crown races. Second, each of three races are on tracks of different lengths. It starts with the Kentucky Derby which is 1 1/4 miles. Then off to Charm City, for the Preakness, where it is raced on a track of a 1 3/16 mile. The horses then head north, up I-95, to the Big Apple, for the longest of the three races, the Belmont Stakes, at 1 1/2 miles. All three tracks demand a different set of skills and need to be won in just a five-week span of traveling from Kentucky to Baltimore to New York for a 820-mile trip into history. It's a test of skill, resilience, speed, durability and, of course, the bond between a horse and its jockey, all with the whole world watching.

Penny Chenery, who bred Secretariat, shared that the training is different because the demand on horses changed through the years with the higher prices that they fetched. There became more emphasis to get a return on the investment from the horse faster and that rushed and hurt their development.

Sir Barton was the first in 1919 to win all three legs. There have only been thirteen horses to ever capture the Triple Crown. But none in such impressive fashion as Secretariat.

To win the Triple Crown you first need to win "The Run for the Roses," the Kentucky Derby. Well, there were 134,476 fans in attendance that day that could—and surely would—attest to the brilliance of this thoroughbred. Secretariat won the 99th running of the Kentucky Derby in a track record time of 1:59 2/5. As the big red horse crossed the finish line, radios across the country were cranked up to full volume to hear the excited voice of Cawood Ledford on United States Armed Forces Radio, "It's Secretariat! And he's got the Kentucky Derby!"

Secretariat was off to Baltimore, with the Kentucky Derby win, and its sights firmly set on the Preakness. Ron Turcotte was aboard but this would not be an easy win for sure. Anderson was on the call as they made the turn out of the starting gates, "Secretariat is last again as they move into the first turn," he said. Turcotte waited until they made the turn towards the backstretch and then as if he was shot out of a cannon, he made his move. Again, Anderson on the call, "Sham with an easy lead now, but here comes Secretariat, he's moving fast, and he's going to the outside, he's going for the lead and it's right now he's looking for it."

Secretariat won the race in spectacular fashion. Turcotte didn't even need to go to the whip as he approached the finish line. There was no question that he was the best three-year-old in the country. The only question was about the final time. The time posted at Pimlico was 1:55 for Secretariat to cover the 1 3/16 race. It was a second slower than the track record set in 1971 by Canonero II. However, the great baseball Triple Crown winner from the Baltimore Orioles, Frank Robinson, who was doubling as the clocker for the *Daily Racing Form,* had Secretariat at 1:53 2/5.

Hold on a second. Not only was that more than a second less on his clock, but it was a different Frank Robinson. It wasn't the former world champion from the Orioles after all. But could his clock be correct? He checked with the chief clocker from the *Daily Racing Form,* Frenchy Schwartz, who had the same time. The next day the Pimlico track clocker E. T. McLean Jr. had the time at 1:54 2/5 but didn't dispute the computer-generated time by the Visumatic machine until the next day. On Monday, the stewards voted to make the official time 1:54 2/5, which was what McLean had clocked. In 2012, the Maryland Racing commission voted unanimously to change the time to a record 1:53 flat using digital technology.

The time was the only controversy in the build up to Belmont. The best racehorse on the planet was Secretariat. But to make it official, Turcotte and "Big Red" needed to prove it at the Belmont Stakes.

As they hit the backstretch, Anderson was on the call again, and he hit his stride in describing the indescribable:

Secretariat is all alone. He's out there almost a sixteenth of a mile away from the rest of the horses. Secretariat is in a position that seems impossible to catch. He's into the stretch. Secretariat leads this field by 18 lengths, and now Twice a Prince has taken second and My Gallant has fallen back to third. They are in the stretch. Secretariat has opened a 22-length lead! He is going to be the Triple Crown winner! Here comes Secretariat to the wire. An unbelievable, an amazing performance! He hits the finish 25 lengths in front!

The excitement in the call came through the TV and to think the lead that fueled his enthusiasm was so large that his in the moment estimate was six lengths short of the official 31-length victory. That was the call that catapulted horseracing into the national spotlight and this horse into history!

After Secretariat broke the quarter of a century Triple Crown drought, Seattle Slew and Affirmed pulled off winning all three legs in back-to-back years. It was 1977 and 1978. It felt like this may become a much more frequent event. But that is not the way the Sports of Kings works. It would be another thirty-seven years until another horse and jockey could capture America's sporting attention and racing's ultimate prize. The year was 2015, and American Pharoah was about to be crowned king of thoroughbred racing. American Pharoah's jockey, Victor Espinoza, was close to winning the Triple Crown twice before, winning the first two legs, but couldn't win the Belmont Stakes either time.

Espinoza had won the Kentucky Derby three times in his career. He won in 2002 guiding War Emblem and then in 2014 he rode California Chrome to victory. Both times he won the Preakness Stakes and needed just one victory at the Belmont to win the Triple Crown.

In 2002, in the 134th running of the Belmont Stakes, Espinoza and War Emblem stumbled out of the starting gate, here's the call that captured the moment, "And they're off and War Emblem's quest for the Triple Crown, he did not break alertly, War Emblem was off near the back of the pack." Espinoza lost his chance at history to a 70–1 long shot, Sarava. A two-dollar bet won you $142.50. It is indeed a long shot to win all three legs but to lose to the biggest long shot ever to win the Belmont Stakes was a tough pill to swallow.

In 2014, at the 146th running of the Belmont Stakes, there was anticipation in the air as Espinoza had his second shot at the historic achievement. California Chrome was the morning line favorite. This time Espinoza would not stumble coming out of the starting gate, he would bolt to the lead on the rail. But by the backstretch he had fallen to fourth place still on the rail but was pinned in. Victor waited and waited to make his move. He stayed within striking distance and on the final turn made his move, but they were four wide and he couldn't overtake Tonalist who surged to the win. California Chrome was 1 1/2 lengths out of the winner's circle. Close but certainly no cigar and they didn't even finish in the money, tying for fourth place with Wicked Strong.

"I think about my experiences and the fact that I was very close twice to winning it," Victor Espinoza said. "When I was close the first time, you know, you learned that nothing is impossible. So, I had to continue to work hard and dedicate myself even more and the second time I was there I thought I got it this time. Again, I had a second chance but the point is that I never gave up. That was my goal in life and it was my dream to build a comeback again and to win the Triple Crown."

His Triple Crown dreams would get a third chance. American Pharoah entered the 2015 Kentucky Derby as the favorite. It had been thirty-seven years since Affirmed won the elusive Triple Crown. There was no way to match that feat without winning the "Run for the Roses." Being the favorite was not a guarantee of victory.

Three times in the seven preceding years the most famous face and name in the racing game, Bob Baffert had left Churchill Downs feeling, well, down. He had two runner-up finishes and a sixth-place finish by another money line favorite. Baffert had the championship pedigree, winning the Derby three times, but the losses were starting to wear on him and his reputation. All that was about to change on May 2, 2015. American Pharoah didn't disappoint, going off as a 5–2 favorite and winning the race by a length and was pulling away as they crossed the finish line.

Baffert had his fourth derby win; now could he and Espinoza win the Triple Crown? Up next was Pimlico.

The 140th running of the Preakness Stakes was the start of what could be a coronation. The eight-horse field was no match for American Pharoah, as they pulled away for an easy seven-length victory. Espinoza had been there before in 2002 and 2014, heading into the Belmont with a chance to etch his name with the all-time great jockeys but he came up short both times.

If the third time was going to be a charm it would come with a lot of history. If he crossed the finish line in first place, Victor Espinoza would become the first Mexican jockey to win the Triple Crown. He would also garner the title of oldest jockey to win the Triple Crown. Could Espinoza and American Pharoah join Secretariat in the annals of history? All that stood in their way was "The Test of the Champion" as the Belmont Stakes is known.

No horse might ever have the impact that Secretariat had on horse racing and sports fans in this county. Tom Petty was right, "The Waiting is the Hardest Part" but it would be well worth the wait for Victor Espinoza and American Pharoah.

SECRETARIAT, AMERICAN PHAROAH HALT TRIPLE CROWN DROUGHTS

BY PETER BOTTE

Thirteen horses have captured the Triple Crown, but few have captured the imagination of the New York crowds quite like slump-busters Secretariat in 1973 and American Pharoah in 2015.

Secretariat's cruise to a 31-length victory at The Belmont—to become the first Triple Crown winner since Citation in 1948—was still marveled at nearly five decades later and is widely recognized as one of the singularly dominant sporting performances of all-time.

Also, the photo of Canadian jockey Ron Turcotte turning around to peer over his shoulder down the stretch as if to wonder what happened to everyone else is one of the legendary and enduring pics in sports history.

"I knew he had a chance at the record," Turcotte beamed on June 9, 1973, after Secretariat broke Count Fleet's Belmont record of a 25-lengths win set in 1943. "[Secretariat] had been fast, but he still had more left when I asked him to go get the record.

"He's just the complete horse, and that seemed to say it all."

The wait for the next two Triple Crown winners in the "Sport of Kings" wasn't quite as long, as Seattle Slew and Affirmed managed victories in the Kentucky Derby, The Preakness, and The Belmont in back-to-back years in 1977 and '78.

After that, however, we waited another thirty-seven years until the Bob Baffert-trained American Pharoah zoomed into our lives in 2015, with Victor Espinoza becoming the first jockey from Mexico and the oldest jockey ever (forty-three) at the time to win the Triple Crown. Mike Smith, at fifty-two, became the oldest to win it three years later when the Baffert-trained Justify—a lineage descendent of Secretariat's—also pulled off the feat in 2018.

"Winning the Triple Crown means everything to me," said Espinoza. "When there are days that are a complete disaster because everything goes wrong, I go to sleep, wake up the next day, shake it off, and then I come back stronger. The feeling that I have winning the Triple Crown will never go away. It will stay there with me probably until the day I die."

347

POSTGAME

Chasing the Dream

VICTOR ESPINOZA (TRIPLE CROWN—WINNING JOCKEY): I took a lot of punches, many times, I got knocked down and hit the ground and got up and moved forward, literally and figuratively.

Those times helped me to be tougher. Just be better and go forward and never stop trying to be able to win the Triple Crown.

Winning the Triple Crown!

VICTOR ESPINOZA: At that moment, there's just no emotions other than, *Did that just happen?* I can't believe I'm the one that did it. I'm the one that won the Triple Crown after so many years.

It's one of those things that I can't even describe because it took so much to be able to get it done, and I'm the lucky one.

The Legacy of American Pharoah

VICTOR ESPINOZA: I think he's a once-in-a-lifetime horse. Especially because I can't even figure out how he has that much power. I think it's his personality. Because I believe in any sport, we need to save energy as much as possible for the finish and don't waste it being nervous. Because if you get nervous, you can waste a lot of energy. American Pharoah was calm. That was the key for him that he never really burned that much energy before the race. Oh, and he just loves to run.

VICTOR ESPINOZA: American Pharoah was probably the top five, maybe like top three, that I ever rode in my life. He was very competitive. By then I rode quite a few good horses, but with that one, I was completely speechless at the way that horse was moving and the amount of power and talent he had, he dominated every single horse in the race.

I mean, the first time I raced him I thought of the Kentucky Derby. When we were in the Arkansas Derby, I knew we could win the Triple Crown. That is when it hit me. This one was my last shot to win the Triple Crown.

Being a Champion

VICTOR ESPINOZA: It affected me a lot because you know I feel like I came to be seen as the best jockey in the United States when I won the Triple Crown.

VICTOR ESPINOZA: Winning the Triple Crown means everything to me.

VICTOR ESPINOZA: I take a lot of pride in being the first jockey from Mexico to win the Triple Crown. It's not just because of where I came from, but it's also about how I started my career, how much I was able to achieve, basically, for me to come out of nowhere—I didn't even know that the Triple Crown existed.

The next thing I know I witnessed myself winning it.

That was probably the ultimate thing for all my hard work and all the ups and downs I had to go through to get there.

VICTOR ESPINOZA: We all think that that's going to happen. But a lot of things can go wrong. So in my career I was always prepared mentally to lose because if I lose it's going to be really hard on me. I could have probably gone home and cried because all that work would just go away in one minute. But when I win it makes things so be much easier, right, a hundred times easier.

It took me twenty-something years riding horses and three times to win the Triple Crown. But every day we learn something new. During my career a lot of bad things happen, but I never stopped trying until I achieved what I wanted—that was a Triple Crown.

VICTOR ESPINOZA: It is amazing how many people that are so excited for me to win that Triple Crown. People I don't even know in New York City see me in the street, and they're so excited. It made me really feel good that so many people recognize me and told me that they were there and witnessed the Triple Crown.

Author's Note: This book was almost completed when Aaron Judge broke Roger Maris's American League home run record; of course we had to add it to the book. We figured you all would be wondering what moment was bumped from the book. Well, here is the answer to your question and your bonus chapter, at no extra charge.

Bonus Chapter

1991 US OPEN TENNIS
SEPTEMBER 2, 1991

JIMMY CONNORS SHOWS BRILLIANCE HAS NO AGE LIMIT

TIME CAPSULE

- Mayor of New York: David Dinkins
- Oscar, Best Picture: *Dances with Wolves*
- Oscar, Best Actor: Jeremy Irons, *Reversal of Fortune*
- Oscar, Best Actress: Kathy Bates, *Misery*
- Grammy, Album of the Year: *Back on the Block*, Quincy Jones
- Grammy, Record of the Year: Phil Collins, "Another Day in Paradise," . . . *But Seriously*
- President of the US: George H. W. Bush
- Price of Gas: $1.14/Gallon
- Heisman Trophy: Desmond Howard, wide receiver/kick returner, Michigan

---

PREGAME

A New Yorker is: Brash, Loud and Confident. Jimmy Connors is: Brash, Loud and Confident. On September 2, 1991, Jimmy Connors was a New Yorker

Jimmy Connors was not from the mean streets of New York. Connors was from the streets of East St. Louis. He was everything that New Yorkers loved, he put his heart and soul into every stroke on the court. His emotions were raw and real. His gave every ounce of effort that his thirty-nine-year-old body would allow in the classic fourth round match at the '91 US Open. It was September 2, 1991—his thirty-ninth birthday—as he stood opposite the twenty-four-year-old Aaron Krickstein.

That night he owned New York like few athletes ever have. The US Open signifies the end of the summer every year in New York, as it wraps up around Labor Day. Connors was at the end of his career, but he was not going to be denied on that September night in Flushing Meadows.

As Connors walked onto the court to play his round of 16 match, the New York fans serenaded him with a rendition of "Happy Birthday." The US

Open was home to Jimmy since the late seventies. He was adopted as their favorite son. However, this night was special. Jimmy Connors at thirty-nine, was making a miraculous run through the US Open field, that led to a young phenom named Aaron Krickstein.

It was not just that Krickstein was good. Get this: at the tender age of sixteen, he won an ATP event in Tel Aviv, Israel, becoming the youngest player to take home an ATP title. Just a year later, he was the youngest player to be ranked in the Top 20, and broke into the Top 10 in August 1984. So, if a match was going to last four hours and forty-one minutes, you would think: Advantage Krickstein.

You'd be wrong.

Now, let's add in that this was way before Tom Brady, Serena Williams, and LeBron James were able to perform at an elite level into their late thirties and even into their forties. It was an epic eleven-day run through the Open for Connors. So the expectations may not have been as high for Jimmy on that night, and with good reason. Besides his age, Connors was coming off of wrist surgery at the end of 1990. He wore a cast for four months, was ranked No. 174 in the world, and only made the US Open field as a qualifier.

Don't forget: between 1973 and 1985, Connors reached the quarterfinals, or better, every year. Connors had the heart and mind of a champion. But could his battered body hold up?

Long before "Jimbo" turned Louis Armstrong Stadium into his own home court in 1991, he had turned the world into his playground. Jimmy had won the 1978 US Open, but had not yet won over the New York fans. During a postmatch interview, in 1978, that was fed into the stadium, Connors said, "Every time I come to New York, I play my best tennis (clapping) whether you like me or not I like you (more applause)." The tide had turned. This guy was one of us!

Connors was a celebrity on and off the court. He dated some of the most beautiful women in the world. It seemed like Connors spent as much time in the gossip pages as he did in the sports pages. He was engaged to Miss World, Marjorie Wallace. I think her title tells you everything you need to know. He then took it a step further, and took the plunge, marrying Playboy model Patti McGuire. But first, his most renown love interest was tennis superstar Chris Evert, known at the time as "America's Sweetheart." Connors and Evert each had a devastating two-handed backhand, and this is not a backhanded compliment. They both won, and a lot, on the court.

They were engaged in 1974. They both won a Grand Slam title at Wimbledon that year. The media had fun with that calling them "The Love-bird Double." Sadly, there was trouble with the "Double," as they broke up in 1975 (though they did get back together in 1976). People followed Connors's love life almost as closely as his tennis life.

At an early age, Connors was pushed into tennis by his mother, Gloria. She was his coach in the early years of his development. Both Jimmy's mother and grandmother were ever-present forces in his tennis life and at his matches. Gloria built the foundation that catapulted Jimmy into national prominence in junior tennis. Connors won both the 12 & under and 14 & under Junior Orange Bowl championships. She eventually turned her son's coaching over to legendary Pancho Segura, at the age of sixteen. The Gloria–Segura coaching combination paid huge dividends, as Jimmy won the Southern California Junior Sectional Boys' 18s championship in 1970. Two years later he turned pro, winning the Jacksonville Open—his first tournament. He didn't stop winning for decades. The next year, he defeated another tennis legend, Arthur Ashe, to take home the 1973 US Pro Singles Championship. Connors was unseeded in the tournament.

How's that for a start to a career?

He was just getting warmed up.

Connors was the ATP No. 1 player in the world for a then-record 160 consecutive weeks from 1974 to 1977. Jimmy won eight Grand Slam singles finals and two Grand Slam doubles titles in his career. He won a total of 109 titles, which is an Open era men's singles record.

Just two years after turning pro, it was a year for the ages for Connors in 1974. His record was 99–4, he won 15 of the 21 tournaments he entered, and he played in the biggest tournaments in the world. Connors won the 1974 Australian Open, Wimbledon, and the US Open in the same year. He was only one tournament short of the Grand Slam. But in 1974, he was banned from participating in the French Open after he joined World Team Tennis. Was being a part of the Baltimore Banners worth losing a place in history as a tennis Grand Slam winner? Probably not. Connors filed a lawsuit to gain entrance in the French Open, but was denied. The French Open lost a chance to have the world's No. 2 player and he lost a chance to make history. Tennis fans also lost out. The only winners were Banners fans in Charm City. Maybe.

Connors won the Australian Open against Phil Dent, then beat Ken Rosewall in both the Wimbledon and US Open Finals that year. Rosewall was, get this for symmetry, thirty-nine years old when he lost both finals to Connors. Connors was just twenty-one when he beat him at Wimbledon. The London crowd was pulling for the veteran Rosewall to give them one more magic moment. Sounds like foreshadowing to the Connors–Krickstein match in 1991, right?

Now to put a finer point on the symmetry, Connors faced the thirty-nine-year Ken Rosewall in the finals of the US Open later that summer. Just like Connors, who would be the exact same age in 1991, the aging veteran, Rosewall, was the clear fan favorite over the younger Connors. Jimmy dismantled him 6–1, 6–0, 6–1—is that any way to treat a legend?—in a little more than an hour. Connors won the championship on the grass courts of the West Side Tennis Club in Forest Hills, Queens, before it moved over to Flushing Meadows.

Connors reached the finals of the US Open every year from 1974 to '78. He reached the finals of Wimbledon four of those years. Connors was on top of the tennis world and loving it.

His biggest rival in the early years was Bjorn Borg. They could not have been more opposite on the court. Borg was emotionless. He was the embodiment of the country club sports roots of tennis. Polite, he never threw a racket or yelled at an umpire. Connors, on the other hand, had turned this gentile sport into a blood sport. They played twelve times, from 1974 to '78. Borg's robotic game was no match for Connors's fury. Borg only took four of those matches. But the two of them that stung the most for Jimmy were held in the finals at the All England Lawn Tennis and Croquet Club. Losing in the 1977 and 1978 Wimbledon Finals helped Borg turn the tide in the rivalry. It also saw Borg supplant Connors as the world's No. 1 player in the world in '77. Connors did get his measure of revenge by beating Borg in the US Open Finals in '78. This added to his victory over Borg in the '76 US Open final.

Connors's next rival, John McEnroe, matched his intensity on the court. In fact, John may even have surpassed Connors's boorish behavior. Connors seemed to play to the crowd, getting them involved and using their energy to motivate him, while Johnny Mac seemed to feed off his belief that everyone was against him. In the 1982 Wimbledon Finals, it was Connors who was principally against him. McEnroe was the No. 1 player in the world but Connors was the best player on that day. Jimmy won his second Wimbledon title. McEnroe got his measure of revenge two years later by taking the Wimbledon Final from Connors. John was six years younger than Jimmy, the best player in the world at that point, and racked up a 20–14 head-to-head record.

Connors was always a showman. He created his own matches against big named players and rivals. They were patterned after the famous "Battle of the Sexes" match, where Bobby Riggs defeated Billie Jean King. In the first match Connors put together, he defeated Rod Laver in a winner-take-all $100,000 showdown in Las Vegas. Connors also mirrored the Battle for the Sexes by taking on Martina Navratilova. Connors won that match 7–5, 6–2. Pretty darn close.

The US Open is where this tale ends. It's a storied history for this championship. There are four Grand Slam events every year. The US Open is the last one. The Connors era was considered the open era when professionals were allowed to compete in Grand Slam events. In 1978, the tournament was moved to the USTA National Tennis Center in Flushing Meadows-Corona Park, in Queens.

Connors won at both locations. He took his first two US Open Championships at the West Side Tennis Club, in 1974 and '76. He then won three more US Open Championships in 1978, '82, and '83. That is eight years before he would make his run through the 1991 US Open field.

Remember, Connors was coming off of wrist surgery and was just a qualifier in the field. He missed the 1990 US Open completely. So to say there were no expectations placed on him in 1991 is an understatement. As you will remember, he entered the Open as the 174th-ranked player in the world. For New York sports fans, this would be an 11-day thrill ride they would never forget.

In the first round, it was Connors vs. McEnroe. The rivalry renewed. Hey, wait a minute. John was busy with his straight sets first-round win versus Glenn Layendecker. Who, you ask? It doesn't matter. What mattered was Jimmy was facing John's brother, Patrick, who was twenty-five years old and a heck of player in his own right. He won 140 singles matches, a French Open championship as a doubles player, and was a Davis Cup captain. Not a bad resume, and was fourteen years younger than Jimmy. The match started at 9:15 p.m. Okay, it wasn't yet bedtime for Jimmy, but he did say good night to McEnroe. The younger McEnroe took the first two sets 6–4, 7–6 in a tiebreaker. Patrick was cruising up three games in the third set. Jimmy knew this could be his last US Open unless he could immediately come up with something magical. Connors fought back and won the third set, 6–4. The crowd also sensed this could be the end without their help. Everyone had to do their part getting behind the old man (in tennis years, of course). Connors won the last two sets 6–2 and 6–4 to escape the first round. The match didn't end until 1:35 in the morning.

"I think this is the biggest comeback, for a lot of reasons," Connors said. "I was going against a McEnroe. Patrick let me in the match the third set, and the crowd won it for me."

"If I was in the crowd, I would have been rooting for Jimmy, too," McEnroe said. "You have to play the player, and that's what I was trying to do. Unfortunately, I didn't put him away when I should have. I thought I had the match won. But if you think you've got Jimmy Connors beat, that is when he is at his most dangerous."

Was Connors tired after his marathon match against McEnroe? Could he find the energy for his second-round match against Michiel Schapers? Even if the name Schapers doesn't ring a bell, he was a heck of a Norwegian tennis player who just three years earlier was ranked 25th in the world by the ATP. So how did Connors do? Well, he won in straight sets.

The third round featured Connors and the New York crowd verses Karel Novacek. Karel was the 10th seed in the tournament and peaked at No. 8 in the world in the ATP ranking. Novacek also won thirteen men's singles titles and six doubles titles. He was a formidable opponent, but not in the first set. Jimmy won easily 6–1. He then won the second set 6–4 and closed him out in straight sets 6–3. Everyone but Karel was happy on that day.

Connors's fairytale run was still alive, Gloria's son was thrilling the county again, and the New York fans still had their man to root for in the round of 16. An hour before the Krickstein match, there was Gloria on the court helping Jimmy with his serve.

Gloria was Connors's coach as a boy.

Gloria was still coaching Connors as a thirty-nine-year-old man.

Gloria was his rock.

Glory was his destiny on that September night in 1991.

. . . AND A VERY HAPPY BIRTHDAY IT WAS FOR JIMMY

By Peter Botte

Aaron Krickstein couldn't sleep, which was wholly understandable after the city that never does was kept awake into the wee hours past midnight during his gripping and exhilarating match against sentimental crowd favorite Jimmy Connors, at the 1991 US Open.

More than thirty years later, those who witnessed Connors last-gasp run at Flushing Meadows in New York—including a nearly five-hour marathon victory on his thirty-ninth birthday over Krickstein in the fourth round—still talk about one of those quintessential "you-had-to-be-there" moments in New York sports lore.

In a telling interview weeks later, Krickstein—a native of Ann Arbor—told future *New York Post* baseball columnist Ken Davidoff of the University of Michigan school paper, the *Michigan Daily*, about his sleepless nights in the ensuing days.

"Well, it was pretty tough at first. It was one of the few matches, probably the only match, I had trouble sleeping for a few nights after it," Krickstein told Davidoff in October of '91. "The night after, I didn't sleep but one minute with all the hype. It was a big match.

"And even though he's thirty-nine, it was labeled Connors-Krickstein, a big Labor Day. CBS match. I was kind of fired up. And I knew since [Boris] Becker had lost, I had a good chance that if I could win this match, even though I had never beaten him, I could possibly go to the semis. And then the way the match turned out, after having so many chances, and then with the crowd, being like they were it was a tough one to lose."

Connors, a five-time US Open winner, was ranked 174th in the world at the start of the tournament, which began with a rousing comeback from two sets down against Patrick McEnroe.

Even winning that match would have represented a fond farewell for Connors, but it only was the beginning en-route to the match with Krickstein, a twenty-four-year-old fellow American. Krickstein normally enjoyed great crowd support in New York, but he estimated that the partisan crowd was "95 percent" behind his Labor Day opponent.

Krickstein actually held a 5–2 lead in the decisive set, but Connors rode the energy of the crowd to win the match 3–6, 7–6(8), 1–6, 6–3, 7–6(4). The crowd then showered him with a rendition of "Happy Birthday" after he captured the match in a stirring fifth-set tiebreaker.

"I guess if there was one person I wouldn't mind losing a match to. Connors and I are pretty good friends," Krickstein said. "But it was a tough one to lose. And there's no doubt, it's one I'll remember for a long time."

THE POSTGAME

Marathon Man!

ANN LIGUORI (TENNIS AND GOLF BROADCASTER): Having a front row seat at the Arthur Ashe Tennis Stadium Court at the Billie Jean King National Tennis Center in Flushing Meadows, NY, from high above in my WFAN broadcast booth for the US Open Tennis Championships every year since 1982, I've seen a lot of history unfold! And before the roof was installed on the Ashe Court, the famous Jimmy Connors-Aaron Krickstein epic match was the "go-to" match they'd replay, over and over again, on the giant screen when there was a rain delay. Those of you who witnessed that September 2, 1991, Round of 16 US Open match between birthday boy Connors, who turned thirty-nine that day, fresh off reconstructive surgery on his wrist, came into the US Open as a wild card entry, ranked 174th in the world, beat twenty-four-year-old Krickstein, 3–6, 7–6, 1–6, 6–3, 7–6, saw one for the ages—all four hours and forty-one minutes of it! Krickstein led 5–2 in the final set but Connors, with his never-say-die attitude, blood-and-guts intensity, and experience, rallied back in that fifth and final set, to win it in a tiebreaker, 7–4. The match, which lasted past 1:30 in the morning, had everything—unlimited momentum changes, Connors berating the referee, incredible athleticism from both players, breathtaking points and the ol' man moving his fans to pandemonium. I was spellbound throughout, watching every second of the match.

AARON KRICKSTEIN (THE *MICHIGAN DAILY*, AS TOLD TO KEN DAVIDOFF): I knew what to expect going in the crowd would be 80–90 percent for him, it was 95 percent. I usually have good support at the US Open, and it was obviously a different atmosphere for me to deal with.

THE 20 GREATEST MOMENTS IN NEW YORK SPORTS HISTORY

JIM NANTZ (CBS SPORTS ANNOUNCER): I did not call that match but I was part of the CBS broadcast team that day when Connors beat Aaron Krickstein. I was calling the grandstand matches that day. When play wrapped up on the grandstand court, I believe it was, Labor Day Monday. I came over just to watch this match, I just knew that we were sitting on history, that at his age, it was an unimaginable, impossible belief. That someone on his thirty-ninth birthday could pull off something like that. It was an amazing feat. And I mean, it was a power jolt through all of New York. Sometimes big events can get lost in the city because it's just so big, there's so many people but the US Open Tennis Tournament, it felt so alive that it felt like the entire city was touched by that moment by Jimmy.

FILIP BONDY (*NY DAILY NEWS* COLUMNIST): Oh, God knows I've seen it often enough, because they used to play it during every rain delay of every tennis match. But lately, we don't get to see it as much because there are roofs on the main courts, and they always have something to show live now. But it used to be that as soon as they went to a rain delay, they automatically switched to Connors-Krickstein. It was a remarkable show and Connors brings emotion to everything. Now, it probably would feel less remarkable, wouldn't it? I hate to say it because of what we've seen from players like Federer, Nadal, and Serena Williams. They've changed what aging in tennis is all about. But back then it was just unheard of that anybody in their thirties, let alone their late thirties, could make a serious run through a major—which is a best-of-five set tournament. Connors was out there sweating his guts out. Of course, the New York fans had adopted him long ago. I mean, he could be a bit of a jerk. There's no denying it. But he brought such emotion to that particular match. Sometimes people underestimate just how good Krickstein was back then. Krickstein was a heck of a player. And that was a great match. I think that when I look back on it, it's probably one of the top five or six events that I've ever been at as a sportswriter.

MARK CANNIZZARO (*NY POST* COLUMNIST): No one played harder than Connors, and New York sports fans loved and respected that. We all, as sports fans, we always want more sports, and that epic, dramatic match felt like it was going to go on for days.

JIMMY CONNORS (DURING A PRESS CONFERENCE): I mean how can you not laugh about this? I mean seriously, I am out here playing against kids who are the greatest players in the world and they are fifteen years younger than I am doing this. I mean what the heck is going on here?

An Adopted New Yorker

FILIP BONDY: He owned the US Open. He owned Flushing Meadows. He owned Ashe Stadium. And he was adopted early actually by New Yorkers. I don't think he was ever a villain in the way that John McEnroe could turn off the crowd. John would just somehow whine and moan and whatever and the crowd turned on John, but they didn't really turn on Jimmy. Jimmy gave the kind of visceral effort out there that the fans loved, the pumping of the fist, the screeching, the screaming, that sort of stuff. He changed the way tennis was viewed and was played in New York, really anywhere. Because until he came around, it was sort of a more gentlemanly sport. It was a sport played by the Borgs of the world. I think that Jimmy was everything that New York and New Yorkers love, putting every ounce of what he had on the court. Even if he did misbehave and, sometimes, he was forgiven much more easily than John McEnroe.

AARON KRICKSTEIN (AS TOLD TO KEN DAVIDOFF): I felt pretty good about my chances, I was playing pretty well in the first set. And in the second set, he started acting up and really got the crowd into it.

If it was any other player, maybe besides McEnroe, he probably would've gotten at least a point or a game or maybe even defaulted for the things he said to the umpire. Then the umpire had the audacity to say he didn't hear him when everyone else on TV did.

I kind of expect that. I didn't think they'd do much about it. I could've seen if they had defaulted him, [the crowd] probably would've done anything from nuking the stadium to killing the referee.

MARK CANNIZZARO: New York loves athletes to bleed passion, and Connors bled passion, wore it on his sleeve when he played. Connors, even though he wasn't a New Yorker, was embraced as a native New Yorker because of the way he played. His gritty, brash style played well in New York and, not coincidentally, he had a lot of success playing in New York. We in New York, if you ask people not from here, can be a little bit in your face with our bold nature. Connors exuded that with the way he played on the court and with the way he treated umpires and spoke to the press.

AARON KRICKSTEIN (AS TOLD TO KEN DAVIDOFF): I mean they were crazy. That was the wildest crowd I've ever played in front of.

ACKNOWLEDGMENTS

I want to start by thanking my wife, Debbie Ehrlich, for watching our five-year son, Jagger, while I spent a year of nights and weekends writing this book. She did the impossible—as any parent can attest to—and appreciate her keeping him out of daddy's office. As the only room in the house he was told he could not be in, it was of course the only room he wanted to spend time in. And, of course, for her constant support of the book throughout the process.

I want to thank my son, who inspired me to write this book in the hope that it can instill a love of sports that my dad, Jay Ehrlich, passed on to me.

I want to thank my mom, Dr. Carole Owens, who was the first to edit every word in this book.

I would like to thank my coauthor, Gary Myers, who edited every word in this book after my mom, as well as fact checking all of the football chapters.

Thank you to David Tyree, who was kind enough to write the foreword for this book.

An additional thank you goes to Peter Botte, who offered a journalist's rendition of a newspaper write-up for each of the twenty moments (as well as the bonus moment).

I want to thank Ken Samelson for the initial proofread and fact check, Tim Rappleye for fact checking all of the hockey chapters, and Ken Davidoff for fact checking all of the baseball chapters. Davidoff also served as "the last line of defense," by editing the entire book after it went through all of the above editing.

I also want to thank Steve Serby, who was kind enough to offer his skills to fact check for any mistakes that might have escaped my team.

I want to specifically thank Jason Katzman, who was our first point of contact at Skyhorse. He believed in the project from the beginning, and as the editor championed it the entire way through. Without him, this book would have never been published and never would have ended up in your hands. Which, by the way, I want to thank you for buying!

I also want to thank the more than one hundred players, writers, broadcasters, and other sports dignitaries that shared their time and memories of these twenty moments. Each and every one of you brought this book to life with your personal insight. I want to make sure each of you are listed below by name here as well as appearing in the chapters. They include (in alphabetical order):

Marv Albert
Edgardo Alfonzo
Glenn Anderson
OJ Anderson
Marty Appel
Gary Apple
Carl Banks
James Blake
Filip Bondy
Emerson Boozer
Greg Buttle
Pete Caldera
Mark Cannizzaro
Harry Carson
Chris Chambliss
Roger Clemens
David Cone
Bob Costas
Howard Cross
Billy Crystal
Mike D'Amato
Ron Darling
Ken Davidoff
Bucky Dent
Steve DeOssie
Zak DeOssie
Lou DiBella
Jim Duquette
Victor Espinoza
Stan Fischler

Ed Ford (son of
    Whitey Ford)
Joan Ford (widow of
    Whitey Ford)
Walt "Clyde" Frazier
Hank Gola
Dwight "Doc"
    Gooden
Butch Goring
Adam Graves
Ron Guidry
Joe Hand Sr.
John Harper
Padraig Harrington
Keith Hernandez
Jon Heyman
Larry Holmes
Jeff Hostetler
Aaron Judge
Michael Kay
Isiah Kiner-Falefa
Mathias Kiwanuka
Brendan Kuty
Don La Greca
Sean Landeta
Bill Leiderman
Justin Leonard
Jim Leyritz
Ann Liguori
Sparky Lyle

Eli Manning
Meredith Marakovits
Leonard Marshall
George Martin
Stéphane Matteau
Anthony McCarron
Phil McConkey
Jiggs McDonald
Mark Messier
Omar Minaya
Sweeny Murti
Joe Namath
Jim Nantz
Jeff Nelson
Karl Nelson
Bobby Nystrom
Shaun O'Hara
Bart Oates
Ian O'Connor
Paul O'Neill
Jesse Orosco
Bob Papa
Jay Payton
J. Russell Peltz
Mike Piazza
Denis Potvin
Ed Randall
Randy Rasmussen
Gary Reasons
Mickey Rivers

John Schmitt

Ron Swoboda

Bobby Valentine

Art Shamsky

Amani Toomer

Bernie Williams

Phil Simms

Bryan Trottier

Mookie Wilson

John Sterling

Justin Tuck

Todd Zeile

Darryl Strawberry

David Tyree

In conclusion, I want to thank all the athletes, coaches, and managers who created these moments that are forever etched in my mind's eye and helped to inspire me to pursue a career in sports television.